THE PRINCETON REVIEW

FLOWERS & SILVER
ANNOTATED PRACTICE
MCATs

1997-98 EDITION

Books in The Princeton Review Series

Cracking the ACT
Cracking the ACT with Sample Tests on CD-ROM
Cracking the CLEP (College-Level Examination Program)
Cracking the GED
Cracking the GMAT
Cracking the GMAT with Sample Tests on Computer Disk
Cracking the GRE
Cracking the GRE with Sample Tests on Computer Disk
Cracking the GRE Biology Subject Test
Cracking the GRE Literature in English Subject Test
Cracking the GRE Psychology Subject Test
Cracking the LSAT
Cracking the LSAT with Sample Tests on Computer Disk
Cracking the LSAT with Sample Tests on CD-ROM
Cracking the MAT (Miller Analogies Test)
Cracking the NTE with Audio CD-ROM
Cracking the SAT and PSAT
Cracking the SAT and PSAT with Sample Tests on Computer Disk
Cracking the SAT and PSAT with Sample Tests on CD-ROM
Cracking the SAT II: Biology Subject Test
Cracking the SAT II: Chemistry Subject Test
Cracking the SAT II: English Subject Tests
Cracking the SAT II: French Subject Test
Cracking the SAT II: History Subject Tests
Cracking the SAT II: Math Subject Tests
Cracking the SAT II: Physics Subject Test
Cracking the SAT II: Spanish Subject Test
Cracking the TOEFL with Audiocassette
Flowers & Silver MCAT
Flowers Annotated MCAT
Flowers Annotated MCATs with Sample Tests on Computer Disk
Flowers Annotated MCATs with Sample Tests on CD-ROM

Culturescope Grade School Edition
Culturescope High School Edition
Culturescope College Edition

LSAT/GRE Analytic Workout
SAT Math Workout
SAT Verbal Workout

All U Can Eat
Don't Be a Chump!
How to Survive Without Your Parents' Money
Speak Now!
Trashproof Resumes

Biology Smart
Grammar Smart
Math Smart
Reading Smart
Study Smart
Word Smart: Building an Educated Vocabulary
Word Smart II: How to Build a More Educated Vocabulary
Word Smart Executive
Word Smart Genius
Writing Smart

American History Smart Junior
Astronomy Smart Junior
Geography Smart Junior
Grammar Smart Junior
Math Smart Junior
Word Smart Junior
Writing Smart Junior

Business School Companion
College Companion
Law School Companion
Medical School Companion

Student Advantage Guide to College Admissions
Student Advantage Guide to the Best 310 Colleges
Student Advantage Guide to America's Top Internships
Student Advantage Guide to Business Schools
Student Advantage Guide to Law Schools
Student Advantage Guide to Medical Schools
Student Advantage Guide to Paying for College
Student Advantage Guide to Summer
Student Advantage Guide to Visiting College Campuses
Student Advantage Guide: Help Yourself
Student Advantage Guide: The Complete Book of Colleges
Student Advantage Guide: The Internship Bible
Hillel Guide to Jewish Life on Campus
International Students' Guide to the United States
The Princeton Review Guide to Your Career

Also available on cassette from Living Language
Grammar Smart
Word Smart
Word Smart II

THE PRINCETON REVIEW

FLOWERS & SILVER ANNOTATED PRACTICE MCATs

1997-98 EDITION

by **THEODORE SILVER, M.D.,**
and the Staff of The Princeton Review

RANDOM HOUSE, INC., NEW YORK 1996

ISBN: 0-679-77784-9

ISSN: 1067-2184

Manufactured in the United States of America on partially recycled paper

9 8 7 6 5 4 3

1997-98 Edition

CONTENTS

PART FIVE

PART ONE

ORIENTATION

INTRODUCTION

In April 1991 the Association of American Medical Colleges first administered its newly revised MCAT. Three months *earlier* (after two years of preparation), The Princeton Review opened its MCAT preparatory course nationwide, complete with four simulated MCATs. At The Princeton Review, we make it our business to know what standardized-test makers are up to, and that's one reason our courses consistently raise scores.

If you're preparing to take the MCAT, start with this book. It will assess your present ability as an MCAT candidate and set you moving on the road to a high score.

HOW THIS BOOK IS ORGANIZED

PART ONE *describes the MCAT* and tells you how to prepare.

PART TWO presents a *full-length simulated MCAT* with answer key and scoring grid.

PART THREE *explains the answers* to the simulated test that appears in Part Two. For every question, we tell you why a particular answer is right and why the others are wrong, so that you can understand your errors and start to correct them. For each of the writing problems, we provide a sample essay written according to The Princeton Review MCAT Essay Formula.

You'll get the most from this book if you pursue its three parts fully and *in their appropriate order*. Read Part One. Take the test provided in Part Two. Score yourself. Then identify your errors, strengths, and weaknesses by reading the explanations provided in Part Three.

PREPARING FOR THE MCAT / WHAT IS THE MCAT?

The MCAT (**M**edical **C**ollege **A**dmissions **T**est) is a seven-hour test that American medical schools use to admit and reject their applicants. If you're planning on attending medical school, you *have* to take the MCAT. It determines where you go—or whether you go at all.

WHO PRODUCES THE MCAT?

The MCAT is officially produced by a group called the Association of American Medical Colleges (AAMC). AAMC is supposed to be responsible for the MCAT. In exercising this responsibility it contracts with other people and testing companies who actually write and administer the test. Since 1991, when the "revised MCAT" was first introduced, AAMC seems to have had some trouble finding people and companies with which it's happy. In 1991 the test was written and administered by American College Testing (ACT) of Iowa. By 1993 it turned over the job of administering the test to Educational Testing Services of New Jersey. Now, for administration of the MCAT, AAMC has gone back to ACT of Iowa, which maintains an office called the MCAT Program Office in Iowa City.

WHAT'S THE MCAT LIKE, AND HOW MANY QUESTIONS DOES IT HAVE?

The MCAT has one component called Scientific Reasoning, another called Verbal Reasoning, and a third that requires you to write two essays.

SCIENTIFIC REASONING

The MCAT's scientific reasoning component is divided into two sections: "Physical Sciences" and "Biological Sciences." Physical Sciences means physics and inorganic chemistry. Biological Sciences means biology and organic chemistry.

The physical sciences section presents ten to eleven reading passages, each pertaining to physics or inorganic chemistry. Every passage is followed by six to ten multiple-choice questions that supposedly concern the passage and the relevant science.

In addition, the physical sciences section presents ten to fifteen questions that *don't* relate to passages. We call these questions "freestanding." Altogether the physical sciences section has seventy-seven questions, and you must answer them in one hour and forty minutes.

The biological sciences section is similarly structured. You get ten to eleven reading passages, each pertaining to biology and/or organic chemistry. For each passage there are six to nine multiple-choice questions. The section also features ten to fifteen freestanding items.

Like the physical sciences section, the biological sciences section presents about exactly 77 questions that you must answer in one hour and forty minutes.

VERBAL REASONING

On its surface, the MCAT's verbal reasoning section resembles reading comprehension tests you've taken in the past. You're given nine to ten passages, and on each passage you're asked five to seven questions. The passages concern the natural sciences, social sciences, and humanities. The total number of questions is sixty-five, and you must answer them in one hour and twenty-five minutes.

ESSAYS

The MCAT features two writing exercises. Each one presents you with a short statement and asks you to write an essay about it. For your first essay you might be given a statement like this:

"A government cannot enforce a law if its citizens oppose it."

And then be instructed to:

> Write a unified essay in which you perform the following tasks: Explain what you think the above statement means. Describe a specific situation in which you believe a government can enforce a law if its citizens oppose it. Discuss what you think determines whether a government can enforce a law that the citizens oppose.

For your second essay you might be given a statement like this:

"No false statement can live indefinitely."

Once again, you'd be told to:

> Write a unified essay in which you perform the following tasks: Explain what you think the above statement means. Describe a specific situation in which you believe a false statement can live indefinitely. Discuss what you think determines whether a false statement can or cannot live indefinitely.

You're allowed thirty minutes to write each essay.

In all, the MCAT features about 30 reading passages, 219 questions, and 2 essays. The total testing time is 7 hours (including an hour for lunch).

HOW IS THE MCAT SCORED?

Every MCAT candidate gets four scores:

- one for verbal reasoning

- one for physical sciences

- one for biological sciences

- one for the two writing samples combined

The verbal and scientific sections are scored on a scale of one to fifteen, on which one is low and fifteen is high. Scores of ten or above ("double-digit scores") are very good. The writing sample is scored on a scale of J–T, on which J is low and T is high.

Here's a table that shows you how the MCAT is designed and scored.

The MCAT			
Section	Questions	Time	Score
Verbal Reasoning	65	85 minutes	1–15
Physical Sciences	77	100 minutes	1–15
Essay Writing	2	60 minutes	J–T
Biological Sciences	77	100 minutes	1–15

NOW, WHAT DOES THE MCAT *REALLY* TEST, AND HOW DO I PREPARE?

There are two answers to that question. AAMC says that the MCAT is just what it claims to be: a test of scientific reasoning, verbal reasoning, and writing ability. AAMC says you should prepare for the science sections by reviewing your college notebooks. It tells you to prepare for the verbal reasoning and writing sections by buying the sample questions and materials it offers for sale.

We at The Princeton Review have a different answer. We know the MCAT. We've taken it apart bit by bit, piece by piece, and shred by shred. We've studied it backward, forward, upside down, and inside out. We know what it tests and what it doesn't test, and we can tell you this:

- The MCAT does *not* test "reasoning"—verbal, scientific, or any other kind.

- Your college notes will not help you achieve a high score.

In order to prepare for the MCAT, you must appreciate the difference between studying *science* and studying *science for the MCAT*. You must review the premedical sciences in a way that is systematically tailored *to the test*. Furthermore, you must study MCAT questions themselves. You should be "wise" to their design and schooled in *techniques* that systematically lead to correct answers.

AAMC doesn't tell you these things. We do. So don't bother reviewing your college notes (as if you still had them) and don't prepare for a test of "reasoning."

AAMC's advice won't help you; ours will.

WAIT A SECOND. AAMC *PRODUCES* THE MCAT. SHOULDN'T I LISTEN TO THEM BEFORE I LISTEN TO YOU?

Good question. The answer is no. AAMC isn't on your side. It's not concerned with you, your score, or your future. AAMC is interested in *promoting the MCAT*. Every year it collects nearly $6 million by charging a lot of money per test to each of approximately 40,000 students. In order to continue collecting that money, AAMC must keep the medical schools believing that the MCAT is worthy of their attention so that the schools, in turn, will continue to require the MCAT of their applicants.

In other words, AAMC doesn't necessarily *want* you to do well on the MCAT. Too many high scores would make the test seem easy, and that would impair the MCAT's credibility. AAMC wants some test takers to get *low* scores. Low scores make the test look hard, and that's *good* for its credibility.

AAMC has no interest in helping you achieve a high score. It's the AAMC's business to peddle their test. *Our* business, on the other hand, is to raise your score. When we give you advice, that's our *only* concern.

SHOULD I BUY THE PRACTICE MATERIALS THAT AAMC SELLS?

Yes, you probably should. For a total of $54, AAMC will sell you three full-length MCATs and two booklets containing additional MCAT-like passages and questions. The materials do *not* include explanatory answers or a scoring grid (which allows you to calculate your scores on the one-to-fifteen scale). Nonetheless, the materials are worth having. To order them, write to:

AAMC
Department 66
Washington, DC 20055

Enclose a check for $54 and a very short letter requesting:

(1) The MCAT Student Manual with Practice Test I

(2) MCAT Practice Test II with Practice Item Booklets

(3) MCAT Practice Test III

You might wish, instead, to call AAMC at 202-828-0416.

AAMC's materials are useful, but, as we said before, their *advice* is not. When it comes to advice about the MCAT, listen to people who are on *your* side. In other words, listen to *us*.

OKAY, I'M LISTENING. HOW *SHOULD* I PREPARE?

Naturally, you have to study physics, chemistry, biology, reading, and writing. But it's important that you approach all of these subjects in a way that's especially *tailored to the MCAT*. You must learn how MCAT questions are structured and how to select correct answers by *thinking like the test writers*.

Let's think first about science. MCAT test writers have a way of using a few simple principles to write a large variety of seemingly difficult questions. These questions are easy to answer if you understand the simple principles on which they're built.

HERE'S AN EXAMPLE: THE PRINCIPLE OF EQUILIBRIUM

Look at this physical science passage and the question that follows.

Passage I

Coal, a major source of energy, can be converted from its solid, raw form to a gaseous form of fuel. This is accomplished by the *water gas reaction* as shown below:

$$C(s) + H_2O(g) \rightleftharpoons CO(g) + H_2(g)$$

Solid carbon is reacted with steam to produce a mixture of carbon monoxide and hydrogen gas. This mixture is what is called "water gas." Water gas is highly combustible. The following table lists the standard heats of formation and free energies of formation of each of the four compounds in the water gas reaction.

	ΔH_f° (KJ/mol)	ΔG_f° (KJ/mol)
$CO(g)$	−110.5	−137.3
$H_2(g)$	0.0	0.0
$C(s)$	0.0	0.0
$H_2O(g)$	−241.8	−228.6

1. Assume a chemist initiates the water gas reaction and then, as the reaction proceeds, invests the surroundings with an extraordinarily high concentration of carbon monoxide. Among the following, which would most likely result?

   I. Water gas will undergo complete and immediate combustion.
   II. Ambient steam concentration will decrease.
   III. Ambient hydrogen concentration will decrease.

   A. I only
   B. III only
   C. I and II only
   D. I and III only

To the student who approaches the MCAT *strategically*, this question is easy. She knows, first of all, that she can answer it *without reading the passage*. She need only:

(1) look at the "water gas reaction" and

(2) understand the principle of equilibrium.

LET'S UNDERSTAND EQUILIBRIUM

Look at this equilibrium equation.

$$A + B \rightleftharpoons C + D$$

On the left side of the equilibrium equation we find A and B. On the right side we find C and D. A and B act together to produce C and D. C and D, meanwhile, act together to produce A and B.

$$A + B \longrightarrow C + D$$
$$A + B \longleftarrow C + D$$

If we add more A to the solution, we're going to get *more* C and D. That's true even if we don't add any more B. Adding more A, by itself, will increase the production of C and D (unless we've used up all of the B, at which point adding more A won't increase the production of C and D).

$$\underset{add\ A}{\searrow} A + B \longrightarrow \uparrow C + \uparrow D$$

If we add more B to the solution, we're also going to get more C and D. That's true even if we don't add any more A. Adding more B, by itself, will increase the production of C and D (unless we've used up all of the A, at which point adding more B won't increase the production of C and D).

$$A + B \longrightarrow \uparrow C + \uparrow D$$

Adding more A *and* B, of course, will also increase the production of C and D.

When we increase the production of C and D, we are "driving the equilibrium to the right." In other words, we're causing increased production of the stuff that's on the right side of the equilibrium equation.

Adding more C or more D to the system has an analogous but opposite effect. If we add more C, we'll increase the production of A and B unless and until we run out of D. If we add more D to the system we'll increase the production of A and B unless and until we run out of C.

THINK ABOUT IT THIS WAY

When you add more A or B to the system, you're making things kind of crowded on the left side of the equation. In order to relieve the crowding, the system decides to move over to the right. Similarly, if you add more C or D to the system, you're making things kind of crowded on the right. The system adjusts by moving to the left.

Now, let's think about this. We know that when we add either C or D, by itself, we get more of A and B. But when we add more C, by itself, what happens to the concentration of D? In other words, when we increase the concentration of a species on the right side of an equation, what happens to the concentration of the *other* species on the right side of the equation?

It goes down.

When we add more C to the system, there will be more collisions between C particles and D particles. That's how we form more A and B. Since we did not add any D to the system, the increased collisions among C and D particles and the increased production of A and B will tend to *reduce* the concentration of D.

In other words, adding more C to the system crowds things up on the right. In order to relieve themselves of the crowding, some C particles and D particles pack up and move over to the left (where they become A and B particles). So, the concentration of D goes down.

The overall concentration of C does *not* go down. The crowding began because we *added* C. It's true that some of the newly added C particles will get together with D and move to the left. But they won't *all* do that. After the equilibrium has shifted, there will be more C particles on the right than there were before we added any C. There will be fewer D particles on the right than there were before we began, and there will, of course, be more A and B particles on the left.

LOOK AGAIN AT THE "WATER GAS REACTION" AND ANSWER THE QUESTION

$$C(s) + H_2O(g) \rightleftharpoons CO(g) + H_2(g)$$

1. Assume a chemist initiates the water gas reaction and then, as the reaction proceeds, invests the surroundings with an extraordinarily high concentration of carbon monoxide. Among the following, which would most likely result?

    I.   Water gas will undergo complete and immediate combustion.
    II. Ambient steam concentration will decrease.
    III. Ambient hydrogen gas concentration will decrease.

    A. I only
    B. III only
    C. I and II
    D. I and III

Choice B is correct. When the chemist exposes the equilibrium to high concentrations of CO, he is, in effect, adding CO to the right side of the equation. The right side gets "crowded," and the equilibrium shifts to the left. That means:

(1) the concentration of hydrogen gas *decreases*

(2) the concentration of steam (gaseous water) *increases*, and

(3) the concentration of solid carbon *increases*.

The equilibrium principle generates a variety of MCAT questions pertaining to inorganic chemistry, organic chemistry, and physics. It underlies *seemingly* complicated MCAT problems involving acids, bases, buffers, syntheses, degradations, kinetics, and thermodynamics. To make the questions seem especially unapproachable, the MCAT writers set them behind a veil of graphs, tables, and diagrams—often useless and irrelevant. You'll bypass such distractions and make your way easily to correct answers *if you see the questions for what they are*—simple applications of the equilibrium principle.

Equilibrium represents *only one* of the simple principles on which MCAT questions are built. There are *many others*. You'll raise your score if you know what they are and how they operate.

ARE THERE TECHNIQUES I SHOULD LEARN FOR THE VERBAL REASONING COMPONENT?

Yes, definitely. The MCAT's verbal reasoning section is susceptible to several systems and strategies. Here, for example, are two devices that help you eliminate wrong answer choices.

DEVICE # 1: *RECOGNIZE STATEMENTS IN THE EXTREME*

When it comes to the MCAT's verbal reasoning section, an answer choice that is immoderate or extreme is seldom correct. When an answer choice pivots on words like "never," "always," "invariably," "only," "total," "ideal," or "perfect," it's almost certainly wrong. In the MCAT world, very few things are *absolute*.

Without even reading a passage, consider this question:

1. The author's claim that "productivity is the soul of civilization" (line 15) introduces his argument that:

    A. economics is the only important aspect of civilized life.
    B. civilizations are built primarily on economic foundations.
    C. people should devote their energies to their own fortunes and not to the problems of others.
    D. human beings are totally dependent on one another for all of their needs.

Choice A is extreme, and you can be pretty sure it's wrong. The idea that economics is the "only" important aspect of civilized life is contrary to MCAT philosophy. Choice D features the words "totally" and "all." It, too, is extreme and almost certainly wrong.

Consider this question and eliminate the choices that are extreme:

2. The author believes that practicing psychiatrists:

    A. cannot possibly help patients unless they are completely objective.
    B. are hopelessly confused over the genesis of mental illness.
    C. are scientists notwithstanding the uncertainties that surround them.
    D. should for the time being treat mental disease in terms of environment.

Choices A and B are extreme. The phrases "cannot possibly," "completely objective," and "hopelessly confused" should tip you off.

DEVICE # 2: RECOGNIZE STATEMENTS THAT AREN'T "NICE"

An answer choice contrary to the kinds of ideas in which "nice people" believe should be eliminated. Consider, for example, these thoughts:

- Violent criminals should not be viewed as human beings.

- Freedom of religion is destructive to a society.

- Children should be encouraged not to make friends with other children whose backgrounds are different from their own.

- Teachers should resort to stern discipline in order to maintain their students' attention.

These ideas just aren't *nice*. They don't conform to progressive and "enlightened" thought. They're never going to be correct answer choices.

With that in mind, consider these two questions. Eliminate

—extremes and

—statements that aren't "nice."

3. The author believes that patients with serious psychiatric disturbances:

   A. are entirely beyond the reach of even the most competent psychotherapists.
   B. may have internal vulnerabilities on which an adverse environment has acted.
   C. are usually to blame for their illnesses and do not deserve treatment.
   D. are not likely to be physically strong.

When you read Choice A, the word "entirely" should ring a warning bell. Choice A is *extreme*, and you should eliminate it.

Choice C isn't "nice." "Nice" people don't blame psychiatric patients for their own illnesses. Such a sentiment won't be a correct answer on the MCAT. Choice C should be eliminated.

4. The passage suggests that criminal attorneys will be most successful in helping their clients if they:

    A. endeavor to give those clients a sense of self-esteem.
    B. identify, personally, with the client's situation.
    C. never offer advice, and limit themselves entirely to asking questions.
    D. treat those clients not like human beings but like diseased organisms.

When you read Choice C the words "never" and "entirely" should trigger an alarm. Choice C is *extreme*. Eliminate it.

Choice D isn't "nice." "Nice" people think all clients should be treated as human beings. Choice D could not possibly be correct.

There are a great many strategies and techniques that lead you to correct answers on the MCAT's verbal reasoning section, and it's important that you use them.

ARE THERE STRATEGIES AND TECHNIQUES FOR THE *WRITING SAMPLE* TOO?

Yes. In order to score well on your MCAT essays it's important, first of all, to know how they're graded. An MCAT essay is normally read by two graders. Each grader spends around ninety seconds (that's right, ninety *seconds*) reading an essay. She then grades it "holistically." Holistic grading is *supposed* to mean that the reader does not make separate evaluations in terms of substance, organization, or grammar. Rather, she's supposed to keep all these criteria somewhere in her mind (for ninety seconds) and then assign a grade based on an overall "sense" of the essay's quality.

AS WE SAID, THAT'S WHAT HOLISTIC GRADING IS *SUPPOSED* TO MEAN

Unfortunately, holistic grading *really* means that MCAT readers won't be giving any serious attention to the quality of your writing or what you're trying to express. In ninety seconds they can't possibly do that. Instead, they'll be grading your essay *based on the impression it makes on them*.

So, writing an MCAT essay means writing something that, in ninety seconds, will *impress* the reader and make her think well of you.

That means you should:

- make your essay easy to read,

- at least give the *appearance* of careful organization, *and*

- use words and phrases that make you seem "wise, serious, and well read."

All of these objectives can be achieved by following an MCAT essay *formula*. Here, for example, is an MCAT essay that's written according to the formula we teach in The Princeton Review MCAT course.

Consider this statement:

> *A society that is well educated will necessarily be free.*
>
> Write a unified essay in which you perform the following tasks: Explain what you think the above statement means. Describe a specific situation in which a well-educated society might not be free. Discuss what you think determines whether or not a well-educated society is free.

Response

The statement indicates that developed intellects seek social and political freedom and, furthermore, that a totalitarian or tyrannical government will ultimately fail in the face of an informed and insightful public. (A similar thought is manifest in Victor Hugo's remark that "One can resist the invasion of armies but not the invasion of ideas.") Those who have honestly and openly explored humanity's intellectual insights and discoveries will likely have the wish and the means to establish free societies.

In order specifically to describe a situation in which the statement does not apply, one need only recognize that the words "educated" and "freedom" are inherently ambiguous. The statement pivots on these words, and its applicability depends on the meanings attached to them. As used in the statement, "education" is subject to interpretation. It might refer to broad knowledge and understanding of history, science, and the arts and letters. On the other hand, it might signify only *formal* schooling, and schools, to be sure, need not educate. The "education" that a given school affords depends on the objectives of those who select its curriculum.

The dictator's school will teach that which fosters reverence for the dictator: intolerance, chauvinism, self-aggrandizement, and fear. Lessons may be rigorous and discipline may be stern. Students are not likely, however, to emerge with the sort of open-minded inquisitiveness that demands political freedom. In that sense, then, "education" need not give rise to freedom.

The phrase "free society" also harbors ambiguity. To some it signifies a capitalistic economy akin to that which operates in the United States. Thus understood, a "free society" does not necessarily accompany an educated populace. The spread of knowledge and learning over this past century seems to have brought widening acceptance of egalitarian principles. That has led, in turn, to widespread socialization of western and eastern economies and to a significant *restriction* on what might be termed economic freedom.

Hence the pertinence of the statement depends in large measure on the meaning attached to its language. If "education" refers to a genuine exposure to humanity's intellectual achievements and "freedom" means social and political liberty, then the statement represents a meaningful comment. If, however, "education" means "school" and "freedom" signifies economic opportunity, the statement is not accurate.

Because this essay was written according to a carefully devised formula,

- it addresses all three of the assigned "tasks."

- it seems to be carefully conceived and organized.

- the writer appears to be "serious" about life, learning, and language.

Those are the ingredients of a high-scoring MCAT essay.

WILL THIS BOOK GIVE ME EVERYTHING I NEED?

To be honest—probably not. Unless you're starting out as a top MCAT student, no *book* can fully prepare you for the MCAT—not this one or any other. If you're serious about earning a high MCAT score, you need a good teacher, powerful materials, personal contact, and *repeated opportunities to take simulated tests that are scored, analyzed, and returned.*

In The Princeton Review MCAT course, for example, students attend sixteen, $3\frac{1}{2}$ hour sessions over an eight-week period. Teachers are dynamic, and classes are small. Each student works his way through twelve hundred pages of carefully designed teaching materials and thousands of exercises. Students are privately tutored, and between meetings they telephone their teachers whenever they feel the need. Separate from their class sessions, students take four simulated MCATs. Each test is scored, analyzed, and returned within a few days so that teacher and students may subject it to thorough review. For fifty-six days our students eat, sleep, and dream the MCAT. Such are the elements of a high MCAT score, and *no book can possibly provide all of them,* regardless of the promises made on its cover.

BUT THIS BOOK IS THE PLACE TO BEGIN

Find out where you stand and what you need. Set aside a full day and *take the simulated MCAT in this book*. Treat it seriously and subject yourself rigorously to MCAT test conditions:

- Start early in the morning, and for the whole day consider yourself absolutely unavailable for anything or anyone else.

- For each section give yourself only as much time as the instructions allow.

- Take the ten-minute breaks as indicated and take a full sixty-minute lunch hour between the Physical Science and Writing Sample sections of the test.

When you've finished the test, score yourself. Use the scoring key on pages 110-111, and derive your scores for Verbal Reasoning, Physical Sciences, and Biological Sciences. (You can't score the writing sample, but we definitely want you to complete that section of the test anyway.)

YES, THEN WHAT?

If both your verbal and science scores are *10 or above* you're in pretty good shape. Depending on your college grades and the medical school you want to attend, you might consider signing up for the MCAT without pursuing special preparation. Naturally, you should review any science that gives you trouble on our simulated test. Then, for a few weeks before you take the real test, sit down and address the sample tests and materials that AAMC provides. If that goes smoothly, take the MCAT as scheduled. You'll probably do well.

On the other hand, if your verbal and science scores are *9 or below,* you've got to raise them. That probably means you should consider a good MCAT course.

CHOOSING AN MCAT COURSE

Generally speaking, a *good* MCAT course will:

1. Provide you with teachers, teaching systems, and teaching materials that organize your work, maintain your attention, and monitor your progress day by day and week by week.

2. Thoroughly immerse you in physics, inorganic chemistry, organic chemistry, biology, reading, and writing—in a way that is strategically designed *for the MCAT.*

3. Show you, systematically, how MCAT questions are structured and teach you how to select correct answers quickly by thinking like the test writers.

4. Give you repeated opportunities to take simulated MCATs that are quickly scored and returned to you for thorough review. Anyone who tries to prepare for the MCAT without repeated MCAT test taking might as well prepare for a

driver's road test without ever getting behind a steering wheel. Hands-on practice with simulated MCATs is essential to raising scores.

Any course that fails to offer these four features is useless, no matter how many papers, booklets, or tapes it provides.

LET'S BE MORE SPECIFIC

Think about science. Some MCAT courses offer you stacks of science outlines and summaries that seem to "cover everything." Such materials are cheap and easy to design because they're only condensed versions of the textbooks you already own. Ironically, these outlines and summaries are much harder to get through than the textbooks themselves. They give you incomplete, watered-down information, and they skip key steps in the explanation process. Most people find them frustrating and confusing. Even if you do get through them (which you won't), they can't help you much. They don't teach science *the way the MCAT tests it.*

Here, for instance, is a sample from an MCAT course we'll call Course X. Try reading it.

9.3.1.1: Human Respiratory Function

A. Anatomy of Respiratory System: Respiratory tract—nares, bronchi (left and right main stem and subdivisions), bronchioles, terminal bronchioles, alveolar sacs and alveolus (site of gas exchange, see below). Bronchial secretions moved by cilia and cough reflex (autonomic, vagal).

B. Inspiratory function: Lung and chest wall have static and dynamic properties. Elasticity permits influx and efflux of gas. Diaphragm contracts (involuntary function, phrenic nerve signal initiated in CNS; medullary respiratory center), creates negative intrapulmonary pressure. Air traverses respiratory tract.

Tidal volume = air normally inspired.

Total capacity = full expansion.

Vital capacity = full exhalation.

Functional residual capacity = gas remaining after exhalation.

Residual volume = gas remaining after full exhalation.

- Resistance to air flow (inspiratory and expiratory) caused by airway caliber. Combined total cross-sectional area increases at deeper levels (bronchioles, alveoli).

- Asthma and Emphysema (Chronic Obstructive Pulmonary Disease) produced by loss of elastic tissue, reduced airway caliber.

The material you just read is junk. It couldn't possibly help you answer a single question on the MCAT. To begin with, it's incomprehensible. No Earthly creature could figure out what it's trying to teach about respiration unless he fully understood and remembered the subject *beforehand* (in which case he wouldn't need a course).

Second, even if Course *X* were understandable, it would be teaching the *wrong information*. The MCAT does require that you know something about respiration. You have to comprehend the structure of the respiratory tract and understand the dynamics of inspiration, expiration, and gas exchange. Course *X* doesn't help you do that. Instead, it presents a hodgepodge of facts, most of which have no bearing on the MCAT. The MCAT will never ask you the meaning of terms like "tidal volume," "total capacity," or "functional residual capacity." (If those terms should happen to appear on the MCAT, their meaning will be explained.)

NOW READ *THIS* MATERIAL ABOUT RESPIRATION:

YOUR BRAIN THINKS YOU SHOULD BREATHE

The signal to breathe originates in the medulla oblongata, which is part of the brain. As you might expect, the signal originates in a part of the medulla that is called the respiratory center. It travels to the diaphragm via a nerve, and that nerve is called the phrenic nerve.

The diaphragm is a muscle. When stimulated by the phrenic nerve, it contracts. Contraction of the diaphragm begins the process of breathing in, which is called inspiration.

249. ❐ **TRUE** ❐ **FALSE** The diaphragm is a muscle.

250. ❐ **TRUE** ❐ **FALSE** The diaphragm receives its signal to contract from the vagus nerve.

251. ❐ **TRUE** ❐ **FALSE** The diaphragm receives its signal to contract from the phrenic nerve.

252. With respect to human respiration, the signal that initiates inspiration arises in the:

   A. cerebral cortex.
   B. medulla oblongata.
   C. trachea.
   D. vagus nerve.

253. Which of the following correctly orders the sequence in which the listed structures act to produce inspiration?

   A. Phrenic nerve, diaphragm, medulla oblongata
   B. Diaphragm, phrenic nerve, medulla oblongata
   C. Phrenic nerve, medulla oblongata, diaphragm
   D. Medulla oblongata, phrenic nerve, diaphragm

LOOK AT THIS SYRINGE

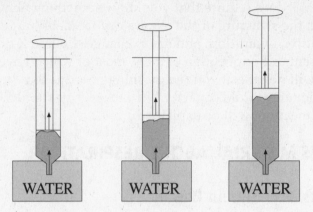

When the plunger rises, it creates negative pressure inside the cylinder. The negative pressure draws the water in, and the syringe fills.

NOW, LOOK AT THE DIAPHRAGM

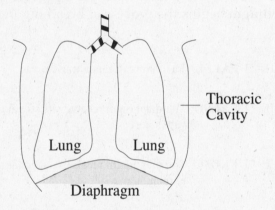

Before the diaphragm contracts, it is shaped like a dome. Then, when it does contract, it flattens out and creates empty space within the thoracic cavity. The empty space creates negative pressure. In order to fill the space and eliminate the negative pressure, the lungs expand.

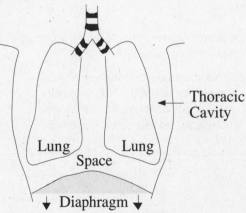

THE LUNGS EXPAND EVEN THOUGH THEY DON'T WANT TO

The lungs have a natural elasticity that tends to keep them from expanding. It's as though they had rubber bands around them "trying" to keep them closed. The negative pressure that arises when the diaphragm contracts causes the lungs to expand, even though they must "stretch" their rubber bands to do that.

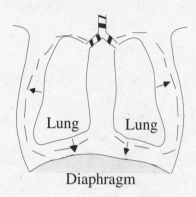

Lung   Lung

Diaphragm

When the lungs do expand, they create a negative pressure inside themselves. In order to eliminate that negative pressure, air rushes into the lungs to fill the newly available space. That completes the process of inspiration.

254. ❑ **TRUE** ❑ **FALSE** During the process of inspiration, the lungs expand because the contraction of the diaphragm produces positive pressure in the thoracic cavity surrounding the lungs.

255. ❑ **TRUE** ❑ **FALSE** The pressure inside the lungs, at the moment they expand, is lower than the pressure in the atmosphere.

256. During the process of inspiration, air moves into the lungs in direct response to:

    A. negative pressure within the thoracic cavity.
    B. positive pressure within the thoracic cavity.
    C. positive pressure within the lungs.
    D. negative pressure within the lungs.

Now—how, exactly, does the air get from the atmosphere to the lungs?

BY CLIMBING AN UPSIDE-DOWN TREE

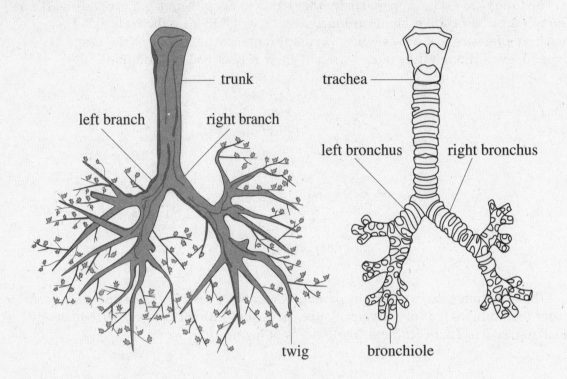

DOES THE RESPIRATORY TRACT HAVE RINGS?

The trachea and bronchi have rings on their outside, and these rings are made of cartilage.

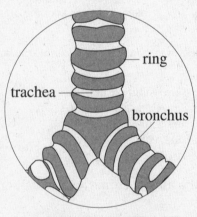

RESPIRATORY TRACT

The rings help keep the trachea and bronchi open.

HOW DOES THE RESPIRATORY TRACT KEEP ITSELF CLEAN?

The respiratory tract begins with the nose. The nose cleans, warms, and moistens incoming air. Large particles are trapped in hairs lining the nostrils.

Particles that make it past the nose get stuck in mucus that lines the lower parts of the respiratory tree. Ciliated cells sweep the dirty mucus back out of the system. Very small particles can make it all the way to the alveoli, and these particles are eaten by phagocytic cells lining the alveoli.

257. ☐ **TRUE** ☐ **FALSE** Between the point where air enters at the nose and then settles in the alveoli, the human respiratory tract undergoes repeated branching.

258. ☐ **TRUE** ☐ **FALSE** Within the human respiratory tract, bronchi outnumber bronchioles, and bronchi outnumber alveoli.

259. Within the human respiratory tract, bronchi branch to form bronchioles, and bronchioles branch to terminate in:

    A. bronchi.
    B. the trachea.
    C. alveoli.
    D. the nose.

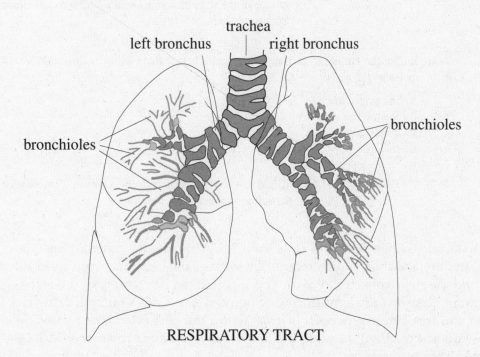

RESPIRATORY TRACT

The entire respiratory tract is like a tree turned upside down. First, air enters the nose and flows into a trunk. The trunk is actually called the trachea. Next, the air reaches a "fork" in the trunk. These right and left branches are called bronchi. The bronchi themselves break up into smaller branches, and these smaller branches split several times more. The tiny twiglike branches are called bronchioles.

DOES THE RESPIRATORY TRACT HAVE LEAVES?

No, but it does have things called alveoli. A little later we'll talk about what the alveoli do.

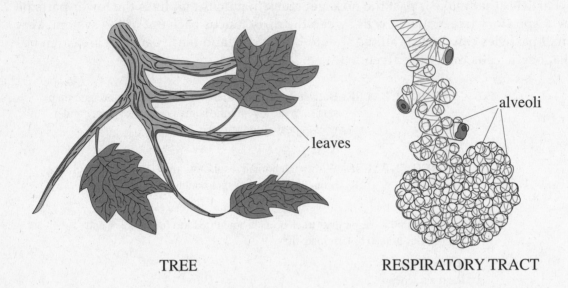

TREE   RESPIRATORY TRACT

260. ❐ TRUE ❐ FALSE Within the human respiratory tract, rings surround the outside of the trachea and bronchi in order to help keep the airway open.

261. Within the human respiratory tract, the structure that cleans, warms, and moistens the air is:

   A. the bronchus.
   B. the trachea.
   C. the alveolus.
   D. the nose.

262. ❐ TRUE ❐ FALSE Mucus-covered ciliated cells prevent only the largest particles from reaching the alveoli.

The material you just read will raise your MCAT score. Its explanations are friendly, understandable, and coherent. They cover the substance you need for the MCAT, and they're likely to stay with you through the day you take the test. Furthermore, they include a multitude of pointed questions that maintain your attention and track your progress. *Together with a teacher's interactive review,* the material you just read will provide the knowledge you need to answer MCAT questions about respiration.

ENOUGH TALK—LET'S TAKE THE FIRST STEP

We've described the MCAT, and we've told you how to prepare for it. Now it's time to get started. Set aside a day and take the sample MCAT that's provided in Part Two of this book. Use the answer sheet provided at the back of the book. Time yourself according to the standard MCAT testing day:

MORNING

Verbal Reasoning:	1 hour, 25 minutes
Break:	10 minutes
Physical Sciences:	1 hour, 40 minutes
Lunch:	1 hour

AFTERNOON

Writing Sample (I):	30 minutes
Writing Sample (II):	30 minutes
Break:	10 minutes
Biological Sciences:	1 hour, 40 minutes

After you've taken the test, score yourself. Then, over the next few days, evaluate your performance carefully by reading the explanatory answers provided in Part Three. They'll show you what you did right and what you did wrong. When you're all done you'll know just where you stand. You'll know where you're strong, you'll know where you're weak, and you'll be ready to plan your route toward a higher score.

From all of us at The Princeton Review: Good luck.

PART TWO

THE PRINCETON REVIEW
MCAT
DIAGNOSTIC TEST 1

Verbal Reasoning I

Time: 85 Minutes
Questions 1–65

VERBAL REASONING

DIRECTIONS: There are nine passages in the Verbal Reasoning test. Each passage is followed by several questions. After reading a passage, select the one best answer to each question. If you are not certain of an answer, eliminate the alternatives that you know to be incorrect and then select an answer from the remaining alternatives. Indicate your selection by blackening the corresponding circle on your answer sheet (DIAGNOSTIC TEST FORM).

Passage I (Questions 1–6)

Controversy over managing public lands is neither an unexpected nor recent development. In the 1970s, debate over land management began to focus on the effects of
5 timber management practices on wildlife. This was most evident in the Pacific Northwest where the public was beginning to express strong concerns about the effects of timber harvest in late-successional forests on
10 northern spotted owls and other vertebrates. The focus on all vertebrates and not just "game animals" distinguished these concerns from earlier wildlife-related issues. In 1976, Congress passed the National Forest Man-
15 agement Act, which mandated the maintenance of biological diversity on lands of the National Forest System. Regulations enacted pursuant to this law specified that viable populations of native and desirable
20 non-native wildlife species would be maintained on planning units (i.e. National Forests) of the National Forest System. Thus, a statutory and regulatory basis was provided for appeals and litigation directed at what
25 the public believed to be the negative effects of timber management practices on wildlife. The many legal challenges that ensued focused primarily on the harvesting of late-successional forests in the Pacific North-
30 west.

The USDA Forest Service responded to this situation in 1981 by chartering a research and development program aimed at studying the role of old-growth forests as wildlife
35 habitat. Early research efforts of this program focused on the ecology of spotted owls, a species at the center of the most intense debate. Although research was underway, legal challenges disrupted forest management
40 activities, and the controversy was played out in legal and political arenas. Science was not called on as part of the solution until nearly a decade later, *after* the development of a political impasse in one of the country's
45 most important timber-producing regions. In 1989, in response to this impasse, an interagency agreement between the major land management agencies established the "Interagency Scientific Committee to Address the
50 Conservation of the Northern Spotted Owl." The charter of this group was later incorporated into law (Section 318 of Public Law 101-121), and a conservation strategy for the northern spotted owl resulted. In 1991, Con-
55 gress intervened directly by commissioning the Scientific Panel on Late-Successional Forest Ecosystems, whose mission was to make broad recommendations about management of the remaining old-growth forests in the
60 Pacific Northwest. And, in 1993, President Bill Clinton intervened and appointed a task force of scientists to evaluate the effects of alternative management scenarios for old-growth forests on all wildlife in the Pacific
65 Northwest. This intervention included an unprecedented visit by a U.S. president to the site of a regional forest management/wildlife controversy for the purpose of facilitating its end (the Forest Conference
70 convened in Portland, Oregon, on April 2, 1993).

GO ON TO THE NEXT PAGE ⇒

It is clear from these events that public concern over the effects of land management on wildlife is enormously important politi-
75 cally, economically, and scientifically. It is also clear that the conservation strategy for the northern spotted owl came too late. Nearly two decades passed from the first concerns over the conservation status of this
80 subspecies until scientists were asked to develop a "scientifically credible" conservation strategy. The necessary commitment to scientific research, which is essential as the basis for any defensible conservation plan, was
85 made too slowly. The resultant sociopolitical turmoil was likely avoidable, at least in part, and the controversy would not have been so intractable if better scientific information had been available earlier.

90 Concerns about wildlife conservation in relation to forest management are limited neither to the Pacific Northwest nor to spotted owls. Appeals and legal challenges of timber management activities, relative to effects on
95 wildlife, are now common throughout the country. The potential for re-enactment of the Pacific Northwest/old-growth scenario exists throughout the western United States. And there is growing public sentiment that
100 serious attention to the conservation of biological diversity is long overdue outside the Pacific Northwest.

1. According to one conservation expert, "we share the universe with extra-terrestrials, we share the planet with terrestrial species; and while outer space challenges our intellects, the Earth is our home." This expert would probably:

   A. support greater use of science in evaluating ecological conflicts.
   B. approve an end to the allocation of scientific resources both to solve ecological problems and to search for extra-terrestrial intelligence.
   C. not consider either ecological analyses or space exploration particularly important.
   D. consider both ecology and space exploration important, but ecology more so.

2. The author of the passage would probably support most strongly a federal law that:

   A. allocates funds for ecological research equal to Commerce Department spending promoting the timber industry.
   B. provides increased tax incentives for the commercial harvesting of forests.
   C. establishes government scholarships for graduate study in environmental science.
   D. assigns to the Army Corps of Engineers the task of researching and resolving ecological controversies.

3. The author's mention of a President's visit to Portland in April, 1993 suggests that such executive attention:

   I. reflects a determination to resolve ecological conflicts through mediation and negotiation.
   II. is warranted due to significant public concern about the ecology.
   III. represents the federal government's willingness to explore alternative-management techniques for forests.

   A. I only
   B. II only
   C. II and III only
   D. I, II, and III

GO ON TO THE NEXT PAGE

4. Which of the following claims is/are explicitly presented in the passage to justify the belief that ecological conflicts could be more efficiently managed through greater reliance on science?

    I. In the case of the spotted owl conflict, legal and political impasses developed in the absence of scientific evidence.

    II. As a rule, scientists are less motivated by political interests than by intellectual curiosity.

    III. The President appointed a task force of scientists, rather than industry representatives or ecology activists, to evaluate proposed alternatives in forest management strategies.

    A. I only
    B. I and II only
    C. I and III only
    D. I, II, and III

5. Which of the following findings would best support the author's belief that a recurrence of the social turmoil experienced in the Northwest is possible elsewhere in the nation?

    A. Most Americans are currently skeptical of the agenda of Big Industry and Big Business.
    B. Public anxiety regarding the sustenance of the ecosphere beyond the Pacific Northwest is growing.
    C. Americans are tantalized by controversy and enjoy a good political battle.
    D. Interest in environmental issues declined in the Northeast region after the decommissioning of the Shoreham nuclear facility on Long Island, New York.

6. According to the passage, which of the following is most likely to be true about the relationship between public pressure and governmental action in ecology policy?

    A. The more intense the public pressure, the greater the governmental intervention.
    B. The more intense the public pressure, the less the governmental intervention.
    C. The less intense the public pressure, the greater the governmental intervention.
    D. There is no apparent connection between the level of public pressure and the amount of governmental intervention.

GO ON TO THE NEXT PAGE

Passage II (Questions 7–12)

Mars has always captured the human imagination. There is its redness. We know now that the color comes from chemical reactions that long ago locked up Mars' oxygen
5 in reddish minerals on its surface, the "rusting" of the planet. To the ancients, the red color meant only one thing: blood. From the earliest times, Mars—named for the Roman god of war—has been associated with blood-
10 shed. Even the astronomical symbol for Mars, a circle with an arrow pointing out at 2 o'clock, is supposed to represent a shield and a spear.

As astronomers acquired telescopes, Mars
15 mythology grew. Humans have a tendency to interpret random images in ways that tell you more about the person doing the interpreting than about the images (think of the Rorschach, or "inkblot," test). Looking at
20 fuzzy images of Mars through early telescopes, astronomers interpreted what they saw in terms of what they knew, and the legend of Mars as a place not unlike Earth—a planet brimming with life—began to grow.
25 By the end of the 18th century, the Anglo-German astronomer William Herschel saw the Martian polar caps, measured the length of the Martian day (it's about 24.5 hours) and argued that dark spots on the Martian sur-
30 face were oceans. His conclusion: Martians "enjoy a situation in many respects similar to our own."

In 1877, Italian astronomer Giovanni Schiaperelli produced the most lasting bit of
35 Martian folklore. He saw what he took to be long, thin, unnaturally straight lines on the Martian surface. He called them *canali*, a word that can translate into English either as "channels" or "canals." Unfortunately, the
40 latter translation was used, and the canals of Mars were born. Obviously if there were canals, there had to be canal builders, so once more Mars was peopled with all manner of intelligent life-forms.

45 The man who took the canals to their limit was the American astronomer Percival Lowell, scion of the old Boston family. Intrigued by Schiaparelli's findings, in 1894 he built a private observatory in Flagstaff, Ari-
50 zona, and commenced a decades-long series of observations. In his 1908 book *Mars as the Abode of Life*, he recorded no fewer than 184 canals.

Throughout the first half of this century,
55 Mars was populated in the popular imagination with all sorts of sentient beings. In his series of novels set on Mars, Edgar Rice Burroughs (creator of "Tarzan") told of bizarre Martian creatures and trees a hundred
60 feet in diameter with "stems and branches and twigs [that] were as smooth and highly polished as the newest of American-made pianos." C. S. Lewis, the shy Cambridge don perhaps best known for the *Chronicles of*
65 *Narnia*, also wrote about incredible Martian plant life: "The purple mass looked for a moment like a plump of organ pipes, then a stack of rolls of cloth set up on end, then like a forest of gigantic umbrellas blown inside
70 out. It was in faint motion....The purple stuff was vegetation...."

In 1938 Mars was the subject of perhaps the most famous radio broadcast in history. Directed by Orson Welles, the show began
75 with music, only to be interrupted by a news flash from the "Mount Jennings Observatory in Chicago" that began the chronicle of a Martian invasion of New Jersey. "The War of the Worlds" touched off real panic. Police
80 switchboards lit up, and people jammed the highways to escape the Martians. Disclaimers on the show seemed to have no effect. The huge impact of "The War of the Worlds" (the radio play was adapted from the book
85 by H.G. Wells) touched off a long series of stories, movies and TV shows based on invasions from Mars. Despite all the fun, there really was no evidence for life on Mars. Lowell apparently had seen what he wanted
90 to see. It is true that the human mind, confronted with a more or less linear series of poorly seen dots, will often connect them into a line. That may be what happened to Lowell. No one else saw canals.

GO ON TO THE NEXT PAGE

95   As late as the 1960s reputable astronomers saw what they thought were changes in vegetation on Mars. Each polar cap in turn shrinks when spring comes to that hemisphere. At the same time, a darkening visible
100 to all spreads from the shrinking cap toward the equator. They reasoned that water from the melting caps was irrigating desert-like vegetation, bringing it to life. (The darkening turned out to be the work of dust storms.)
105   Still being touted as proof of ancient civilizations on Mars is "The Face," a rocky outcrop that looks remarkably like a human face when illuminated from the side.

7. Which of the following statements best summarizes the main idea of the passage?

   A. Humans historically have viewed Mars subjectively, according to their own individual beliefs.

   B. Humans historically have viewed Mars subjectively, according to the opinions of leading philosophers of the time.

   C. Humans historically have viewed Mars objectively, based on folklore handed down from generation to generation.

   D. Humans historically have viewed Mars objectively, based solely on available scientific data.

8. As described in the passage, representations of Mars in popular art support the author's point that:

   A. media presentations can prove disruptive of social peace and order.

   B. the unknown serves as a mirror to reflect the human imagination.

   C. the unknown is at times best illuminated by mythology rather than by science.

   D. canals probably do exist on Mars.

9. As used in the passage, the word folklore (line 35) most nearly means:

   A. history.

   B. fallacy.

   C. fact.

   D. narrative.

10. Which of the following statements, if true, would most WEAKEN the author's contention that Mars is less known than created by us?

   A. Dust storms do not, in fact, occur on Mars.

   B. Percival Lowell never saw canals through his telescope but read a tale of such structures in an ancient folklore anthology.

   C. Most people believe that intelligent beings populate Mars.

   D. Information recently generated by satellite has produced information that corresponds closely to Lewis' depictions of the planet.

GO ON TO THE NEXT PAGE

11. In organizing a group of astronauts to visit Mars, the author would most likely advise them to approach the planet with:

    A. assurance, because it is unlikely that any biological threat to humankind exists there.

    B. caution, because despite centuries of speculation about Mars from both artistic and scientific orientations, relatively little is known for certain about the planet.

    C. aggression, because it is probable that dangerous microorganisms or hostile creatures populate Mars.

    D. reverence, because Mars has reflected so numerous and such varied perspectives of the earthly imagination.

12. A 1933 treatise on the solar system describes Mars as "potentially the greatest threat to Earth's civilization" and that any life on Mars would "surely possess the will and the incentive to overcome the military forces of the nations of the Earth." If the author were to include this analysis in the passage, he would probably use it to:

    A. justify the long association of Mars with warfare and military science.

    B. illustrate the point that humans often see aliens as beings like themselves.

    C. emphasize that what we think we know about Mars often is the product of our imagination.

    D. explain the author's own opinion about Mars.

GO ON TO THE NEXT PAGE

Passage III (Questions 13–18)

The ability to make art is one of our most distinctive features, for it separates us from all other creatures across an unbridgeable evolutionary gap.

5 Just as an embryo retraces much of the human evolutionary past, so the budding artist reinvents the first stages of art. Soon, however, he completes that process and begins to respond to the culture around him.
10 Even children's art is subject to the taste and outlook of the society that shapes his or her personality. In fact, we tend to judge children's art according to the same criteria as adult art— only in appropriately simpler terms—and with
15 good reason, for if we examine its successive stages, we find that the youngster must develop all the skills that go into adult art: coordination, intellect, personality, imagination, creativity, and aesthetic judgment. Seen
20 this way, the making of a youthful artist is a process as fragile as growing up itself, and one that can be stunted at any step by the vicissitudes of life. No wonder that so few continue their creative aspirations into adult-
25 hood.

Given the many factors that feed into it, art must play a very special role in the artist's personality. Sigmund Freud, the founder of modern psychiatry, conceived of art prima-
30 rily in terms of sublimation outside of consciousness. Such a view hardly does justice to artistic creativity, since art is not simply a negative force at the mercy of our neuroses but a positive expression that integrates di-
35 verse aspects of personality. Indeed, when we look at the art of the mentally ill, we may be struck by its vividness: but we instinctively sense that something is wrong, because the expression is incomplete.

40 Artists may sometimes be tortured by the burden of their genius, but they can never be truly creative under the thrall of psychosis. The imagination is one of our most mysterious facets. It can be regarded as the connector
45 between the conscious and the subconscious, where most of our brain activity takes place.

It is the very glue that holds our personality, intellect, and spirituality together. Because the imagination responds to all three, it acts in
50 lawful, if unpredictable, ways that are determined by the psyche and the mind. Thus, even the most private artistic statements can be understood on some level, even if only an intuitive one.

55 The imagination is important, as it allows us to conceive of all kinds of possibilities in the future and to understand the past in a way that has real survival value. It is a fundamental part of our makeup. The ability to make
60 art, in contrast, must have been acquired relatively recently in the course of human evolution. The record of the earliest art is lost to us. Human beings have been walking the earth for some two million years, but the old-
65 est prehistoric art that we know of was made only about 35,000 years ago, though it was undoubtedly the culmination of a long development no longer traceable. Even the most "primitive" ethnographic art represents a late
70 stage of development within a stable society.

Who were the first artists? In all likelihood, they were shamans. Like the legendary Orpheus, they were believed to have divine powers of inspiration and to be able to enter
75 the underworld of the subconscious in a death-like trance, but, unlike ordinary mortals, they were then able to return to the realm of the living.

Even today the artist remains a magician
80 whose work can mystify and move us—an embarrassing fact to civilized people, who do not readily relinquish their veneer of rational control.

In a larger sense art, like science and reli-
85 gion, fulfills our innate urge to comprehend ourselves and the universe. This function makes art especially significant and, hence, worthy of our attention. Art has the power to penetrate to the core of our being, which rec-
90 ognizes itself in the creative act. For that reason, art represents its creator's deepest understanding and highest aspirations; at the same time, the artist often plays an important

GO ON TO THE NEXT PAGE

role as the articulator of our shared beliefs
95 and values, which he expresses through an
ongoing tradition to us, his audience. A masterpiece, then, is a work that contributes to
our vision of life and leaves us profoundly
moved. Moreover, it can bear the closest scru-
100 tiny and withstand the test of time.

13. The main idea of the passage is that:

    A. artists serve as mediators between our
       daily reality and the world of the un-
       conscious.
    B. as human society has evolved and be-
       come more sophisticated, so has human
       artistic expression.
    C. artistic expression reflects the psycho-
       logical processes and make-up of its
       creator.
    D. the essential appeal of art is its power
       to mystify.

14. In the context of the passage, the word
    genius refers primarily to:

    A. the recognition and appreciation of an
       artist's ability by critics and the public
       at large.
    B. the psychic sensitivity an artist devel-
       ops to reality.
    C. the intellectual attainments of indi-
       vidual artists.
    D. the neurotic and psychotic manifesta-
       tions of artistic perception.

15. The passage implies that art relates to its
    audience:

    A. by delivering both a personal and a uni-
       versal communication from artist to
       audience.
    B. less intensely today because, no longer
       associated with magic, its power to mys-
       tify and to move has dwindled.
    C. by providing insight into another's cre-
       ativity only, while science and religion
       allow us to comprehend ourselves and
       the universe.
    D. irrespective of an audience's emotional
       and spiritual needs.

16. The passage suggests that the ability to
    create art:

    A. evolved before the imagination evolved.
    B. evolved primarily as a survival skill.
    C. has been documented to exist as early
       as two million years ago, when humans
       first inhabited the Earth.
    D. was the result of a long developmental
       process that began when stable societ-
       ies formed.

17. According to the passage, why is art embar-
    rassing to some people who pride them-
    selves on their civilized rationality?

    A. Art's essential mystery frustrates those
       who like to appear cultivated.
    B. Art makes many social sophisticates feel
       ignorant.
    C. Art's simultaneous universality and in-
       dividual relevance seems paradoxical
       to some who pride themselves on their
       logical powers.
    D. Art is able to access the most funda-
       mental and private essence of the self.

18. The discussion of Sigmund Freud's view of
    art and artists shows primarily that:

    A. art represents an integrative psychologi-
       cal function rather than an uncontrolled
       psychic expression.
    B. art which sublimates psychological am-
       biguity is superior to that which
       generates mystery.
    C. successful psychotherapy would enable
       an artist to sublimate the need for artis-
       tic expression.
    D. development of individual artistic con-
       sciousness retraces much of humans'
       evolutionary past.

GO ON TO THE NEXT PAGE

Passage IV (Questions 19–25)

Organisms which live on land exist where weathering and erosion are dominant processes. Even though in some terrestrial environments sediment is deposited in quan-
5 tity, the remains of creatures and plants which lived on land are comparatively rare. In the sea, however, there is often rapid deposition of sediment which is not removed and which entombs a multitude of organisms, many of
10 which become preserved. Rapid burial of the organism prevents it from being eaten by scavengers or broken by sedimentary processes. In order for a fossil to form, a chemical balance has to be maintained between the
15 organic material and the strata in which it becomes trapped. An organism with hard parts such as a shell or skeleton, which is also strong enough not to be readily broken, stands the best chance of being preserved.
20 At the other extreme, however, minute creatures such as *Foraminfera* are often preserved in great abundance. In a few well-documented cases soft-bodied creatures have been well preserved. The Burgess shales high in
25 the Rockies of British Columbia, Canada, are unique in containing a wealth of delicate creatures which lived on the Cambrian sea bed and were carried by a series of mud slides to be preserved at the base of a submarine cliff.
30 Another famous example is that of the Solnhofen limestone in Germany, where dragonflies and feathers are preserved in extremely fine-grained sediment.

35 Whole organisms may occasionally be fossilized, as in the amber on the Baltic coast where insects are trapped in what was originally resin on pine trees. In the southern states of the USA natural pools of tar occur
40 on the land surface. During the Tertiary period mammals stumbled into the sticky swamp and became perfectly preserved, locked away from air and bacteria. Similar processes preserve Arctic mammals trapped in permafrost in Siberia. There are other ex-
45 amples of such complete preservation, but most fossils have undergone change before they are preserved.

The chemical composition of the hard
50 parts of many organisms is such that they can exist in equilibrium with a variety of rocks and environments in the Earth's crust. Calcium carbonate is common in shell-fish and vertebrate skeletons, while silica is
55 present in the structure of Radiolaria and sponges. The horny nitrogen-bearing carbohydrate, chitin, which occurs in many arthropod exoskeletons, is very stable in a number of geological situations. Nevertheless, changes often take place in the organism,
60 or the fragments of it.

Petrifaction occurs when the organic remains are impregnated with minerals brought in by fluids and solutions seeping through
65 the strata. Such solutions commonly carry calcite, silica, and iron minerals, and partial or complete changes can be effected. Though the fossils thus formed may retain their outward shape, the fine detail of the original
70 may be lost. Examples of petrification include the iron pyrite shells of molluscs in Jurassic clays and shales, and opal tree stumps from Australia and the USA. The solutions which percolate through the fossil-bearing strata do not only introduce new
75 minerals. Often they remove calcite shells leaving a curved hollow in the sediment. This mould may later become infilled with one of a variety of minerals, thus preserving at least the surface detail and shape of the organic
80 matter. The chemistry of living organisms is based on carbon, and many fossils of, for example, plants, fish, and graptolites are preserved as a thin black film of this element. After burial in the sediment the more volatile
85 chemicals are released and the carbon percentage thus increases. The outlines of large marine reptiles are sometimes thus preserved, but the best known carbonized fossils are the delicate ferns and the other plants from Car-
90 boniferous strata.

Fossils can occur without any part of the organism remaining. Footprints, tracks, and burrows are trace fossils, indicating where
95 creatures have existed. These can give valuable information as to the size and structure of the animal.

GO ON TO THE NEXT PAGE

19. According to the passage, each of the following factors favors the preservation of fossils EXCEPT for:

    A. high quantity of sediment deposition.
    B. natural pools of swamp tar.
    C. chemical balance between organic material and surrounding strata.
    D. high velocity of sediment deposition.

20. According to the information given in the passage, the Burgess shales in British Columbia contain:

    A. creatures native to the Canadian Rockies.
    B. fossils preserved in the Cambrian sea bed.
    C. fossils preserved at the base of an underwater cliff.
    D. minute, soft-bodied creatures called *Foraminfera*.

21. The author mentions the Siberian permafrost in order to provide an example of:

    A. the preservation of hard-shell organisms.
    B. a preservative shell permeable to bacteria and air.
    C. incomplete fossil preservation.
    D. complete fossil preservation.

22. According to the passage, silica present in the structure of Radiolaria and sponges serves:

    A. to provide a chitin-like preservative exoskeleton.
    B. to maintain equilibrium with material in the Earth's crust.
    C. as a pseudo-vertebral morphological structure.
    D. as an absolute barrier against changes in the fossil.

23. According to the passage, the carbonization of fossils derives from:

    A. evaporation of unstable chemicals from organic remains.
    B. deposition of a carbon shell on organic remains.
    C. deposition of calcite, silica, and iron minerals in organic remains.
    D. removal of calcite shells, leaving a curved, C-shaped hollow in the sediment.

24. According to the passage, the fluid that percolates through fossil-bearing strata:

    A. removes all traces of fossils in its path.
    B. has no effect on fossils in its path.
    C. often leaves the calcite shells of a fossil in its path undisturbed.
    D. can erase the fine details of a fossil in its path.

25. The synthesis of geology, chemistry, biology, physics, marine science, and other disciplines necessary to develop an understanding of fossils as described would be most similar to the study of:

    A. Greek mythology, Elizabethan drama, and "found" poetry to develop an approach to modern literary sensibility.
    B. mathematics, logic, and computer science to develop a theory of artificial intelligence.
    C. resistance, magnetism, and electron-flow to develop an understanding of electricity.
    D. the mechanisms of different antibiotics to develop a theory of infectious disease.

GO ON TO THE NEXT PAGE

Passage V (Questions 26–35)

It has been twenty years since the publication of Jacques Derrida's *Of Grammatology* set off the boom in literary theory, the full effects of which are only now becoming
5 apparent. Whether or not most of us have actually read a word of Derrida, or of Paul de Man, Michel Foucault, or Fredric Jameson, our collective sense of what art is and does has been dramatically altered by their work.

10 The aim of what has, rather grandly, come to be called "theory" is the skeptical interrogation of various cultural forms—history writing, legal discourse, advertising imagery, and, perhaps most significantly, art. Over
15 the past two decades, theorists have sought to reveal art's long-suppressed kinship with propaganda, pornography, and the language of imperial oppression. Seen in theory's bleaching light, great poets no longer appear
20 as ideals of wisdom or of human triumph against the odds. Now they're to be approached as shrewd deceivers; tour guides to dreamy, detached lotus worlds, apologists for race and gender oppression, bagmen for
25 the bourgeoisie. Current criticism, under the rubric of cultural studies, has continued the trend. Today's professorial commentators on literature—or film or rock or hip-hop—assume the truth of high theory without feeling
30 a need to argue for it. And as the various purported mystifications of popular culture fall under theory's skeptical beam, practitioners savor a sense of rebellion, of old laws broken and new freedoms won.

35 But before theory's triumph is complete, we ought to back up and see the battle between poetry and the professors in a larger historical context. When we do, it becomes clear that theory isn't the unprecedented in-
40 tellectual revolution that its proponents often assume. Rather, it's an installment in a struggle that's as old as Western culture itself—the struggle between the philosophers and the poets that Plato, in the fourth cen-
45 tury B.C., said was already ancient.

To Plato, the poets were a band of deceivers. Theory offered illusions, mere imitations of imitations, whereas life's highest purpose is to seek eternal truths. For his own part,
50 Plato claimed to offer access to concepts that could help one to live a better life. Through philosophical conversation, you approach pure knowledge of the Good, the Truer, the Beautiful. Conversely, the knowledge that
55 you glean from reading literature is messy, undefined, without focus. You may encounter numerous instances of just action in Homer, but by simply reading Homer you'll never find out what all those instances have
60 in common: you'll never make the step from anecdotal to general knowledge, never become a philosopher.

Until the theory boom, literary critics provided a third element in the poet/philosopher
65 debate. Responsive to both art and intellection, critics from Aristotle to Virginia Woolf effectively defended poetry, not only from popular indifference but from dismissive philosophy. With the onset of theory, the critical
70 contingency is fast disappearing. There are now plenty of poets and no end of philosopher/theorists, but art's public defenders, writers whose first allegiance is to the aesthetic experiences that have shaped them, are
75 becoming ever more rare.

26. The central thesis of the passage is that:

   A. art has a long-standing relationship with propaganda and the language of imperial oppression.
   B. art is closely related to propaganda.
   C. current literary theory has long-standing historical precedents.
   D. high theory has an inherent truth that need not be put to debate.

GO ON TO THE NEXT PAGE ➡

27. Implicit in the statement that new theory views literary artists as cultural conmen and flunkies is the notion that:

    A. great novels and poetry do not truly reflect the milieu from which they emerge.

    B. poets and dramatists reject point-of-view narration in favor of objective truths.

    C. literature caters to the cultural biases of the ruling class.

    D. the ruling class does not, by and large, embrace the moral values and social norms that its literature advocates.

28. Given the claims made in the passage, statements such as, "Their poetry is a tissue of pretty lies," "Literature deceives the unwary reader," "The writer's product is pure illusion," represent:

    A. establishment propaganda distributed by apologists for oppressors.

    B. perceptions of literary art unexpressed prior to the late 20th century.

    C. ancient views of literature.

    D. criticism typical of Virginia Woolf.

29. According to the passage, a critic who endorses the new theory would most likely believe that:

    A. writers should be loyal to their most influential aesthetic experience.

    B. Homeric poetry is like advertising.

    C. Homeric poetry offers both dramatic action and eternal truth.

    D. contemporary poetry needs defense from disinterested and derisive readers.

30. The ideas discussed in this passage would likely be of most use to:

    A. a cultural historian.

    B. a scholar of Greek epic poetry.

    C. a graduate student in philosophy.

    D. a writer of contemporary drama.

31. An appropriate description of the historical relationship between literary artists and their critics derived from the passage would state that:

    I. artists and critics do not always agree on the purpose, function and meaning of art.

    II. artists and critics may have opposing viewpoints.

    III. artists and critics may play mutually supportive roles.

    A. I only

    B. II only

    C. I and II only

    D. I, II, and III

32. Faced with the field of theory today, Plato would most likely respond by:

    A. embracing it, because it views poets as clever deceivers.

    B. embracing it, because it seeks to foster debate concerning the truth of high theory.

    C. rejecting it, because it is skeptical of art and artists.

    D. rejecting it, because it takes poets for apologists and dreamers.

GO ON TO THE NEXT PAGE →

33. Based on the passage, a member of "the critical contingency" would probably discuss a novel from the point-of-view of:

    A. the importance of the author's political assumptions.

    B. the importance of the author's aesthetic experience.

    C. a member of a historically oppressed class.

    D. a member of the philosopher class.

34. Which of the following statements is NOT presented as evidence of historical debate between writers and critics?

    A. Plato believed that poetry offered illusions of illusions.

    B. The struggle between philosophers and poets began before Plato's time.

    C. Homeric poetry engages the reader viscerally, and not critically.

    D. The work of Derrida, de Man, and Foucault has changed our understanding of the parameters of literature.

35. According to the passage, in the long debate between those who scorn literature and those who defend it:

    I. the defenders are a threatened species.

    II. Aristotle has not been immune to popular indifference.

    III. critics dismissed Virginia Woolf as irrelevant to the social norms of her time.

    A. II only

    B. III only

    C. I and II only

    D. I, II, and III

GO ON TO THE NEXT PAGE

Passage VI (Questions 36–45)

The depression, in the strict sense, began as a stock market and financial crisis. Prices of stocks had been pushed upward by years of continuing expansion and high dividends.
5 At the beginning of 1929 prices on the European stock exchanges began to weaken. But the real crisis, or turning point, came with the crash on the New York Stock Exchange in October 1929. Here, values had been driven
10 to fantastic heights by excessive speculation. Not only professional speculators, but quite ordinary people, in the United States, as an easy way to make a good deal of money, bought stock with borrowed funds. Some-
15 times, trading on "margin," they "owned" five or ten times as much stock as the amount of their own money put into it; the rest they borrowed from brokers, and the brokers borrowed from banks, the purchased stock in
20 each case serving as collateral. With money so easy to obtain, people pushed up stock prices by bidding against each other and enjoyed huge fortunes on paper; but if prices fell, even a little, the hapless owners would
25 be obliged to sell their stock to pay off the money they had borrowed. Hence the weakening of values on the New York Stock Exchange set off uncontrollable tidal waves of selling, which drove stock prices down
30 irresistibly and disastrously. In a month stock values dropped by 40 percent, and in three years, from 1929 to 1932, the average value of fifty industrial stocks traded on the New York Stock Exchange dropped from 252 to 61. In
35 these same three years 5,000 American banks closed their doors.

The crisis passed from finance to industry, and from the United States to the rest of the world. The export of American capital
40 came to an end. Americans not only ceased to invest in Europe but sold the foreign securities that they had. This pulled the foundations from under the postwar revival of Germany and hence indirectly of much of
45 Europe. Americans, their incomes falling, ceased to buy foreign goods; from Belgium to Borneo people saw their American markets slip away, and prices tumbled. In 1931

the failure of a leading Vienna bank, the
50 Creditanstalt, sent a wave of shivers, bankruptcies, and business calamities over Europe. Everywhere business firms and private people could not collect what was owed them, or even draw on money that they thought
55 they had in the bank. They could not buy, and so the factories could not sell. Factories slowed down or closed entirely. Between 1929 and 1932, the latter year representing the depth of the depression, world produc-
60 tion is estimated to have declined by 38 percent, and the world's international trade fell by two-thirds. In the United States the national income fell from $85 billion to $37 billion.

65 Unemployment, a chronic disease ever since the war, assumed the proportion of pestilence. In 1932 there were 30 million unemployed persons statistically reported in the world; and this figure did not include the
70 further millions who could find work only for a few hours in the week, or the masses in Asia or Africa for whom no statistics were to be had. The worker's wages were gone, the farmer's income now touched bottom; and
75 the decline of mass purchasing power forced more idleness of machinery and more unemployment. People in the prime of life spent years out of work. Young people could not find jobs or establish themselves in an occu-
80 pation. Skills and talents of older people grew rusty. Millions were reduced to living, and supporting their families, on the pittances of charity, doles, or relief. Great modern cities saw an outburst of sidewalk art, in
85 which, at busy street corners, jobless ablebodied men drew pictures on the pavement with colored chalk, in the hope of attracting a few sixpence or dimes. People were crushed in spirit by a feeling of uselessness; months
90 and years of fruitless job hunting left them demoralized, bored, discouraged, embittered, frustrated, and resentful. Never had there been such waste, not merely of machinery which now stood still, but of the trained and
95 disciplined labor force on which all modern societies were built. And people chronically out of work naturally turned to new and disturbing political ideas.

GO ON TO THE NEXT PAGE

36. The author's central thesis is that:

    A. speculation in the stock market by trading on "margin" entails inherent risks which lead inevitably to pandemic socioeconomic turbulence.

    B. radical political ideas will always surge to the forefront in modern societies with large skilled labor forces which undergo periods of significant unemployment.

    C. in 1929 deficiencies of data collection regarding third-world unemployment led to underestimates in the duration and severity of global depression.

    D. the economic and social consequences of the 1929 stock market crash, both domestic and international, were inextricably linked in a domino-like way.

37. The passage suggests that the Great Depression most likely affected the European economy for which of the following reasons?

    A. European industry was largely dependent on the American consumer market for its prosperity.

    B. European workers could not compete effectively with the cheap, surplus third-world labor force.

    C. The American stock market was highly invested in the European consumer market.

    D. American investors lost faith in European currencies and manufacturing quality.

38. Which of the following assertions does the author support with an example?

    I. Ready availability of capital leads to massive speculation.
    II. The failure of a large bank can provoke general investor panic.
    III. A global depression results in abandonment of family farms.

    A. I only
    B. III only
    C. I and II only
    D. II and III only

39. Stock prices in 1929 just prior to the crash are described as "fantastic." What is the most likely reason for the choice of this word?

    A. The word implies the unrealistic magnitude of investor speculation.

    B. The market offered a superb, irresistible avenue to financial independence.

    C. The price supports involved a bizarre relationship between European industry and third-world labor.

    D. Many who speculated in the market believed that divine and occult powers safeguarded the American economy.

40. According to the passage, which of the following is cited as a consequence of the stock market crash of 1929?

    I. Between 1929 and 1932 American production fell by 38 percent.
    II. Global trade declined by 66 percent.
    III. Famine pervaded Africa and Asia.

    A. I only
    B. II only
    C. I an III only
    D. II and III only

GO ON TO THE NEXT PAGE

41. The author suggests that unemployment became a pestilence during the Great Depression because it:

    A. spread throughout the world.
    B. assumed chronic proportions.
    C. led to starvation and suicide.
    D. destroyed the tissue of society.

42. What does the discussion of unemployment imply about political developments during the 1930s?

    A. Charismatic demagogues manipulated popular discontent for their own ends.
    B. Profound economic insecurity allowed politicians to isolate and blame segments of society as scapegoats.
    C. Widespread social dislocations stimulated a search for new solutions.
    D. Extremist philosophies triumphed over good sense, justice, and fairness.

43. The author argues that the stock market crash of 1929 led to a virtually universal desperation in society. Which of the following claims, if true, would most WEAKEN the argument?

    A. Retraining in needed skills was relatively easy to obtain.
    B. Relocation was an option for most workers.
    C. Wholesale social renovation emerged as a political goal.
    D. People were willing to do anything to make ends meet.

44. According to the author's account, the global unemployment statistics during the Depression were likely:

    A. understated, due to the cultural reluctance of unemployed masses in Africa and Asia to divulge that information to international agencies.
    B. understated, due to a lack of available statistics in Asia and Africa, and the failure to account for huge numbers of underemployed workers.
    C. inflated, due to the number of European immigrants who wrongfully claimed unemployment in order to obtain relief money.
    D. inflated, due to adjustments by politicians in Europe and America who sought to secure better relief programs for their regions.

45. Today's international economy is more deficit-financed and interdependent than ever before, and becoming increasingly so. What worry might this information reasonably arouse among economic historians?

    A. Whether unscrupulous multinational industrialists might manipulate global economic conditions to favor their own interests
    B. Whether global investment institutions will become the ultimate judges of political decisions
    C. Whether economic and political safeguards installed after the Great Depression are sufficient to prevent another global collapse
    D. Whether the global depletion of natural resources will lead to inevitable economic chaos and sociopolitical crisis

GO ON TO THE NEXT PAGE

Passage VII (Questions 46–51)

Science education is clearly influenced by a single overriding premise: the primary function of formal science education, whether precollege or college, is to ensure a steady
5 supply of scientists and science-related professionals, including, of course, science educators. Everything else done in science education, regardless of its educational worth or numbers of students involved, turns out
10 to be secondary to this goal. Not that this is its avowed purpose, of course. Science educators persistently try to persuade themselves, and the community at large, to believe that there is a loftier purpose to sci-
15 ence education, namely, to educate the general public—to achieve widespread scientific literacy—and indeed many educators have visions of such an ideal. But the reality behind such grand objectives is that the prac-
20 tical goal of producing future scientists must (and does) come first. Urging students into science as a profession is clearly part of the responsibility of science educators, but one must bear in mind that here we are dealing
25 with only about 5 to 10 percent of the high school student population. To face the issue squarely, it is obvious that science departments, whether in our schools or colleges, are no different from most other disciplines
30 in seeking to increase the enrollment of non-majors in their courses; their underlying motive is more to attract critical masses of faculty and adequate equipment budgets for research than to satisfy some compelling edu-
35 cational need of the general (non-science) student.

The competition is keen in most faculties to be included in the distribution requirements for all students, and equally acute in
40 most science departments to design courses that will attract these students regardless of whether such courses will have a lasting effect on them. Think for a moment if the science departments in our high schools had
45 to justify their existence by serving only the 10 percent or so who claim to be science-bound, or if our college science departments served only its majors. Most science departments would collapse for lack of a critical
50 mass of faculty, and the training of science professionals would have to be given over to a relatively few specialized state or national high schools and colleges. So, unseemly as it may be, a major factor in the pursuit of scien-
55 tific literacy is self-justification and perpetuation of the science and science education professions. Many university science departments survive only by virtue of the "point credits" they earn through their intro-
60 ductory courses. How else to account for such promotional course titles as Physics for Poets, Kitchen Chemistry, Biology for Living, etc. Not that this is altogether improper, for it is essential that university science de-
65 partments be able to support "critical masses" of faculty to carry on research and prepare future scientists. Whether this is equally true for all students at the high school level is open to question.

70 A second premise concerns general education in science. If the purpose of such education is to create a scientifically literate public, the principal target audience, namely the student population, may be ill-chosen. However one chooses to define scientific lit-
75 eracy, its main objective seems clear enough: society (and the individual) will somehow benefit if its members are sufficiently literate to participate intelligently in science-based societal issues. Assuming this is true...and
80 on the surface it seems perfectly sensible, is the proper target audience the student or the adult population? Obviously, if the purpose of such literacy is to benefit society, it is really only the adult population that is in a
85 position to contribute to the public good. So while students may attain some level of scientific literacy relating to the individual science courses they take in school, what good is it if they fail to retain this knowledge into
90 adulthood?

The mistake we make is in assuming that because some, perhaps even many, of our students perform well in school science, they have achieved a measure of scientific literacy

GO ON TO THE NEXT PAGE

that will serve them as adults....Most science teachers leave their classes feeling that they have communicated successfully with some number of non-science students, and most
100 likely they have. But the end effect of this is a delusion. Good school performance, even a reasonable level of scientific literacy while one is a student, provides no assurance that the individual will retain enough science
105 when he or she becomes a responsible adult, presumably contributing to the overall good of society. It would be different if science education for the general student were justified solely on the grounds of a cultural or
110 intellectual imperative, but while many may believe that it should be, science educators in general fear that doing so would spell its doom by relegating it to purely elective status in the schools.

115 Here lies the crux of the matter. Whatever we may do to turn students on to science, to make them acutely aware of the world around them, and get them to at least appreciate what the scientific enterprise is about, if
120 not so much science itself, we are guided in the schools by immediate feedback rather than long-term retention. After all, to be pragmatic about it, having literate students who turn out to be scientific illiterates as
125 adults does not do much for society. We know that the staying power of science courses is very poor, but what is particularly depressing is the fact that although most students lapse back into scientific illiteracy soon
130 after they graduate, they nevertheless think they are reasonably literate in science.

46. The author's claim that science educators must set "practical goal[s]" before aspiring to loftier objectives (lines 19-20) is supported by which of the following observations?

A. There is a relative lack of competition from other departments for the science majors' interest.

B. General students seek large numbers of science courses.

C. Science departments seek large numbers of science faculty.

D. Society has a compelling need to achieve widespread scientific literacy.

47. The author most likely believes that one of the main purposes of teaching general science to critical masses of students is to:

A. enable large numbers of citizens to participate intelligently in a scientifically oriented economy.

B. provide an understanding of empirical methodology to all students as an essential problem-solving skill.

C. familiarize non-science majors with newly challenging ethical issues generated by scientific technology.

D. justify the maintenance of a large academic and research establishment in science.

48. Given the information in the passage, most non-science majors who study general science in either high school or college will most likely:

A. enroll in pseudo-scientific courses such as "Physics for Poets," etc.

B. do so to meet course distribution and "point credits" requirements.

C. subscribe to popular science periodicals after graduation.

D. retain little science knowledge after graduation.

GO ON TO THE NEXT PAGE

49. Based on information in the passage, if science departments taught fewer "promotional course[s]" (line 61) to undergraduates, which of the following outcomes would likely occur?

   A. Colleges and universities would produce significantly higher numbers of scientifically literate graduates.
   B. All students would graduate with significantly greater scientific literacy.
   C. Science departments might risk decreased budgetary support from administrations.
   D. Non-science departments might be overwhelmed by increasing student enrollments.

50. The author suggests that restricting high school science departments to only science majors would result in:

   A. the demise of many high school science departments.
   B. the proliferation of specialized state or national high schools.
   C. improved high school science curricula.
   D. better utilization of academic resources.

51. Suppose the majority of high school graduates were found to demonstrate an educated interest in science and science-related issues fifteen years post-graduation. This new information would most CHALLENGE the claim that:

   A. schools are guided more by immediate feedback than by long-term results.
   B. most scientifically illiterate graduates believe themselves to be scientifically knowledgeable.
   C. having literate students who become scientifically illiterate adults does not do much for society.
   D. the staying power of science courses is very poor.

Passage VIII (Questions 52–59)

As the largest land animal on the planet, the elephant is a potent symbol of the animal kingdom, distinguished by its size, prehensile trunk, ivory tusks, and enormous ears.
5 In the West, where the elephant is an exotic creature known only from books, movies, circuses, and zoos, its image suffers distortion and even exploitation. Whether romanticized or trivialized, the elephant is rarely presented
10 in its complex reality. But in Africa, where humans and elephants—or their respective ancestors—have coexisted for a million years or more, the elephant is known in fuller dimensions. It has been a source of food,
15 material, and riches; a fearsome rival for resources; and a highly visible, provocative neighbor. Inevitably it has had an impact on the artistic imagination. Even in areas where the elephant has now vanished, it persists as
20 a symbol in expressive culture. As interpreted in African sculpture, masquerade, dance, and song, its image undergoes a startling range of transformations. But no matter how it is represented, its size and power are
25 the features most likely to be dramatized, for they not only inspire respect, but stand, for better or worse, as emblems for human values.

The elephant is of course only one crea-
30 ture within the vast drama of intricate relationships that link the animal world with the human one. It should not be isolated from the hierarchy of fauna that give it context not just in actuality but also in its
35 symbolic life. In its symbolic functions it is at times interchangeable with other creatures, depending on culture and circumstance: qualities ascribed in one instance to the elephant may be given in another to the leopard
40 or duiker. Even within a single culture the meanings ascribed to it can shift. Or it may be just one of an array of animals treated more or less equally, much like those of the Biblical Noah's ark—a theme that has been
45 explored in glass paintings from Senegal, thorn carvings from Nigeria, and popular paintings from Ethiopia.

The elephant may be considered as a microcosm—a large one, to be sure. By virtue
50 of its sheer size and prominence, the roles it plays in art and historical processes are magnified. In the broader terms of the macrocosm one might ask how humans relate to their environment and the fauna they share it with;
55 and above all, how they interpret that relationship. In Africa as elsewhere, people represent their relationship to animals in multiple ways, and their complex experience of it can be read in the symbolic language of
60 their respective cultures. Although elephant imagery may have its origins in actual observation, it is just as often a product of the imagination, and African depictions of the elephant have as much to say about human
65 society as about the animal itself. Ultimately, historical events, social responsibilities, religious beliefs, and political relationships are the primary subjects of elephant imagery.

For some, this may appear problematic.
70 Within the scientific community, finding *human* traits in *animals* is often seen as sentimental anthropomorphizing even though it is, according to Levi-Strauss, a fundamental activity of the human mind. On
75 the other hand, finding *animal* traits in *humans* tends to be seen outside the scientific community as pernicious and degrading. Mary Midgley puts it quite succinctly:

Unquestionably there does remain a non-
80 scientific but powerful tendency to resent and fear all close comparison between our own species and any other. Unquestionably we often tend to feel—at times extremely strongly—that the gap between our own spe-
85 cies and all others is enormous.

Yet in African cultures, the perception of this "enormous gap" provokes much thoughtful and creative response. Of all creatures, the elephant, so huge, so remote, and yet so
90 apparently human, most dramatizes the gap between the species. Donal Cosentino surveying the elephant in oral traditions, sees it as the Gray Planet, whose sightings are full of mystery and portent. But the phenom-

GO ON TO THE NEXT PAGE

95 enon is by no means confined to oral literature; indeed, many visual representations are
driven by the impulse to mediate the breach
between worlds.

52. The passage suggests that Africans'
longstanding coexistence with elephants has
caused them to regard elephants with:

A. appreciation.
B. contempt.
C. fear.
D. reverence.

53. Suppose that the elephants in a particular
region of Africa were to disappear. How
would this new information affect the
author's claims about the animal's impact
on the artistic product of humans living in
the area?

A. Owing to their scarcity, talismanic objects carved from elephant tusks would
acquire considerable value as magical
totems.
B. Communities would barter their local
products for cultural works and artisan crafts from communities who
remained physically close to elephants.
C. The dance and song of the local inhabitants would gradually lose all traces of
elephant imagery.
D. Elephant imagery would continue to
play an important role in the local culture.

54. Suppose it is discovered that muralists in a
number of African communities portrayed
jaguars as provisioners of food, material,
and wealth, as dangerous competitors for
resources, and as dramatically inspirational
cohabitants. How would this information
affect the author's claims about the interchangeability of symbolic function?

A. It would support the claim that culture
and circumstance help determine which
qualities are ascribed to which animals.
B. It would support the claim that some
people believe the gap between animals
and humans to be enormous.
C. It would weaken the claim that
Senegalese glass paintings are comparable in their imagery to Noah's Ark.
D. It would weaken the claim that the elephant may be viewed as a microcosm.

55. The claim that elephant imagery in African
culture reveals information about Africans'
social lives is based mainly on:

A. western European cultural analysis.
B. African representations of the micro-
cosm.
C. Nigerian thorn carvings.
D. Ethiopian popular art.

56. According to the passage, European societies differ from African societies in that the
former would be less likely to:

A. become captivated by the elephant's size
and power.
B. devote considerable resources to maintain artificial environments for captive
elephants.
C. use elephant characteristics to
emblemize human values.
D. adopt the elephant as a children's cultural icon.

GO ON TO THE NEXT PAGE

57. Levi-Strauss and Mary Midgley are cited in the passage in order to support the point that:

   A. African cultures tend to anthropomorphize to a much greater degree than do European cultures.
   B. science scholars have systematically identified a number of human qualities in animals.
   C. the human capacity to liken human characteristics to animal traits is a complex and contradictory phenomenon.
   D. anthropological scholars have achieved a general consensus of opinion with regard to anthropomorphism.

58. The passage suggests that a gap exists between all of the following EXCEPT:

   A. African and western versions of elephant imagery.
   B. size of an elephant and its symbolic import.
   C. actual elephants and elephant imagery.
   D. the perspective of elephant as microcosm and as macrocosm.

59. The passage as a whole suggests that humans view their relationship to animals:

   A. in nearly universal symbols across different cultures.
   B. in varied ways that depend on each culture's symbolic forms.
   C. in superficial and simplistic terms.
   D. in purely practical terms.

GO ON TO THE NEXT PAGE

Passage IX (Questions 60–69)

Advances in computers and data networks inspire visions of a future "information economy" in which everyone will have access to gigabytes of all kinds of information
5 anywhere and anytime. But information has always been a notoriously difficult commodity to deal with, and, in some ways, computers and high-speed networks make the problems of buying, selling, and distributing informa-
10 tion goods worse rather than better.

To start with, the very abundance of digital data exacerbates the most fundamental constraint on information commerce—the limits of human comprehension. As Nobel
15 laureate economist Herbert A. Simon puts it: "What information consumes is rather obvious: it consumes the attention of its recipients. Hence a wealth of information creates a poverty of attention, and a need to allocate that
20 attention efficiently among the overabundance of information sources that might consume it." Technology for producing and distributing information is useless without some way to locate, filter, organize, and sum-
25 marize it. A new profession of "information managers" will have to combine the skills of computer scientists, librarians, publishers, and database experts to help us discover and manage information. These human agents
30 will work with software agents that specialize in manipulating information—offspring of indexing programs such as Archie, Veronica, and various "World Wide Web crawlers" that aid Internet navigators today.

35 The evolution of the Internet itself poses serious problems. Now that the Internet has been privatized, several companies are competing to provide the backbones that will carry traffic between different local networks,
40 but workable business models for interconnection—who pays how much for each packet transmitted, for example—have yet to be developed. If interconnection standards are developed that make it cheap and easy to
45 transmit information across independent networks, competition will flourish. If technical or economic factors make interconnection difficult, so that transmitting data across multiple networks is expensive or too slow,
50 the largest suppliers can offer a significant performance advantage; they may be able to use this edge to drive out competitors and monopolize the market.

Similar problems arise at the level of the
55 information goods themselves. There is a growing need for open standards for formats used to represent text, images, video, and other collections of data, so that one producer's data will be accessible to another's
60 software. As with physical links, it is not yet clear how to make sure companies have the right economic incentives to negotiate widely usable standards.

In addition to standards for distribution
65 and manipulation of information, we must develop standards for networked economic transactions: the actual exchange of money for digital goods....There are already more than a dozen proposals for ways to conduct
70 secure financial transactions on the Internet. Some of them, such as the DigiCash system, involve complex encryption techniques; others, such as that used by First Virtual, are much simpler. Many of these protocols are
75 implemented entirely in software; others enlist specialized hardware to support electronic transactions. "Smart" credit cards with chips embedded in them can perform a variety of authentication and accounting tasks....

80 Even when the financial infrastructure becomes widely available, there is still the question of how digital commodities will be priced....Will data be rented or sold? Will articles be bundled together, as is done today
85 in magazines and newspapers, or will consumers purchase information on an article-by-article basis? Will users subscribe to information services, or will they be able to buy data spontaneously? How will pay-
90 ment be divided among the various parties involved in the transaction, such as authors, publishers, libraries, on-line services, and so on? Not one of these questions has a defini-

GO ON TO THE NEXT PAGE

tive answer, and it is likely that many market
95 experiments will fail before viable solutions
emerge.

The shared nature of information technology makes it critical to address issues of
standardization and interoperability sooner
100 rather than later. Each consumer's willingness to use a particular piece of
technology—such as the Internet—depends
strongly on the number of other uses. New
communications tools, such as fax machines,
105 VCRs, and the Internet itself, have typically
started out with long periods of relatively
low use followed by exponential growth,
which implies that changes are much cheaper
and easier to make in the early stages. Fur-
110 thermore, once a particular technology has
penetrated a significant portion of the market, it may be very difficult to dislodge.
Fortunes in the computer industry have been
made and lost from the recognition that
115 people do not want to switch to a new piece
of hardware or software—even if it is demonstrably superior—because they will lose
both the time they have invested in the old
ways and the ability to share data easily with
120 others....If buyers, sellers, and distributors of
information make the wrong choices now,
repairing the damage later could be very
costly.

This discussion about managing, distrib-
125 uting, and trading in information is
overshadowed by the more fundamental issue of how much data authors and publishers
will be willing to make available in electronic
form. If intellectual property protection is
130 too lax, there may be inadequate incentives
to produce new electronic works; conversely,
if protection is too strict, it may impede the
free flow and fair use of information. A compromise position must be found somewhere
135 between those who suggest that all information should be free and those who advocate
laws against the electronic equivalent of
browsing at a magazine rack.

Extending existing copyright and patent
140 law to apply to digital technologies can only
be a stopgap measure. Law appropriate for
the paper-based technology of the 18th century will not be adequate to cope with the
digital technology of the 21st; already the
145 proliferation of litigation over software pat-
ents and even over the shape of computer
screen trash cans makes the need for wholesale revisions apparent.

60. The author's main point about the information economy is that:

A. cooperation among competing information suppliers and hardware designers
is essential if the new information
economy is to flourish.
B. the competitive commodity in the information age is human attention, and
the greater the amount of data available, the higher the relative value of
attention.
C. the nature of the information services
market lends itself to monopolization
by smart entrepreneurs and large suppliers.
D. new information technologies create
new legal, commercial, and managerial
problems that will require new solutions.

61. The passage suggests that with regard to
information technology consumers will do
which of the following?

A. Use a new technology more readily if
many others also use it
B. Readily switch from an older product
to a newer and improved one
C. Embrace new communication tools as
soon as the tools are introduced on the
market
D. Initially respond enthusiastically to a
new product and then lose interest in it
as it remains on the market

GO ON TO THE NEXT PAGE

62. The passage suggests that workable models to interconnect local Internet networks need further development because without them:

    A. consumers will have to determine which backbone system most fits their needs.
    B. uncontrolled competition will confuse consumers with information overload.
    C. price wars will destroy the industry's ability to develop new services and products.
    D. monopolies will arise, and quality and price control may suffer.

63. The need for financial incentives to motivate information producers is cited by the author as evidence for the claim that:

    A. ready access to digital information should be balanced against protection of intellectual property rights.
    B. the Internet represents the electronic equivalent of a library periodical rack.
    C. intellectual property protection that is too lax will restrict consumer access to digital information.
    D. access to fair use of digital information ideally should be universal and free.

64. The existence of which of the following phenomena would most strongly CHALLENGE the information in the passage?

    A. Infrastructure design incorporating cost-effective modification capability
    B. Masses of users who are reluctant to use new systems and programs
    C. New inventions rendering current systems obsolete within 20 years
    D. Relatively user-friendly interoperability

65. According to the passage, a "smart" credit card (line 77) would best be described as one that:

    A. contains chips which can perform a variety of computational tasks.
    B. recognizes software protocols capable of delivering financial services.
    C. enlists and enables special hardware to carry out electronic transactions.
    D. involves complex digital encryption techniques.

STOP
IF YOU FINISH BEFORE TIME IS CALLED, YOU MAY CHECK YOUR WORK ON THIS TEST ONLY.
DO NOT TURN TO ANY OTHER TEST IN THIS BOOK.

Physical Sciences I

Time: 100 Minutes
Questions 66–142

PHYSICAL SCIENCES

DIRECTIONS: Most questions in the Physical Sciences test are organized into groups, each preceded by a descriptive passage. After studying the passage, select the one best answer to each question in the group. Some questions are not based on a descriptive passage and also are independent of each other. You must also select the one best answer to these questions. If you are not certain of an answer, eliminate the alternatives that you know to be incorrect and then select an answer from the remaining alternatives. Indicate your selection by blackening the corresponding circle on your answer sheet (DIAGNOSTIC TEST FORM). A periodic table is provided for your use. You may consult it whenever you wish.

PERIODIC TABLE OF THE ELEMENTS

1 H 1.0																	2 He 4.0
3 Li 6.9	4 Be 9.0											5 B 10.8	6 C 12	2 N 14.0	8 O 16	9 F 19.0	10 Ne 20.0
11 Na 22.0	12 Mg 24.3											13 Al 27.0	14 Si 28.1	15 P 31.0	16 S 32.1	17 Cl 35.5	18 Ar 39.0
19 K 39.1	20 Ca 40.1	21 Sc 45.0	22 Ti 47.9	23 V 50.9	24 Cr 52.0	25 Mn 54.9	26 Fe 55.8	27 Co 58.9	28 Ni 58.7	29 Cu 63.5	30 Zn 65.4	31 Ga 69.7	32 Ge 72.6	33 As 74.9	34 Se 79.0	35 Br 79.9	36 Kr 83.8
37 Rb 85.5	38 Sr 87.6	39 Y 88.9	40 Zr 91.2	41 Nb 92.9	42 Mo 95.9	43 Tc 97.0	44 Ru 101.0	45 Rh 102.9	46 Pd 106.4	47 Ag 107.9	48 Cd 112.4	49 In 114.8	50 Sn 118.7	51 Sb 121.8	52 Te 127.6	53 I 126.9	54 Xe 131.3
55 Cs 132.9	56 Ba 137.3	57 La 138.9	72 Hf 178.5	73 Ta 180.9	74 W 183.9	75 Re 186.2	76 Os 190.2	77 Ir 192.2	78 Pt 195.1	79 Au 197.0	80 Hg 200.6	81 Tl 204.4	82 Pb 207.2	83 Bi 209.0	84 Po 209.0	85 At 210.0	86 Rn 222.0
87 Fr 223.0	88 Ra 226.0	89 Ac 227.0															

58 Ce 140.1	59 Pr 140.9	60 Nd 144.2	61 Pm 145.0	62 Sm 150.4	63 Eu 152.0	64 Gd 157.3	65 Tb 158.9	66 Dy 162.5	67 Ho 164.9	68 Er 167.3	69 Tm 168.9	70 Yb 173.0	71 Lu 175.0
90 Th 232.0	91 Pa 231.0	92 U 238.0	93 Np 237.0	94 Pu 244.0	95 Am 243.0	96 Cm 247.0	97 Bk 247.0	98 Cf 251.0	99 Es 254.0	100 Fm 253.0	101 Md 256.0	102 No 253.0	103 Lr 257.0

GO ON TO THE NEXT PAGE

Passage 1 (Questions 66–71)

Acid rain results from the accumulation of a high concentration of acids in the atmosphere. This accumulation follows the interaction of nitrogen and sulfur oxides to produce acids. Sulfur dioxide and nitrogen oxide emitted from power plants combine with other compounds to generate complex chemical reactions. The reaction rate is most rapid in the liquid phase. In the presence of solar radiation, sulfur dioxide may be converted to sulfur trioxide when it combines with reactive substances such as ozone.

The chemistry of acid rain is shown below:

Reaction I

$$SO_3 + H_2O \rightarrow H_2SO_4$$

SO_3 is extremely reactive and, in the presence of water, produces H_2SO_4. This reaction leads to the liberation of heat. Liquid H_2SO_4 boils at 290° C. Gaseous H_2SO_4 dissociates into SO_3 and water vapor at about 350°C and a pressure of 300 atm.

Sulfuric acid is an extremely important chemical product. When reacted with metals it acts as a strong oxidizing agent.

Reaction II

$$2\ H_2SO_4 + 2\ Ag \rightarrow Ag_2SO_4 + SO_2 + 2\ H_2O$$

At high temperatures, it can also react with salts to liberate volatile acids such as HCl.

Reaction III

$$H_2SO_4 + NaCl \rightarrow HCl + NaHSO_4$$

66. If 216 grams of silver react with excess sulfuric acid, how many grams of water are produced?

 A. 9 g
 B. 18 g
 C. 27 g
 D. 36 g

67. As Reaction III progresses, which of the following is true of the sodium and chlorine ions?

 A. Sodium ions are reduced and chlorine ions are oxidized.
 B. Sodium and chlorine ions are oxidized.
 C. Sodium and chlorine ions are reduced.
 D. Sodium and chlorine ions are neither oxidized nor reduced.

68. With respect to sulfuric acid, which of the following is NOT true?

 A. It is a buffer.
 B. It is a strong acid.
 C. It is a polyprotic acid.
 D. It is a proton donor.

69. An aqueous solution of H_2SO_4 is titrated with a 0.1 M solution of sodium hydroxide, as shown below. Which of the following is true at point 2?

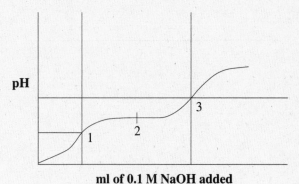

ml of 0.1 M NaOH added

 A. $[H_2SO_4] = [HSO_4^-]$
 B. $[H_2SO_4] = [SO_4^{2-}]$
 C. $[HSO_4^-] = [SO_4^{2-}]$
 D. $[H^+] = [OH^-]$

GO ON TO THE NEXT PAGE

70. At constant high temperature, a sample of 1 mole of sulfuric acid completely dissociates into gaseous sulfur trioxide and water vapor. In terms of average speed, how do sulfur trioxide molecules compare to molecules of water?

A. Sulfur trioxide molecules have a faster average speed.

B. Sulfur trioxide molecules have a slower average speed.

C. The two gases have equal average speeds.

D. The relationship between the average speeds cannot be determined.

71. Assuming Reaction I is at equilibrium, which of the following changes to the reaction conditions will increase the concentration of sulfuric acid?

A. Decreasing the pressure

B. Decreasing the concentration of SO_3

C. The addition of a catalyst

D. Decreasing the temperature

Passage II (Questions 72–78)

A magnetic field may be used to identify charged particles. In an experimental procedure, particles were sent into a magnetic field perpendicular to the field's direction. The figure below shows the paths of three particles, X, Y, and Z, which were sent into the field.

The magnetic field is directed into the page, which is signified by the symbol ⊗ for vector B.

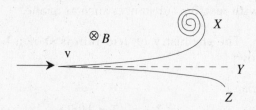

When moving through a magnetic field, any charged particle experiences a force whose magnitude is give by:

$$F = qvB\sin\phi$$

The angle ϕ is the angle between the direction of the particle's velocity and the direction of the magnetic field. The variables q, v, and B represent the magnitudes of the charge on the particle, the velocity of the particle, and the magnetic field strength, respectively.

When a relatively low energy particle is sent into a magnetic field it travels a spiral path that degenerates in circular fashion as shown for particle X in the figure above. The motion is circular in nature because the principal force affecting the particle is perpendicular to the direction of its motion.

GO ON TO THE NEXT PAGE

72. A particle is fired into the magnetic field. Its initial velocity is directed at an angle φ to the magnetic field lines. Which of the following graphs best represents the change in the magnitude of the force on the particle as φ is increased from 0° to 90°?

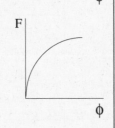

73. Keeping all other factors constant, which of the following would increase the size of the spiral in which particle X travels?

A. Increasing the strength of the magnetic field
B. Giving the particle more kinetic energy
C. Giving the particle less kinetic energy
D. Increasing the charge on the particle

74. Particle Z is given an initial velocity of 1×10^3 m/s perpendicular to the magnetic field lines. If the field strength is 5.5 T and particle Z has a charge of 1 coul, what is the net force on particle Z when it first enters the field?

A. 0 N
B. 5.5×10^3 N
C. 1.1×10^3 N
D. 2.5×10^3 N

75. If particle P were given a velocity component into the page, with a magnitude equal to the magnitude of its velocity in the direction of path Y, the force first felt by the particle would:

A. decrease by a factor of 4.
B. decrease by a factor of 2.
C. remain the same.
D. increase by a factor of 2.

76. Observing paths followed by particles X and Z, an experimenter would be justified in concluding that the two particles:

A. have charges of equal magnitude.
B. entered the field with different kinetic energies.
C. are oppositely charged.
D. are positively charged.

77. A particle of mass .001 kg and charge 1 coul enters the magnetic field traveling 1000 m/s. The particle spirals and comes to a complete stop in 0.05 seconds. How much work is done by friction in bringing the particle to a stop?

A. 20 J
B. 25 J
C. 500 J
D. 1000 J

GO ON TO THE NEXT PAGE

78. Which of the following diagrams represents the force experienced by a positively charged particle traveling through a magnetic field?

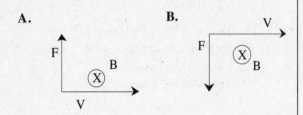

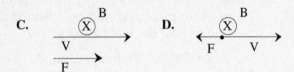

Passage III (Questions 79–82)

A chemist conducted experiments to determine the heat of formation and Gibbs' free energy for eight substances: H_2, Fe_2O_3, C_2H_4, CO_2, $KClO_4$, N_2O_4, H_2O, and Fe.

Experiment 1

Each substance was synthesized from its constituent elements, and its heat of formation was measured and recorded in Table 1.

Substance	H_f° (kJ/mol)
$H_2(g)$	0.0
$Fe_2O_3(c)$	−824.2
$C_2H_4(g)$	52.3
$CO_2(g)$	−393.5
$KClO_4(c)$	−432.8
$N_2O_4(g)$	9.2
$H_2O(l)$	−285.9
Fe (s)	0.0

(c) = crystalline; (g) = gaseous; (s) = solid; (l) = liquid

Table 1

Experiment 2

For each synthesis studied in Experiment 1, the change in entropy was measured and the Gibbs' free energy was calculated. The results are tabulated in Table 2.

Substance	G_f° (kJ/mol)
$H_2(g)$	0.0
$Fe_2O_3(c)$	−742.2
$C_2H_4(g)$	68.2
$CO_2(g)$	−394.4
$KClO_4(c)$	−303.1
$N_2O_4(g)$	97.9
$H_2O(l)$	−236.8
Fe (s)	0.0

Table 2

GO ON TO THE NEXT PAGE

79. When a molecule is formed from previously uncombined atoms by chemical reaction:

    A. bonds are formed and energy is released.
    B. bonds are broken and energy is released.
    C. bonds are formed and energy is absorbed.
    D. bonds are broken and energy is absorbed.

80. According to Table 2, the formation of CO_2 (g) from elemental carbon and oxygen:

    A. is not spontaneous under standard conditions.
    B. is spontaneous under standard conditions.
    C. requires a catalyst.
    D. occurs only at very high temperatures.

81. If a particular synthesis proceeds spontaneously only at high temperatures, which of the following should be anticipated?

    A. ΔS is positive; ΔH is negative.
    B. ΔS is positive; ΔH is positive.
    C. ΔS is negative; ΔH is negative.
    D. ΔS is negative; ΔH is positive.

82. What is the change in enthalpy associated with the formation of $N_2O_4(g)$ from its constituent elements?

    A. –9.2 kJ
    B. –4.6 kJ
    C. 9.2 kJ
    D. 18.4 kJ

Passage IV (Questions 83–88)

Three common types of radioactive decay are listed below. These processes occur in a fission reactor that uses U-235 as a fuel. Fission of such uranium atoms will occur if they are struck by a high-energy neutron.

Gamma Rays

Gamma rays (γ) are high-energy photons. These particles carry away excess energy when a nucleus moves to a lower energy level. The following reaction is one possible outcome when U-235 is struck by a high-energy neutron.

$$^{235}_{92}\text{U} + ^{1}_{0}\text{n} \rightarrow ^{92}_{36}\text{Kr} + ^{141}_{56}\text{Ba} + 3^{1}_{0}\text{n} + ^{0}_{0}\gamma$$

There are many other massless and chargeless particles that can carry energy away from a nucleus. A neutrino (μ) is such a particle.

Alpha Decay

Some nuclei can spontaneously emit alpha particles ($^{4}_{2}\alpha$). Alpha particles are the nuclei of helium atoms.

A nucleus of U-235 will split when struck by a high-speed neutron. However, this process creates many more high-speed neutrons than it consumes. To keep the reaction from running out of control, most reactors contain control rods made of a material that will absorb the excess neutrons. Boron can be used to absorb high energy neutrons and instead produce low-energy alpha particles.

$$^{10}_{5}\text{B} + ^{1}_{0}\text{n} \rightarrow ^{11}_{5}\text{B}$$
$$^{11}_{5}\text{B} \rightarrow ^{7}_{3}\text{Li} + ^{4}_{2}\alpha$$

GO ON TO THE NEXT PAGE

Beta Decay

A beta particle (β) is an energetic electron. When a nuclei emits a beta particle, it will lose one neutron and gain one proton. Although the probability is very small, U-235 could emit a beta particle and decay to an isotope of neptunium.

$$^{235}_{92}\text{U} \rightarrow ^{235}_{93}\text{Np} + ^{0}_{-1}\beta$$

(Note: proton mass = 1.0073 amu;
electron rest mass = 9.11×10^{-31} kg;
1 amu = 931 MeV; 1eV = 1.6×10^{-19} J.)

83. Two particles travel through a magnetic field in the same direction. If particle 1 experiences a net force and particle 2 does not, which of the following could represent the particles' identities?

A. Particle 1 is a beta particle and particle 2 is an alpha particle.
B. Particle 1 is a gamma particle and particle 2 is a neutrino.
C. Particle 1 is a beta particle and particle 2 is a neutrino.
D. Particle 1 is a gamma particle and particle 2 is an alpha particle.

84. Two helium nuclei fuse and release energy in the form of photons. Which of the following describes the main energy transfer that takes place?

A. Kinetic to potential
B. Electrical to kinetic
C. Mass to electromagnetic
D. Kinetic to electrical

85. $^{236}_{90}$Th emits two beta particles and two alpha particles. Which of the following nuclei results?

A. $^{226}_{87}$Fr
B. $^{226}_{88}$Ra
C. $^{228}_{88}$Ra
D. $^{224}_{86}$Rn

86. One half of a Tl sample decays to Pb in 3.1 mins through the emission of beta particles. If an initially pure sample of Tl contains 7 g of lead after 9.3 mins, what was the approximate mass of the original sample?

A. 7 g
B. 8 g
C. 28 g
D. 32 g

87. An element decays to an isotope of itself, releasing alpha and beta particles. In terms of the number of particles released, the ratio of alpha particles to beta particles is:

A. $\frac{1}{2}$
B. 1
C. 2
D. 4

88. If 2.8 MeV are needed to produce 1 photon, how many photons can be produced when 1 gram of matter is converted to energy?

A. 2×10^{26}
B. 2×10^{32}
C. 2×10^{35}
D. 4×10^{35}

GO ON TO THE NEXT PAGE

Questions 89 through 93 are **NOT** based on a descriptive passage.

89. Light traveling through water in a swimming pool has the following measured values:

    frequency = 5.0×10^{14} Hz
    wavelength = 4.5×10^{-7} m
    velocity = 2.25×10^{8} m/s

    The wave propagates across the surface of the water into air. If the speed of light in air is 3×10^{8} m/s, what is the frequency of the wave traveling in air?

    A. 2.5×10^{14} Hz
    B. 3.8×10^{14} Hz
    C. 5.0×10^{14} Hz
    D. 6.7×10^{14} Hz

90. A trigonal bipyramid is the characteristic of which orbital hybridization?

    A. sp
    B. sp^2
    C. sp^3
    D. dsp^3

91. Which of the following electronic configurations belongs to a diamagnetic element in its ground state?

    A. $1s^2 2s^1$
    B. $1s^2 2s^2 2p^1$
    C. $1s^2 2s^2 2p^4$
    D. $1s^2 2s^2 2p^6$

92. Three mechanical waves are passed through the same medium at equal velocities. Their respective amplitudes are 1 cm, 2 cm, and 4 cm. What is the smallest possible amplitude of the resultant wave?

    A. 0 cm
    B. 1 cm
    C. 7 cm
    D. 8 cm

93. When magnesium (Mg) and chlorine (Cl) are compared in terms of electronegativity and atomic radius, which of the following is true?

    A. Magnesium has greater electronegativity and smaller atomic radius.
    B. Magnesium has greater electronegativity and greater atomic radius.
    C. Magnesium has lesser electronegativity and smaller atomic radius.
    D. Magnesium has lesser electronegativity and greater atomic radius.

GO ON TO THE NEXT PAGE

Passage V (Questions 94–100)

Machines transform energy into work, and reduce the input force required to perform a task. Ideally, the *work* done in performing a given task is unchanged by the use of a machine, and is given by the relationship: (work) = (force) × (distance). In general, therefore, a reduction in force input requires an increase in distance traveled.

Inclined planes are perhaps the simplest of all machines and, among other purposes, allow individuals who use wheelchairs access to buildings.

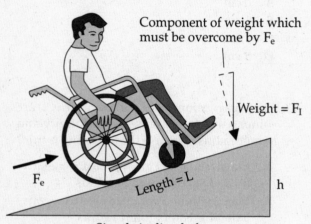

Simple inclined plane

The ramp allows the wheelchair user to climb to a height h while applying a force that is significantly smaller than the combined weight of the person and the wheelchair. The user must, however, move upward along the plane a distance greater than h. The energy used to exploit this machine is provided entirely by the person climbing the plane.

A more complex machine that might be used to lift a wheelchair would involve the use of an electric motor driving an elevator. The elevator converts electrical energy ultimately to potential energy of the wheelchair and its user. In this case, the user does not provide any of the energy used to drive the chair upward.

The ideal mechanical advantage for a machine (IMA) is given by the ratio of the distance traversed by the input force d_i to the distance traversed by the output force d_o:

$$IMA = d_i / d_o$$

In the case of the ramp pictured above, $d_i = L$ and $d_o = h$.

For real machines, some of the input force must be used to overcome dissipative forces, such as friction. The actual mechanical advantage (AMA) is given by the ratio of the output force F_o to the input force F_i:

$$AMA = F_o / F_i$$

The efficiency of a machine is given by the ratio of the work done by the output force W_o to the work done by the input force W_i. This is also equal to the ratio of the actual mechanical advantage to the ideal mechanical advantage.

$$Efficiency = W_o / W_i = AMA / IMA$$

The wheel and handle arrangement of the simple wheelchair shown below is similar in principle to the simple machine known as the wheel and axle, except that because of design considerations for the wheelchair shown, the input force can not be smaller than the output force.

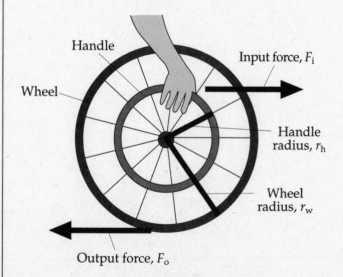

Figure 2

GO ON TO THE NEXT PAGE

94. For the wheelchair pictured in Figure 2, the radial distance to the handle is exactly twice the distance to the edge of the tire. The force applied to the ground F_o will be:

A. half the force applied to the handle F_i.
B. equal to the force applied to the handle F_i.
C. twice the force applied to the handle F_i.
D. four times the force applied to the handle F_i.

95. The human body is approximately 75% efficient in converting its stored chemical energy to mechanical work. A person who weighs 80 N rolls himself up a ramp with a length of 10 m to a height of 1.5 m. If the ramp is a 95% efficient machine and the wheelchair weighs 40 N, how much energy does the person expend?

A. $(80 + 40)(1.5)(95/100)(75/100)$ J
B. $(80 + 40)(1.5)(100/95)(100/75)$ J
C. $(80 + 40)(10)(95/100)(75/100)$ J
D. $(80 + 40)(10)(100/95)(100/75)$ J

96. A first wheelchair user climbs an inclined plane to a height of 3 m. A second wheelchair user is raised straight up in the chair to the same height by an electric lift. The potential energy gained by the first wheelchair user is:

A. greater than the energy gained by the second because a greater distance has been traveled.
B. greater than the energy gained by the second because electric energy is not easily converted into potential energy.
C. less than the energy gained by the second because electric energy is easily converted into potential energy.
D. equal to the energy gained by the second because the wheelchair has been raised to the same height.

97. If the radius of the wheel pictured in Figure 2 is 40 cm, what is the distance traveled by the wheelchair over the course of 6 complete wheel rotations?

A. 7 m
B. 11 m
C. 15 m
D. 21 m

98. An ideal wheelchair ramp bridges a height of 1.2 m. If the ramp is 24 m in length, how much force must be applied by a 60 N man in a 40 N wheelchair to climb the ramp?

A. 5 N
B. 10 N
C. 20 N
D. 50 N

99. Which of the following changes MUST increase the ideal mechanical advantage of the ramp pictured in Figure 1?

A. Increase L and increase h.
B. Decrease L and decrease h.
C. Decrease L and increase h.
D. Increase L and decrease h.

100. For the wheelchair shown in Figure 2, which of the following is most likely the design consideration that makes the output force smaller than the input force?

A. Only one wheel is shown in Figure 2.
B. The handle radius can not be larger than the wheel radius.
C. The input force will vary depending on the weight of the person seated in the wheelchair.
D. A rotational force can only be applied perpendicular to the axis of rotation.

GO ON TO THE NEXT PAGE

Passage VI (Questions 101–105)

For standard acid-base indicators, the equilibrium reaction is $HIn_A \leftrightarrow H^+ + In_B^-$, where HIn_A is the acid of the indicator with color A, and In_B^- is the conjugate base with color B. Two acid-base indicators are thymol blue (A = red and B = yellow) and bromothymol blue (A = yellow and B = blue).

If an acid is added to an indicator solution, the equilibrium shifts, and color A is produced. Adding a base shifts the equilibrium in the other direction and produces color B.

Acid-base indicators often change color at pH values significantly different from the equivalence points of many titratable acids. Acid-base indicators are most useful for measuring pH changes caused by strong acids such as HCl and H_2SO_4 in aqueous solutions. Near the equivalence point, strong acids exhibit a long, steep rise in their titration curves such that most indicators will change color at some point in this region of the curve. Weaker acids such as acetic acid ($HC_2H_3O_2$) exhibit a much shorter rise. The indicator used with weak acids must change color in a pH range that lies closer to the equivalence point.

A scientist titrated 50 ml of 0.1M HCl with 0.1M NaOH using an unknown acid–base indicator HIn_A. The equivalence point was determined to occur at pH 7.0. A change in color occurred at a pH below the equivalence point.

101. What pH would most likely cause a color change in the unknown indicator?

  A. 5
  B. 7
  C. 9
  D. 14

102. Which of the following colors would result from the formation of the conjugate base of bromothymol blue?

  A. Spectral red
  B. Blue
  C. Yellow
  D. Green

103. At pH 7.0, the solution's color most probably indicates the presence of:

  A. HIn_A
  B. In_A^-
  C. In_B^-
  D. HIn_B

104. Two additional indicators were used. For HCl, phenolphthalein changed color above the equivalence point, and methyl red changed color below the equivalence point. At the equivalence point, which forms of the indicators produce color?

  A. The base of phenolphthalein and the acid of methyl red.
  B. The base of methyl red and the acid of phenolphthalein.
  C. The acids of both indicators.
  D. The bases of both indicators.

GO ON TO THE NEXT PAGE

105. According to the information presented below, which of the following indicators will be present in the acid form in an aqueous titration solution that reached pH 5.0?

Indicator	Acid Color	Base Color	K_{ind}	pH Range
Thymol blue	Red	Yellow	2×10^{-2}	1.2 – 2.8
Methyl orange	Red	Orange	3.5×10^{-4}	3.1 – 4.4
Bromothymol blue	Yellow	Blue	8×10^{-8}	6.0 – 7.6

A. Thymol blue, because the conjugate acid remains protonated at the pH value of the solution.

B. Thymol blue, because the conjugate base is deprotonated at the pH value of the solution.

C. Bromothymol blue, because the conjugate acid remains protonated at the pH value of the solution.

D. Bromothymol blue, because the conjugate base is deprotonated at the pH value of the solution.

Passage VII (Questions 106–109)

A U-shaped glass tube with stems A and B has a diameter of 0.1 m and is filled with a liquid of density 5.0×10^3 kg/m³. The liquid settles to a height of h_o in both stems A and B. A piston of negligible mass is then fitted into stem A forming a perfect seal. By moving the piston up or down, work is done by or on the fluid according to the following equation:

$$W = (P_i - P_f) \Delta V$$

where P_i and P_f are the initial and final pressures on the fluid, and V is the displaced volume of fluid in stem A. (Note: Assume that the density of the fluid remains constant.)

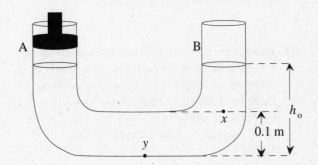

106. The piston is pulled upward to reduce the pressure on the fluid so that the new fluid heights in stems A and B are h_1 and h_2 respectively. Which of the following relate h_o, h_1, and h_2?

A. $h_o < h_1 < h_2$
B. $h_1 < h_o < h_2$
C. $h_2 < h_o < h_1$
D. $h_o = h_2 = h_1$

GO ON TO THE NEXT PAGE

107. If both stems A and B have fluid at height h_o, what is the difference in pressure between points x and y? (Assume atmospheric pressure is 1.013×10^5 Pa.)

   A. 5.0×10^3 Pa
   B. 1.0×10^5 Pa
   C. 1.5×10^5 Pa
   D. 2.5×10^5 Pa

108. The pressure exerted by the fluid at point x is directed:

   A. vertically upward only.
   B. vertically downward only.
   C. horizontally only.
   D. to and from all directions.

109. The piston is removed and the liquid reaches a height of 20 m in each stem. A small hole appears at point y, and a steady flow of fluid escapes. Ignoring friction, what is the velocity at which fluid leaves the U-tube? (Consider that gravitational acceleration = 10 m/s^2)

   A. 10 m/s
   B. 12 m/s
   C. 17 m/s
   D. 20 m/s

Passage VIII (Questions 110–114)

The phase-related properties of water have been subjected to considerable scientific scrutiny. The table below lists several of these properties.

Property	Properties of Water
Density	0.99707 g/cm^3 at 25° C* 1.00000 g/cm^3 at 4° C 0.99987 g/cm^3 at 0° C
Heat of Fusion	6.008 kJ/mol at 0° C
Heat of Vaporization	44.02 kJ/mol at 25° C 44.94 kJ/mol at 0° C
Vapor Pressure	23.76 mm Hg at 25° C** 6.54 mm Hg at 5° C 4.58 mm Hg at 0° C

*Density decreases as temperature rises above 25° C.
**Vapor pressure increases as temperature rises above 25° C.

In the solid phase, water shows an open lattice structure which is facilitated by the extensive amount of hydrogen bonding within the lattice.

If liquid water is heated, the cohesive forces diminish progressively. For example, when liquid water is heated from 20° C to 60° C, its viscosity decreases more than 50 percent while the surface tension decreases approximately 5 percent. These trends continue as temperature increases further.

Liquid water gives rise to a vapor pressure. If a mixture of gases is collected over water, the vapor pressure of the water contributes to the total pressure of the gaseous mixture. At 0° C, water vapor contributes 4.58 mm Hg to the total pressure of the mixture. Near 100° C, the water vapor contribution to total gas pressure approaches 760 mm Hg.

GO ON TO THE NEXT PAGE ▷

110. The dependence of the viscosity and surface tension of water on temperature is best illustrated by which of the following figures?

A.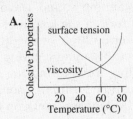

C.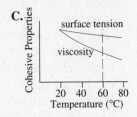

B.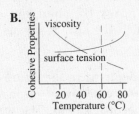

D.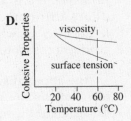

111. Which phenomenon accounts for the decrease in density of water as its temperature decreases from 4° C to 0° C?

A. Hydrogen bonding
B. Covalent bonding
C. Freezing point depression
D. Heat of fusion

112. When H_2O moves from the solid to the liquid phase at 0° C, under standard equilibrium conditions, what enthalpy change occurs?

A. The reaction releases 6.008 kJ/mol.
B. The reaction absorbs 6.008 kJ/mol.
C. The reaction releases 44.02 kJ/mol.
D. The reaction absorbs 44.02 kJ/mol.

113. In a laboratory, the vapor pressure of a sample of water is gradually increased until it reaches atmospheric pressure. At this point, the water:

A. melts.
B. freezes.
C. boils.
D. condenses.

114. Under standard pressure, 1.00 gram of water at 4° C occupies a smaller volume than it does at 25° C. Such a finding confirms that at 25° C water:

A. has a lower density.
B. has a higher vapor pressure.
C. has a greater molecular weight.
D. undergoes ionization.

Questions 115 through 119 are **NOT** based on a descriptive passage.

115. How many orbitals are there in the *d* subshell of an atom?

A. 3
B. 5
C. 6
D. 10

116. A car of mass *m* is rolling down a ramp that is elevated at an angle of 60°. What is the magnitude of the car's acceleration parallel to the ramp?

A. $g \cos 60°$
B. $g \sin 60°$
C. $mg \cos 60°$
D. $mg \sin 60°$

117. Which of the following is most stable?

A. Mg^-
B. Mg^0
C. Mg^+
D. Mg^{2+}

GO ON TO THE NEXT PAGE

118. Which of the following is NOT a vector quantity?

   A. Force
   B. Energy
   C. Velocity
   D. Acceleration

119. The atomic radius of $_{11}^{22}\text{Na}$ is approximately twice that of $_{18}^{40}\text{Ar}$, primarily because:

   A. the ionization energy of Ar is greater than that of Na.
   B. Ar is inert, whereas Na easily forms an ion.
   C. the valence electrons of Na are more effectively shielded from the nucleus than the valence electrons of Ar.
   D. Ar has 18 protons attracting its electrons, whereas Na has only 11 protons.

Passage IX (Questions 120–125)

A hollow tube with one closed end can be used to set up a standing sound wave. A standing wave will form if the length of the tube is an odd-integer multiple of one-quarter the wavelength of the sound entering the tube. When a standing wave forms, the column of air inside the tube is said to resonate. Almost all musical instruments work on this principle. For example, a guitar player produces different notes by changing the frequencies at which the strings on his instrument resonate.

The apparatus depicted in the figure below exploits the phenomenon of resonance to calculate the speed of sound. The water level in the tube can be lowered by releasing water through the valve located near the bottom. Lowering the water level effectively lengthens the tube. The tuning fork is struck and held near the open end of the tube. The tuning fork emits sound waves at 400 Hz. As the water level is lowered, it is observed that the air in the tube resonates at multiples of a fixed length.

GO ON TO THE NEXT PAGE ➤

120. What is the period of the wave produced by the tuning fork?

    A. 0.0007 sec

    B. 0.0025 sec

    C. 0.0070 sec

    D. 0.0400 sec

121. Which of the following figures best represents a standing sound wave inside the tube?

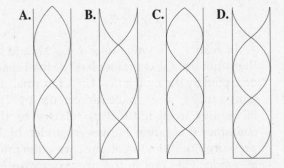

122. If the tube's diameter were increased, which of the following would be true regarding the period and/or frequency of the standing wave inside it?

    A. Its wavelength would increase.

    B. Its wavelength would decrease.

    C. Its period would increase.

    D. Its wavelength and period would remain unchanged.

123. As the water level in the tube is lowered, resonance occurs at intervals of 0.4 m. This implies that the speed of sound in air is:

    A. 160 m/s.

    B. 320 m/s.

    C. 390 m/s.

    D. 440 m/s.

124. Assume the experiment is conducted in a room filled with helium. The density of helium gas is much less than that of air. What changes will occur to the standing wave?

    A. The distance between antinodes will increase.

    B. The distance between antinodes will decrease.

    C. The distance between antinodes will remain the same.

    D. No standing wave will form.

125. Which of the following would indicate that the tuning fork is rapidly moving away from the end of the tube?

    A. The amplitude of the sound waves reaching the tube is greater than expected.

    B. The amplitude of the sound waves reaching the tube is less than expected.

    C. The frequency of the sound waves reaching the tube is greater than expected.

    D. The frequency of the sound waves reaching the tube is less than expected.

GO ON TO THE NEXT PAGE

Passage X (Questions 126–131)

In studying the properties of gases, scientists often employ the ideal gas equation, $PV = nRT$. In this equation, n represents the number of moles of the gas present, P represents pressure, V represents volume, T represents absolute temperature, and R is the gas constant, equal to 0.082 L-atm/K-mol.

If n increases while T is held constant, the quantity PV will increase. If pressure and temperature are held constant, volume must increase to satisfy the ideal gas equation. Similarly, if temperature and volume are held constant if n increases, pressure must also increase. Figure 1 represents the relationship between n and PV while temperature is held constant.

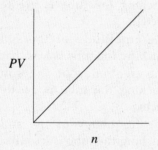

Figure 1

Scientists and engineers often work with gases at high pressures. Gases under these conditions show large departures from the ideal gas equation. The equation would better describe gases at high pressure if P is replaced by $P + (an^2/V^2)$, and V is replaced by $V-nb$. The constants a and b are van der Waals constants, which vary with the identity of the gas. The values of PV/RT in terms of pressure for nitrogen and hydrogen gases at 300° K are shown in Figure 2. The dotted line plots values predicted by the ideal gas law.

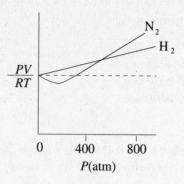

Figure 2

In reality, the value used for V should be the volume of the container less the total space occupied by the molecules. Under normal circumstances, the space taken up by the molecules is insignificant, relative to the container's volume. However, under high-pressure situations, a volume correction must be made. This fact is the primary cause for the deviation between the predicted and observed results in Figure 2.

Substance	Constant a	Constant b
Helium	0.0341	0.02370
Neon	0.211	0.0171
H_2	0.244	0.0266
N_2	1.39	0.0391
Cl_2	6.49	0.0562

GO ON TO THE NEXT PAGE

126. A sample of gas is held in a container at constant temperature of 300°K, and gas is slowly removed from the container. Which of the following figures best depicts change in pressure as gas is removed?

A.

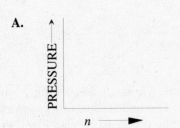

B.

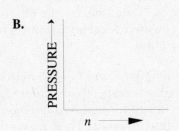

C.

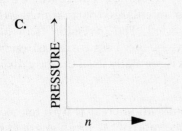

D.

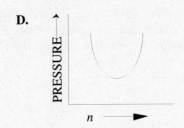

127. A researcher wishes to compare real gas behavior to gas behavior predicted by the ideal gas law. The researcher subjects a gas sample to relatively high pressure and then compares the pressure actually measured to that which would be predicted according to the ideal gas law. The pressure *actually measured* is probably:

   A. greater than that predicted by the ideal gas law because of repulsive forces among gas particles.
   B. greater than that predicted by the ideal gas law because of attractive forces among gas particles.
   C. less than that predicted by the ideal gas law because of repulsive forces among gas particles.
   D. less than that predicted by the ideal gas law because of attractive forces among gas particles.

128. A decrease in the number of moles of a gas at constant temperature and volume will decrease which of the following unit measures?

   A. liters
   B. moles per liter
   C. Joules per mole
   D. Kelvins

129. Which of the following will likely demonstrate the greater departure from the behavior of an ideal gas: hydrogen gas or helium gas?

   A. Helium gas, because the van der Waals corrections are lower than for hydrogen.
   B. Helium gas, because it is an inert gas.
   C. Hydrogen gas, because the van der Waals corrections are greater than for helium.
   D. Hydrogen gas, because hydrogen shows decreased intermolecular forces at higher pressures.

GO ON TO THE NEXT PAGE

130. The pressure of a gas at a temperature of 27°C is measured to be P. If the temperature is increased to 127°C while all other factor are kept constant, what will be the new pressure of the gas?

   A. $\dfrac{1}{5}P$

   B. $\dfrac{3}{4}P$

   C. $\dfrac{4}{3}P$

   D. $5P$

131. According to the passage, what would be the van der Waals correction for the volume of 2 moles of neon gas at very high pressure?

   A. $V - (0.02370)$
   B. $V - (0.0171)$
   C. $V - (2)(0.02370)$
   D. $V - (2)(0.0171)$

Passage XI (Questions 132–137)

The prototypical astronomical telescope is designed as shown in Figure 1 below.

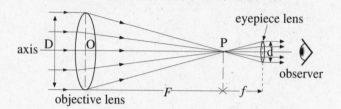

The objective lens, O, has a long positive focal length. The incident parallel rays emanating from the object to be visualized enter from the left and traverse the objective lens. The eyepiece is located nearer the observer. It has a short positive focal length and acts as a magnifying glass.

The focal lengths F and f of the objective lens and eyepiece respectively coincide at point P. The image formed by the objective lens is real and inverted. This image then acts as the object for the eyepiece which transforms it into an enlarged virtual image that remains inverted. The inversion is of little practical consequence because the astronomical telescope is normally used to study distant objects.

The magnification created by a telescope is given by the ratio of the focal length of the objective lens F to the focal length of the eyepiece f. For the telescope pictured above, F is equal to 40 cm and f is equal to 2 cm. The lenses are made of glass with a refractive index of 1.5.

GO ON TO THE NEXT PAGE

132. In the telescope pictured above, the objective lens is a:

A. converging lens and the eyepiece is a diverging lens.

B. converging lens and the eyepiece is a converging lens.

C. diverging lens and the eyepiece is a diverging lens.

D. diverging lens and the eyepiece is a converging lens.

133. An investigator works with a telescope equipped with a variety of removable lenses. Among the following combinations, the investigator will achieve greatest magnification with:

A. an objective with large focal length and an eyepiece with large focal length.

B. an objective with small focal length and an eyepiece with small focal length.

C. an objective with large focal length and an eyepiece with small focal length.

D. an objective with small focal length and an eyepiece with small focal length.

134. An object is to be observed using only an eyepiece lens. If the object lies at a distance 1.5 cm from the eyepiece lens, the image will be located:

A. 1 cm from the eyepiece.

B. 2 cm from the eyepiece.

C. 3 cm from the eyepiece.

D. 6 cm from the eyepiece.

135. What is the power of the eyepiece of the telescope pictured above?

A. 2 diopters

B. 5 diopters

C. 20 diopters

D. 50 diopters

136. If the objective lens were replaced with a lens composed of a material with a refractive index greater than 1.5, which of the following would be expected to occur?

A. The focal length of the lens would decrease.

B. The focal length of the lens would increase.

C. The diameter of the lens would decrease.

D. The diameter of the lens would increase.

137. The speed of light through glass:

A. is greater than the speed of light in air.

B. is less than the speed of light in air.

C. may be greater or less than the speed of light in air.

D. is equal to the speed of light in air.

GO ON TO THE NEXT PAGE

138. Based on the table below, which of the following species is the strongest oxidizing agent?

Half-Reaction	Standard Potential
$Br_2(l) + 2e^- \rightarrow 2Br^-(aq)$	1.08
$Ag_2O(s) + H_2O + 2e \rightarrow 2Ag(s) + 2OH^-(aq)$	0.34
$Cu^{2+}(aq) + e^- \rightarrow Cu^+(aq)$	0.15
$H_2(g) + 2e^- \rightarrow 2H^-(aq)$	0.00

   A. H_2
   B. Cu^{2+}
   C. Br_2
   D. Ag_2O

139. An atom is in its ground state with all the orbitals filled through the second principal energy level ($n = 2$). How many electrons are contained in this atom?

   A. 8
   B. 10
   C. 12
   D. 14

140. A uranium-238 nucleus emits an alpha particle and decays to thorium-234. The alpha particle leaves the nucleus traveling 4.68×10^5 m/s. At what speed would the thorium nucleus recoil? (Note: Assume the masses of a proton and a neutron to be equal.)

   A. 1.5×10^3 m/s
   B. 4.0×10^3 m/s
   C. 8.0×10^3 m/s
   D. 2.5×10^4 m/s

141. A constant current of 5 amperes is passing through a 10 ohm resistor. How much energy is dissipated in the resistor over the course of 10 seconds?

   A. 250 J
   B. 500 J
   C. 1000 J
   D. 2500 J

142. As an ideal fluid flowing in a cylindrical pipe through a constant pressure differential moves from a region of larger diameter to a region of smaller diameter, which of the following will occur?

   A. Flow will remain constant and fluid velocity will increase.
   B. Flow will remain constant and fluid velocity will remain constant.
   C. Flow will increase and fluid velocity will increase.
   D. Flow will increase and fluid velocity will remain constant.

GO ON TO THE NEXT PAGE

STOP
IF YOU FINISH BEFORE TIME IS CALLED, YOU MAY CHECK YOUR WORK ON THIS TEST ONLY.
DO NOT TURN TO ANY OTHER TEST IN THIS BOOK.

Writing Sample I

Time: 60 Minutes
2 Prompts, Separately Timed:
30 Minutes Each

WRITING SAMPLE

DIRECTIONS: This is a test of your writing skills. The test consists of two parts. You will have 30 minutes to complete each part.

Your responses to the Writing Sample prompts will be written in ANSWER DOCUMENT 2. Your response to Part 1 must be written only on the answer sheets marked "1," and your response to Part 2 must be written only on the answer sheets marked "2." You may work only on Part 1 during the first 30 minutes of the test and only on Part 2 during the second 30 minutes. If you finish writing on Part 1 before time is up, you may review your work on that part, but do not begin work on Part 2. If you finish writing on Part 2 before time is up, you may review your work only on that part of the test.

Use your time efficiently. Before you begin writing each of your responses, read the assignment carefully to understand exactly what you are being asked to do. You may use the space beneath each writing assignment to make notes in planning each response.

Because this is a test of your writing skills, your response to each part should be an essay of complete sentences and paragraphs, as well organized and clearly written as you can make it in the allotted time. *You may make corrections or additions neatly between the lines of your responses, but do not write in the margins of the answer booklet.*

There are four pages in your answer booklet to write your responses, two pages for each part of the test. You are not expected to use all of the pages, but to ensure that you have enough room for each essay, do not skip lines.

Essays that are illegible cannot be scored.

Part 1

Consider this statement:

People get the government they deserve.

Write a unified essay in which you perform the following tasks: Explain what you think the above statement means. Describe a specific situation in which people do not get the government they deserve. Discuss what you think determines whether or not people get the government they deserve.

_____

_____

_____

_____

_____

_____

_____

_____

_____

_____

_____

_____

_____

_____

_____

_____

_____

_____

_____

_____

_____

_____

STOP
IF YOU FINISH BEFORE TIME IS CALLED, YOU MAY CHECK YOUR WORK ON PART 1 ONLY.

Part 2

Consider this statement:

Honesty is essential to friendship.

Write a unified essay in which you perform the following tasks: Explain what you think the above statement means. Describe a specific situation in which honesty is not essential to friendship. Discuss what you think determines whether or not honesty is essential to friendship.

_____

_____

_____

_____

_____

_____

_____

_____

_____

_____

_____

_____

_____

_____

_____

_____

_____

_____

_____

_____

_____

_____

STOP
IF YOU FINISH BEFORE TIME IS CALLED, YOU MAY CHECK YOUR WORK ON PART 2 ONLY.

Biological Sciences I

Time: 100 Minutes
Questions 143–219

BIOLOGICAL SCIENCES

DIRECTIONS: Most questions in the Biological Sciences test are organized into groups, each preceded by a descriptive passage. After studying the passage, select the one best answer to each question in the group. Some questions are not based on a descriptive passage and are also independent of each other. You must also select the one best answer to these questions. If you are not certain of an answer, eliminate the alternatives that you know to be incorrect and then select an answer from the remaining alternatives. Indicate your selection by blackening the corresponding circle on your answer sheet (DIAGNOSTIC TEST FORM). A periodic table is provided for your use. You may consult it whenever you wish.

PERIODIC TABLE OF THE ELEMENTS

1 H 1.0																	2 He 4.0
3 Li 6.9	4 Be 9.0											5 B 10.8	6 C 12	2 N 14.0	8 O 16	9 F 19.0	10 Ne 20.0
11 Na 22.0	12 Mg 24.3											13 Al 27.0	14 Si 28.1	15 P 31.0	16 S 32.1	17 Cl 35.5	18 Ar 39.0
19 K 39.1	20 Ca 40.1	21 Sc 45.0	22 Ti 47.9	23 V 50.9	24 Cr 52.0	25 Mn 54.9	26 Fe 55.8	27 Co 58.9	28 Ni 58.7	29 Cu 63.5	30 Zn 65.4	31 Ga 69.7	32 Ge 72.6	33 As 74.9	34 Se 79.0	35 Br 79.9	36 Kr 83.8
37 Rb 85.5	38 Sr 87.6	39 Y 88.9	40 Zr 91.2	41 Nb 92.9	42 Mo 95.9	43 Tc 97.0	44 Ru 101.0	45 Rh 102.9	46 Pd 106.4	47 Ag 107.9	48 Cd 112.4	49 In 114.8	50 Sn 118.7	51 Sb 121.8	52 Te 127.6	53 I 126.9	54 Xe 131.3
55 Cs 132.9	56 Ba 137.3	57 La 138.9	72 Hf 178.5	73 Ta 180.9	74 W 183.9	75 Re 186.2	76 Os 190.2	77 Ir 192.2	78 Pt 195.1	79 Au 197.0	80 Hg 200.6	81 Tl 204.4	82 Pb 207.2	83 Bi 209.0	84 Po 209.0	85 At 210.0	86 Rn 222.0
87 Fr 223.0	88 Ra 226.0	89 Ac 227.0															

58 Ce 140.1	59 Pr 140.9	60 Nd 144.2	61 Pm 145.0	62 Sm 150.4	63 Eu 152.0	64 Gd 157.3	65 Tb 158.9	66 Dy 162.5	67 Ho 164.9	68 Er 167.3	69 Tm 168.9	70 Yb 173.0	71 Lu 175.0
90 Th 232.0	91 Pa 231.0	92 U 238.0	93 Np 237.0	94 Pu 244.0	95 Am 243.0	96 Cm 247.0	97 Bk 247.0	98 Cf 251.0	99 Es 254.0	100 Fm 253.0	101 Md 256.0	102 No 253.0	103 Lr 257.0

GO ON TO THE NEXT PAGE ⟶

Passage I (Questions 143-148)

Within animals that have closed circulatory systems, the space that lies both outside the cells of the body and outside the circulatory system is called the interstitial compartment. This compartment normally has fluid in it. The precise volume of this fluid represents a balance between two factors.

The first of these factors is the *fluid pressure* within the blood vessels, which tends to force fluid out of the vessels and into the interstitial space. The second factor is the *colloid pressure*, which is created by the higher levels of protein in the blood as compared with the interstitial space. The interiors of blood vessels retain their higher protein levels because the vessels are not normally permeable to protein. The difference in protein levels between the interior of blood vessels and the interstitial space creates a gradient that tends to draw fluid into the vessels from the interstitial space.

The role of colloid pressure in determining interstitial fluid volume has been studied through a technique in which (1) the circulatory system of an animal cadaver is opened at the arterial end and at the venous end, and (2) fluid is pumped in through the arterial opening and through the vasculature, and then drained out at the venous opening.

Experiment 1

The circulatory systems of three 60 kg animal cadavers were infused with fluids having different protein concentrations, according to the technique described above. Cadaver A received fluid with the lowest protein concentration, and Cadaver C received fluid with the highest concentration. At ten-minute intervals, the cadavers were weighed to determine how much interstitial fluid had been drawn into the circulatory system and drained through the venous opening. The infused fluid was also weighed. The results are tabulated in Table 1.

| Infusion Time | Body Weight | | |
	Cadaver A	Cadaver B	Cadaver C
10 min.	60 kg	60 kg	60 kg
20 min.	53 kg	47 kg	36 kg
30 min.	44 kg	32 kg	28 kg
40 min.	31 kg	23 kg	27 kg
50 min.	24 kg	23 kg	27 kg
60 min.	24 kg	23 kg	27 kg
70 min.	24 kg	23 kg	27 kg

Table 1

Experiment 2

The circulatory system of one 75 kg cadaver—Cadaver D—was infused with fluid lacking any protein, according to the same technique described above. The cadaver was weighed at ten-minute intervals. The results are tabulated in Table 2.

| Infusion Time | Body Weight |
	Cadaver D
10 min.	75 kg
20 min.	75 kg
30 min.	75 kg
40 min.	75 kg
50 min.	75 kg
60 min.	75 kg
70 min.	75 kg

Table 2

GO ON TO THE NEXT PAGE

143.   In humans, the peptide bonds of ingested proteins are first cleaved by which of the following enzymes?

A. Lactase
B. Pepsin
C. Dipeptidase
D. Lipase

144.   Colloid pressure tends to draw fluid into the blood vessels by:

A. passive diffusion along a concentration gradient.
B. passive diffusion along an electrical gradient.
C. facilitated transport along an electrochemical gradient.
D. active diffusion, mediated by an ATP-dependent pump.

145.   A professor theorized that if a patient's capillaries became suddenly permeable to protein, the patient would manifest edema. Is this a plausible hypothesis?

A. No; fluid will move across a membrane only in response to an ion gradient.
B. No; protein permeability would have no effect on hydrostatic pressure within the blood vessel.
C. Yes; protein in the interstitial space would fuel the active transport of fluid into the interstitial space.
D. Yes; colloid pressure inside the capillaries would decrease, and fluid would leak into the interstitial space.

146.   The blood proteins that produce colloid pressure are synthesized by a sequential mechanism that involves the direct activity of:

A. cellular proteases.
B. smooth endoplasmic reticulum.
C. messenger RNA.
D. cytochromes.

147.   Given the results of Experiments 1 and 2, a researcher would be most justified in concluding that:

A. Cadaver D had a higher protein concentration in its interstitial fluid than did Cadavers A, B, or C.
B. Cadaver A contained more interstitial fluid than did Cadaver B, which contained more interstitial fluid than did Cadaver C.
C. Cadavers A, B, and C were composed of at least 50 percent interstitial fluid by weight.
D. Cadaver C was composed of approximately 80 percent interstitial fluid by weight.

148.   If, in a normal patient, proteins were suddenly infused into the interstitial space, which of the following physiological compensations could prevent the resulting edema?

A. Reduction of hydrostatic pressure within the blood vessels
B. Passive diffusion of proteins from the blood vessels to the interstitial space
C. Facilitated diffusion of protein from the blood vessels to the interstitial space
D. Increased protein synthesis within the red blood cells

GO ON TO THE NEXT PAGE

Passage II (Questions 149-155)

Metabolism is the process that organisms utilize to derive free energy from the oxidation of fuel molecules. In eukaryotic cells, metabolism includes the process of oxidative phosphorylation. This process occurs on the mitochondrial respiratory chain and forms ATP by transferring electrons from NADH and $FADH_2$ to oxygen. The mitochondrial respiratory chain, with inhibitors, is illustrated in Figure 1.

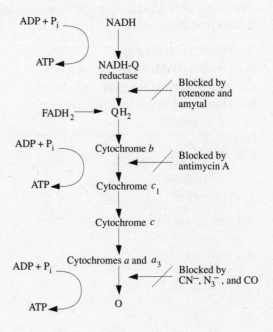

Figure 1

To elucidate the site inhibited by antimycin A, an antibiotic, researchers carried out the following protocols:

• Mitochondrial extracts containing intact respiratory chains were exposed to antimycin A in the presence of NADH and $FADH_2$.

• Oxygen consumption before and after antibiotic administration was measured, and mitochondrial cytochrome structure was analyzed by X-ray crystallography.

It was found that the inhibited structure was cytochrome b, which possesses the heme-containing center pictured in Figure 2.

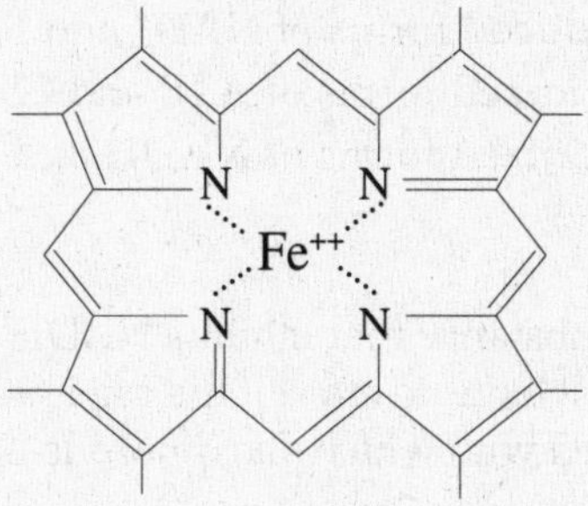

Figure 2

There was a significant drop in oxygen consumption upon administration of antimycin A.

149. Formation of ATP from ADP and inorganic phosphate occurs via:

A. hydrolysis, which involves the removal of a molecule of water.
B. hydrolysis, which involves the addition of a molecule of water.
C. dehydration synthesis, which involves the removal of a molecule of water.
D. dehydration synthesis, which involves the addition of a molecule of water.

150. Which of the following phosphorous-containing compounds can entirely circumvent the effects of rotenone, as seen in Figure 1?

A. $FADH_2$
B. Both NADH and ADP
C. Both ADP and $FADH_2$
D. $FADH_2$, NADH, and ADP

GO ON TO THE NEXT PAGE

151. Aerobic organisms generate the greatest number of ATPs when monosaccharide oxidation produces:

    A. reduced levels of antioxidants.
    B. reduced forms of NAD^+ and FAD.
    C. oxidized forms of ATP and GTP.
    D. oxidized forms of NADH and $FADH_2$.

152. A substance that inhibits NADH-Q reductase will have no effect if the cell is adequately supplied with which phosphorous-containing compound?

    A. $FADH_2$
    B. NADPH
    C. ADP
    D. NADH

153. The presence of fully functioning respiratory chains in the mitochondrial extracts was vital to the success of the experiment. If cytochrome c_1 had been missing, the researchers most likely would have found that:

    A. extra cytochrome c had accumulated.
    B. NADH and $FADH_2$ could not enter the system.
    C. Antimycin A had produced increased oxygen consumption.
    D. Antimycin A had had no effect.

154. To further characterize cytochrome b, the researchers reacted its sulfur-containing amino acids with performic acid and then broke apart the polypeptide into individual amino acid residues. The most likely means of performing this latter task is to:

    A. reduce cysteine residues.
    B. decarboxylate acidic residues.
    C. oxidize amide linkages.
    D. hydrolyze amide linkages.

155. The heme portions of cytochrome molecules are able to transfer electrons among themselves because of:

    A. thioether linkages.
    B. pi-electron delocalization.
    C. enol-intermediate racemization.
    D. shortened bond length.

GO ON TO THE NEXT PAGE

Passage III (Questions 156-160)

A milk inspector was sent by the state Food and Drug Administration to a dairy plant to randomly sample containers of both raw and pasteurized milk to certify that milk production was being conducted under sanitary conditions. Milk contamination may be the result of several types of bacterial growth. The first organism to flourish in milk is usually *Streptococcus lactis,* which ferments the sugar lactose to lactic acid. The chemical environment produced by fermentation is conducive to the growth of the nonspore-forming, gram-positive organism *LactobacilExperimentlus,* which then predominates. Facultative, anaerobic, sporeforming bacteria such as *Streptococcus faecalis* may also be present. Fresh milk, which contains emulsified fat droplets, tends to be anaerobic and has a pH of about 7. Pasteurization is the most common procedure that kills nonspore-forming pathogenic bacteria. The FDA's laboratory conducted the examination according to the procedure below:

1. Take 10 samples of raw and pasteurized milk.
2. Shake each sample vigorously to obtain a homogeneous sample of milk.
3. Using a pipette, transfer 10 mls of each sample of milk to 20 sterilized test tubes.
4. Heat the tubes and hold at 50° C for 15 minutes in a water bath and then add sufficient melted vaspar to form a 1/2-inch layer on the milk in each tube.
5. Incubate all tubes at 37° C for at least 3 days.
6. Make thin smears and stain with methylene blue and gram stain.

156. Which of the following best describes the appearance of *Lactobacillus* when stained and then viewed with a light microscope?

- **A.** Spherical
- **B.** S-shaped
- **C.** Rodlike
- **D.** Asymmetrical

157. The proliferation of *Lactobacillus* in milk samples indicates:

- **A.** high lactose concentration.
- **B.** a drop in the pH.
- **C.** predominance of spore-forming bacteria.
- **D.** the absence of *Streptococcus faecalis.*

158. If one of the raw milk samples were heated to 100° C for 30 minutes and then incubated, which of the following graphs would best represent resulting spore-forming and nonspore-forming bacteria populations?

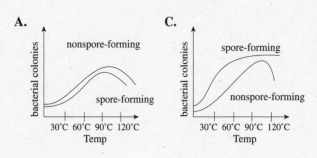

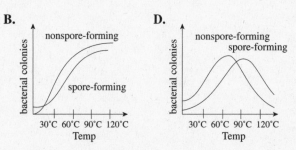

GO ON TO THE NEXT PAGE

159. The gram-staining procedure used in the laboratory enables the inspector to:

    A. identify bacterial species present in the incubate.

    B. distinguish between aerobic and anaerobic organisms.

    C. differentiate pathogenic from non-pathogenic colonies.

    D. distinguish between bacterial and viral organisms.

160. Which of the following environmental factors will affect the growth of *S. faecalis*?

    I. Nutritional content of the milk
    II. The process of pasteurization
    III. Ambient oxygen concentration

    A. I only
    B. I and II only
    C. I and III only
    D. I, II, and III

Questions 161 through 166 are **NOT** based on a descriptive passage.

161. The *eclipsed* conformation of *n*-butane is illustrated below, in the figure on the left. Which of the circled positions in the figure on the right corresponds to the terminal methyl group in the *anti* conformation?

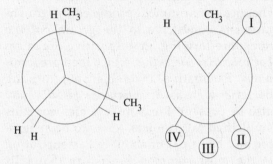

    A. I
    B. II
    C. III
    D. IV

162. All of the following structures secrete enzymes that serve digestive functions EXCEPT the:

    A. pancreas.
    B. stomach.
    C. thymus.
    D. salivary glands.

163. Alkyl halides are more reactive than their corresponding alkanes because the halides more readily participate in:

    A. pyrolysis.
    B. combustion reactions.
    C. hydrophobic bonding.
    D. nucleophilic substitution.

GO ON TO THE NEXT PAGE

164. When lettuce is placed in deionized water it remains crisp because:

- A. the cells lose H_2O.
- B. the cells swell with H_2O.
- C. the stomates close in response to excess water.
- D. the chloroplasts generate greater levels of ATP.

165. Among the following, which statement(s) can be said to apply to the molecule depicted schematically below?

$$
\begin{array}{c}
Br \\
| \\
H - C - CH_3 \\
| \\
CH_2Cl
\end{array}
$$

- I. It rotates the plane of polarized light to the left.
- II. It exhibits chirality.
- III. It is optically active.

- A. I only
- B. I and II only
- C. I and III only
- D. II and III only

166. Which statement below most accurately describes the characteristic features of striated muscle cells?

- A. Striated muscle cells are stimulated by the autonomic nervous system and contain few mitochondria.
- B. Striated muscle cells are mononucleate and arranged in syncytial bundles.
- C. Striated muscle cells have alternating A-bands and I-bands arranged in a transverse pattern.
- D. Striated muscle cells are similar to smooth muscle cells except they lack internal stores of calcium.

Passage IV (Questions 167-171)

Invasive candidiasis is a disease in humans that is caused by several members of the fungal candida species, including *Candida albicans* and *Candida tropicalis*. Candida are easily detected in tissue samples because of their sturdy cell walls, which contain polysaccharides and ergosterol.

In pathological circumstances, candida are found both in the unicellular yeast form and the multicellular, nonbranching pseudohyphal form. In the yeast form, candida divide by *asexual budding*, which involves replication of DNA by mitosis without the formation of germ cells. The pseudohyphal form grows in nonbranching strands and reproduces mostly by *asexual budding*. However, the pseudohypha can also form fruiting bodies that produce gametes (spores). These spores are haploid and can fuse to form a diploid zygote. Both the yeast and pseudohyphal forms of candida can invade many different organ systems via the blood stream.

All of the following drugs have been used in the treatment of candidal infections. These drugs either attack the fungal cell wall or interfere with replication or transcription.

1. Amphotericin B binds to ergosterol in the outer membrane and increases fungal cell wall permeability.
2. Ketoconazole interferes with ergosterol synthesis and, thus, increases cell wall permeability.
3. 5-Fluorocytosine (5-FC) is a synthetic pyrimidine that interferes with the synthesis of RNA in fungal cells.

GO ON TO THE NEXT PAGE

5-FC is deaminated by fungal cells to yield 5-fluorouracil (5-FU). An intermediate product of 5-FU binds to the enzyme thymidylate synthetase, blocking its ability to catalyze the formation of thymidine. The structure of 5-FC is shown in Figure 1.

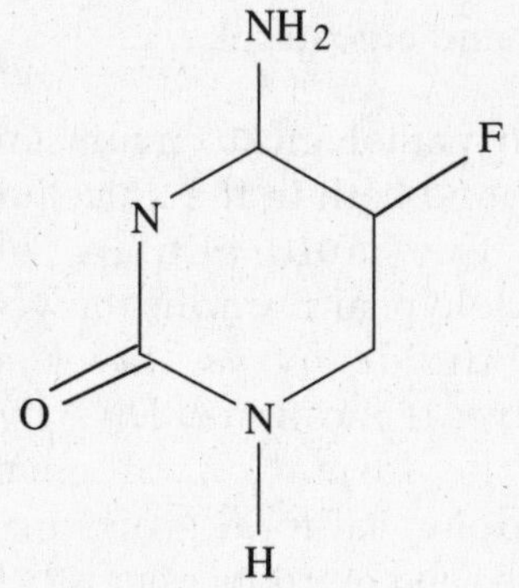

Figure 1

167. Which of the following treatments would NOT effectively treat candidal infections?

   A. Administration of a drug that attacks the outer cell wall of the fungus

   B. Administration of a drug that interferes with fungal replication and transcription

   C. Exposure to a bacteriotoxic agent

   D. Exposure to oral fungistatic drugs

168. Attacking the gamete-producing stage of candida does NOT rid the body of candidal infection because:

   A. the fungus does not reproduce by the formation of gametes.

   B. the fungus can be killed only during periods of asexual reproduction via budding.

   C. the fungus produces gametes that are insensitive to all known drugs.

   D. the fungus most often exists in a form that reproduces asexually.

169. 5-FC attacks the candida fungus by decreasing:

   A. the availability of ATP.

   B. the availability of DNA and RNA precursors.

   C. the availability of necessary amino acids.

   D. the availability of 5-FU.

170. After absorption of 5-FC, which step must then occur for 5-FC to terminate DNA synthesis?

   A. One pyrimidine must be substituted for another pyrimidine.

   B. A purine must be converted into a pyrimidine.

   C. Uracil must be converted into thymidine.

   D. Thymidylate synthetase must be phosphorylated to be inactivated.

171. According to the passage, the yeast form of candida in the human body reproduces by retaining:

   A. the same number of chromosomes per nucleus, while randomly dividing the genome between two daughter cells.

   B. the same number of chromosomes per nucleus, without randomly dividing the genome between two daughter cells.

   C. half the number of chromosomes per nucleus, without randomly dividing the genome between two daughter cells.

   D. half the number of chromosomes per nucleus, while randomly dividing the genome between two daughter cells.

GO ON TO THE NEXT PAGE

Passage V (Questions 172-178)

Physiological changes during the human menstrual cycle are affected by levels of sex hormones. The following procedure measured the secretion of estrogens during the menstrual cycle, and during pregnancy and menopause.

Test subjects with approximately equal weights and levels of daily activity were chosen. Pregnant subjects were tested at the 160th day of the gestational period or at term. Another group of subjects was tested after showing postmenopausal signs and symptoms for at least two months prior to testing. Menstruating subjects were tested either at the onset of menstruation, at the peak of ovulation, or at the luteal maximum. The luteal maximum represents the greatest amount of estrogen secretion during the second half of the menstrual cycle.

During the test period, urine samples were taken every four hours. Urinary levels of five naturally occurring estrogens were measured using the Kober test. The Kober test produces a pink color in the presence of estrogens, including the oxidative product estriol. Estradiol is the most potent estrogen, while estrone is weaker and estriol is the weakest of the three. The results of the procedure are shown in Table 1, with the value of estrogen levels averaged for each test group.

Estrogen excreted per 24 hours					
Time measurement	Estriol	Estrone	Estradiol	16-Epiestriol	16α-Hydroxy -estrone
Onset of menstruation	7 µg	6 µg	3 µg	*	*
Ovulation peak	28 µg	21 µg	10 µg	*	*
Luteal maximum	23 µg	15 µg	8 µg	*	*
Pregnancy, 160 days	8 mg	0.8 mg	0.3 mg	*	*
Pregnancy, term	31 mg	2.5 mg	0.85 mg	0.80 mg	1.8 mg
Postmenopause	4.3 µg	3.0 µg	0.7 µg	*	*

Table 1

172. Which of the following ovarian cell organelles will show the greatest levels of activity during the secretion of estrogen?

A. Lysosomes
B. Golgi apparatus
C. Centrioles
D. Ribosomes

173. Which test groups showed the greatest levels of estrogen synthesis and secretion?

I. Onset of menstruation
II. Ovulation peak
III. Pregnancy, 160 days
IV. Pregnancy, term

A. I and III only
B. I and IV only
C. II and III only
D. III and IV only

174. From Table 1, which variable would prove to be the best marker for the term stage of normal pregnancy, as indicated by the Kober test?

A. The oxidation of estradiol
B. The presence of estriol
C. The presence of 16 α-hydroxyestrone
D. A positive Kober reaction

175. Would estrogen levels in males increase at the onset of puberty?

A. Yes, because the increased levels of testosterone in the pubertal male are partially converted to estrogens.
B. Yes, because estrogen is the predominant male sex hormone produced by pubertal males.
C. No, because estrogen hormones are not produced in human males.
D. No, because estrogen concentration does not vary from pre-puberty to puberty in the male.

GO ON TO THE NEXT PAGE

176. In Table 1, which of the following pairs of subject groups showed the greatest difference in the ratio of estrone to 16-epiestriol levels?

A. Pregnancy/160 days and post-menopause
B. Pregnancy/term and pregnancy/160 days
C. Post-menopause and pregnancy/160 days
D. Onset of menstruation and post-menopause

177. What change in the ratio of estrone to estradiol is expected to occur as women enter post-menopause, according to the passage?

A. The ratio increases, because estradiol levels decrease relatively more than estrone levels decrease.
B. The ratio increases, because estradiol levels decrease while estrone levels are unaffected.
C. The ratio is unchanged, because both estrogen hormone levels decrease in the postmenopausal period.
D. The ratio decreases, because estrone levels decrease more than estradiol levels.

178. Researchers further studied estrogen levels in subjects at the luteal minimum of estrogen secretion and at the 210th day of pregnancy. Which findings would NOT indicate a trend similar to that found during the original procedures?

A. The levels of estriol are greater than the levels of estradiol in both pregnant and luteal minimum groups.
B. The levels of estradiol are lower than those of estrone in the pregnant group.
C. The estrone levels are elevated in the pregnant group compared with the luteal minimum group.
D. The ratio of 16-epiestriol levels between the pregnant and luteal minimum groups is 1:2.

Passage VI (Questions 179-184)

The figure illustrates a procedure used in the preparation of organic compounds from alkyl halides. These compounds are useful intermediates for the synthesis of a variety of organic products.

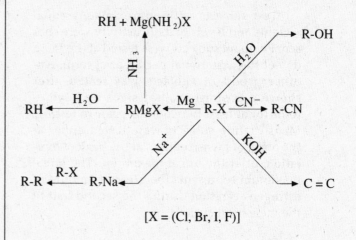

$$[X = (Cl, Br, I, F)]$$

Figure 1

179. When alkyl halides react with potassium hydroxide to yield alkene derivatives, the potassium hydroxide acts as:

A. an acid.
B. a base.
C. a proton donor.
D. a reductant.

180. If one were to substitute heavy water (D_2O) in the last steps of the Grignard reaction, the reaction would lead to the synthesis of:

A. R-R.
B. R-OD.
C. R-D.
D. R-H.

GO ON TO THE NEXT PAGE

181. Alkyl halides are not usually prepared by direct halogenation of alkanes because:

- A. alkanes are not very reactive compounds.
- B. alkanes have low boiling points.
- C. alkanes are desaturated by halogenation.
- D. alkanes do not dissolve in polarized solutions.

182. The synthesis of ethane from ethyl bromide requires the addition of:

- A. Mg and H_2O.
- B. Mg and RCH_2Cl.
- C. Na^+ and RCH_2Cl.
- D. Na^+ and CH_3Br.

183. Alkyl halides are insoluble in water because:

- A. they are hydrophilic.
- B. they are ionic compounds.
- C. they are unable to form hydrogen bonds.
- D. they contain electron-withdrawing groups.

184. Identification of alkyl halides is based on all of the following physical properties EXCEPT:

- A. boiling point.
- B. density.
- C. spectroscopy.
- D. mass.

Passage VII (Questions 185-190)

Carbohydrate absorption is controlled by several factors, including levels of blood glucose. Insulin and glucagon secretion regulates plasma glucose levels in response to blood glucose availability. This is accomplished by a negative feedback control mechanism that regulates cellular metabolism.

In response to high levels of blood glucose, the pancreas secretes insulin into the blood stream, which acts to increase the availability of plasma glucose to tissues. Glucagon is secreted in response to low levels of blood glucose and acts to decrease plasma glucose availability to tissue cells.

Experiments on laboratory animals illustrate how insulin and glucagon together regulate carbohydrate metabolism. The experimental administration of insulin to laboratory mice has been shown to induce hypoglycemic shock and convulsions. Alternatively, the administration of glucose to animals in hypoglycemic shock causes immediate and dramatic recovery.

Experiment 1

Step 1: A single dose of insulin (50-100 IU/Kg) was administered to an experimental group of laboratory mice. Blood was drawn at 15-minute intervals in order to assay the levels of plasma glucose up until the onset of convulsions.

Step 2: Immediately thereafter, the mice were injected with glucose solution. Glucose administration was continued until convulsions ceased to occur.

Results: Experimental insulin administration caused severe hypoglycemic shock, which was dramatically remedied by the administration of glucose.

Experiment 2 was identical to Experiment 1 except that glucose was initially administered instead of insulin, thereby inducing hyperglycemia, which was immediately reversed by insulin injection.

GO ON TO THE NEXT PAGE ➡

185. Which of the following would NOT account for elevated levels of insulin in the blood?

 A. Ingesting a heavy meal
 B. Injecting insulin at bedtime
 C. Arising after an all-night fast
 D. Breaking a fast

186. Which of the following individuals would have the highest levels of glucagon in the blood stream?

 A. A man running in the last third of a marathon
 B. A pregnant woman after eating breakfast
 C. A bedridden patient two hours after a meal
 D. A child after eating dessert

187. The administration of insulin in Experiment 2 is able to reverse hyperglycemia because:

 A. insulin inhibits glucose uptake by body cells.
 B. insulin enhances glucose uptake by body cells.
 C. glucagon production by the liver is inhibited by insulin.
 D. levels of intracellular glucose are reduced by insulin.

188. Which of the following best supports the premise that insulin and glucagon are produced by two different types of pancreatic islet cells?

 A. Certain islet cells have secretory products similar to those secreted by nervous system cells.
 B. High blood glucose increases the activity of some islet cells while low blood glucose increases the activity of different islet cell types.
 C. Insulin and glucagon have opposing actions in the body.
 D. Insulin and glucagon are composed of different polypeptide chains.

189. Body cells can respond in vivo to exogenously administered insulin because insulin is a polypeptide that interacts with cells via:

 A. a bilayer membrane that allows simple inward diffusion of insulin.
 B. a bilayer membrane that allows endocytosis of insulin.
 C. cell receptors that are activated in close association with insulin.
 D. cell receptors that degrade insulin on contact.

190. What happened to the blood glucose levels in the blood after insulin administration in Experiment 1?

 A. Glucose was moved primarily into the liver and not other body tissues.
 B. Glucose was moved primarily into the kidneys, as in diabetes insipidus.
 C. Glucose was moved into body cells because insulin prevented blood cell degradation of glucose.
 D. Glucose was moved into body cells because insulin increased the cells' uptake of glucose.

GO ON TO THE NEXT PAGE

Questions 191 through 195 are **NOT** based on a descriptive passage.

191. Bacteriophages are viruses that attack bacteria. They attach to the surface of a bacterium and inject their genetic material into the host. Bacteriophages differ from other organisms in that:

A. they only contain RNA, which replicates inside a host cell.

B. they have only RNA and must utilize a host cell's machinery to generate DNA.

C. they lack the cellular metabolic machinery found in both eukaryotic and prokaryotic organisms.

D. they possess bounding membranes and internal organelles including ribosomes and vacuoles.

192. Consider the reaction below.

$$CH_3CH_2CH_2OH \xrightarrow[CH_2Cl_2]{PCC} CH_3CH_2CHO$$

Which of the following observations about the infrared spectrum of the reaction mixture would indicate that the reaction shown above occurred?

A. The appearance of a C=O stretch and C–H stretch

B. The appearance of an aliphatic C–H stretch

C. The appearance of an O–H stretch

D. The disappearance of an N–H stretch

193. The process of respiration consists of both inspiration and expiration. Inspiration is:

A. a passive process due to negative pressure in the thoracic cavity.

B. a passive process due to positive pressure in the thoracic cavity.

C. an active process due to negative pressure in the thoracic cavity.

D. an active process due to positive pressure in the thoracic cavity.

194. Sickle cell anemia is a blood disorder due to a point mutation in a single gene. It is inherited as an autosomal recessive trait. A woman heterozygous for the disorder most likely has:

A. full-blown sickle cell anemia.

B. sickle cell trait, a carrier disease.

C. no signs or symptoms of the disease.

D. a predominance of sickle-shaped red blood cells.

195. Which of the following is NOT a resonance structure of phenol?

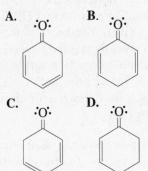

GO ON TO THE NEXT PAGE

Passage VIII (Questions 196-200)

Coronary atherosclerosis refers to an accumulation of cholesterol plaques within the coronary arteries and is the principal cause of myocardial infarction ("heart attack"). Coronary atherosclerosis is more common in patients with preexisting high blood pressure and, some authorities believe, in patients who experience high levels of stress. The condition is known to relate closely to the concentration of lipid in the blood.

The blood stream carries lipids in five different types of lipoprotein particles: (1) chylomicrons, (2) very low-density lipoproteins (VLDL), (3) low-density lipoproteins (LDL), (4) intermediate-density lipoproteins (IDL), and (5) high-density lipoproteins (HDL). All five types of lipoprotein particles share a basic structure. A core of nonpolar lipid is surrounded by a surface coat of phospholipid. At one end the surface phospholipid molecules are polar and therefore soluble in the plasma. At the other end, they are nonpolar and therefore lipid-soluble.

The lipoprotein most often and most strongly associated with coronary atherosclerosis, and hence with the incidence of myocardial infarction, is LDL. The coronary arteries supply the heart muscle itself with blood to meet its metabolic needs. When flow through the coronary arteries is sufficiently compromised by atherosclerosis, a portion of the muscle is damaged or dies for lack of blood supply.

LDL promotes the formation of atherosclerotic plaques in the coronary arteries. HDL particles, on the other hand, tend to prevent atherosclerosis. The lipid imbalance that most commonly leads to coronary atherosclerosis is an excess of LDL relative to HDL.

How derangements in plasma lipoproteins induce atherosclerosis is the subject of investigation. Whatever the precise mechanism, clinical management requires that the physician effectively employ laboratory procedures to identify high-risk states. With three simple blood tests the physician can identify virtually all patients at risk of developing coronary atherosclerosis. The tests are: (1) total serum cholesterol, (2) HDL cholesterol, and (3) fasting triglycerides. A fourth value, LDL cholesterol, is derived from this formula:

$$LDL\ cholesterol = (total\ serum\ cholesterol - HDL\ cholesterol)$$

From 60 percent to 70 percent of serum cholesterol is found in LDL particles, which explains the strong relationship between total serum cholesterol and LDL content. As is shown in Figure 1, the correlation between serum cholesterol and morbidity from atherosclerosis varies with the age group to which the patient belongs.

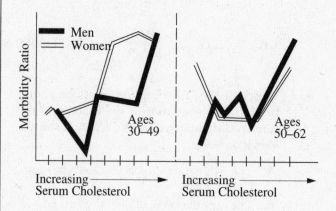

Figure 1

GO ON TO THE NEXT PAGE

196. High total serum cholesterol puts a patient at risk for myocardial infarction because it reflects:

   A. low blood content of high-density lipoproteins.

   B. low blood content of low-density lipoproteins.

   C. high blood content of high-density lipoproteins.

   D. high blood content of low-density lipoproteins.

197. If an elderly woman with abnormally high levels of LDL has little coronary atherosclerosis, she most likely:

   A. has high levels of HDL, counteracting the effects of the LDL.

   B. follows a diet that is low in cholesterol-containing foods.

   C. has no atherosclerosis in arteries outside the heart.

   D. has failed to undergo a complete diagnostic screening for blood lipid status.

198. Coronary atherosclerosis constitutes a medical problem because it threatens to:

   A. render the heart less sensitive to stress.

   B. produce imbalance in the patient's blood lipid profile.

   C. compromise the heart muscle's oxygen supply.

   D. subject the patient to high blood pressure.

199. Coronary atherosclerosis is virtually unknown among peoples living in non-industrialized nations. This indicates that in comparison with industrialized populations these peoples probably have:

   A. a lower incidence of heart attack.

   B. a lower incidence of hypertension.

   C. higher levels of VLDL.

   D. higher levels of IDL.

200. If coronary atherosclerosis produces myocardial infarction, what is the status of the affected heart muscle?

   A. High pH

   B. Low pH

   C. High O_2 concentration

   D. Low CO_2 concentration

GO ON TO THE NEXT PAGE ⟶

Passage IX (Questions 201-207)

In studying the effects of molecular substituents on the acidity of carboxylic acids, researchers have compared equilibrium reactions for the deprotonation of a number of dicarboxylic acids. A standard reaction for comparison purposes is the deprotonation of malonic acid.

$$HOOCCH_2COOH + H_2O \rightleftharpoons HOOCCH_2COO^- + H_3O^+$$

Reaction I

The equilibrium rate constant for Reaction I is symbolized as K_1. The anion in Reaction I can be further deprotonated; the equilibrium constant for this reaction is symbolized as K_2, a value substantially lower than the original K_1.

$$HOOCCH_2COO^- + H_2O \rightleftharpoons {}^-OOCCH_2COO^- + H_3O^+$$

Reaction II

The constants K_1 and K_2 are determined according to the following equations:

$$K_1 = \frac{[HOOCCH_2COO^-][H_3O^+]}{[HOOCH_2COOH]}$$

$$K_2 = \frac{[{}^-OOCCH_2COO^-][H_3O^+]}{[HOOCH_2COO^-]}$$

The ratios above are determined under equilibrium conditions and do not apply to nonequilibrium conditions.

Table 1 lists the values of K_1 and K_2 for several dicarboxylic acids.

Compound	Formula	K_1	K_2
Oxalic Acid	HOOC – COOH	5400×10^{-5}	5.2×10^{-5}
Malonic Acid	HOOCCH$_2$COOH	140×10^{-5}	0.2×10^{-5}
Succinic Acid	HOOC(CH$_2$)$_2$COOH	64×10^{-5}	0.23×10^{-5}
Maleic Acid	HOOCCH=CHCOOH	1000×10^{-5}	0.055×10^{-5}
Fumaric Acid	HOOCCH=CHCOOH	96×10^{-5}	4.1×10^{-5}

Table 1

Note: The structures of fumaric and maleic acid are shown below:

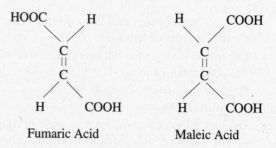

Fumaric Acid   Maleic Acid

201. Based on the passage, one could estimate a dicarboxylic acid's K_1 value by determining:

A. its concentration in a nonequilibrium mixture.
B. the stability of the anion form.
C. its tendency to undergo decarboxylation.
D. its crystallization structure.

GO ON TO THE NEXT PAGE

202. Glutaric acid is a dicarboxylic acid with the formula $HOOC(CH_2)_3COOH$. This acid is most likely to have a K_1 constant closest in value to which substance listed in the table?

A. Fumaric acid
B. Maleic acid
C. Succinic acid
D. Oxalic acid

203. If equal concentrations of succinic acid, malonic acid, and maleic acid were heated in a weakly basic solution, which of the following products would be in the greatest concentration at equilibrium?

A. $HOOCCH_2COO^-$
B. $HOOC(CH_2)_2COO^-$
C. $HOOCCH=CHCOO^-$
D. $HOOC-COOH$

204. Based on information in the passage, it would be difficult to estimate K_1 for a molecule with the formula $HOOCCH_2NHCOOH$ because:

A. its anion stability is not directly comparable to that of succinic acid.
B. it cannot exist in the deprotonated form.
C. it must form an insoluble compound.
D. it represents an unstable compound.

205. In an aqueous mixture of maleic and fumaric acid, the equilibrium proportions can best be determined by which method?

A. Radioactive tagging of the corresponding alkene
B. Hydration of the anion solution
C. Acidification of the solution
D. Nuclear magnetic resonance spectroscopy of the equilibrium solution

206. The value of K_1 of the dicarboxylic compound glutamic acid is substantially lower than the K_1 of glutaric acid because:

A. glutamate is readily convertible into a nonpolar zwitterion.
B. glutamate's deprotonated form is less stable than the glutarate anion.
C. glutamate is an amino acid.
D. glutamic acid is a stronger acid than glutaric acid.

207. One can most reasonably estimate the value of K_2 for acetic acid (CH_3COOH) to be:

A. higher than K_1 for acetic acid.
B. higher than K_2 for maleic acid.
C. lower than K_2 for oxalic acid.
D. less than zero.

GO ON TO THE NEXT PAGE

Passage X (Questions 208-215)

Bacillus subtilis is a gram-positive bacterium that reproduces itself through replication of a double-stranded chromosome. Reproduction does not require the formation of gametes. The haploid cells of *B. subtilis* undergo asexual division in which the haploid number is preserved and two daughter cells are formed from one parent. *B. subtilis* does not form a diploid state and does not undergo a reduction division. In studying *B. subtilis* scientists have also studied bacteriophage SP8, a virus that infects *B. subtilis*. Of particular interest is that the virus performs transcription from a single strand of intact double-stranded viral DNA using host cell enzymatic machinery.

Experiment 1

To determine the role of each DNA strand in transcription, researchers denatured the viral DNA and hybridized the separated strands, termed Light and Heavy, to tritiated RNA isolated from SP8-infected *B. subtilis*. The density of the separated strands was determined, and the hybridized DNA-RNA strands were analyzed in the presence of RNAse, a hydrolytic enzyme. The graphs in Figure 1 and Figure 2 summarize the results obtained for both Light and Heavy strands of viral DNA.

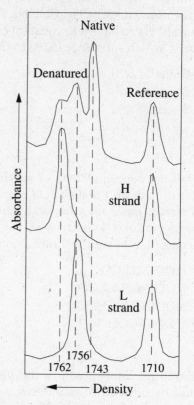

Figure 1

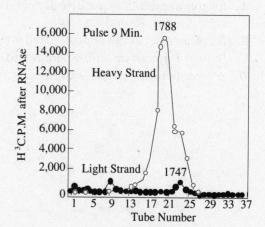

Figure 2

GO ON TO THE NEXT PAGE

Experiment 2

SP8-infected *B. subtilis*, carrying the viral DNA, was induced to undergo division, and the viral DNA Light strand of one daughter cell was extensively mutated. The other daughter's viral DNA Light strand was unaffected. There were no phenotypic differences between the daughter cells, including reproduction rates.

Experiment 3

SP8-infected *B. subtilis* was again induced to undergo division. The Light strand of viral DNA of one daughter cell was extensively mutated, and the Heavy strand of viral DNA of the second daughter was also mutated. The two daughter cells were induced to undergo a second round of division. Only the daughter cell with the mutated viral DNA Light strand produced offspring. The two Light strand mutants were again induced to replicate and successfully produced offspring.

208.   If a segment of the denatured viral DNA strand had a base sequence ATAA, what would have been the complementary RNA sequence?

A. GTGG
B. TATT
C. UAUU
D. TUTT

209.   At the end of Experiment 3, how many offspring reproduced through the formation of gametes?

A. 0
B. 2
C. 4
D. 12

210.   Suppose the lower-density Light strand mutant in Figure 1 cannot undergo transcription. The most likely explanation is that it does not:

A. bind DNA.
B. bind RNA.
C. bind protein.
D. replicate.

211.   All of the following are true with regard to bacteriophage SP8 EXCEPT:

A. It infects the *B. subtilis* bacterium.
B. Gram staining its cell wall helps to permit its identification.
C. It contained viral DNA.
D. It possesses a tail structure.

212.   Which of the following findings best supports the conclusion that the viral DNA Heavy strand normally produces transcribed mRNA, whereas the viral DNA Light strand does not?

A. Neither the Heavy strand nor the Light strand of viral DNA can excise point mutations.
B. Neither the Heavy strand nor the Light strand of viral DNA hybridizes with labeled RNA.
C. Only the viral DNA Light strand can direct protein synthesis.
D. Only the mutated viral DNA Heavy strand produces phenotypic changes.

213.   How can one determine that mutations of the viral DNA Light strand do not affect phenotypic expression in the host?

A. By locating the mutation on the host DNA
B. By comparing Light strand mutants with Heavy strand mutants
C. By comparing the mutant phenotype with the unmutated form
D. By studying the production of RNA polymerase

GO ON TO THE NEXT PAGE

214. By studying Figures 1 and 2, a scientist decided that the normal bacteriophage SP8 DNA consists of a double-stranded chromosome. For this conclusion to be true, which of the following assumptions must be correct?

A. Hybridization of DNA with RNA involves the formation of covalent bonds.
B. Radiolabeling affects the size of the RNA-DNA hybrid produced.
C. Mutation does not lead to changes in DNA sequence.
D. Denaturation breaks apart the double helix without hydrolyzing covalently attached base pairs.

215. For bacteriophage SP8, if the mutated Heavy strand codes for a protein that destroys DNA polymerases while the Light strand does not, then the mutant will:

A. show increased production of DNA.
B. show decreased evolutionary "fitness" compared with the Light strand mutant.
C. show increased evolutionary "fitness" compared with the normal virus.
D. show an increased tendency to undergo meiosis.

GO ON TO THE NEXT PAGE

Questions 216 through 219 are **NOT** based on a descriptive passage.

216. Which of the following processes does NOT occur on the ribosomes during protein synthesis?

   A. Translation of mRNA
   B. Peptide bond formation
   C. Attachment of tRNA anticodons to mRNA codons
   D. Transcription of mRNA

217. During embryonic gastrulation, invagination occurs as a result of which of the following processes?

   A. Release of a hormone
   B. Migration of cells
   C. Reproduction of cells
   D. Asymmetric division of cells

218. Surgically implanted pacemakers are frequently used in the treatment of heart disease. Which of the following normal heart structures carries out the same function as a pacemaker?

   A. The bundle of His
   B. The atrioventricular node
   C. The sinoatrial node
   D. The sinoventricular node

219. The hormone that most directly stimulates the formation of sperm in the testes is which of the following?

   A. Estrogen
   B. Testosterone
   C. Luteinizing hormone
   D. Follicle-stimulating hormone

STOP
IF YOU FINISH BEFORE TIME IS CALLED, YOU MAY CHECK YOUR WORK ON THIS TEST ONLY.
DO NOT TURN TO ANY OTHER TEST IN THIS BOOK.

SCORE CONVERSION CHART

Verbal Reasoning

Total Correct	Scaled Score
65	15
64	14
62–63	13
60–61	12
58–59	11
55–57	10
50–54	9
45–49	8
39–44	7
33–38	6
27–32	5
22–26	4
17–21	3
11–16	2
0–10	1

Physical Sciences

Total Correct	Scaled Score
76–77	15
73–75	14
69–72	13
63–68	12
57–62	11
51–56	10
46–50	9
39–45	8
34–38	7
28–33	6
23–27	5
18–22	4
13–17	3
8–12	2
0–7	1

Biological Sciences

Total Correct	Scaled Score
76–77	15
74–75	14
70–73	13
67–69	12
63–66	11
58–62	10
53–57	9
46–52	8
40–45	7
34–39	6
28–33	5
24–27	4
20–23	3
15–19	2
0–14	1

The Princeton Review
Diagnostic Test Form ○ Side 1

1.

YOUR NAME: _____
(Print)   Last   First   M.I.

SIGNATURE: _____   DATE: ___ / ___ / ___

HOME ADDRESS: _____
(Print)   Number and Street

_____
City   State   Zip Code

PHONE NO.: _____
(Print)

IMPORTANT: Please fill in these boxes exactly as shown on the back cover of your test book.

2. TEST FORM

_____

3. TEST CODE

4. REGISTRATION NUMBER

5. YOUR NAME

First 4 letters of last name				FIRST INIT	MID INIT

(Columns with bubbles A through Z)

6. DATE OF BIRTH

MONTH	DAY		YEAR	
JAN				
FEB				
MAR				
APR				
MAY				
JUN				
JUL				
AUG				
SEP				
OCT				
NOV				
DEC				

7. SEX

○ MALE
○ FEMALE

Begin with number 1 for each new section of the test. Leave blank any extra answer spaces.

SECTION 1

1 A B C D E   26 A B C D E   51 A B C D E   76 A B C D E
2 A B C D E   27 A B C D E   52 A B C D E   77 A B C D E
3 A B C D E   28 A B C D E   53 A B C D E   78 A B C D E
4 A B C D E   29 A B C D E   54 A B C D E   79 A B C D E
5 A B C D E   30 A B C D E   55 A B C D E   80 A B C D E
6 A B C D E   31 A B C D E   56 A B C D E   81 A B C D E
7 A B C D E   32 A B C D E   57 A B C D E   82 A B C D E
8 A B C D E   33 A B C D E   58 A B C D E   83 A B C D E
9 A B C D E   34 A B C D E   59 A B C D E   84 A B C D E
10 A B C D E   35 A B C D E   60 A B C D E   85 A B C D E
11 A B C D E   36 A B C D E   61 A B C D E   86 A B C D E
12 A B C D E   37 A B C D E   62 A B C D E   87 A B C D E
13 A B C D E   38 A B C D E   63 A B C D E   88 A B C D E
14 A B C D E   39 A B C D E   64 A B C D E   89 A B C D E
15 A B C D E   40 A B C D E   65 A B C D E   90 A B C D E
16 A B C D E   41 A B C D E   66 A B C D E   91 A B C D E
17 A B C D E   42 A B C D E   67 A B C D E   92 A B C D E
18 A B C D E   43 A B C D E   68 A B C D E   93 A B C D E
19 A B C D E   44 A B C D E   69 A B C D E   94 A B C D E
20 A B C D E   45 A B C D E   70 A B C D E   95 A B C D E
21 A B C D E   46 A B C D E   71 A B C D E   96 A B C D E
22 A B C D E   47 A B C D E   72 A B C D E   97 A B C D E
23 A B C D E   48 A B C D E   73 A B C D E   98 A B C D E
24 A B C D E   49 A B C D E   74 A B C D E   99 A B C D E
25 A B C D E   50 A B C D E   75 A B C D E   100 A B C D E

The Princeton Review
Diagnostic Test Form ○ Side 2

Completely darken bubbles with a No. 2 pencil. If you make a mistake, be sure to erase mark completely. Erase all stray marks.

Begin with number 1 for each new section of the test. Leave blank any extra answer spaces.

SECTION 2

1	A	B	C	D	E	26	A	B	C	D	E	51	A	B	C	D	E	76	A	B	C	D	E
2	A	B	C	D	E	27	A	B	C	D	E	52	A	B	C	D	E	77	A	B	C	D	E
3	A	B	C	D	E	28	A	B	C	D	E	53	A	B	C	D	E	78	A	B	C	D	E
4	A	B	C	D	E	29	A	B	C	D	E	54	A	B	C	D	E	79	A	B	C	D	E
5	A	B	C	D	E	30	A	B	C	D	E	55	A	B	C	D	E	80	A	B	C	D	E
6	A	B	C	D	E	31	A	B	C	D	E	56	A	B	C	D	E	81	A	B	C	D	E
7	A	B	C	D	E	32	A	B	C	D	E	57	A	B	C	D	E	82	A	B	C	D	E
8	A	B	C	D	E	33	A	B	C	D	E	58	A	B	C	D	E	83	A	B	C	D	E
9	A	B	C	D	E	34	A	B	C	D	E	59	A	B	C	D	E	84	A	B	C	D	E
10	A	B	C	D	E	35	A	B	C	D	E	60	A	B	C	D	E	85	A	B	C	D	E
11	A	B	C	D	E	36	A	B	C	D	E	61	A	B	C	D	E	86	A	B	C	D	E
12	A	B	C	D	E	37	A	B	C	D	E	62	A	B	C	D	E	87	A	B	C	D	E
13	A	B	C	D	E	38	A	B	C	D	E	63	A	B	C	D	E	88	A	B	C	D	E
14	A	B	C	D	E	39	A	B	C	D	E	64	A	B	C	D	E	89	A	B	C	D	E
15	A	B	C	D	E	40	A	B	C	D	E	65	A	B	C	D	E	90	A	B	C	D	E
16	A	B	C	D	E	41	A	B	C	D	E	66	A	B	C	D	E	91	A	B	C	D	E
17	A	B	C	D	E	42	A	B	C	D	E	67	A	B	C	D	E	92	A	B	C	D	E
18	A	B	C	D	E	43	A	B	C	D	E	68	A	B	C	D	E	93	A	B	C	D	E
19	A	B	C	D	E	44	A	B	C	D	E	69	A	B	C	D	E	94	A	B	C	D	E
20	A	B	C	D	E	45	A	B	C	D	E	70	A	B	C	D	E	95	A	B	C	D	E
21	A	B	C	D	E	46	A	B	C	D	E	71	A	B	C	D	E	96	A	B	C	D	E
22	A	B	C	D	E	47	A	B	C	D	E	72	A	B	C	D	E	97	A	B	C	D	E
23	A	B	C	D	E	48	A	B	C	D	E	73	A	B	C	D	E	98	A	B	C	D	E
24	A	B	C	D	E	49	A	B	C	D	E	74	A	B	C	D	E	99	A	B	C	D	E
25	A	B	C	D	E	50	A	B	C	D	E	75	A	B	C	D	E	100	A	B	C	D	E

SECTION 3

1	A	B	C	D	E	26	A	B	C	D	E	51	A	B	C	D	E	76	A	B	C	D	E
2	A	B	C	D	E	27	A	B	C	D	E	52	A	B	C	D	E	77	A	B	C	D	E
3	A	B	C	D	E	28	A	B	C	D	E	53	A	B	C	D	E	78	A	B	C	D	E
4	A	B	C	D	E	29	A	B	C	D	E	54	A	B	C	D	E	79	A	B	C	D	E
5	A	B	C	D	E	30	A	B	C	D	E	55	A	B	C	D	E	80	A	B	C	D	E
6	A	B	C	D	E	31	A	B	C	D	E	56	A	B	C	D	E	81	A	B	C	D	E
7	A	B	C	D	E	32	A	B	C	D	E	57	A	B	C	D	E	82	A	B	C	D	E
8	A	B	C	D	E	33	A	B	C	D	E	58	A	B	C	D	E	83	A	B	C	D	E
9	A	B	C	D	E	34	A	B	C	D	E	59	A	B	C	D	E	84	A	B	C	D	E
10	A	B	C	D	E	35	A	B	C	D	E	60	A	B	C	D	E	85	A	B	C	D	E
11	A	B	C	D	E	36	A	B	C	D	E	61	A	B	C	D	E	86	A	B	C	D	E
12	A	B	C	D	E	37	A	B	C	D	E	62	A	B	C	D	E	87	A	B	C	D	E
13	A	B	C	D	E	38	A	B	C	D	E	63	A	B	C	D	E	88	A	B	C	D	E
14	A	B	C	D	E	39	A	B	C	D	E	64	A	B	C	D	E	89	A	B	C	D	E
15	A	B	C	D	E	40	A	B	C	D	E	65	A	B	C	D	E	90	A	B	C	D	E
16	A	B	C	D	E	41	A	B	C	D	E	66	A	B	C	D	E	91	A	B	C	D	E
17	A	B	C	D	E	42	A	B	C	D	E	67	A	B	C	D	E	92	A	B	C	D	E
18	A	B	C	D	E	43	A	B	C	D	E	68	A	B	C	D	E	93	A	B	C	D	E
19	A	B	C	D	E	44	A	B	C	D	E	69	A	B	C	D	E	94	A	B	C	D	E
20	A	B	C	D	E	45	A	B	C	D	E	70	A	B	C	D	E	95	A	B	C	D	E
21	A	B	C	D	E	46	A	B	C	D	E	71	A	B	C	D	E	96	A	B	C	D	E
22	A	B	C	D	E	47	A	B	C	D	E	72	A	B	C	D	E	97	A	B	C	D	E
23	A	B	C	D	E	48	A	B	C	D	E	73	A	B	C	D	E	98	A	B	C	D	E
24	A	B	C	D	E	49	A	B	C	D	E	74	A	B	C	D	E	99	A	B	C	D	E
25	A	B	C	D	E	50	A	B	C	D	E	75	A	B	C	D	E	100	A	B	C	D	E

FOR TPR USE ONLY	V1	V2	V3	V4	M1	M2	M3	M4	M5	M6	M7	M8

The Princeton Review
Diagnostic Test Form ○ Side 1

1.

YOUR NAME: _____
(Print)   Last   First   M.I.

SIGNATURE: _____   DATE: ___/___/___

HOME ADDRESS: _____
(Print)   Number and Street

_____
City   State   Zip Code

PHONE NO.: _____
(Print)

5. YOUR NAME

First 4 letters of last name				FIRST INIT	MID INIT
A	A	A	A	A	A
B	B	B	B	B	B
C	C	C	C	C	C
D	D	D	D	D	D
E	E	E	E	E	E
F	F	F	F	F	F
G	G	G	G	G	G
H	H	H	H	H	H
I	I	I	I	I	I
J	J	J	J	J	J
K	K	K	K	K	K
L	L	L	L	L	L
M	M	M	M	M	M
N	N	N	N	N	N
O	O	O	O	O	O
P	P	P	P	P	P
Q	Q	Q	Q	Q	Q
R	R	R	R	R	R
S	S	S	S	S	S
T	T	T	T	T	T
U	U	U	U	U	U
V	V	V	V	V	V
W	W	W	W	W	W
X	X	X	X	X	X
Y	Y	Y	Y	Y	Y
Z	Z	Z	Z	Z	Z

IMPORTANT: Please fill in these boxes exactly as shown on the back cover of your test book.

2. TEST FORM

3. TEST CODE

4. REGISTRATION NUMBER

6. DATE OF BIRTH

MONTH	DAY	YEAR
○ JAN		
○ FEB		
○ MAR	0 0	0 0
○ APR	1 1	1 1
○ MAY	2 2	2 2
○ JUN	3 3	3 3
○ JUL	4	4 4
○ AUG	5	5 5
○ SEP	6	6 6
○ OCT	7	7 7
○ NOV	8	8 8
○ DEC	9	9 9

7. SEX
○ MALE
○ FEMALE

Begin with number 1 for each new section of the test. Leave blank any extra answer spaces.

SECTION 1

1 A B C D E   26 A B C D E   51 A B C D E   76 A B C D E
2 A B C D E   27 A B C D E   52 A B C D E   77 A B C D E
3 A B C D E   28 A B C D E   53 A B C D E   78 A B C D E
4 A B C D E   29 A B C D E   54 A B C D E   79 A B C D E
5 A B C D E   30 A B C D E   55 A B C D E   80 A B C D E
6 A B C D E   31 A B C D E   56 A B C D E   81 A B C D E
7 A B C D E   32 A B C D E   57 A B C D E   82 A B C D E
8 A B C D E   33 A B C D E   58 A B C D E   83 A B C D E
9 A B C D E   34 A B C D E   59 A B C D E   84 A B C D E
10 A B C D E   35 A B C D E   60 A B C D E   85 A B C D E
11 A B C D E   36 A B C D E   61 A B C D E   86 A B C D E
12 A B C D E   37 A B C D E   62 A B C D E   87 A B C D E
13 A B C D E   38 A B C D E   63 A B C D E   88 A B C D E
14 A B C D E   39 A B C D E   64 A B C D E   89 A B C D E
15 A B C D E   40 A B C D E   65 A B C D E   90 A B C D E
16 A B C D E   41 A B C D E   66 A B C D E   91 A B C D E
17 A B C D E   42 A B C D E   67 A B C D E   92 A B C D E
18 A B C D E   43 A B C D E   68 A B C D E   93 A B C D E
19 A B C D E   44 A B C D E   69 A B C D E   94 A B C D E
20 A B C D E   45 A B C D E   70 A B C D E   95 A B C D E
21 A B C D E   46 A B C D E   71 A B C D E   96 A B C D E
22 A B C D E   47 A B C D E   72 A B C D E   97 A B C D E
23 A B C D E   48 A B C D E   73 A B C D E   98 A B C D E
24 A B C D E   49 A B C D E   74 A B C D E   99 A B C D E
25 A B C D E   50 A B C D E   75 A B C D E   100 A B C D E

Completely darken bubbles with a No. 2 pencil. If you make a mistake, be sure to erase mark completely. Erase all stray marks.

Begin with number 1 for each new section of the test. Leave blank any extra answer spaces.

SECTION 2

1 Ⓐ Ⓑ Ⓒ Ⓓ Ⓔ	26 Ⓐ Ⓑ Ⓒ Ⓓ Ⓔ	51 Ⓐ Ⓑ Ⓒ Ⓓ Ⓔ	76 Ⓐ Ⓑ Ⓒ Ⓓ Ⓔ
2 Ⓐ Ⓑ Ⓒ Ⓓ Ⓔ	27 Ⓐ Ⓑ Ⓒ Ⓓ Ⓔ	52 Ⓐ Ⓑ Ⓒ Ⓓ Ⓔ	77 Ⓐ Ⓑ Ⓒ Ⓓ Ⓔ
3 Ⓐ Ⓑ Ⓒ Ⓓ Ⓔ	28 Ⓐ Ⓑ Ⓒ Ⓓ Ⓔ	53 Ⓐ Ⓑ Ⓒ Ⓓ Ⓔ	78 Ⓐ Ⓑ Ⓒ Ⓓ Ⓔ
4 Ⓐ Ⓑ Ⓒ Ⓓ Ⓔ	29 Ⓐ Ⓑ Ⓒ Ⓓ Ⓔ	54 Ⓐ Ⓑ Ⓒ Ⓓ Ⓔ	79 Ⓐ Ⓑ Ⓒ Ⓓ Ⓔ
5 Ⓐ Ⓑ Ⓒ Ⓓ Ⓔ	30 Ⓐ Ⓑ Ⓒ Ⓓ Ⓔ	55 Ⓐ Ⓑ Ⓒ Ⓓ Ⓔ	80 Ⓐ Ⓑ Ⓒ Ⓓ Ⓔ
6 Ⓐ Ⓑ Ⓒ Ⓓ Ⓔ	31 Ⓐ Ⓑ Ⓒ Ⓓ Ⓔ	56 Ⓐ Ⓑ Ⓒ Ⓓ Ⓔ	81 Ⓐ Ⓑ Ⓒ Ⓓ Ⓔ
7 Ⓐ Ⓑ Ⓒ Ⓓ Ⓔ	32 Ⓐ Ⓑ Ⓒ Ⓓ Ⓔ	57 Ⓐ Ⓑ Ⓒ Ⓓ Ⓔ	82 Ⓐ Ⓑ Ⓒ Ⓓ Ⓔ
8 Ⓐ Ⓑ Ⓒ Ⓓ Ⓔ	33 Ⓐ Ⓑ Ⓒ Ⓓ Ⓔ	58 Ⓐ Ⓑ Ⓒ Ⓓ Ⓔ	83 Ⓐ Ⓑ Ⓒ Ⓓ Ⓔ
9 Ⓐ Ⓑ Ⓒ Ⓓ Ⓔ	34 Ⓐ Ⓑ Ⓒ Ⓓ Ⓔ	59 Ⓐ Ⓑ Ⓒ Ⓓ Ⓔ	84 Ⓐ Ⓑ Ⓒ Ⓓ Ⓔ
10 Ⓐ Ⓑ Ⓒ Ⓓ Ⓔ	35 Ⓐ Ⓑ Ⓒ Ⓓ Ⓔ	60 Ⓐ Ⓑ Ⓒ Ⓓ Ⓔ	85 Ⓐ Ⓑ Ⓒ Ⓓ Ⓔ
11 Ⓐ Ⓑ Ⓒ Ⓓ Ⓔ	36 Ⓐ Ⓑ Ⓒ Ⓓ Ⓔ	61 Ⓐ Ⓑ Ⓒ Ⓓ Ⓔ	86 Ⓐ Ⓑ Ⓒ Ⓓ Ⓔ
12 Ⓐ Ⓑ Ⓒ Ⓓ Ⓔ	37 Ⓐ Ⓑ Ⓒ Ⓓ Ⓔ	62 Ⓐ Ⓑ Ⓒ Ⓓ Ⓔ	87 Ⓐ Ⓑ Ⓒ Ⓓ Ⓔ
13 Ⓐ Ⓑ Ⓒ Ⓓ Ⓔ	38 Ⓐ Ⓑ Ⓒ Ⓓ Ⓔ	63 Ⓐ Ⓑ Ⓒ Ⓓ Ⓔ	88 Ⓐ Ⓑ Ⓒ Ⓓ Ⓔ
14 Ⓐ Ⓑ Ⓒ Ⓓ Ⓔ	39 Ⓐ Ⓑ Ⓒ Ⓓ Ⓔ	64 Ⓐ Ⓑ Ⓒ Ⓓ Ⓔ	89 Ⓐ Ⓑ Ⓒ Ⓓ Ⓔ
15 Ⓐ Ⓑ Ⓒ Ⓓ Ⓔ	40 Ⓐ Ⓑ Ⓒ Ⓓ Ⓔ	65 Ⓐ Ⓑ Ⓒ Ⓓ Ⓔ	90 Ⓐ Ⓑ Ⓒ Ⓓ Ⓔ
16 Ⓐ Ⓑ Ⓒ Ⓓ Ⓔ	41 Ⓐ Ⓑ Ⓒ Ⓓ Ⓔ	66 Ⓐ Ⓑ Ⓒ Ⓓ Ⓔ	91 Ⓐ Ⓑ Ⓒ Ⓓ Ⓔ
17 Ⓐ Ⓑ Ⓒ Ⓓ Ⓔ	42 Ⓐ Ⓑ Ⓒ Ⓓ Ⓔ	67 Ⓐ Ⓑ Ⓒ Ⓓ Ⓔ	92 Ⓐ Ⓑ Ⓒ Ⓓ Ⓔ
18 Ⓐ Ⓑ Ⓒ Ⓓ Ⓔ	43 Ⓐ Ⓑ Ⓒ Ⓓ Ⓔ	68 Ⓐ Ⓑ Ⓒ Ⓓ Ⓔ	93 Ⓐ Ⓑ Ⓒ Ⓓ Ⓔ
19 Ⓐ Ⓑ Ⓒ Ⓓ Ⓔ	44 Ⓐ Ⓑ Ⓒ Ⓓ Ⓔ	69 Ⓐ Ⓑ Ⓒ Ⓓ Ⓔ	94 Ⓐ Ⓑ Ⓒ Ⓓ Ⓔ
20 Ⓐ Ⓑ Ⓒ Ⓓ Ⓔ	45 Ⓐ Ⓑ Ⓒ Ⓓ Ⓔ	70 Ⓐ Ⓑ Ⓒ Ⓓ Ⓔ	95 Ⓐ Ⓑ Ⓒ Ⓓ Ⓔ
21 Ⓐ Ⓑ Ⓒ Ⓓ Ⓔ	46 Ⓐ Ⓑ Ⓒ Ⓓ Ⓔ	71 Ⓐ Ⓑ Ⓒ Ⓓ Ⓔ	96 Ⓐ Ⓑ Ⓒ Ⓓ Ⓔ
22 Ⓐ Ⓑ Ⓒ Ⓓ Ⓔ	47 Ⓐ Ⓑ Ⓒ Ⓓ Ⓔ	72 Ⓐ Ⓑ Ⓒ Ⓓ Ⓔ	97 Ⓐ Ⓑ Ⓒ Ⓓ Ⓔ
23 Ⓐ Ⓑ Ⓒ Ⓓ Ⓔ	48 Ⓐ Ⓑ Ⓒ Ⓓ Ⓔ	73 Ⓐ Ⓑ Ⓒ Ⓓ Ⓔ	98 Ⓐ Ⓑ Ⓒ Ⓓ Ⓔ
24 Ⓐ Ⓑ Ⓒ Ⓓ Ⓔ	49 Ⓐ Ⓑ Ⓒ Ⓓ Ⓔ	74 Ⓐ Ⓑ Ⓒ Ⓓ Ⓔ	99 Ⓐ Ⓑ Ⓒ Ⓓ Ⓔ
25 Ⓐ Ⓑ Ⓒ Ⓓ Ⓔ	50 Ⓐ Ⓑ Ⓒ Ⓓ Ⓔ	75 Ⓐ Ⓑ Ⓒ Ⓓ Ⓔ	100 Ⓐ Ⓑ Ⓒ Ⓓ Ⓔ

SECTION 3

1 Ⓐ Ⓑ Ⓒ Ⓓ Ⓔ	26 Ⓐ Ⓑ Ⓒ Ⓓ Ⓔ	51 Ⓐ Ⓑ Ⓒ Ⓓ Ⓔ	76 Ⓐ Ⓑ Ⓒ Ⓓ Ⓔ
2 Ⓐ Ⓑ Ⓒ Ⓓ Ⓔ	27 Ⓐ Ⓑ Ⓒ Ⓓ Ⓔ	52 Ⓐ Ⓑ Ⓒ Ⓓ Ⓔ	77 Ⓐ Ⓑ Ⓒ Ⓓ Ⓔ
3 Ⓐ Ⓑ Ⓒ Ⓓ Ⓔ	28 Ⓐ Ⓑ Ⓒ Ⓓ Ⓔ	53 Ⓐ Ⓑ Ⓒ Ⓓ Ⓔ	78 Ⓐ Ⓑ Ⓒ Ⓓ Ⓔ
4 Ⓐ Ⓑ Ⓒ Ⓓ Ⓔ	29 Ⓐ Ⓑ Ⓒ Ⓓ Ⓔ	54 Ⓐ Ⓑ Ⓒ Ⓓ Ⓔ	79 Ⓐ Ⓑ Ⓒ Ⓓ Ⓔ
5 Ⓐ Ⓑ Ⓒ Ⓓ Ⓔ	30 Ⓐ Ⓑ Ⓒ Ⓓ Ⓔ	55 Ⓐ Ⓑ Ⓒ Ⓓ Ⓔ	80 Ⓐ Ⓑ Ⓒ Ⓓ Ⓔ
6 Ⓐ Ⓑ Ⓒ Ⓓ Ⓔ	31 Ⓐ Ⓑ Ⓒ Ⓓ Ⓔ	56 Ⓐ Ⓑ Ⓒ Ⓓ Ⓔ	81 Ⓐ Ⓑ Ⓒ Ⓓ Ⓔ
7 Ⓐ Ⓑ Ⓒ Ⓓ Ⓔ	32 Ⓐ Ⓑ Ⓒ Ⓓ Ⓔ	57 Ⓐ Ⓑ Ⓒ Ⓓ Ⓔ	82 Ⓐ Ⓑ Ⓒ Ⓓ Ⓔ
8 Ⓐ Ⓑ Ⓒ Ⓓ Ⓔ	33 Ⓐ Ⓑ Ⓒ Ⓓ Ⓔ	58 Ⓐ Ⓑ Ⓒ Ⓓ Ⓔ	83 Ⓐ Ⓑ Ⓒ Ⓓ Ⓔ
9 Ⓐ Ⓑ Ⓒ Ⓓ Ⓔ	34 Ⓐ Ⓑ Ⓒ Ⓓ Ⓔ	59 Ⓐ Ⓑ Ⓒ Ⓓ Ⓔ	84 Ⓐ Ⓑ Ⓒ Ⓓ Ⓔ
10 Ⓐ Ⓑ Ⓒ Ⓓ Ⓔ	35 Ⓐ Ⓑ Ⓒ Ⓓ Ⓔ	60 Ⓐ Ⓑ Ⓒ Ⓓ Ⓔ	85 Ⓐ Ⓑ Ⓒ Ⓓ Ⓔ
11 Ⓐ Ⓑ Ⓒ Ⓓ Ⓔ	36 Ⓐ Ⓑ Ⓒ Ⓓ Ⓔ	61 Ⓐ Ⓑ Ⓒ Ⓓ Ⓔ	86 Ⓐ Ⓑ Ⓒ Ⓓ Ⓔ
12 Ⓐ Ⓑ Ⓒ Ⓓ Ⓔ	37 Ⓐ Ⓑ Ⓒ Ⓓ Ⓔ	62 Ⓐ Ⓑ Ⓒ Ⓓ Ⓔ	87 Ⓐ Ⓑ Ⓒ Ⓓ Ⓔ
13 Ⓐ Ⓑ Ⓒ Ⓓ Ⓔ	38 Ⓐ Ⓑ Ⓒ Ⓓ Ⓔ	63 Ⓐ Ⓑ Ⓒ Ⓓ Ⓔ	88 Ⓐ Ⓑ Ⓒ Ⓓ Ⓔ
14 Ⓐ Ⓑ Ⓒ Ⓓ Ⓔ	39 Ⓐ Ⓑ Ⓒ Ⓓ Ⓔ	64 Ⓐ Ⓑ Ⓒ Ⓓ Ⓔ	89 Ⓐ Ⓑ Ⓒ Ⓓ Ⓔ
15 Ⓐ Ⓑ Ⓒ Ⓓ Ⓔ	40 Ⓐ Ⓑ Ⓒ Ⓓ Ⓔ	65 Ⓐ Ⓑ Ⓒ Ⓓ Ⓔ	90 Ⓐ Ⓑ Ⓒ Ⓓ Ⓔ
16 Ⓐ Ⓑ Ⓒ Ⓓ Ⓔ	41 Ⓐ Ⓑ Ⓒ Ⓓ Ⓔ	66 Ⓐ Ⓑ Ⓒ Ⓓ Ⓔ	91 Ⓐ Ⓑ Ⓒ Ⓓ Ⓔ
17 Ⓐ Ⓑ Ⓒ Ⓓ Ⓔ	42 Ⓐ Ⓑ Ⓒ Ⓓ Ⓔ	67 Ⓐ Ⓑ Ⓒ Ⓓ Ⓔ	92 Ⓐ Ⓑ Ⓒ Ⓓ Ⓔ
18 Ⓐ Ⓑ Ⓒ Ⓓ Ⓔ	43 Ⓐ Ⓑ Ⓒ Ⓓ Ⓔ	68 Ⓐ Ⓑ Ⓒ Ⓓ Ⓔ	93 Ⓐ Ⓑ Ⓒ Ⓓ Ⓔ
19 Ⓐ Ⓑ Ⓒ Ⓓ Ⓔ	44 Ⓐ Ⓑ Ⓒ Ⓓ Ⓔ	69 Ⓐ Ⓑ Ⓒ Ⓓ Ⓔ	94 Ⓐ Ⓑ Ⓒ Ⓓ Ⓔ
20 Ⓐ Ⓑ Ⓒ Ⓓ Ⓔ	45 Ⓐ Ⓑ Ⓒ Ⓓ Ⓔ	70 Ⓐ Ⓑ Ⓒ Ⓓ Ⓔ	95 Ⓐ Ⓑ Ⓒ Ⓓ Ⓔ
21 Ⓐ Ⓑ Ⓒ Ⓓ Ⓔ	46 Ⓐ Ⓑ Ⓒ Ⓓ Ⓔ	71 Ⓐ Ⓑ Ⓒ Ⓓ Ⓔ	96 Ⓐ Ⓑ Ⓒ Ⓓ Ⓔ
22 Ⓐ Ⓑ Ⓒ Ⓓ Ⓔ	47 Ⓐ Ⓑ Ⓒ Ⓓ Ⓔ	72 Ⓐ Ⓑ Ⓒ Ⓓ Ⓔ	97 Ⓐ Ⓑ Ⓒ Ⓓ Ⓔ
23 Ⓐ Ⓑ Ⓒ Ⓓ Ⓔ	48 Ⓐ Ⓑ Ⓒ Ⓓ Ⓔ	73 Ⓐ Ⓑ Ⓒ Ⓓ Ⓔ	98 Ⓐ Ⓑ Ⓒ Ⓓ Ⓔ
24 Ⓐ Ⓑ Ⓒ Ⓓ Ⓔ	49 Ⓐ Ⓑ Ⓒ Ⓓ Ⓔ	74 Ⓐ Ⓑ Ⓒ Ⓓ Ⓔ	99 Ⓐ Ⓑ Ⓒ Ⓓ Ⓔ
25 Ⓐ Ⓑ Ⓒ Ⓓ Ⓔ	50 Ⓐ Ⓑ Ⓒ Ⓓ Ⓔ	75 Ⓐ Ⓑ Ⓒ Ⓓ Ⓔ	100 Ⓐ Ⓑ Ⓒ Ⓓ Ⓔ

FOR TPR USE ONLY	V1	V2	V3	V4	M1	M2	M3	M4	M5	M6	M7	M8

DIAGNOSTIC TEST ANSWERS

PART THREE

MCAT
DIAGNOSTIC TEST I
ANSWERS AND EXPLANATIONS

DIAGNOSTIC TEST I ANSWERS

Section 1 Verbal Reasoning		Section 2 Physical Sciences		Section 3 Biological Sciences	
1. D	34. D	66. D	105. C	143. B	182. A
2. C	35. C	67. D	106. C	144. A	183. C
3. D	36. D	68. A	107. A	145. D	184. D
4. C	37. A	69. C	108. D	146. C	185. C
5. B	38. C	70. B	109. D	147. C	186. A
6. A	39. A	71. D	110. C	148. A	187. B
7. A	40. B	72. D	111. A	149. C	188. B
8. B	41. A	73. B	112. B	150. A	189. C
9. B	42. C	74. B	113. C	151. B	190. D
10. D	43. A	75. C	114. A	152. A	191. C
11. B	44. B	76. C	115. B	153. D	192. A
12. C	45. C	77. C	116. B	154. D	193. C
13. C	46. C	78. A	117. D	155. B	194. B
14. B	47. D	79. A	118. B	156. C	195. D
15. A	48. D	80. B	119. D	157. B	196. D
16. D	49. C	81. B	120. B	158. C	197. A
17. D	50. A	82. D	121. D	159. A	198. C
18. A	51. D	83. C	122. D	160. A	199. A
19. A	52. A	84. C	123. B	161. C	200. B
20. C	53. D	85. C	124. A	162. C	201. B
21. D	54. A	86. B	125. D	163. D	202. C
22. B	55. B	87. A	126. A	164. B	203. C
23. A	56. C	88. A	127. D	165. D	204. A
24. D	57. C	89. C	128. B	166. C	205. D
25. B	58. B	90. D	129. C	167. C	206. B
26. C	59. B	91. D	130. C	168. D	207. C
27. C	60. D	92. B	131. D	169. B	208. C
28. C	61. A	93. D	132. B	170. A	209. A
29. B	62. D	94. A	133. C	171. B	210. B
30. A	63. A	95. B	134. D	172. B	211. B
31. D	64. A	96. D	135. D	173. D	212. D
32. A	65. A	97. B	136. A	174. C	213. C
33. D		98. A	137. B	175. A	214. D
		99. D	138. C	176. B	215. B
		100. B	139. B	177. A	216. C
		101. A	140. C	178. D	217. B
		102. B	141. D	179. B	218. C
		103. C	142. A	180. C	219. B
		104. B		181. A	

VERBAL REASONING EXPLANATIONS I

1. According to one conservation expert, "we share the universe with extra-terrestrials, we share the planet with terrestrial species; and while outer space challenges our intellects, the Earth is our home." This expert would probably:

   A. support greater use of science in evaluating ecological conflicts.
   B. approve an end to the allocation of scientific resources both to solve ecological problems and to search for extra-terrestrial intelligence.
   C. not consider either ecological analyses or space exploration particularly important.
   D. consider both ecology and space exploration important, but ecology more so.

D is correct. This question requires you to extrapolate from your reading and general knowledge the ideas that: 1) conservationists believe ecology to be important; and 2) scientific analysis of ecological problems is socially useful and desirable. The question itself adds that this particular expert finds extra-terrestrial issues both challenging and relevant to human life.

The wrong answer choices: Choice A is a tempting alternative because it offers a statement which is most likely accurate—this expert would support greater scientific involvement in ecological problems. Based on the information given in the question, though, choice D is a more direct answer. Although it is conceivable that some conservationists are opposed to governmental support of scientific inquiry, the passage leads you to the opposite conclusion. Choice B and C directly contradict the implications in both the passage and the question about the expert's sense of priorities.

2. The author of the passage would probably support most strongly a federal law that:

A. allocates funds for ecological research equal to Commerce Department spending promoting the timber industry.

B. provides increased tax incentives for the commercial harvesting of forests.

C. establishes government scholarships for graduate study in environmental science.

D. assigns to the Army Corps of Engineers the task of researching and resolving ecological controversies.

C is correct. Most of the passage concerns the importance of scientific research in evaluating ecological disputes. Therefore, a law providing for increased training and research activity in this area would likely win support from the author.

The wrong answer choices: The author might well favor measures presented in choices A and D, because the general tone of the passage supports governmental action to protect the environment. Neither one, however, is so directly related to the passage as is choice C. Nothing in the passage indicates that the author would support the law described in choice B.

3. The author's mention of a President's visit to Portland in April, 1993 suggests that such executive attention:

I. reflects a determination to resolve ecological conflicts through mediation and negotiation.

II. is warranted due to significant public concern about the ecology.

III. represents the federal government's willingness to explore alternative-management techniques for forests.

A. I only
B. II only
C. II and III only
D. I, II, and III

D is correct. The next-to-last sentence of paragraph 2 states that the President "appointed...scientists to evaluate...alternative management scenarios" which corresponds to statement III. The following sentence of the text says the President visited the site of the "controversy for the purpose of facilitating its end," which supports statement I. Sentence 1 of paragraph 3 asserts that "public concern:...is enormously important," a sentiment echoed by statement II.

4. Which of the following claims is/are explicitly presented in the passage to justify the belief that ecological conflicts could be more efficiently managed through greater reliance on
science?

   I. In the case of the spotted owl
   conflict, legal and political
   impasses developed in the
   absence of scientific evidence.
   II. As a rule, scientists are less
   motivated by political interests
   than by intellectual curiosity.
   III. The President appointed a task
   force of scientists, rather than
   industry representatives or
   ecology activists, to evaluate
   proposed alternatives in forest
   management strategies.

   A. I only
   B. I and II only
   C. I and III only
   D. I, II, and III

C is correct. Sentence 4 of paragraph 2 notes that scientists were not called into the spotted-owl controversy until "after the development of a political impasse." The next-to-last sentence of this paragraph clearly identifies the presidential task force as composed by scientists, not others. Thus, statements I and III are supported by the passage.

5. Which of the following findings would best support the author's belief that a recurrence of the social turmoil experienced in the Northwest is possible elsewhere in the nation?

   A. Most Americans are currently skeptical of the agenda of Big Industry and Big Business.
   B. Public anxiety regarding the sustenance of the ecosphere beyond the Pacific Northwest is growing.
   C. Americans are tantalized by controversy and enjoy a good political battle.
   D. Interest in environmental issues declined in the Northeast region after the decommissioning of the Shoreham nuclear facility on Long Island, New York.

B is correct. Sentence 1 of the last paragraph asserts that conservationist concern is not limited "to the Pacific Northwest nor to spotted owls." The next sentence states that ecological legal actions are "common throughout the country." In the last sentence we learn that people "outside the Pacific Northwest" are becoming interested in protecting "biological diversity."

The wrong answer choices: Although choices A and C are plausible, neither offers the "best" answer. Choice D is contrary to the author's belief.

6. According to the passage, which of the following is most likely to be true about the relationship between public pressure and governmental action in ecology policy?

   A. The more intense the public pressure, the greater the governmental intervention.
   B. The more intense the public pressure, the less the governmental intervention.
   C. The less intense the public pressure, the greater the governmental intervention.
   D. There is no apparent connection between the level of public pressure and the amount of governmental intervention.

A is correct. Paragraph 3 refers to the effect of public pressure on governmental intervention in environmental problems. The last sentence of that paragraph states that "sociopolitical turmoil was likely avoidable" had the government implemented scientific analysis earlier that it did, implying that only the public turmoil elicited political intervention.

The wrong answer choices: Choices B, C, and D contradict information in the passage.

Passage II (Questions 7-12)

7. Which of the following statements best sum-
    marizes the main idea of the passage?

    A. Humans historically have viewed Mars
        subjectively, according to their own indi-
        vidual beliefs.
    B. Humans historically have viewed Mars
        subjectively, according to the opinions of
        leading philosophers of the time.
    C. Humans historically have viewed Mars
        objectively, based on folklore handed down
        from generation to generation.
    D. Humans historically have viewed Mars ob-
        jectively, based solely on available scientific
        data.

A is correct. In paragraph 2, the author asserts, "Humans...interpret random images
in ways that tell you more about the person...than about the images." At the end of
paragraph 6, the author again brings up this notion: "Lowell has apparently seen what
he wanted to see. It is true that the human mind, confronted with a...series of poorly
seen dots, will often connect them into a line. That may be what happened to Lowell.
No one else saw canals."

The wrong answer choices: Choices C and D contradict the author's principal
message: objectivity and science had little or nothing to do with hypotheses about life
on Mars. Choice B is wrong because imaginings were based on that which people
wished to believe, not on authoritative commentary.

8. As described in the passage, representations
    of Mars in popular art support the author's
    point that:

    A. media presentations can prove disruptive
        of social peace and order.
    B. the unknown serves as a mirror to reflect
        the human imagination.
    C. the unknown is at times best illuminated
        by mythology rather than by science.
    D. canals probably do exist on Mars.

B is correct. According to sentences 6 and 7 of paragraph six , starting in the late
'30's "a long series of stories, movies and TV shows based on invasions from Mars"
became popular. And, "Despite all the fun, there really was no evidence for life on
Mars." Contrast this information with the preceding paragraph's descriptions of
Martian tales and you'll see that B is clearly correct.

The wrong answer choices: A offers a statement which might tempt you, referring to paragraph 6: "'The War of the Worlds' touched off real panic. Police switchboards lit up, and people jammed the highways to escape the Martians." But this kind of disruption occurred only after Welles' play and is not characteristic of all the popular myths described. The author nowhere makes the point presented in choice C. At the end of paragraph 6 the author debunks the idea of Martian canals, contradicting choice D.

9. As used in the passage, the word folklore (line 35) most nearly means:

   A. history.
   B. fallacy.
   C. fact.
   D. narrative.

B is correct. The passage discusses the mythology (not fact, but imaginary ideas) that arose about Mars over the centuries. In the context of the passage, and among the choices offered, the word that most closely approximates "folklore" is "fallacy," something that is not objectively or logically true.

10. Which of the following statements, if true, would most WEAKEN the author's contention that Mars is less known than created by us?

    A. Dust storms do not, in fact, occur on Mars.
    B. Percival Lowell never saw canals through his telescope but read a tale of such structures in an ancient folklore anthology.
    C. Most people believe that intelligent beings populate Mars.
    D. Information recently generated by satellite has produced information that corresponds closely to Lewis' depictions of the planet.

D is correct. If Lewis had somehow ascertained the true nature of Mars, and his descriptions were confirmed by satellite data, then the author's belief that we create Mars in our own image, rather than know it objectively, would be less compelling than appears from the passage.

The wrong answer choices: A is wrong, because if the scientific findings regarding dust storms—mentioned in the next-to-last paragraph—turned out to be false, it would provide another example of how the human imagination had seen something that wasn't really there, thus strengthening the author's contention. Choice C would indicate that Lowell's theories were founded on a wholly imaginative text, again strengthening, not weakening, the author's belief. Choice C would suggest that most people's imaginations run in a similar direction, and would not weaken the author's contention.

11. In organizing a group of astronauts to visit Mars, the author would most likely advise them to approach the planet with:

   A. assurance, because it is unlikely that any biological threat to humankind exists there.

   B. caution, because despite centuries of speculation about Mars from both artistic and scientific orientations, relatively little is known for certain about the planet.

   C. aggression, because it is probable that dangerous microorganisms or hostile creatures populate Mars.

   D. reverence, because Mars has reflected so numerous and such varied perspectives of the earthly imagination.

B is correct. One of the author's main points is that Mars remains relatively unknown, despite all the imaginative speculations about it.

The wrong answer choices: Choices A and C are incorrect because each in its own way assumes that the nature of Mars is well understood by humans. Choice D might tempt you because it reflects some of the passage's meaning, but it is not so direct or good an answer as B.

12. A 1933 treatise on the solar system describes Mars as "potentially the greatest threat to Earth's civilization" and that any life on Mars would "surely possess the will and the incentive to overcome the military forces of the nations of the Earth." If the author were to include this analysis in the passage, he would probably use it to:

   A. justify the long association of Mars with warfare and military science.

   B. illustrate the point that humans often see aliens as beings like themselves.

   C. emphasize that what we think we know about Mars often is the product of our imagination.

   D. explain the author's own opinion about Mars.

C is correct. The question calls for simple common sense. The treatise to which the question refers was published between the two World Wars, a time at which some analysts believed that disarmament represented an imprudent course in a dangerous world and a vast universe. According to the passage, the treatise seems to be more imaginative than factual.

The wrong answer choices: Choice A seeks to confuse the Romans' depiction of Mars with a twentieth century analysis. Choice B sounds good, but its point is not so closely reflected in the passage as is that of choice C. Choice D is a non-sequitur; nowhere does the author offer any such opinion about Mars.

Passage III (Questions 13-18)

13. The main idea of the passage is that:

   A. artists serve as mediators between our daily reality and the world of the unconscious.
   B. as human society has evolved and become more sophisticated, so has human artistic expression.
   C. artistic expression reflects the psychological processes and make-up of its creator.
   D. the essential appeal of art is its power to mystify.

   C is correct. In sentences 4 and 6 of paragraph 2, the author lists "the skills that go into adult art: coordination, intellect, personality, imagination, creativity, and aesthetic judgment." According to the passage, the making of an artist is "a process as fragile as growing up itself." Sentence 3 of paragraph 3 states that art is "a positive expression that integrates diverse aspects of personality." Furthermore, in sentence 5 of the following paragraph, the author observes that "the imagination...acts in lawful, if unpredictable, ways that are determined by the psyche and the mind."

   The wrong answer choices: Although sentence 3 of paragraph 4 says that the imagination is "the connector between the conscious and the subconscious"; and sentence 3 of paragraph 6 adds that artists were believed "able to enter the underworld of the subconscious...but, unlike ordinary mortals, they were then able to return to the realm of the living," this motif represents a subordinate theme and not the main idea of the passage; choice A is wrong. Paragraphs 1, 2, and 5 contain information which may lead you to choose B as the answer, but this idea is more implied than directly addressed in the passage. The next-to-last paragraph claims that "the artist remains a magician whose work can mystify and move us," but this notion, expressed in choice D, is not the text's main idea.

14. In the context of the passage, the word genius refers primarily to:

   A. the recognition and appreciation of an artist's ability by critics and the public at large.
   B. the psychic sensitivity an artist develops to reality.
   C. the intellectual attainments of individual artists.
   D. the neurotic and psychotic manifestations of artistic perception.

B is correct. In sentence 3 of paragraph 2, the passage states that the artist's imagination "is subject to the taste and outlook of the society that shapes his or her personality," that forms, that is, his or her sensibility. The word "genius" appears in the opening sentence of paragraph 4, in which the author asserts that a psychotic sensibility can not make truly great art. Later in the same paragraph, imagination appears as "the very glue that holds our personality, intellect, and spirituality together," another way of saying "psychic sensibility." Sentences 3 and 4 of the last paragraph add that "Art has the power to penetrate to the core of our being," and "represents its creator's deepest understanding and highest aspirations...our shared beliefs and values," the outside reality an artist creates from, about, and to.

The wrong answer choices: Although the final three sentences of the passage discuss the artist's relation to an audience, and by implication, to critics, and implies that an artistic genius will be well received by both, choice A is not the best answer in relation to this passage. The word genius may refer, generally, to one's intellectual capability and/or achievements, but in this passage it is not used in that sense. Choice C is incorrect. Paragraph 4 directly contradicts choice D as explained above.

> 15. The passage implies that art relates to its audience:
>
>   A. by delivering both a personal and a universal communication from artist to audience.
>   B. less intensely today because, no longer associated with magic, its power to mystify and to move has dwindled.
>   C. by providing insight into another's creativity only, while science and religion allow us to comprehend ourselves and the universe.
>   D. irrespective of an audience's emotional and spiritual needs.

A is correct. The last sentence of paragraph 4 notes that "even the most private artistic statements can be understood on some level, even if only an intuitive one," implying a relationship between the intensely personal and the universal. Later, sentence 4 of the last paragraph emphasizes that "art represents its creator's deepest understanding and highest aspirations; at the same time, the artist often plays an important role as the articulator of our shared beliefs and values, which he expresses through an ongoing tradition to us, his audience."

The wrong answer choices: Choice B is clearly contradicted by the next-to-last paragraph: "Even today the artist remains a magician whose work can mystify and move us." Choice C claims that we can find no universal truth in art. Choice D is ruled out by the passage's next-to-last sentence: "A masterpiece, then, is a work that contributes to our vision of life and leaves us profoundly moved."

16. The passage suggests that the ability to create art:

    A. evolved before the imagination evolved.
    B. evolved primarily as a survival skill.
    C. has been documented to exist as early as two million years ago, when humans first inhabited the Earth.
    D. was the result of a long developmental process that began when stable societies formed.

D is correct. Sentences 5 and 6 point the way of paragraph 5: "[Prehistoric art]...was the culmination of a long development"; and "Even the most 'primitive' ethnographic art represents a late stage of development within a stable society."

The wrong answer choices: Paragraph 5 states that "The imagination is important...in a way that has real survival value....The ability to make art, in contrast, must have been acquired relatively recently in the course of evolution." Choices A and B contradict that text. Sentence 5 of paragraph 5 establishes that the oldest prehistoric art is dated only 35,000 years ago, which excludes choice C.

17. According to the passage, why is art embarrassing to some people who pride themselves on their civilized rationality?

    A. Art's essential mystery frustrates those who like to appear cultivated.
    B. Art makes many social sophisticates feel ignorant.
    C. Art's simultaneous universality and individual relevance seems paradoxical to some who pride themselves on their logical powers.
    D. Art is able to access the most fundamental and private essence of the self.

D is correct. The next-to-last paragraph refers to "civilized people, who do not readily relinquish their veneer of rational control," and three sentences later observes that "Art has the power to penetrate to the core of our being." Taken together, these two assertions make D the best choice.

The wrong answer choices: Choices A, B and C may all reflect some element of truth, but they are truths not touched on in the passage.

18. The discussion of Sigmund Freud's view of art and artists shows primarily that:

   A. art represents an integrative psychological function rather than an uncontrolled psychic expression.
   B. art which sublimates psychological ambiguity is superior to that which generates mystery.
   C. successful psychotherapy would enable an artist to sublimate the need for artistic expression.
   D. development of individual artistic consciousness retraces much of humans' evolutionary past.

A is correct. Sentence 3 of paragraph 3 states that "art is not simply a negative force at the mercy of our neuroses but a positive expression that integrates diverse aspects of personality." This assertion immediately follows the allusion to Freud, and serves, generally, to negate Freud's hypothesis as presented.

The wrong answer choices: Choice B does not follow logically from the passage; nowhere is it supported by the text. Choice C seeks to confuse you with a hodgepodge of tempting terminology. Paragraph 2 actually does reflect the assertion offered in option D but is completely unrelated to the discussion of Freud.

Passage IV (Questions 19–25)

19. According to the passage, each of the following factors favors the preservation of fossils EXCEPT for:

   A. high quantity of sediment deposition.
   B. natural pools of swamp tar.
   C. chemical balance between organic material and surrounding strata.
   D. high velocity of sediment deposition.

A is correct. REMEMBER: The question requires you to identify which factor is NOT cited in the passage as fostering fossilization. Sentence 2 of paragraph 1 contains the key statement: "Even though...sediment is deposited in quantity, the remains of creatures and plants which lived on land are comparatively rare."

The wrong answer choices: Sentences 2 and 3 of paragraph 2 note that "natural pools of tar occur on the land surface....mammals stumbled into the sticky swamp and became perfectly preserved." Thus, option B is a cited factor, and an incorrect choice here. Sentence 5 of paragraph 1 states that "a chemical balance has to be maintained between the organic material and the strata in which it becomes trapped." Sentence 3 of paragraph 1 observes: "In the sea...rapid deposition of sediment...entombs a multitude of organisms, many of which become preserved." Thus, C and D are both cited factors in the passage as well, and so are excluded under this question.

20. According to the information given in the passage, the Burgess shales in British Columbia contain:

    A. creatures native to the Canadian Rockies.
    B. fossils preserved in the Cambrian sea bed.
    C. fossils preserved at the base of an underwater cliff.
    D. minute, soft-bodied creatures called *Foraminfera.*

C is correct. Sentence 9 of paragraph 1 asserts that "The Burgess shales . . . were carried by a series of mud slides to be preserved at the base of a submarine cliff."

The wrong answer choices: The same sentence makes it clear that these were "creatures which lived on the Cambrian sea bed," thus ruling out choice A. Choice B is negated by the same sentence as explained above. The *Foraminfera* are mentioned in the sentence immediately preceding the one under discussion, but without reference or relevance to the Burgess shales.

21. The author mentions the Siberian permafrost in order to provide an example of:

    A. the preservation of hard-shell organisms.
    B. a preservative shell permeable to bacteria and air.
    C. incomplete fossil preservation.
    D. complete fossil preservation.

D is correct. Sentences 3 and 4 of paragraph 2 inform you that "mammals...became perfectly preserved, locked away from air and bacteria. Similar processes preserve Arctic mammals trapped in permafrost in Siberia."

The wrong answer choices: Sentence 1 of paragraph 3 refers to "The chemical composition of the hard parts of many organisms" as offering preservative benefits, but without relation to the permafrost. So choice A is wrong. Choice B is a bit tricky, because while the permafrost offers complete preservation, it is not "a preservative shell" in the sense of the word as used in paragraph 3, nor is it permeable. Choice C is clearly wrong as explained above.

22. According to the passage, silica present in the structure of Radiolaria and sponges serves:

   A. to provide a chitin-like preservative exoskeleton.
   B. to maintain equilibrium with material in the Earth's crust.
   C. as a pseudo-vertebral morphological structure.
   D. as an absolute barrier against changes in the fossil.

B is correct. The question requires you to extrapolate the correct answer from information in Sentences 1 and 2 of paragraph 3. In the context of describing how components of hard-shelled creatures can allow fossils to equilibrate chemically with elements in the Earth's crust, the author indicates that "silica...present in the structure of Radiolaria and sponges" serves that purpose.

The wrong answer choices: A is wrong because while silica may serve a similar function as does chitin, it does not provide an exoskeleton. Choice C seeks to confuse you by comparing silica to the vertebral structures containing calcium carbonate. The last sentence of paragraph 3 points out the error in choice D: Despite the hard shell elements, "changes often take place in the organism."

23. According to the passage, the carbonization of fossils derives from:

   A. evaporation of unstable chemicals from organic remains.
   B. deposition of a carbon shell on organic remains.
   C. deposition of calcite, silica and iron minerals in organic remains.
   D. removal of calcite shells, leaving a curved, C-shaped hollow in the sediment.

A is correct. The question requires you to know that volatility correlates with ready evaporability. The last three sentences of paragraph 4 establish that carbonization occurs when organic matter is buried in sediment, and as "the more volatile chemicals are released...the [remaining] carbon percentage thus increases."

The wrong answer choices: Choice B is wrong because carbon is already present in organic matter during evaporative carbonization, not deposited thereon. Choices C and D describe processes associated with fossilization, not carbonization.

24. According to the passage, the fluid that percolates through fossil-bearing strata:

    A. removes all traces of fossils in its path.
    B. has no effect on fossils in its path.
    C. often leaves the calcite shells of a fossil in
       its path undisturbed.
    D. can erase the fine details of a fossil in its
       path.

D is correct. Paragraph 4 provides the answer. According to sentences 2 and 3,
fluid passing through fossil-bearing strata can change the developing fossils, and
"partial or complete changes may be effected. Though the fossils thus formed may
retain their outward shape, the fine detail of the original may be lost."

The wrong answer choices: Choices A and B contradict the text just cited. Choice C is
excluded because sentence 6 of paragraph 4 states that the fluid often removes calcite
shells in its path.

25. The synthesis of geology, chemistry, biology,
physics, marine science, and other disciplines
necessary to develop an understanding of fossils as described would be most similar to the
study of:

    A. Greek mythology, Elizabethan drama, and
       "found" poetry to develop an approach to
       modern literary sensibility.
    B. mathematics, logic, and computer science
       to develop a theory of artificial intelligence.
    C. resistance, magnetism, and electron-flow
       to develop an understanding of electricity.
    D. the mechanisms of different antibiotics to
       develop a theory of infectious disease.

B is correct. The parallel presented in choice B is most like the interdisciplinary
curriculum cited in the question because it includes a variety of academic fields.

The wrong answer choices: Choice A offers only different areas within the single field
of literature. Similarly, choice C presents interrelated areas of electrical physics only.
Choice D also confines itself to a single discipline.

Passage V (Questions 26–33)

26. The central thesis of the passage is that:

   A. art has a long-standing relationship with propaganda and the language of imperial oppression.
   B. art is closely related to propaganda.
   C. current literary theory has long-standing historical precedents.
   D. high theory has an inherent truth that need not be put to debate.

C is correct. Paragraphs 3 and 4 make it clear that literary theory is not a new phenomenon. According to the last sentence of paragraph 3, for example, "[Theory is] an installment in a struggle that's as old as Western culture itself—the struggle...that Plato, in the fourth century B.C., said was already ancient."

The wrong answer choices: Sentence 2 of paragraph 2 might tempt you to choose A, but careful reading makes clear that these are theorists' viewpoints not the author's own. Sentences 2 and 3 of paragraph 5 exclude choice B as the central thesis with this text: "Responsive to both art and intellection, critics from Aristotle to Virginia Woolf effectively defended poetry, not only from popular indifference but from dismissive philosophy. With the onset of theory, the critical contingency is fast disappearing." Although sentence 6 of paragraph 2 asserts that "today's professorial commentators on literature—or film or rock or hip-hop—assume the truth of high theory without feeling a need to argue for it," that assumption may not be taken as the central thesis of the text. Indeed, Choice D directly contradicts the author's view.

27. Implicit in the statement that new theory views literary artists as cultural conmen and flunkies is the notion that:

   A. great novels and poetry do not truly reflect the milieu from which they emerge.
   B. poets and dramatists reject point-of-view narration in favor of objective truths.
   C. literature caters to the cultural biases of the ruling class.
   D. the ruling class does not, by and large, embrace the moral values and social norms that its literature advocates.

C is correct. Sentence 4 of paragraph 2 claims that in the view of new theory, artists become "shrewd deceivers; tour guides to dreamy, detached lotus worlds, apologists for race and gender oppression, bagmen for the bourgeoisie."

The wrong answer choices: A is incorrect because, according to the new theory, if writers truly reflected the milieu in which they lived theorists would not label them conmen. Similarly, theorists who found objective truths in art would not likely call the artist a flunky, and so choice B is wrong. Theorists might or might not agree with option D, but this phenomenon would be a by-product of the one expressed in option C, which is a better choice.

28. Given the claims made in the passage, statements such as, "Their poetry is a tissue of pretty lies," "Literature deceives the unwary reader," "The writer's product is pure illusion," represent:

    A. establishment propaganda distributed by apologists for oppressors.
    B. perceptions of literary art unexpressed prior to the late 20th century.
    C. ancient views of literature.
    D. criticism typical of Virginia Woolf.

C is correct. The opening sentence of paragraph 4 tells you that "To Plato, the poets were a band of deceivers....[who]...offered illusions, mere imitations of imitations, whereas life's highest purpose is to seek eternal truths."

The wrong answer choices: A is incorrect, because according to the claims in the passage, establishment propaganda would defend, not attack, poetry and literature. Choice B is wrong, as is evident from the sentence cited above. Choice D is not supported by the passage. In fact, the last paragraph establishes that "...Virginia Woolf effectively defended poetry, not only from popular indifference, but from disimissive philosophy."

29. According to the passage, a critic who endorses the new theory would most likely believe that:

    A. writers should be loyal to their most influential aesthetic experience.
    B. Homeric poetry is like advertising.
    C. Homeric poetry offers both dramatic action and eternal truth.
    D. contemporary poetry needs defense from disinterested and derisive readers.

B is correct. According to the author's account of Platonic criticism (paragraph 4, sentence 6), "You may encounter numerous instances of just action in Homer, but by simply reading Homer you'll never find out what all those instances have in common: you'll never make the step from anecdotal to general knowledge, never become a philosopher." As presented by the passage, in their ongoing debate with poets, philosophers criticized Homeric action epics in much the same way as today's theorists dismiss action adventure movies and popular novels: as "propaganda, pornography, and the language of imperial oppression."

The wrong answer choices: The final sentence of the passage presents "art's public defenders, writers whose first allegiance is to the aesthetic experiences that have shaped them" as those who do not subscribe to new theory, so choice A is ruled out. The explanation given above negates choice C. The final paragraph implies that new theorists are disinterested and dismissive, not defenders against such attitudes. Choice D, then, will not do.

30. The ideas discussed in this passage would likely be of most use to:

    A. a cultural historian.
    B. a scholar of Greek epic poetry.
    C. a graduate student in philosophy.
    D. a writer of contemporary drama.

A is correct. This question is not simple, because the ideas in the passage would probably be of interest to all of those referred to in the answer options. However, because the passage primarily concerns itself with an historical analysis of culture, the ideas would likely be of *most* use to a cultural historian.

The wrong answer choices: Choices B, C and D are all tempting for obvious reasons, but A is the best bet.

31. An appropriate description of the historical relationship between literary artists and their critics derived from the passage would state that:

    I.   artists and critics do not always agree on the purpose, function and meaning of art.
    II. artists and critics may have opposing viewpoints.
    III. artists and critics may play mutually supportive roles.

    A. I only
    B. II only
    C. I and II only
    D. I, II, and III

D is correct. At first glance, statements II and III may appear mutually contradictory. However, sentence 2 of the final paragraph points out that "Responsive to both art and intellection, critics from Aristotle to Virginia Woolf effectively defended poetry, not only from popular indifference but from dismissive philosophy," supporting statement III. And sentence 3 of paragraph 3 asserts that the conflict between artists and critics is "a struggle that's as old as Western culture itself," endorsing statement II. Statement I represents the mediation between II and III.

32. Faced with the field of theory today, Plato would most likely respond by:

    A. embracing it, because it views poets as clever deceivers.
    B. embracing it, because it seeks to foster debate concerning the truth of high theory.
    C. rejecting it, because it is skeptical of art and artists.
    D. rejecting it, because it takes poets for apologists and dreamers.

A is correct. Paragraph 4 establishes that Plato thought poets were "a band of deceivers." Paragraph 2 reveals that theorists considered poets to be "shrewd deceivers."

The wrong answer choices: In paragraph 2 the author asserts that new theorists "assume the truth of high theory without feeling a need to argue for it." That eliminates choice B. Choices C and D are more or less equivalent and both contradict the passage.

33. Based on the passage, a member of "the critical contingency" would probably discuss a novel from the point-of-view of:

    A. the importance of the author's political assumptions.
    B. the importance of the author's aesthetic experience.
    C. a member of a historically oppressed class.
    D. a member of the philosopher class.

B is correct. As used in the next-to-last sentence of the passage, this phrase refers to those critics who, opposed to the new theorists, defend the aesthetic experience as the writer's primary allegiance.

The wrong answer choices: Choice A: New theorists, not the "critical contingency," would likely consider a writer's political assumptions to be of primary importance. Choice C: A member of the critical contingency might of belong to an oppressed class, but given the context of the passage, such a person would more likely belong to the educated class. Choice D: The passage generally equates philosophers with new theorists, not with the critical contingency.

34. Which of the following statements is NOT pre-
    sented as evidence of historical debate between
    writers and critics?

    A. Plato believed that poetry offered illusions
       of illusions.
    B. The struggle between philosophers and
       poets began before Plato's time.
    C. Homeric poetry engages the reader viscer-
       ally, and not critically.
    D. The work of Derrida, de Man, and Fou-
       cault has changed our understanding of
       the parameters of literature.

D is correct. In sentence 2 of paragraph 1 the author acknowledges that "our
collective sense of what art is and does has been dramatically altered by" the work of
Derrida, de Man, and Foucault, and later juxtaposes an historical view (paragraph 3,
sentence 1): "But before theory's triumph is complete, we ought to back up and see
the battle between poetry and the professors in a larger historical context." Therefore,
the reference in the first paragraph to the three theorists precedes the reference to the
long-term conflict, and is not given as evidence of the historical debate.

The wrong answer choices: Choices A, B and C are all cited in the passage to support
the author's theme.

35. According to the passage, in the long debate
    between those who scorn literature and those
    who defend it:

    I. the defenders are a threatened
       species.
    II. Aristotle has not been immune to
        popular indifference.
    III. critics dismissed Virginia Woolf
         as irrelevant to the social norms
         of her time.

    A. II only
    B. III only
    C. I and II only
    D. I, II, and III

C is correct. In support of statement I, the final sentence of the passage states that
"art's public defenders...are becoming ever more rare." Two sentences earlier, the
author points out that Aristotle needed defense from "popular indifference," making
statement II also true.

The wrong answer choices: Choice A ignores the final sentence of the passage. Choice
B contradicts the final paragraph which equates "critics" with *defenders* of Virginia
Woolf. Choice D includes statement III, which is false.

Passage VI (Questions 36–45)

36. The author's central thesis is that:

    A. speculation in the stock market by trading on "margin" entails inherent risks which lead inevitably to pandemic socioeconomic turbulence.

    B. radical political ideas will always surge to the forefront in modern societies with large skilled labor forces which undergo periods of significant unemployment.

    C. in 1929 deficiencies of data collection regarding third-world unemployment led to underestimates in the duration and severity of global depression.

    D. the economic and social consequences of the 1929 stock market crash, both domestic and international, were inextricably linked in a domino-like way.

D is correct. Sentence 9 of the opening paragraph puts you on the right track: "the weakening of values on the...Stock Exchange set off uncontrollable...selling, which drove stock prices down irresistibly and disastrously." Sentence 1 of paragraph 2 makes the point unmistakably apparent: "The crisis passed from finance to industry, and from the United States to the rest of the world."

*The wrong answer choice*s: While the author locates the ultimate cause for the economic disaster of the '30s in overextended investment margins (paragraph 1, sentences 5-7), that conviction cannot be identified as the central thesis. In addition, the word "inevitably" should alert you to doublecheck answer A before selecting it, because what might have been true about stock market dynamics in 1929 might not be true at all times. Choice B might tempt you because of the author's final sentence: "And people chronically out of work naturally turned to new and disturbing political ideas." Again, this idea does not qualify as the central thesis. Also, the universal "always" should alert you to doublecheck the answer. Choice C involves statistical deficiencies in the third-world, and seems at first to echo sentence 2 of paragraph 3, which refers to "the masses in Asia or Africa for whom no statistics were to be had." A close reading, however, shows this to be a false similarity.

37. The passage suggests that the Great Depression most likely affected the European economy for which of the following reasons?

A. European industry was largely dependent on the American consumer market for its prosperity.

B. European workers could not compete effectively with the cheap, surplus third-world labor force.

C. The American stock market was highly invested in the European consumer market.

D. American investors lost faith in European currencies and manufacturing quality.

A is correct. Sentence 5 of paragraph 2 asserts that "Americans, their incomes falling, ceased to buy foreign goods; from Belgium to Borneo people saw their American markets slip away, and prices tumbled."

The wrong answer choices: Choice B offers an idea which some believe is true today, but which bears no relation to the passage. Choice C is something of a nonsense statement, which sounds relevant to the passage, and might even be taken as true by less-than-careful scrutiny. (American investment in the European stock market—not consumer market—declined drastically after the crash.) Nowhere does the passage suggest that Americans' inability to afford European securities was tied to a loss of faith in European money or products.

38. Which of the following assertions does the author support with an example?

I. Ready availability of capital leads to massive speculation.

II. The failure of a large bank can provoke general investor panic.

III. A global depression results in abandonment of family farms.

A. I only
B. III only
C. I and II only
D. II and III only

C is correct. Sentences 5 and 8 of paragraph 1 observe that "values had been driven to fantastic heights by excessive speculation....With money so easy to obtain, people pushed up stock prices by bidding against each other." Thus, statement I is true. Statement II is supported by sentence 6 of paragraph 2: "In 1931 the failure of a leading Vienna bank, the Creditanstalt, sent a wave of shivers, bankruptcies, and business calamities over Europe." The passage does not support Statement III.

39. Stock prices in 1929 just prior to the crash are described as "fantastic." What is the most likely reason for the choice of this word?

    A. The word implies the unrealistic magnitude of investor speculation.

    B. The market offered a superb, irresistible avenue to financial independence.

    C. The price supports involved a bizarre relationship between European industry and third-world labor.

    D. Many who speculated in the market believed that divine and occult powers safeguarded the American economy.

A is correct. The word is contained in sentence 5 of the opening paragraph: "values had been driven to fantastic heights by excessive speculation." The question requires that you understand from the surrounding text, the lack of realism that characterized investor behavior during the period leading up to the crash.

The wrong answer choices: Sentence 6 of the same paragraph acknowledges that many saw the stock market as "an easy way to make a good deal of money." But the context of the paragraph does not support the meaning of the word suggested in choice B. The passage does not discuss the relationship between third-world labor and European industry, so choice C is incorrect. There may be some truth lurking in choice D, but nothing in the passage remotely resembles it.

40. According to the passage, which of the following is cited as a consequence of the stock market crash of 1929?

    I. Between 1929 and 1932 American production fell by 38 percent.

    II. Global trade declined by 66 percent.

    III. Famine pervaded Africa and Asia.

    A. I only
    B. II only
    C. I an III only
    D. II and III only

B is correct. The question requires that you recognize the conversion from fractions to percentage and relate it to the next-to-last sentence of paragraph 2: "the world's international trade fell by two-thirds." Only statement II is supported by the passage.

41. The author suggests that unemployment be-
    came a pestilence during the Great Depression
    because it:

    A. spread throughout the world.
    B. assumed chronic proportions.
    C. led to starvation and suicide.
    D. destroyed the tissue of society.

A is correct. The first two sentences in paragraph 3 make the author's point regarding the worldwide spread of unemployment.

The wrong answer choices: Sentence 1 of paragraph 3 states that unemployment had been "chronic" ever since the war, so choice B is wrong. Choices C and D offer situation statements that not only fit the metaphorical use of "pestilence" but also probably aptly characterize the Great Depression. Nonetheless, the passage does not directly mention either of them.

42. What does the discussion of unemployment
    imply about political developments during the
    1930s?

    A. Charismatic demagogues manipulated
       popular discontent for their own ends.
    B. Profound economic insecurity allowed
       politicians to isolate and blame segments
       of society as scapegoats.
    C. Widespread social dislocations stimulated
       a search for new solutions.
    D. Extremist philosophies triumphed over
       good sense, justice, and fairness.

C is correct. The final sentence of the passage contains the key phrase: "And people chronically out of work naturally turned to new and disturbing political ideas."

The wrong answer choices: Choices A and B represent elements of historical truth about that decade and might tempt you to choose them. The passage, however, does not discuss those occurrences. Choice D suggests another historical phenomenon, which temporarily afflicted parts of the world at the time, but is not mentioned in the text.

43. The author argues that the stock market crash of 1929 led to a virtually universal desperation in society. Which of the following claims, if true, would most WEAKEN the argument?

A. Retraining in needed skills was relatively easy to obtain.

B. Relocation was an option for most workers.

C. Wholesale social renovation emerged as a political goal.

D. People were willing to do anything to make ends meet.

A is correct. The question requires that you understand the logic of the author's argument and be able to identify which option runs counter to it. The author's thesis is that the general desperation was so profound precisely because there were no "needed skills" during the Depression. According to the passage's next-to-last sentence: "Never had there been such waste, not merely of machinery which now stood still, but of the trained and disciplined labor force on which all modern societies were built." So if, in fact, jobs had existed during the '30s for which retraining would have qualified workers, the societal desperation would not have been nearly so pervasive as it was, and the author's argument would be faulty.

The wrong answer choices: Even if relocation was available to workers, as is stated in option B, unemployment was widespread, and so merely moving from one place to another would not have lessened the universality of the desperation. The final sentence suggests that conditions did, in fact, stimulate political innovation, a fact which is harmonious with the author's contentions, and which rules out choice C. The situation represented in choice D reflects a society beset by a desperate populace, and in no way weakens the author's logic.

44. According to the author's account, the global unemployment statistics during the Depression were likely:

A. understated, due to the cultural reluctance of unemployed masses in Africa and Asia to divulge that information to international agencies.

B. understated, due to a lack of available statistics in Asia and Africa, and the failure to account for huge numbers of underemployed workers.

C. inflated, due to the number of European immigrants who wrongfully claimed unemployment in order to obtain relief money.

D. inflated, due to adjustments by politicians in Europe and America who sought to secure better relief programs for their regions.

B is correct. The second sentence of paragraph 3 states that "In 1932 there were 30 million unemployed persons statistically reported in the world; and this figure did not include the further millions who could find work for only a few hours in the week, or the masses in Asia or Africa for whom no statistics were to be had."

The wrong answer choices: There is no support in the passage for any of the other options.

45. Today's international economy is more deficit-financed and interdependent than ever before, and becoming increasingly so. What worry might this information reasonably arouse among economic historians?

   A. Whether unscrupulous multinational industrialists might manipulate global economic conditions to favor their own interests

   B. Whether global investment institutions will become the ultimate judges of political decisions

   C. Whether economic and political safeguards installed after the Great Depression are sufficient to prevent another global collapse

   D. Whether the global depletion of natural resources will lead to inevitable economic chaos and sociopolitical crisis

C is correct. The question requires that you recognize and identify the economic factors and financial dynamics underlying the Depression as discussed in the passage. The debt and interdependence built into today's global economy resemble some of the factors which precipitated the crash of 1929.

The wrong answer choices: Choices A, B, and D may all represent legitimate and reasonable concerns of economic historians and others, but none of them, in the context of the passage, offers so direct a response to the question as does option C.

Passage VII (Questions 46–51)

46. The author's claim that science educators must set "practical goal[s]" before aspiring to loftier objectives (lines 19-20) is supported by which of the following observations?

    A. There is a relative lack of competition from other departments for the science majors' interest.
    B. General students seek large numbers of science courses.
    C. Science departments seek large numbers of science faculty.
    D. Society has a compelling need to achieve widespread scientific literacy.

C is correct. The key phrase is found in the last sentence of paragraph 1, where the author points out that generally, a science department's primary "underlying motive is more to attract critical masses of faculty and adequate equipment budgets for research than to satisfy some compelling educational need of the general (non-science) student."

The wrong answer choices: Option A is disproven a moment earlier in the same sentence: "science departments, whether in our schools or colleges, are no different from most other disciplines in seeking to increase the enrollment of non-majors in their courses," and in the first sentence of paragraph 2: "The competition is keen in most faculties to be included in the distribution requirements for all students." This last citation, implying that most general students take science only to fulfill distribution requirements, also rules against option B. Sentences 4 and 5 of paragraph 1, and sentence 4 of paragraph 2, indicate that the ideal of creating a scientifically literate society is less a genuine goal of science educators than it is a "self-justification and perpetuation of the science and science education professions." Thus, choice D is debunked.

47. The author most likely believes that one of the main purposes of teaching general science to critical masses of students is to:

   A. enable large numbers of citizens to participate intelligently in a scientifically oriented economy.
   B. provide an understanding of empirical methodology to all students as an essential problem-solving skill.
   C. familiarize non-science majors with newly challenging ethical issues generated by scientific technology.
   D. justify the maintenance of a large academic and research establishment in science.

D is correct. See the explanation of wrong answers to #46 above.

The wrong answer choices: Sentence 3 of paragraph 3 presents the idea which might lead you to choose either option A or C: "society (and the individual) will somehow benefit if its members are sufficiently literate to participate intelligently in science-based societal issues." However, the remainder of this paragraph, together with paragraph 4, dismisses this lofty objective as a "delusion" given the reality of poor knowledge retention after graduation. Choice B is a perfectly sensible goal but is never discussed as such in the passage.

48. Given the information in the passage, most non-science majors who study general science in either high school or college will most likely:

   A. enroll in pseudo-scientific courses such as "Physics for Poets," etc.
   B. do so to meet course distribution and "point credits" requirements.
   C. subscribe to popular science periodicals after graduation.
   D. retain little science knowledge after graduation.

D is correct. The fourth sentence of the last paragraph begins, "We know that the staying power of science courses is very poor."

The wrong answer choices: The phenomenon of pseudo-science courses is mentioned in sentence 6 of paragraph 2, but the author never claims that the majority of non-science majors enroll in such courses: so if you choose option A you allow yourself to be misled. Sentence 5 of that same paragraph mentions "point credits" as the basis on which university departments must justify their positions and budgets, not a requirement with which students must comply. According to choice D, non-science majors subscribe to popular science magazines after graduation, but the passage makes no such statement.

49. Based on information in the passage, if science departments taught fewer "promotional course[s]" (line 60) to undergraduates, which of the following outcomes would likely occur?

   A. Colleges and universities would produce significantly higher numbers of scientifically literate graduates.
   B. All students would graduate with significantly greater scientific literacy.
   C. Science departments might risk decreased budgetary support from administrations.
   D. Non-science departments might be overwhelmed by increasing student enrollments.

C is correct. According to sentence 5 of paragraph 2, "Many university science departments survive only by virtue of the 'point credits' they earn through their introductory courses." In the context of the passage, the author clearly implies that in the absence of such gut courses, science departments might have a difficult time filling their rolls, and thus justifying high budgets.

The wrong answer choices: Neither choice A nor B is discussed in the passage. Choice D might be a by-product of a decrease in pseudo-science courses, but the passage does not directly suggest it. C remains the better answer.

50. The author suggests that restricting high school science departments to only science majors would result in:

   A. the demise of many high school science departments.
   B. the proliferation of specialized state or national high schools.
   C. improved high school science curricula.
   D. better utilization of academic resources.

A is correct. The information you need to answer this question is found in sentence 3 of paragraph 2: "Most science departments would collapse for lack of a critical mass of faculty..."

The wrong answer choices: That same sentence continues, "...the training of science professionals would have to be given over to a relatively few specialized state or national high schools and colleges." Option B speaks of a "proliferation" of such specialty schools, not "few" of them. Option C presents a dubious proposition that is not endorsed anywhere in the passage. Some might argue for the merits of option D, but the author does not.

51. Suppose the majority of high school graduates were found to demonstrate an educated interest in science and science-related issues fifteen years post-graduation. This new information would most CHALLENGE the claim that:

    A. schools are guided more by immediate feedback than by long-term results.
    B. most scientifically illiterate graduates believe themselves to be scientifically knowledgeable.
    C. having literate students who become scientifically illiterate adults does not do much for society.
    D. the staying power of science courses is very poor.

D is correct. This option is the most directly affected by the new information.

The wrong answer choices: Option A offers a tempting alternative, and while the assertion it presents arguably would be challenged by the new information, option D is still the better choice. The new information would not affect the validity of the statements in options B and C.

Passage VIII (Questions 52–59)

52. The passage suggests that Africans' longstanding coexistence with elephants has caused them to regard elephants with:

    A. appreciation.
    B. contempt.
    C. fear.
    D. reverence.

A is correct. According to sentences 4 and 5 of paragraph 1, to Africans, "the elephant is known in fuller dimensions. It has been a source of food, materials, and riches; a fearsome rival for resources; and a highly visible, provocative neighbor." The choice that best characterizes the full range of an elephant's impact on Africans is A.

The wrong answer choices: Although "fearsome" is mentioned in the description of the elephant's role in African people's lives, choice C can be ruled out because fear is, according to the passage, by no means the defining attitude of Africans toward elephants. Choices B and D are not supported by the passage, because neither hate nor worship characterize Africans' relationship to the elephant.

53. Suppose that the elephants in a particular region of Africa were to disappear. How would this new information affect the author's claims about the animal's impact on the artistic product of humans living in the area?

   A. Owing to their scarcity, talismanic objects carved from elephant tusks would acquire considerable value as magical totems.
   B. Communities would barter their local products for cultural works and artisan crafts from communities who remained physically close to elephants.
   C. The dance and song of the local inhabitants would gradually lose all traces of elephant imagery.
   D. Elephant imagery would continue to play an important role in the local culture.

D is correct. Sentence 7 of paragraph 1 furnishes the justification: "Even in areas where the elephant has now vanished, it persists as a symbol in expressive culture."

The wrong answer choices: Neither A nor B is supported by the passage. Choice C is excluded because it directly contradicts the substance of paragraph 1, sentence 7.

54. Suppose it is discovered that muralists in a number of African communities portrayed jaguars as provisioners of food, material, and wealth, as dangerous competitors for resources, and as dramatically inspirational cohabitants. How would this information affect the author's claims about the interchangeability of symbolic function?

   A. It would support the claim that culture and circumstance help determine which qualities are ascribed to which animals.
   B. It would support the claim that some people believe the gap between animals and humans to be enormous.
   C. It would weaken the claim that Senegalese glass paintings are comparable in their imagery to Noah's Ark.
   D. It would weaken the claim that the elephant may be viewed as a microcosm.

A is correct. Sentence 5 of paragraph 1 explains that in African culture, the elephant is known as "a source of food, material, and riches; a fearsome rival for resources; and a highly visible, provocative neighbor." The question represents these same characteristics in different words and ascribes them to the jaguar, in effect making the elephant interchangeable with the jaguar in a different cultural milieu.

The wrong answer choices: None of the statements presented by the other options would be affected by the new information.

> **55.** The claim that elephant imagery in African culture reveals information about Africans' social lives is based mainly on:
>
> **A.** western European cultural analysis.
> **B.** African representations of the microcosm.
> **C.** Nigerian thorn carvings.
> **D.** Ethiopian popular art.

B is correct. The question requires you to follow a fairly subtle line of reasoning in the passage. Paragraph 3 opens by considering the elephant as a "microcosm." The final two sentences of the paragraph contain the relevant information: "African depictions of the elephant have as much to say about human society as about the animal itself....[and] historical events, social responsibilities, religious beliefs, and political relationships are the primary subjects of elephant imagery."

The wrong answer choices: Option A might tempt you, but you don't know if the author writes from a European, African, Asian, Latin, or other perspective. Nigerian carvings (option C) and Ethiopian art (option D) doubtless have much to tell us about African lives, but in the passage the author's claim about elephant imagery is based *mainly* on option B.

> **56.** According to the passage, European societies differ from African societies in that the former would be less likely to:
>
> **A.** become captivated by the elephant's size and power.
> **B.** devote considerable resources to maintain artificial environments for captive elephants.
> **C.** use elephant characteristics to emblemize human values.
> **D.** adopt the elephant as a children's cultural icon.

C is correct. Sentence 4 of paragraph 1 tells you that in Africa "the elephant is known in fuller dimensions" than in Europe, and as such, the paragraph's final sentence concludes, has come to "stand, for better or worse, as emblems for human values."

The wrong answer choices: Sentences 1 and 2 of the opening paragraph rule out options A and B. Your general knowledge should lead you to discard option D, even if you missed the above citations.

57. Levi-Strauss and Mary Midgley are cited in the passage in order to support the point that:

 A. African cultures tend to anthropomorphize to a much greater degree than do European cultures.
 B. science scholars have systematically identified a number of human qualities in animals.
 C. the human capacity to liken human characteristics to animal traits is a complex and contradictory phenomenon.
 D. anthropological scholars have achieved a general consensus of opinion with regard to anthropomorphism.

C is correct. Paragraph 4 presents the contradictory points of view. On the one hand, "finding *human* traits in *animals* is...a fundamental activity of the human mind." At the same time, among non-scientists, "finding *animal* traits in *humans* tends to be seen...as pernicious and degrading."

The wrong answer choices: Nothing in the passage supports any of the other options; in fact, the paragraph just cited tends to contradict them.

58. The passage suggests that a gap exists between all of the following EXCEPT:

 A. African and western versions of elephant imagery.
 B. size of an elephant and its symbolic import.
 C. actual elephants and elephant imagery.
 D. the perspective of elephant as microcosm and as macrocosm.

B is correct. Remember that you are looking for a statement that is *not* correct. The passage begins with the phrase, "As the largest land animal on the planet, the elephant is a potent symbol..." In addition, the second sentence of paragraph 3 states, "By virtue of its sheer size and prominence the role [the elephant] plays in art and historical processes are magnified." The question requires you to understand the difference between the author's conception of the elephant as microcosm, and as macrocosm. As microcosm, the elephant is "so apparently human" (sentence 2, last paragraph). As macrocosm, the creature remains "so huge, so remote," and "most dramatizes the gap between the species." The paragraph says that oral and "visual representations are driven by the impulse to mediate the breach between worlds." The only answer choice that sounds this theme is D.

The wrong answer choices: Each of the other reflects statements or viewpoints that are expressed in the passage.

59. The passage as a whole suggests that humans view their relationship to animals:

    A. in nearly universal symbols across different cultures.
    B. in varied ways that depend on each culture's symbolic forms.
    C. in superficial and simplistic terms.
    D. in purely practical terms.

B is correct. Sentence 4 of paragraph 3 states the case unambiguously: "In Africa as elsewhere, people represent their relationship to animals in multiple ways, and their complex experience of it can be read in the symbolic language of their respective cultures."

The wrong answer choices: Choices A and C contradict the above citation, and run counter to the general sense of the passage. Paragraphs 4 and 5 make option D incorrect.

Passage IX (Questions 60–69)

60. The author's main point about the information economy is that:

    A. cooperation among competing information suppliers and hardware designers is essential if the new information economy is to flourish.
    B. competitive commodity in the information age is human attention, and the greater the amount of data available, the higher the relative value of attention.
    C. the nature of the information services market lends itself to monopolization by smart entrepreneurs and large suppliers.
    D. new information technologies create new legal, commercial, and managerial problems that will require new solutions.

D is correct. All of the options offered reflect ideas discussed in the passage, but option D best summarizes the overall central theme: "in some ways, computers and high-speed networks make the problems of buying, selling and distributing information goods worse rather than better" (sentence 2, paragraph 1).

The wrong answer choices: Sentence 3 of paragraph 3, and really the entire paragraph, makes the point that "If interconnection standards are developed that make it cheap and easy to transmit information across independent networks, competition will flourish." But this realization, like option A, articulates one of many ideas in the passage, not the central thesis. Sentence 3 of paragraph 2 acknowledges that "a wealth of information creates a poverty of attention," and this insight, like option B, represents a sub-theme of the text. Sentence 4 of paragraph 3 warns that "If technical or economic factors make interconnection difficult" monopolistic tendencies might develop, but this advisory, like option C, cannot be said to summarize the author's main idea.

61. The passage suggests that with regard to information technology consumers will do which of the following?

   A. Use a new technology more readily if many others also use it
   B. Readily switch from an older product to a newer and improved one
   C. Embrace new communication tools as soon as the tools are introduced on the market
   D. Initially respond enthusiastically to a new product and then lose interest in it as it remains on the market

A is correct. Sentence 2 of paragraph 7 contains the vital information: "Each consumer's willingness to use a particular piece of technology—such as the Internet—depends strongly on the number of other uses."

The wrong answer choices: Sentence 3 of the same paragraph eliminates choices C and D: "New communication tools...have typically started out with long periods of relatively low use followed by exponential growth.." Sentences 4 and 5 of paragraph 7 make option B incorrect: "once a ...technology has penetrated a significant portion of the market, it may be very difficult to dislodge...people do not want to switch to a new piece of hardware or software—even if it is demonstrably superior."

62. The passage suggests that workable models to interconnect local Internet networks need further development because without them:

   A. consumers will have to determine which backbone system most fits their needs.
   B. uncontrolled competition will confuse consumers with information overload
   C. price wars will destroy the industry's ability to develop new services and products.
   D. monopolies will arise, and quality and price control may suffer.

D is correct. According to the last sentence of paragraph 3, in the absence of internetwork models large suppliers might achieve such market dominance as to "drive out competitors and monopolize the market," a circumstance which could lead to a decline in quality and affordability.

The wrong answer choices: Choice A presents a likely development given the conditions of the question, but does not so directly reflect the passage's ideas as does option D. If you confuse the issues of information overload and market competition as presented in the passage you might be misled to choose B. Choice C cannot be eliminated because the author does not discuss price wars or ruinous competition.

63. The need for financial incentives to motivate information producers is cited by the author as evidence for the claim that:

    A. ready access to digital information should be balanced against protection of intellectual property rights.

    B. the Internet represents the electronic equivalent of a library periodical rack.

    C. intellectual property protection that is too lax will restrict consumer access to digital information.

    D. access to fair use of digital information ideally should be universal and free.

A is correct. The answer is found in the final sentence of paragraph 8, in which the author declares that "A compromise position must be found...between those who suggest that all information should be free and those who advocate laws against the electronic equivalent of browsing at a magazine rack."

The wrong answer choices: The text just cited excludes choices D and B. Choice C misinterprets the meaning of paragraph 8, sentence 2. There, the author states that excessively strict intellectual property protection will act to limit free flow of information to consumers.

64. The existence of which of the following phenomena would most strongly CHALLENGE the information in the passage?

    A. Infrastructure design incorporating cost-effective modification capability

    B. Masses of users who are reluctant to use new systems and programs

    C. New inventions rendering current systems obsolete within 20 years

    D. Relatively user-friendly interoperability

A is correct. The question calls on you to determine which assertion would MOST STRONGLY challenge the passage information. If it became relatively easy and cost-effective to modify existing computer systems to make them compatible with new technologies and other systems, then most of the author's arguments would be moot, because "technical or economic factors [which] make interconnection difficult" would not exist, and the need for "open standards for formats used to represent text, images, video, and other collections of data, so that one producer's data will be accessible to another's software" would be obviated.

The wrong answer choices: Choice B would support the author's view that "the limits of human comprehension" are "the most fundamental constraint on information commerce..." Choices C and D tend to support the author's arguments, because: (1) obsolescence would only highlight the need for consumer and hardware adaptability; and (2) a producer who offered readily interoperable systems would be following the author's advice.

65. According to the passage, a "smart" credit card (line 77) would best be described as one that:

    A. contains chips which can perform a variety of computational tasks.
    B. recognizes software protocols capable of delivering financial services.
    C. enlists and enables special hardware to carry out electronic transactions.
    D. involves complex digital encryption techniques.

A is correct. The question asks you to identify the "best description, and the last sentence of paragraph 5 keys the answer: "'Smart' credit cards with chips embedded in them can perform a variety of authentication and accounting tasks."

The wrong answer choices: Although each of the other choices sounds plausible, and echos statements in the text regarding computerized, electronic financial dealings, none is so good a description of "smart" card technology as choice A.

Passage I (Questions 66-71)

66. If 216 grams of silver react with excess sulfuric acid, how many grams of water are produced?

    A. 9 g
    B. 18 g
    C. 27 g
    D. 36 g

D is correct. If sulfuric acid is in excess, all 2 moles of silver react. Examine the periodic table and note that silver's atomic weight is approximately 108 g/mol. Two hundred sixteen grams of silver represents 2 moles. Water's molecular weight is 18 g/mol. Examine Reaction II. The equation demonstrates that 2 moles of silver produce 2 moles of water. Knowing that water's molecular weight is 18 g/mol, you calculate that 2 moles of water have mass of 36 g.

67. As Reaction III progresses, which of the following is true of the sodium and chlorine ions?

    A. Sodium ions are reduced and chlorine ions are oxidized.
    B. Sodium and chlorine ions are oxidized.
    C. Sodium and chlorine ions are reduced.
    D. Sodium and chlorine ions are neither oxidized nor reduced.

D is correct. Neither sodium nor chlorine changes its oxidation state over the course of the reaction. Sodium retains its oxidation state of +1 and chlorine retains its oxidation state of –1. To know that a species undergoes no change in oxidation state means that it has neither oxidized nor reduced.

68. With respect to sulfuric acid, which of the following is NOT true?

    A. It is a buffer.
    B. It is a strong acid.
    C. It is a polyprotic acid.
    D. It is a proton donor.

A is correct. Review chemistry and recall that a buffer arises from a solution containing a weak acid and its conjugate base or a weak base and its conjugate acid. Sulfuric acid is a *strong* acid; in aqueous solution, it ionizes completely.

The wrong answer choices: Choice B is wrong because it makes an accurate statement; sulfuric acid is a strong acid. Choice C, too, makes an accurate statement. Sulfuric acid is a polyprotic acid since it may give up one hydrogen ion to yield HSO_4^- and yet another to yield SO_4^{2-}. Choice D is wrong as well. Sulfuric acid conforms to the definition of a Bronsted-Lowry acid and is, therefore, a "proton donor."

69. An aqueous solution of H_2SO_4 is titrated with a 0.1 M solution of sodium hydroxide, as shown below. Which of the following is true at point 2?

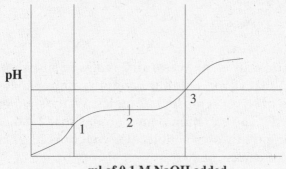

pH

ml of 0.1 M NaOH added

A. $[H_2SO_4] = [HSO_4^-]$
B. $[H_2SO_4] = [SO_4^{2-}]$
C. $[HSO_4^-] = [SO_4^{2-}]$
D. $[H^+] = [OH^-]$

C is correct. At the titration curve's first "bump" all H_2SO_4 molecules have reacted with the base, each generating an HSO_4^- ions. At point 2, 50% of the HSO_4^- ions have reacted with the base to form SO_4^{2-} ion. Therefore the concentrations of the two anions are equal.

70. At constant high temperature, a sample of 1 mole of sulfuric acid completely dissociates into gaseous sulfur trioxide and water vapor. In terms of average speed, how do sulfur trioxide molecules compare to molecules of water?

A. Sulfur trioxide molecules have a faster average speed.
B. Sulfur trioxide molecules have a slower average speed.
C. The two gases have equal average speeds.
D. The relationship between the average speeds cannot be determined.

B is correct. Review inorganic chemistry and recall: at any given temperature, all gas molecules have the same *kinetic energy*. For any body (a gas molecule, a rocket ship, or a planet) kinetic energy $= \frac{1}{2}mv^2$. For two gas molecules at a given kinetic energy, therefore, the mass of one is inversely proportional to the square of the other's velocity. Since the mass of a water molecule (18 gram atomic units) is less than that of a sulfur trioxide molecule (80 gram atomic units), its *velocity* must be greater. The water molecules' average speed is approximately twice that of the sulfur trioxide molecules.

71. Assuming Reaction I is at equilibrium, which of the following changes to the reaction conditions will increase the concentration of sulfuric acid?

    A. Decreasing the pressure
    B. Decreasing the concentration of SO_3
    C. The addition of a catalyst
    D. Decreasing the temperature

D is correct. Look closely at Reaction I and paragraph 2. Then, recall LeChatelier's principle. Paragraph 2 tells you that Reaction I is exothermic. *In a sense*, then, heat is one of the reaction's products. Decreased temperature is akin to removal of a product; it drives the reaction forward ("to the right"). *For a reversible exothermic reaction, decreased temperature favors the forward reaction and increased temperature favors the reverse reaction. A reciprocal phenomenon applies to endothermic reactions.* This reaction is exothermic, and decreased temperature increases H_2SO_4 production.

The wrong answer choices: Choice A is wrong because decreased pressure would favor the production of gas and thus drive the reaction to the left. Choice B is wrong because decreased concentration of reactant will drive the reaction to the left. Choice C is wrong too. In the presence of a catalyst a reaction "takes less time" to "get" to equilibrium. Once the reaction reaches equilibrium, however, *concentrations* are as they would be without catalysis.

Passage II (Questions 72-78)

72. A particle is fired into the magnetic field. Its initial velocity is directed at an angle ϕ to the magnetic field lines. Which of the following graphs best represents the change in the magnitude of the force on the particle as ϕ is increased from 0° to 90°?

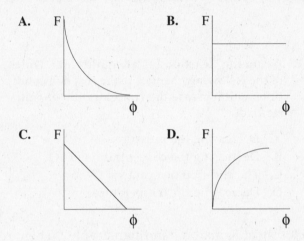

D is correct. The equation set forth in the passage, shows that force is proportional to sin ϕ. Choice D shows is the only graph that shows force increasing with angle ϕ and, furthermore, it is consistent with a sine curve.

73. Keeping all other factors constant, which of the following would increase the size of the spiral in which particle X travels?

  A. Increasing the strength of the magnetic field
  B. Giving the particle more kinetic energy
  C. Giving the particle less kinetic energy
  D. Increasing the charge on the particle

B is correct. Increasing kinetic energy means increasing velocity, which, in turn, means that for every degree of circular motion it travels, the particle will cover more distance and, therefore, increase the radius of the circle in which it travels each instant. That, in turn, increases the size of the spiral. (The spiral's size would also increase if the force on the particle were reduced.)

The wrong answer choices: Choices A and D are wrong because increased field strength or increased charge would increase force on the particle and thereby reduce the spiral's size. Choice C is wrong for the reason that B is right: reduced kinetic energy means decreased velocity and "tightening" the spiral.

74. Particle Z is given an initial velocity of 1×10^3 m/s perpendicular to the magnetic field lines. If the field strength is 5.5 T and particle Z has a charge of 1 coul, what is the net force on particle Z when it first enters the field?

 A. 0 N
 B. 5.5×10^3 N
 C. 1.1×10^3 N
 D. 2.5×10^3 N

B is correct. The passage provides an equation and the question assigns values to the variables: plug them in. $F = qvB\sin\phi$

$$F = (1 \text{ coul}) \times (1 \times 10^3 \text{ m/sec}) \times (5.5 \text{ T})(\sin 90°);$$
$$F = 5.5 \times 10^3 \text{ N}$$

75. If particle P were given a velocity component into the page, with a magnitude equal to the magnitude of its velocity in the direction of path Y, the force first felt by the particle would:

 A. decrease by a factor of 4.
 B. decrease by a factor of 2.
 C. remain the same.
 D. increase by a factor of 2.

C is correct. A velocity directed *into the page*, is parallel to the direction of the magnetic field, and angle ϕ is zero. Applying the equation provided in the passage, shows that the force associated with such a velocity is zero. That, in turn, means that the added velocity would bring no change to the force felt by the particle.

76. Observing paths followed by particles X and Z, an experimenter would be justified in concluding that the two particles:

 A. have charges of equal magnitude.
 B. entered the field with different kinetic energies.
 C. are oppositely charged.
 D. are positively charged.

C is correct. The magnetic field force causes the two particles to move in opposite directions. That can only mean that their charges are opposite; one is positive and the other negative.

The wrong answer choices: Choices A and B are wrong. Neither charge magnitude nor kinetic energy explains the particles' divergent paths and the divergent path does not justify conclusions as to those quantities. Choice D is wrong for the reason that C is right. The particles travel in opposite directions and must be oppositely charged.

77. A particle of mass .001 kg and charge 1 coul enters the magnetic field traveling 1000 m/s. The particle spirals and comes to a complete stop in 0.05 seconds. How much work is done by friction in bringing the particle to a stop?

    A. 20 J
    B. 25 J
    C. 500 J
    D. 1000 J

C is correct. Review of physics will remind you that work, a measure of (force) × (distance) is equivalent, also, to change in kinetic energy (ΔKE). In this context calculate it thus:

$$W = \Delta KE = KE_f - KE_i \qquad\qquad W = (1/2)mv^2 - 0 \text{ J}$$
$$W = (1/2)(.001 \text{ kg})(1000 \text{ m/sec})^2 \qquad\qquad W = 500 \text{ J}$$

78. Which of the following diagrams represents the force experienced by a positively charged particle traveling through a magnetic field?

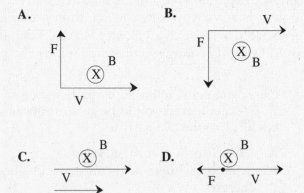

A is correct. The particle experiences a force that is perpendicular to both the particle's velocity and the field lines, so choices C and D are wrong. Correctly apply the right hand rule to choose between choices A and B and you will decide on A.

Passage III (Questions 79-82)

79. When a molecule is formed from previously uncombined atoms by chemical reaction:

    A. bonds are formed and energy is released.
    B. bonds are broken and energy is released.
    C. bonds are formed and energy is absorbed.
    D. bonds are broken and energy is absorbed.

A is correct. When a molecule is created from uncombined atoms, bonds must be formed. When bonds are formed, energy is always released.

80. According to Table 2, the formation of $CO_2 (g)$ from elemental carbon and oxygen:

    A. is not spontaneous under standard conditions.
    B. is spontaneous under standard conditions.
    C. requires a catalyst.
    D. occurs only at very high temperatures.

B is correct. The standard free energy change ($G_f°$) is negative, which indicates that the process is spontaneous under standard conditions.

The wrong answer choices: Choice A would be correct if $G_f°$ were positive. Choices C and D do not pertain to Table 2. The table offers no information about catalysts or reaction temperature.

81. If a particular synthesis proceeds spontaneously only at high temperatures, which of the following should be anticipated?

    A. ΔS is positive; ΔH is negative.
    B. ΔS is positive; ΔH is positive.
    C. ΔS is negative; ΔH is negative.
    D. ΔS is negative; ΔH is positive.

B is correct. A chemical reaction is spontaneous only if Gibbs free energy (ΔG) is negative. Gibbs' free energy is a function of enthalpy (H), entropy (S), and temperature (T, in °K): $\Delta G = \Delta H - T\Delta S$. Whether Gibbs free energy is negative or positive depends on the "balance" struck between changes in enthalpy and entropy.

When ΔH and ΔS are both positive, then (a) at relatively *low* temperature, ΔH will play the more important role and ΔG will be positive, making the reaction non-spontaneous (b) at higher temperature, ΔS will prevail, making ΔG negative and the reaction spontaneous.

82. What is the change in enthalpy associated with the formation of 2 moles of $N_2O_4(g)$ from its constituent elements?

   A. –9.2 kJ
   B. –4.6 kJ
   C. 9.2 kJ
   D. 18.4 kJ

D is correct. Examine Table 1, and note: when 1 mole of $N_2O_4(g)$ is formed the enthalpy change is 9.2 kJ. Simple reasoning and arithmetic reveal that when 2 moles are formed, the enthalpy change is $(2)x$ (9.2kJ) = 18.4 kJ.

Passage IV (Questions 83-88)

83. Two particles travel through a magnetic field. If particle 1 experiences a net force and particle 2 does not, which of the following could represent the particles' identities?

   A. Particle 1 is a beta particle and particle 2 is an alpha particle.
   B. Particle 1 is a gamma particle and particle 2 is a neutrino.
   C. Particle 1 is a beta particle and particle 2 is a neutrino.
   D. Particle 1 is a gamma particle and particle 2 is an alpha particle.

C is correct. Charged particles experience force when traveling through a magnetic field. Uncharged particles don't. Beta particles are charged (negatively) and neutrinos are not.

The wrong answer choices: Choice A is wrong because it describes particle 2 as an alpha particle. Alpha particles *are* charged (positively). Choices B and D are wrong because each describes particle 1 as a gamma ray. Gamma rays are uncharged.

84. Two helium nuclei fuse and release energy in the form of photons. Which of the following describes the main energy transfer that takes place?

   A. Kinetic to potential
   B. Electrical to kinetic
   C. Mass to electromagnetic
   D. Kinetic to electrical

C is correct. The question describes a nuclear fusion reaction. Nuclear fusion (and fission) reactions illustrate the equivalency of mass and energy as described by Einstein's famous equation, $E = mc^2$. In this nuclear fusion reaction light energy is evolved; the reaction converts mass to energy and, more specifically, to energy in the form of electromagnetic radiation.

85. $_{90}^{236}$Th emits two beta particles and two alpha particles. Which of the following nuclei results?

   A. $_{87}^{226}$Fr

   B. $_{88}^{226}$Ra

   C. $_{88}^{228}$Ra

   D. $_{86}^{224}$Rn

C is correct. Depict the process in writing:

$$_{90}^{236} \xrightarrow{\enclose{circle}{2\beta}} {}_{92}^{236} \xrightarrow{\enclose{circle}{2\alpha}} {}_{n}^{m}$$

Note that atomic *numbers* must be in balance:

$$n = 90 - (2)(-1) - (2)(2)$$
$$n = 90 + 2 - 4$$
$$n = 88$$

Look at the periodic table and find atomic number 88. It belongs to Radium (Ra). Atomic *weights* also must be in balance:

$$m = 236 - (2)(0) - (2)(4)$$
$$m = 236 - 8$$
$$m = 228$$

The answer is Ra – 228.

86. One half of a Tl sample decays to Pb in 3.1 mins through the emission of beta particles. If an initially pure sample of Tl contains 7 g of lead after 9.3 mins, what was the approximate mass of the original sample?

    A. 7 g
    B. 8 g
    C. 28 g
    D. 32 g

B is correct. Since beta particles have negligible mass, you should assume that the mass of the Pb that appears is equal to the mass of the Tl that decays. That means 7 g of T1 decayed. Since T1 has a half-life of 3.1 minutes, 9.3 minutes represents 3 half-lives. In three half-lives, 7/8 of the original sample decays. Simple algebra reveals that:

$$\left(\frac{7}{8}\right)(x) = 7g; \quad x = 8g$$

87. An element decays to an isotope of itself, releasing alpha and beta particles. In terms of the number of particles released, the ratio of alpha particles to beta particles is:

    A. $\dfrac{1}{2}$
    B. 1
    C. 2
    D. 4

A is correct. Because the element decayed to an isotope of itself, its atomic number is constant. Alpha decay decreases the atomic number by two. Beta decay increases atomic number by one. Atomic number will be constant only if there are two beta decays for every alpha decay.

88. If 2.8 MeV are needed to produce 1 photon, how many photons can be produced when 1 gram of matter is converted to energy?

    A. 2×10^{26}
    B. 2×10^{32}
    C. 2×10^{35}
    D. 4×10^{35}

A is correct. Photons have energy but no mass. When a question concerns the conversion of mass to energy, remember Einstein's formula:

$$E = mc^2 \qquad E = (.001 \text{ kg})(3 \times 10^8 \text{ m/s})^2 \qquad E = 9 \times 10^{13} \text{J}$$

Next, determine how many photons correspond to 9×10^{13} J of energy:

$$(9 \times 10^{-13} \text{ J}) \times (1 \text{ photon}/ 2.8 \text{ MeV}) \times (1 \text{ eV}/1.6 \times 10^{-19} \text{ J}) \times$$
$$(1 \text{ MeV}/10^6 \text{ eV}) = 2 \times 10^{26} \text{ photons}$$

Isn't that nice?

Questions 89 through 93 are NOT based on a descriptive passage

89. Light traveling through water in a swimming pool has the following measured values:

   frequency $= 5.0 \times 10^{14}$ Hz
   wavelength $= 4.5 \times 10^{-7}$ m
   velocity $= 2.25 \times 10^8$ m/s

   The wave propagates across the surface of the water into air. If the speed of light in air is 3×10^8 m/s, what is the frequency of the wave traveling in air?

   A. 2.5×10^{14} Hz
   B. 3.8×10^{14} Hz
   C. 5.0×10^{14} Hz
   D. 6.7×10^{14} Hz

C is correct. Wave velocity is the product of frequency and wavelength. When a light wave passes from one medium to another its wavelength or velocity may change, but its frequency does not. The wave equation applies and the wave's frequency in the air is equal to its frequency in the water.

90. A trigonal bipyramid is the characteristic of which orbital hybridization?

   A. sp
   B. sp^2
   C. sp^3
   D. dsp^3

D is correct. A trigonal bipyramid structure requires *five* hybrid orbitals. Among the configurations listed in the choices, only dsp^3 offers the five. The number of pure orbitals contributing to hybridization equals the total number of hybrid orbitals finally formed.

91. Which of the following electronic configurations belongs to a diamagnetic element in its ground state?

    A. $1s^2 2s^1$
    B. $1s^2 2s^2 2p^1$
    C. $1s^2 2s^2 2p^4$
    D. $1s^2 2s^2 2p^6$

D is correct. Diamagnetic elements have no unpaired electrons, and that's the situation reflected in choice D.

The wrong answer choices: Choices A and B show an odd number of electrons, meaning that some electrons are unpaired. Choice C is wrong even though it shows an even number of electrons. According to Hund's rule, electrons occupy orbitals singly until all orbitals within the relevant subshell are occupied by one electron. When the *p* subshell carries four electrons, two are unpaired.

92. Three mechanical waves are passed through the same medium at equal velocities. Their respective amplitudes are 1 cm, 2 cm, and 4 cm. What is the smallest possible amplitude of the resultant wave?

    A. 0 cm
    B. 1 cm
    C. 7 cm
    D. 8 cm

B is correct. Combine the waves so as to cause the greatest destructive interference: (4 cm) − (2 cm) − (1 cm) = 1 cm

93. When Magnesium (Mg) and Chlorine (Cl) are compared in terms of electronegativity and atomic radius, which of the following is true?

    A. Magnesium has greater electronegativity and smaller atomic radius.
    B. Magnesium has greater electronegativity and greater atomic radius.
    C. Magnesium has lesser electronegativity and smaller atomic radius.
    D. Magnesium has lesser electronegativity and greater atomic radius.

D is correct. Magnesium sits on the left side of the periodic table and Cl on the right. As you move from left to right across a period, atomic radius decreases because, even though electrons are added, they are in the same electron shell and the expanding number of protons draws them progressively closer to the nucleus, "tightening" the electron shells. Electronegativity increases, because as a given shell fills and positive nuclear charge increases, the atom progressively decreases its "willingness" to lose an electron.

Passage V (Questions 94-100)

94. For the wheelchair pictured in Figure 2, the radial distance to the handle is exactly twice the distance to the edge of the tire. The force applied to the ground F_o will be:

   A. half the force applied to the handle F_i.
   B. equal to the force applied to the handle F_i.
   C. twice the force applied to the handle F_i.
   D. four times the force applied to the handle F_i.

A is correct. Review physics and recall the quantity called "torque." It concerns forces applied to and experienced by objects in rotatory motion. Torque is equal to (force) × (lever arm). In the case of a circular object rotating about its axis, lever arm is equal to radius of the circle to which force is applied. If force is applied at the handle, lever arm is equal to the distance between the center and the handle. If force is applied at the tire lever arm is equal to the distance between the center and the tire. Applying the symbols shown in the drawing:

$$F_i r_h = F_o r_w, \text{ but } r_w = 2r_h. \text{ Therefore, } F_o = F_i / 2$$

95. The human body is approximately 75% efficient in converting its stored chemical energy to mechanical work. A person who weighs 80 N rolls himself up a ramp with a length of 10 m to a height of 1.5 m. If the ramp is a 95% efficient machine and the wheelchair weighs 40 N, how much energy does the person expend?

   A. $(80 + 40)(1.5)(95/100)(75/100)$ J
   B. $(80 + 40)(1.5)(100/95)(100/75)$ J
   C. $(80 + 40)(10)(95/100)(75/100)$ J
   D. $(80 + 40)(10)(100/95)(100/75)$ J

B is correct. Because the two machines (human body and ramp) are not ideal, the work done will be greater than the potential energy achieved.

$$(\text{work done}) \times (75/100)(95/100) = (mg) \times (h);$$
$$(\text{work done}) = (80 + 40) \times (1.5) (100/95) \times (100/75) \text{ J}$$

Note that the ramp's length does not affect the result, but that the height to be achieved *does*.

96. A first wheelchair user climbs an inclined plane to a height of 3 m. A second wheelchair user is raised straight up in the chair to the same height by an electric lift. The potential energy gained by the first wheelchair user is:

    A. greater than the energy gained by the second because a greater distance has been traveled.
    B. greater than the energy gained by the second because electric energy is not easily converted into potential energy.
    C. less than the energy gained by the second because electric energy is easily converted into potential energy.
    D. equal to the energy gained by the second because the wheelchair has been raised to the same height.

D is correct. An object's gravitational potential energy (GPE) depends only on its weight (mg) and height (h). (GPE = *mgh*). The manner by which the chair and user obtain their height is irrelevant to the potential energy they gain on moving upward. If you wish to conceive of the potential energy in terms of the work done on the wheelchair and rider [(force) × (distance)], recall that as compared to the straight upward pull, the inclined plane reduces applied force and increases the distance over which it acts, so the work done is the same. For the two users, the *products* (force) × (distance) are equal, although the individual quantities (force) and (distance) are not.

97. If the radius of the wheel pictured in Figure 2 is 40 cm, what is the distance traveled by the wheelchair over the course of 6 complete wheel rotations?

    A. 7 m
    B. 11 m
    C. 15 m
    D. 21 m

B is correct. The question calls for simple geometry.

Circumference = $2\pi r$ = (2) × (3.14) × (0.4 m) = 2.5 m

Distance = (6 revolutions)C = (6 rev)(2.5 m/rev) = 15 m

98. An ideal wheelchair ramp bridges a height of 1.2 m. If the ramp is 24 m in length, how much force must be applied by a 60 N man in a 40 N wheelchair to climb the ramp?

A. 5 N
B. 10 N
C. 20 N
D. 50 N

A is correct. Fd = Fd. Use the relationship:

(input force) × (input distance) = (output force) × (output distance)

(input force) × (24 m) = (60 N + 40 N) × (1.2 m)

(input force) = 5 N

99. Which of the following changes MUST increase the ideal mechanical advantage of the ramp pictured in Figure 1?

A. Increase L and increase h.
B. Decrease L and decrease h.
C. Decrease L and increase h.
D. Increase L and decrease h.

D is correct. From the passage, appreciate that IMA is directly proportional to L and inversely proportional to h. If L is increased and h is decreased, *IMA* must increase.

The wrong answer choices: Choices A is wrong, because, in terms of the fraction F(L/h) it refers to increasing L and increasing h. If the factor by which h is increased exceeds the factor by which L is increased, the fraction's value will decrease. Choice B is wrong for analogous reasons. Choice C is wrong, because a decrease in numerator and an increase in denominator will reduce the fraction's value.

100. For the wheelchair shown in Figure 2, which of the following is most likely the design consideration that makes the output force smaller than the input force?

    A. Only one wheel is shown in Figure 2.
    B. The handle radius can not be larger than the wheel radius.
    C. The input force will vary depending on the weight of the person seated in the wheelchair.
    D. A rotational force can only be applied perpendicular to the axis of rotation.

B is correct. Knowing that $F_i r_h = F_o r_w$, you may conclude the input force will fall below output force only if the handle radius is larger than the wheel radius.

The wrong answer choices: Choices A and C are true statements but do not answer the question. Choice D is a false statement.

Passage VI (Questions 101-105)

101. What pH would most likely cause a color change in the unknown indicator?

    A. 5
    B. 7
    C. 9
    D. 14

A is correct. In the last two sentences of the passage, you're told that the color change occurred at a pH below the equivalence pH of 7.0. Among the choices, only A represents a pH below 7.0.

102. Which of the following colors would result from the formation of the conjugate base of bromothymol blue?

    A. Spectral red
    B. Blue
    C. Yellow
    D. Green

B is correct. In paragraph 1 of the passage you learn that the conjugate base (In_B^-) of bromothymol blue is blue.

103. At pH 7.0, the solution's color most probably indicates the presence of:

   A. HIn_A
   B. In_A^-
   C. In_B^-
   D. HIn_B^-

C is correct. The indicator is in its conjugate base form at pH just below pH 7.0. Hence, it has the symbol In_B^-.

The wrong answer choices: Choice A describes the *acid* form of the indicator. Choices B and D present species not mentioned in the passage; they are, in fact, meaningless.

104. Two additional indicators were used. For HCl, phenolphthalein changed color above the equivalence point, and methyl red changed color below the equivalence point. At the equivalence point, which forms of the indicators produce color?

   A. The base of phenolphthalein and the acid of methyl red
   B. The base of methyl red and the acid of phenolphthalein
   C. The acids of both indicators
   D. The bases of both indicators

B is correct. Methyl red changes color below the equivalence point. *At* the equivalence point, it is present in conjugate base form. Phenolphthalein changes color above the equivalence point and, *at* the equivalence point, remains in its acid form.

105. According to the information presented below, which of the following indicators will be present in the acid form in an aqueous titration solution that reached pH 5.0?

Indicator	Acid Color	Base Color	K_{ind}	pH Range
Thymol blue	Red	Yellow	2×10^{-2}	$1.2 - 2.8$
Methyl orange	Red	Orange	3.5×10^{-4}	$3.1 - 4.4$
Bromothymol blue	Yellow	Blue	8×10^{-8}	$6.0 - 7.6$

A. Thymol blue, because the conjugate acid remains protonated at the pH value of the solution
B. Thymol blue, because the conjugate base is deprotonated at the pH value of the solution
C. Bromothymol blue, because the conjugate acid remains protonated at the pH value of the solution
D. Bromothymol blue, because the conjugate base is deprotonated at the pH value of the solution

C is correct. The right-hand column of the table describes the pH range at which each indicator is converted to its conjugate base form. At pH 5, bromothymol blue is not yet converted. It remains in its *acid* form.

The wrong answer choices: Choices A and B are wrong. The table shows you that well below pH 5, thymol blue is completely converted to its conjugate base form. Choice D is contrary to the question.

Passage VII (Questions 106-109)

106. The piston is pulled upward to reduce the pressure on the fluid so that the new fluid heights in stems A and B are h_1 and h_2 respectively. Which of the following relate h_o, h_1, and h_2?

A. $h_o < h_1 < h_2$
B. $h_1 < h_o < h_2$
C. $h_2 < h_o < h_1$
D. $h_o = h_2 = h_1$

C is correct. Examine the figure. Within stem A, the upward movement of the piston reduces pressure between the piston and liquid surface. It creates a "negative pressure." As the piston rises, so does the fluid, to a height of h_1. The fluid height in stem B must drop to h_2. Assuming that fluid remains in stem B and does not drop below x, h_1 *must* be greatest, and h_2 lowest.

107. If both stems A and B have fluid at height h_o, what is the difference in pressure between points x and y? (Assume atmospheric pressure is 1.013×10^5 Pa.)

A. 5.0×10^3 Pa
B. 1.0×10^5 Pa
C. 1.5×10^5 Pa
D. 2.5×10^5 Pa

A is correct. Review physics and recall that for any two points in a stagnant fluid, the pressure difference, $\Delta P, = \rho g \Delta h$, *where* ρ is the density of the fluid, g is the acceleration due to gravity, and Δh is the difference in height between the two points. Therefore:

$$\Delta P = (5.0 \times 10^3 \text{kg/m}^3) \times (10\text{m/s}^2) \times (0.1\text{m}) = 5 \times 10^3 \text{ Pa}$$

108. The pressure exerted by the fluid at point x is directed:

   A. vertically upward only.
   B. vertically downward only.
   C. horizontally only.
   D. to and from all directions.

D is correct. At any point within a fluid, *fluid pressure* is always exerted from all directions: up, down, and sideways.

The wrong answer choices: Choices A, B, and C all assign a single direction to the fluid pressure. Each choice is wrong. Fluid pressure is always to and from all directions.

109. The piston is removed and the liquid reaches a height of 20 m in each stem. A small hole appears at point y, and a steady flow of fluid escapes. Ignoring friction, what is the velocity at which fluid leaves the U-tube? (Consider that gravitational acceleration = 10 m/s^2)

   A. 10 m/s
   B. 12 m/s
   C. 17 m/s
   D. 20 m/s

D is correct. Your review of physics will reacquaint you with Bernoulli's equation and Toricelli's theorem. The velocity of an escaping fluid as is described here as equal to:

$$(2g \times \text{the height of the fluid above})$$
$$\text{Velocity} = (2 \times 10 \text{ m/s}^2 \times 20 \text{ m})^{1/2} = 20 \text{ m/s}.$$

Passage VIII (Questions 110-114)

110. The dependence of the viscosity and surface tension of water on temperature is best illustrated by which of the following figures?

A.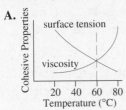

C.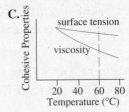

B.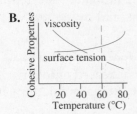

D.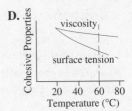

C is correct. Paragraph 3 presents the relevant information. You're told that from 20° C to 60° C, viscosity decreases by more than 50 percent, while surface tension decreases by only 5 percent. Choice C shows a graph wherein viscosity decreases much more quickly than does surface tension.

The wrong answer choices: Choices A and B shows greater cohesion with increased temperature. No such trend is observed. Choice D shows that in the temperature range 20° C to 60° C, surface tension falls more quickly than viscosity. That is not correct.

111. Which phenomenon accounts for the decrease in density of water as its temperature decreases from 4° C to 0° C?

A. Hydrogen bonding
B. Covalent bonding
C. Freezing point depression
D. Heat of fusion

A is correct. According to paragraph 2 hydrogen bonding produces the open lattice structure of solid water. Deduce that the open lattice structure must begin to form as the water molecule approaches its freezing point.

112. When H_2O moves from the solid to the liquid phase at 0° C, under standard equilibrium conditions, what enthalpy change occurs?

   A. The reaction releases 6.008 kJ/mol.
   B. The reaction absorbs 6.008 kJ/mol.
   C. The reaction releases 44.02 kJ/mol.
   D. The reaction absorbs 44.02 kJ/mol.

B is correct. The question requires that you (1) read the table effectively to ascertain water's heat of fusion and (2) know that when water melts, heat must be absorbed.

The wrong answer choices: Choices A and C indicate that heat is *released* as ice melts. Choice D reflects water's of vaporization instead of its heat of fusion.

113. In a laboratory, the vapor pressure of a sample of water is gradually increased until it reaches atmospheric pressure. At this point, the water:

   A. melts.
   B. freezes.
   C. boils.
   D. condenses.

C is correct. When the vapor pressure of a liquid is raised so it equals the pressure of the surroundings, it boils. Indeed, you might *define* boiling as the process that occurs when a liquid's vapor pressure is equal to the pressure of its surroundings. (You might also think of it as the process that occurs when all molecules of a liquid sample have sufficient kinetic energy to escape to the gas phase.)

114. Under standard pressure, 1.00 gram of water at 4° C occupies a smaller volume than it does at 25° C. Such a finding confirms that at 25° C water:

   A. has a lower density.
   B. has a higher vapor pressure.
   C. has a greater molecular weight.
   D. undergoes ionization.

A is correct. The question requires that you know the meaning of density in mathematical terms. Density represents mass per volume. If mass is constant, decreased volume means increased density; increased volume means decreased density.

The wrong answer choices: Choice B is true statement, but it doesn't explain how 1.00 g of water experiences a change in volume with a change in temperature. Choices C and D are wrong because temperature change has no bearing on molecular weight or ionization.

Questions 115 through 119 are NOT based on a descriptive passage.

115. How many orbitals are there in the *d* subshell of an atom?

A. 3
B. 5
C. 6
D. 10

B is correct. The *s* subshell has 1 orbital, the *p* subshell has 3, the *d* subshell 5, and the *f* subshell 7. Every orbital has "room" for 2 electrons and the *s* subshell therefore accommodates 2 electrons, the *p* subshell accommodates 6, the *d* accommodates 10 and the *f* 14.

116. A car of mass m is rolling down a ramp that is elevated at an angle of 60°. What is the magnitude of the car's acceleration parallel to the ramp?

A. $g \cos 60°$
B. $g \sin 60°$
C. $mg \cos 60°$
D. $mg \sin 60°$

B is correct. The force parallel to the ramp is equal to $mg \sin 60°$.

$$ma = mg \sin 60°$$
$$a = g \sin 60°$$

117. Which of the following is most stable?

A. Mg^-
B. Mg^0
C. Mg^+
D. Mg^{2+}

D is correct. Magnesium is most stable when its outermost electron shell is full. The shell fills when a magnesium ion loses two electrons and thus takes on the electron configuration of the noble gas neon, thereby achieving a "stable octet."

118. Which of the following is NOT a vector quantity?

    A. Force
    B. Energy
    C. Velocity
    D. Acceleration

B is correct. A vector quantity has magnitude *and direction*. Unlike the other listed quantities, energy has magnitude, but *no direction*.

119. The atomic radius of $_{11}^{22}$Na is approximately twice that of $_{18}^{40}$Ar, primarily because:

    A. the ionization energy of Ar is greater than that of Na.
    B. Ar is inert, whereas Na easily forms an ion.
    C. the valence electrons of Na are more effectively shielded from the nucleus than the valence electrons of Ar.
    D. Ar has 18 protons attracting its electrons, whereas Na has only 11 protons.

D is correct. Refer to the periodic table for this question. Within a period, movement from left to right normally corresponds to a decrease in atomic radius because additional protons "pull" on the outermost electrons.

The wrong answer choices: Choices A and B are wrong because ionization energy and chemical reactivity fail to explain the observed difference in atomic radii. Choice C is wrong because Na and Ar belong to the same period (horizontal row) of the periodic table. Their valence electrons experience equal shielding.

Passage IX (Questions 120-125)

120. What is the period of the wave produced by the tuning fork?

A. 0.0007 sec
B. 0.0025 sec
C. 0.0070 sec
D. 0.0400 sec

B is correct. Wave frequency refers to the number of cycles a wave produces over time. Period, on the other hand, refers to the time taken to complete one cycle. Period (T) is therefore the reciprocal of frequency.

$$T = 1/400 \text{ Hz} = .0025 \text{ s}$$

121. Which of the following figures best represents a standing sound wave inside the tube?

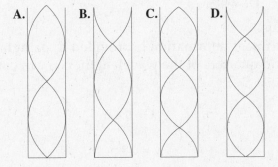

D is correct. Review physics and be reminded that a standing wave ordinarily forms a node at a fixed boundary and an antinode at an unfixed boundary. The closed end of the tube represents a fixed boundary, and the open end represents an unfixed boundary. Expect a node at the closed end of the tube and an antinode at the open end.

122. If the tube's diameter were increased, which of the following would be true regarding the period and/or frequency of the standing wave inside it?

    A. Its wavelength would increase.
    B. Its wavelength would decrease.
    C. Its period would increase.
    D. Its wavelength and period would remain unchanged.

D is correct. The wavelength and period of the tube will be affected by the length of the tube, but not the diameter.

123. As the water level in the tube is lowered, resonance occurs at intervals of 0.4 m. This implies that the speed of sound in air is:

    A. 160 m/s.
    B. 320 m/s.
    C. 390 m/s.
    D. 440 m/s.

B is correct. The pertinent information is provided in paragraph 1. Knowing that resonance occurs at odd quarters of the wavelength, you can conclude that:

$$\frac{1}{2}\lambda = 0.4 \text{ m}$$

$$\lambda = 0.8 \text{ m}$$

The frequency of the wave is provided to you:

$$v = f\lambda$$
$$v = (0.8 \text{ m})(400 \text{ Hz})$$
$$v = (0.8 \text{ m})(400 \text{ s}^{-1})$$
$$v = 320 \text{ m/s}$$

124. Assume the experiment is conducted in a room filled with helium. The density of helium gas is much less than that of air. What changes will occur to the standing wave?

   A. The distance between antinodes will increase.
   B. The distance between antinodes will decrease.
   C. The distance between antinodes will remain the same.
   D. No standing wave will form.

A is correct. A medium's composition and density determine the speed at which it facilitates wave propagation. Helium gas is less dense than air, so sound waves travel faster through helium than through air. Since you know that $v = \lambda f$; you know also that if v increases and f remains constant, λ must increase. Increased wavelength produces separation of antinodes.

125. Which of the following would indicate that the tuning fork is rapidly moving away from the end of the tube?

   A. The amplitude of the sound waves reaching the tube is greater than expected.
   B. The amplitude of the sound waves reaching the tube is less than expected.
   C. The frequency of the sound waves reaching the tube is greater than expected.
   D. The frequency of the sound waves reaching the tube is less than expected.

D is correct. The question refers to the Doppler effect. If a wave's source travels away from an observer, the frequency of the sound reaching the observer is less than the frequency emitted at the source. The Doppler effect does *not* change the amplitude of a wave.

Passage X (Questions 126-131)

126. A sample of gas is held in a container at constant temperature of 300°K, and gas is slowly removed from the container. Which of the following figures best depicts change in pressure as gas is removed?

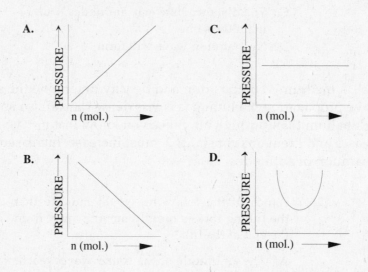

A is correct. According to the ideal gas equation, pressure is directly proportional to *n* (number of moles). As the number of moles of gas decreases, pressure must decrease. Look for a graph that depicts direct proportion. It should be linear and sloped upward.

The wrong answer choices: Choice B presents a graph that depicts inverse proportionality. Choices C and D do not show proportionality at all.

127. A researcher wishes to compare real gas behavior to gas behavior predicted by the ideal gas law. The researcher subjects a gas sample to relatively high pressure and then compares the pressure actually measured to that which would be predicted according to the ideal gas law. The pressure *actually measured* is probably:

   A. greater than that predicted by the ideal gas law because of repulsive forces among gas particles.
   B. greater than that predicted by the ideal gas law because of attractive forces among gas particles.
   C. less than that predicted by the ideal gas law because of repulsive forces among gas particles.
   D. less than that predicted by the ideal gas law because of attractive forces among gas particles.

D is correct. The ideal gas law is based on the assumptions that: (1) gas particles themselves have no volume, and (2) gas particles do not attract one another. In fact gas particles (1) do have (very small) volume of their own and (2) attract one another via van der Waals forces, dipole interactions, and London dispersion forces. Such attractive forces are especially significant under conditions of high pressure and produce actual pressures that are lower than those obtained via the ideal gas equation.

128. A decrease in the number of moles of a gas at constant temperature and volume will decrease which of the following unit measures?

   A. liters
   B. moles per liter
   C. Joules per mole
   D. Kelvins

B is correct. This question tests your knowledge of units. Consider the equation: $PV = nRT$. If T, R, and V are fixed, and n is decreased, it is true that the number of moles of gas per fixed volume decreases. In other words, there is a decrease in the number of moles per liter. P would also decrease, but no answer choice describes units of pressure such as atmospheres, mm Hg, or Torr.

129. Which of the following will likely demonstrate the greater departure from the behavior of an ideal gas: hydrogen gas or helium gas?

    A. Helium gas, because the van der Waals corrections are lower than for hydrogen.

    B. Helium gas, because it is an inert gas.

    C. Hydrogen gas, because the van der Waals corrections are greater than for helium.

    D. Hydrogen gas, because hydrogen shows decreased intermolecular forces at higher pressures.

C is correct. Paragraph 3 describes the corrections that apply to the ideal gas law. a and b are van der Waals constants. The table shows the values of a and b for He and H_2. Greater deviation from ideal gas behavior corresponds to greater values for a and b. The values of a and b are greater for hydrogen than for helium.

130. The pressure of a gas at a temperature of 27°C is measured to be P. If the temperature is increased to 127°C while all other factor are kept constant, what will be the new pressure of the gas?

    A. $\dfrac{1}{5}P$

    B. $\dfrac{3}{4}P$

    C. $\dfrac{4}{3}P$

    D. $5\,P$

C is correct. Remember that (1) temperature and pressure are directly proportional, and (2) that you must convert temperature to the kelvin scale.

$$P_2/P_1 = T_2/T_1$$

$$P_2 = \frac{400}{300}P_1$$

$$P_2 = \frac{4}{3}P_1$$

131. According to the passage, what would be the van der Waals correction for the volume of 2 moles of neon gas at very high pressure?

A. $V - (0.02370)$
B. $V - (0.0171)$
C. $V - (2)(0.02370)$
D. $V - (2)(0.0171)$

D is correct. In paragraph 3 you learn to correct the ideal gas law. V is replaced by $V - nb$, where n represents the number of moles in the sample and b is a constant listed in the table. For 2 moles of neon, the corrected volume should be $V - 2(0.0171)$.

The wrong answer choices: A and C are wrong because they use the constant for helium, not neon. B is wrong because it accounts for only one mole of neon.

Passage XI (Questions 132-137)

132. In the telescope pictured above, the objective lens is a:

A. converging lens and the eyepiece is a diverging lens.
B. converging lens and the eyepiece is a converging lens.
C. diverging lens and the eyepiece is a diverging lens.
D. diverging lens and the eyepiece is a converging lens.

B is correct. The illustration reveals that light rays are bent inward as they pass through both lenses. Both lenses cause the rays to converge.

133. An investigator works with a telescope equipped with a variety of removable lenses. Among the following combinations, the investigator will achieve greatest magnification with:

A. an objective with large focal length and an eyepiece with large focal length.
B. an objective with small focal length and an eyepiece with small focal length.
C. an objective with large focal length and an eyepiece with small focal length.
D. an objective with small focal length and an eyepiece with small focal length.

C is correct. The passage's last paragraph tells you that magnification is equal to the fraction: F(focal length objective lens)/f (focal length of eyepiece). Magnification is greatest when that fraction is greatest. Fractions, of course, increase with increasing numerator and decreasing denominator. Choice C represents a fraction with large numerator and small denominator.

134. An object is to be observed using only an eyepiece lens. If the object lies at a distance 1.5 cm from the eyepiece lens, the image will be located:

A. 1 cm from the eyepiece.
B. 2 cm from the eyepiece.
C. 3 cm from the eyepiece.
D. 6 cm from the eyepiece.

D is correct. Apply the lens equation:

$$1/f = 1/o + 1/i; \qquad 1/2 = 1/(1.5) + 1/i; \qquad i = 6$$

135. What is the power of the eyepiece of the telescope pictured above?

A. 2 diopters
B. 5 diopters
C. 20 diopters
D. 50 diopters

D is correct. The power of a lens in diopters is equal to the reciprocal of its focal length. Remember that focal length is measured in meters.

$$P = 1 / f = 1 / (0.02) = 50$$

136. If the objective lens were replaced with a lens composed of a material with a refractive index greater than 1.5, which of the following would be expected to occur?

    A. The focal length of the lens would decrease.
    B. The focal length of the lens would increase.
    C. The diameter of the lens would decrease.
    D. The diameter of the lens would increase.

A is correct. The focal point is the point at which incoming rays "meet" one another. A lens with a higher index of refraction would produce greater refraction of incoming light rays and thus cause the rays to meet "sooner." The increased refraction reduces focal length.

The wrong answer choices: Choice B makes a statement that is opposite to the truth. Choices C and D refer to lens diameter which is unrelated to refractive index.

137. The speed of light through glass:

    A. is greater than the speed of light in air.
    B. is less than the speed of light in air.
    C. may be greater or less than the speed of light in air.
    D. is equal to the speed of light in air.

B is correct. The speed of light in any medium is equal to F (speed of light in a vacuum)/n (refractive index of medium). For any medium, therefore, the speed at which it conducts light is inversely proportional to refractive index. A vacuum is said to have a refractive index of 1. All *matter* has a higher index. The refractive index of air is slightly greater than 1 and that of glass is a little greater still.

Questions 138 through 142 are NOT based on a descriptive passage.

138. Based on the table below, which of the following species is the strongest oxidizing agent?

Half-Reaction	Standard Potential
$Br_2(l) + 2e^- \rightarrow 2Br^-(aq)$	1.08
$Ag_2O(s) + H_2O + 2e \rightarrow 2Ag(s) + 2OH^-(aq)$	0.34
$Cu^{2+}(aq) + e^- \rightarrow Cu^+(aq)$	0.15
$H_2(g) + 2e^- \rightarrow 2H^-(aq)$	0.00

A. H_2
B. Cu^{2+}
C. Br_2
D. Ag_2O

C is correct. A strong oxidizing agent is itself readily reduced; it readily gives up electrons to a reducing agent. Among the listed species, Br_2, has the greatest reduction potential: 1.08 V. The table provides reduction potentials which, in turn, describes the species tendency to undergo reduction. Identify the species with the greatest reduction potential, and you have identified the strongest oxidizing agent.

139. An atom is in its ground state with all the orbitals filled through the second principal energy level ($n = 2$). How many electrons are contained in this atom?

A. 8
B. 10
C. 12
D. 14

B is correct. The question describes an atom for which the second shell is complete. That means the first shell is complete as well. The first shell contains only the s subshell (2 electrons). The second shell contains the s subshell (another 2 electrons) and the p subshell (6 electrons). 2 + 2 + 6 = 10. Alternatively, sketch the configuration that fills the second energy level:

$$1s^2 2s^2 2p^6; \ 2 + 2 + 6 = 10$$

140. A uranium-238 nucleus emits an alpha particle and decays to thorium-234. The alpha particle leaves the nucleus traveling 4.68×10^5 m/s. At what speed would the thorium nucleus recoil? (Note: Assume the masses of a proton and a neutron to be equal.)

A. 1.5×10^3 m/s
B. 4.0×10^3 m/s
C. 8.0×10^3 m/s
D. 2.5×10^4 m/s

C is correct. This question asks only that you understand conservation of momentum. Initial momentum = 0, so final momentum = 0.

$$m_1 v_1 = m_2 v_2$$
$$v_1 = m_2 v_2 / m_1$$
$$v_1 = (4 \text{ amu})(4.68 \times 10^5 \text{ m/s}) / (234 \text{ amu})$$
$$v_1 = 8 \times 10^3 \text{ m/s}$$

141. A constant current of 5 amperes is passing through a 10 ohm resistor. How much energy is dissipated in the resistor over the course of 10 seconds?

A. 250 J
B. 500 J
C. 1000 J
D. 2500 J

D is correct. Power is a measure of energy per unit of time. In electrical contexts, units are so defined as to allow for the expression of power as $P = I^2R = (5)^2(10)$ W = 250 J/s. We ascertain the dissipated energy when we multiply 250 J/s by the applicable time, 10 seconds: E = (250 J/s)(10 sec) = 2500 J.

142. As an ideal fluid flowing in a cylindrical pipe through a constant pressure differential moves from a region of larger diameter to a region of smaller diameter, which of the following will occur?

A. Flow will remain constant and fluid velocity will increase.

B. Flow will remain constant and fluid velocity will remain constant.

C. Flow will increase and fluid velocity will increase.

D. Flow will increase and fluid velocity will remain constant.

A is correct. Flow expresses the volume of fluid that passes a given point in a given time period. It is measured in units of volume per unit of time. For fluid flowing within a single ideal system, flow is constant at all points, even though the area or caliber of the conductor might vary from place to place. Where the conductor is narrow, flow has the same value it has where the conductor is wide. For any given length, a relatively narrow section of pipe or hose holds fewer molecules than does a relatively wide section. Since flow in one section is equal to flow in the other, the molecules in the narrow section must move through it at a relatively greater velocity.

WRITING SAMPLE EXPLANATIONS I

The following essays were written according to The Princeton Review's MCAT Essay Formula. As described in Part I, they are designed to make a "good impression" on a reader who will spend approximately *ninety seconds* evaluating them. Notice that each essay:

- performs, in appropriate order, all three "tasks" described in the MCAT instructions,

- provides frequent paragraphing,

- uses formal language, and

- cites a quotation from some famed authority.

WRITING SAMPLE EXAMPLE #1

PEOPLE GET THE GOVERNMENT THEY DESERVE.

Essay:

The statement indicates that in all societies people constitute the ultimate power, that they bear responsibility for their destiny, and that a government, however corrupt or abusive, reflects that which the people choose or tolerate. (The notion that people are generally responsible for their own fate is manifest also in Mohandas K. Gandhi's remark that "Good government is no substitute for self-government.")

If in a democracy a legislature or leader should fail to serve the people's interest, the people might be said to "deserve" the result because it is they who vote. Likewise, it might be argued that even a totalitarian dictator is incapable of installing *himself* in power. He must at some point have the active or passive approval of the citizenry.

In order specifically to describe a situation in which the statement does not apply, one need only recognize that the words "people" and "deserve" are inherently ambiguous. The statement pivots on these words, and its applicability depends on the meanings attached to them.

As used in the statement, "people" is subject to interpretation. No government comes to power with the unanimous approval of the populace, and in many situations, past and present, minority political groups have sought actively to overthrow a sitting government. It is unfair to suggest, for example, that occupied

Europe's underground movements were in any way responsible for Nazi governance. Participants in such movements sought aggressively to defeat the Nazis, and in no sense can they be said to have "deserved" life under the occupying power even though they were *people* and for a time it was their government.

The word "deserve" also harbors ambiguity. If it carries some *moral* implication then it is proper to say that there are a great many situations to which the statement does not apply. The fact that a people should be ignorant, naive, or misguided does not mean that they are morally deficient or that in some moral sense they "deserve" a government hostile to their interests.

For example, during the 1988 presidential election campaign many Americans were misled by one candidate's promise of "no new taxes" and did not believe those who warned them that new taxes would be necessary regardless of who became president. When the candidate won, he broke his promise. Voters who were then disturbed by tax increases did not deserve their disappointment in the sense that they were bad or evil for believing that a candidate would keep his word.

Hence the pertinence of the statement depends in large measure on the meaning attached to its language. If "people" refers to the majority of the people, and if "deserve" refers only to the concept of responsibility, then perhaps the statement represents a meaningful comment. If however, "people" means *all people* and "deserve" imparts some moral justice, the statement is not a useful insight.

WRITING SAMPLE EXAMPLE #2
HONESTY IS ESSENTIAL TO FRIENDSHIP.
Essay:

The statement indicates that a genuine bond of friendship requires truthfulness and that in its absence friendship is false. (The statement seems implicitly, also, to extol true friendship as Ben Jonson did when he wrote, "True happiness consists not in the multitude of friends but in the worth and choice.") The statement suggests that two people are not truly friends, for example, if they are unable to confide in one another or if one habitually deceives the other.

In order specifically to describe a situation in which the statement does not apply, one need only recognize that the words "honesty" and "friendship" are inherently ambiguous. The statement pivots on these words, and its applicability depends on the meanings attached to them.

As used in the statement, "honesty" is subject to interpretation. There is probably no person living or dead who has ever revealed to any other person all the details of every thought or experience he has ever had. It is doubtful that any person is capable of such openness. It probably is not fair to suggest that one who has difficulty sharing certain of his thoughts and feelings cannot have and cannot be a friend.

Furthermore, there are occasions on which total truthfulness between two persons would violate the confidence of a third. One who has been trusted with the secret of another in a personal or professional context is wrong to reveal it even to a true friend. One's friendship with another person is not impaired because he guards the secret of a third. Indeed, if that were not so, one could never have more than one friend.

The word "friendship" also harbors ambiguity. In some contexts the term simply describes social acquaintances. In others it imports deep, long-lasting, confidential relations. Social acquaintances can and do proceed on only small amounts of honesty. Hence when a "group of old high school friends" gets together for a reunion, it can scarcely be said that a high degree of personal honesty is essential to their interaction. Yet they still might call themselves "friends." Deep confidential relationships, on the other hand, do call for a significant commitment to truthfulness, and friendship conceived in that sense does require honesty.

Hence the pertinence of the statement depends in large measure on the meaning attached to its language. The statement represents a legitimate comment if "honesty" refer to a substantial commitment to truthfulness (with due regard for the rights of others) and if "friendship" refers to relatively deep and confidential relationships. If however, "honesty" means total candor in all respects and "friendship" denotes any and every relationship tagged with the label "friend," the statement does not furnish a useful insight.

BIOLOGICAL SCIENCES EXPLANATIONS I

Passage I (Questions 143-148)

143. In humans, the peptide bonds of ingested proteins are first cleaved by which of the following enzymes?

   A. Lactase
   B. Pepsin
   C. Dipeptidase
   D. Lipase

B is correct. The question has nothing to do with the passage. To answer correctly you need only know this: pepsin is the gastric enzyme that initially cleaves peptide bonds.

The wrong answer choices: After you've studied digestive enzymes, you'll know that choices A and D are wrong because lactase and lipase do not act on proteins, but on other substrates. Dipeptidases cleave dipeptides in the small intestine.

144. Colloid pressure tends to draw fluid into the blood vessels by:

   A. passive diffusion along a concentration gradient.
   B. passive diffusion along an electrical gradient.
   C. facilitated transport along an electrochemical gradient.
   D. active diffusion, mediated by an ATP-dependent pump.

A is correct. This question requires that you read paragraph 2. The protein concentration gradient between the interior of blood vessels and interstitial fluid produces passive diffusion.

The wrong answer choices: Choice B is wrong because the gradient is not electrical. Choices C and D are wrong because in this case fluid movement depends on neither a carrier molecule nor the expenditure of energy.

145. A professor theorized that if a patient's capillaries became suddenly permeable to protein, the patient would manifest edema. Is this a plausible hypothesis?

A. No; fluid will move across a membrane only in response to an ion gradient.

B. No; protein permeability would have no effect on hydrostatic pressure within the blood vessel.

C. Yes; protein in the interstitial space would fuel the active transport of fluid into the interstitial space.

D. Yes; colloid pressure inside the capillaries would decrease, and fluid would leak into the interstitial space.

D is correct. You'll find the relevant information in paragraph 2. The presence of protein in the interstitial space would draw water in an "attempt" to balance the colloid pressure differences.

The wrong answer choices: Choices A and B should be eliminated because they present false statements. Why do we say that? Because fluid may move across a membrane in response to a number of influences. An ion gradient is only *one* such influence. Protein permeability will alter hydrostatic pressure within a blood vessel. Choice C is wild and unjustified.

146. The blood proteins that produce colloid pressure are synthesized by a sequential mechanism that involves the direct activity of:

A. cellular proteases.

B. smooth endoplasmic reticulum.

C. messenger RNA.

D. cytochromes.

C is correct. The question is unrelated to the passage. It draws on your knowledge of the fact that messenger RNA directs protein synthesis from amino acid constituents.

The wrong answer choices: After studying cellular biology, you'll know that choices A, B, and D are wrong because none is associated with protein synthesis: Proteases degrade protein, smooth endoplasmic reticulum forms part of the intracellular membrane, and cytochromes are a part of the electron transport chain.

147. Given the results of Experiments 1 and 2, a researcher would be most justified in concluding that:

    A. Cadaver D had a higher protein concentration in its interstitial fluid than did Cadavers A, B, or C.
    B. Cadaver A contained more interstitial fluid than did Cadaver B which contained more interstitial fluid than did Cadaver C.
    C. Cadavers A, B, and C were composed of at least 50 percent interstitial fluid by weight.
    D. Cadaver C was composed of approximately 80 percent interstitial fluid by weight.

C is correct. The tables show that all three cadavers had a weight of at least 60 kg before infusion began and that all had a weight of less than 30 kg after 70 minutes. During the interim, interstitial fluid was removed from all cadavers. That means that all of the cadavers were originally composed of at least 50 percent interstitial fluid (because at least *half* of the total weight in fluid was drawn off from each of cadavers A, B, and C).

The wrong answer choices: Choices A, B, and D are wrong simply because there is nothing in the table that supports any of the statements they represent.

148. If, in a normal patient, proteins were suddenly infused into the interstitial space, which of the following physiological compensations could prevent the resulting edema?

    A. Reduction of hydrostatic pressure within the blood vessels
    B. Passive diffusion of proteins from the blood vessels to the interstitial space
    C. Facilitated diffusion of protein from the blood vessels to the interstitial space
    D. Increased protein synthesis within the red blood cells

A is correct. Paragraph 2 explains hydrostatic force. Reduced hydrostatic pressure within the blood vessels decreases the fluid volume forced into the interstitial space.

The wrong answer choices: Choices B and C are wrong because paragraph 2 states that in a normal person blood vessels are impermeable to protein. That means neither passive nor facilitative diffusion will move protein from blood vessels to the interstitial fluid. Choice D is wrong because red blood cells do not directly regulate fluid balance between blood cells and interstitial space.

Passage II (Questions 149-155)

149. Formation of ATP from ADP and inorganic phosphate occurs via:

    A. hydrolysis, which involves the removal of a molecule of water.
    B. hydrolysis, which involves the addition of a molecule of water.
    C. dehydration synthesis, which involves the removal of a molecule of water.
    D. dehydration synthesis, which involves the addition of a molecule of water.

C is correct. Once you review organic chemistry, you will recall that phosphate is added to ADP in the process of dehydration synthesis, in which a molecule of water is removed.

150. Which of the following phosphorous-containing compounds can entirely circumvent the effects of rotenone, as seen in Figure 1?

    A. $FADH_2$
    B. Both NADH and ADP
    C. Both ADP and $FADH_2$
    D. $FADH_2$, NADH, and ADP

A is correct. According to Figure 1, $FADH_2$ enters the respiratory chain *after* the step at which rotenone acts. Therefore, application of rotenone has no effect on the activity of $FADH_2$.

The wrong answer choices: Choices B and D are incorrect. The first ADP enters the respiratory chain at the point where rotenone would effectively inhibit it, and NADH would be affected in the second step of the respiratory chain. Choice C also is wrong. ADP does not entirely escape inhibition by rotenone, while $FADH_2$ does.

151. Aerobic organisms generate the greatest number of ATPs when monosaccharide oxidation produces:

    A. reduced levels of antioxidants.
    B. reduced forms of NAD^+ and FAD.
    C. oxidized forms of ATP and GTP.
    D. oxidized forms of NADH and $FADH_2$.

B is correct. Paragraph 1 tells you that NADH and $FADH_2$ transfer electrons to produce ATP. NADH and $FADH_2$ can be referred to as reduced forms of NAD^+ and FAD. In other words, the reduced form of a molecule is associated with H^+ and has potential for greatest energy release.

The wrong answer choices: Choices A and C should be eliminated. They're wild and irrelevant. Choice D is also incorrect. Oxidized forms of NADH and $FADH_2$ correspond to NAD^+ and FAD. These molecules have already lost their H^+ and with it their potential for energy release.

152. A substance that inhibits NADH-Q reductase will have no effect if the cell is adequately supplied with which phosphorous-containing compound?

    A. $FADH_2$
    B. NADPH
    C. ADP
    D. NADH

A is correct. The diagram indicates that $FADH_2$ bypasses inhibition of NADH-Q reductase. That's because $FADH_2$ enters the respiratory chain *beyond* the site of NADH-Q reductase inhibition. (A blocked bridge won't stop you from reaching your destination if your route *doesn't cross the bridge*.)

The wrong answer choices: Choice B should be eliminated because NADPH is not a component of the respiratory chain. Choices C and D are wrong because NADH and ADP enter the respiratory chain "upstream" of the site at which NADH-Q reductase inhibition occurs.

153. The presence of fully functioning respiratory chains in the mitochondrial extracts was vital to the success of the experiment. If cytochrome c_1 had been missing, the researcher most likely would have found that:

A. extra cytochrome c had accumulated.
B. NADH and $FADH_2$ could not enter the system.
C. Antimycin A had produced increased oxygen consumption.
D. Antimycin A had had no effect.

D is correct. Figure 1 shows you that antimycin A blocks the step bridging cytochrome b and cytochrome c_1. If cytochrome c_1 were missing, then that step of the respiratory chain "connecting" cytochrome b to cytochrome c_1 would fail before exposure to antimycin A.

The wrong answer choices: Choice A should be eliminated because it's wild. cytochrome c is a component of the respiratory chain and does not vary in number in response to changes in other respiratory chain components. Choice B makes a false statement. Entry of NADH and $FADH_2$ into the respiratory chain is not affected by absence of cytochrome c_1 farther down the chain. Choice C makes also a false statement. The passage states that the effect of antimycin A is to *decrease* oxygen consumption.

154. To further characterize cytochrome b, the researchers reacted its sulfur-containing amino acids with performic acid and then broke apart the polypeptide into individual amino acid residues. The most likely means of performing this latter task is to:

A. reduce cysteine residues.
B. decarboxylate acidic residues.
C. oxidize amide linkages.
D. hydrolyze amide linkages.

D is correct. After reviewing the biochemistry of cells, you'll know that a "peptide bond" is an "amide bond." (It's the amide bond that holds amino acids together to make proteins.) If one hydrolyzes peptide bonds, one is hydrolyzing amide bonds.

The wrong answer choices: Choice A should be eliminated. It's wild and irrelevant. Choice B is also wrong. The process of breaking a polypeptide into its component amino acids does not involve decarboxylation. Choice C can be eliminated because the breakage of an amide linkage occurs through *hydrolysis*, not oxidation.

155. The heme portions of cytochrome molecules are able to transfer electrons among themselves because of:

   A. thioether linkages.
   B. pi-electron delocalization.
   C. enol-intermediate racemization.
   D. shortened bond length.

B is correct. The question is unrelated to the passage. It requires that you know that the heme portions of cytochromes are characterized by pi-electron delocalization which stabilize the structure.

The wrong answer choices: Choice A is incorrect. Thioethers are thiol derivatives and are not associated with heme resonance structure. Choice C is also wrong. An enol-intermediate represents one of the forms that carbonyl molecules assume. It is *not* associated with heme resonance structure. Choice D is wild and irrelevant.

Passage III (Questions 156-160)

156. Which of the following best describes the appearance of *Lactobacillus* when stained and then viewed with a light microscope?

   A. Spherical
   B. S-shaped
   C. Rodlike
   D. Asymmetrical

C is correct. There is nothing in the passage that helps you answer this question. You need only know that *Lactobacillus* belongs to the bacterial group "bacilli." After reviewing microbiology, you'll recall that bacilli are rod-shaped.

The wrong answer choices: Choices A and B are wrong because spherically shaped and S-shaped bacteria describe the appearance of cocci and spirilli, respectively. Choice D is wrong because symmetry of form has no bearing on the classification of bacteria.

157. The proliferation of *Lactobacillus* in milk samples indicates:

    A. high lactose concentration.
    B. a drop in the pH.
    C. predominance of spore-forming bacteria.
    D. the absence of *Streptococcus faecalis*.

B is correct. Paragraph 1 describes the environmental conditions that promote growth of *Lactobacilli*. A reduced pH provides a receptive environment for *Lactobacilli*.

The wrong answer choices: Choice A should be eliminated because it contradicts paragraph 1, which tells you that lactose must be converted to lactic acid to spur *Lactobacilli* growth. Choices C and D are wrong because in relation to the growth of *Lactobacillus*, the passage does not mention spore forming bacteria or *Streptococcus faecalis*.

158. If one of the raw milk samples were heated to 100° C for 30 minutes and then incubated, which of the following graphs would best represent resulting, spore-forming and nonspore-forming bacteria populations?

A.

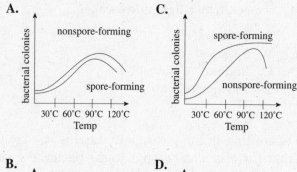

C.

B.

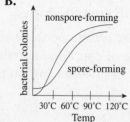

D.

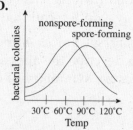

C is correct. The essential information is provided in paragraph 1. You're told that pasteurization kills nonspore-forming bacteria. You may infer that spore-forming bacteria are better able to resist the high temperatures of pasteurization.

The wrong answer choices: Choices A and B should be eliminated because the graphs they present indicate high survival rates for the nonspore-forming bacteria. Paragraph 1 states that nonspore-forming bacteria do *not* survive pasteurization. Choice D is wrong because it indicates that pasteurization kills spore-forming bacteria.

159. The gram-staining procedure used in the laboratory enables the inspector to:

   A. identify bacterial species present in the incubate.
   B. distinguish between aerobic and anaerobic organisms.
   C. differentiate pathogenic from nonpathogenic colonies.
   D. distinguish between bacterial and viral organisms.

A is correct. The question has nothing to do with the passage. It requires that you review microbiology and know that gram staining will allow bacterial identification.

The wrong answer choices: Choices B and C are wrong because gram staining does not elucidate metabolic processes. Choice D should be eliminated because gram staining targets bacteria, not viruses.

160. Which of the following environmental factors will affect the growth of *S. faecalis*?

   I. Nutritional content of the milk
   II. The process of pasteurization
   III. Ambient oxygen concentration

   A. I only
   B. I and II only
   C. I and III only
   D. I, II, and III

A is correct. The relevant information is provided in paragraph 1. You're told that *S. faecalis* grows in milk, which contains emulsified fat droplets. Therefore, option I is correct. Option II is incorrect because *S. faecalis* is a *spore-forming* bacteria. The passage states that pasteurization kills *non*spore-forming bacteria. Option III also is wrong. *S. faecalis* is *anaerobic*; it does not require oxygen.

Questions 161 through 166 are NOT based on a descriptive passage

161. The *eclipsed* conformation of *n*-butane is illustrated below, in the figure on the left. Which of the circled positions in the figure on the right corresponds to the terminal methyl group in the *anti* conformation?

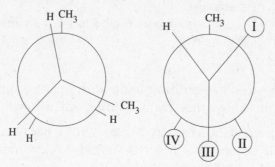

A. I
B. II
C. III
D. IV

C is correct. Butane has two methyl groups that rotate freely about the carbon-carbon single bond. When it comes to butane, the *eclipsed* conformation means that the methyl groups overlap. The *anti* conformation means the methyl groups are situated "across" from one another. With reference to the picture, the position that's directly across from the *n*-butane's methyl group is position III. That's why C is right.

162. All of the following structures secrete enzymes that serve digestive functions EXCEPT the:

A. pancreas.
B. stomach.
C. thymus.
D. salivary glands.

C is correct. After reviewing mammalian physiology, you'll know that the thymus is a site at which lymphocytes mature.

The wrong answer choices: Choices A, B, and D are wrong because all of the named structures produce enzymes important to digestion. The pancreas secretes enzymes that decompose starch, protein, and fat. The stomach secretes pepsin, which digests protein. The salivary glands secrete amylase, which digests starch.

163. Alkyl halides are more reactive than their corresponding alkanes because the halides more
readily participate in:

    A. pyrolysis.
    B. combustion reactions.
    C. hydrophobic bonding.
    D. nucleophilic substitution.

D is correct. Alkyl halides are more reactive than their corresponding alkanes because they all feature the functional group OH^-, which makes them readily susceptible to nucleophilic substitution. That's why D is right.

The wrong answer choices: Choice A is wrong because pyrolysis refers to decomposition by heat. Alkyl halides are no more susceptible to that sort of decomposition than are the alkanes. Choice B is wrong because combustion refers to reaction with oxygen (burning) to produce carbon dioxide and water. Alkyl halides are no more combustible than are their corresponding alkanes. Choice C is wrong because there is no such thing as "hydrophobic bonding."

164. When lettuce is placed in deionized water it
remains crisp because:

    A. the cells lose H_2O.
    B. the cells swell with H_2O.
    C. the stomates close in response to excess
water.
    D. the chloroplasts generate greater levels of
ATP.

B is correct. After reviewing cell membranes, you'll know that a medium of pure water is hypotonic compared with a cell placed within it. Water will enter the cell in an "attempt" to balance the high solute concentration within the cell.

The wrong answer choices: Choice A is wrong for this reason: Water would leave the cell only if the cell's solute concentration were *lower* than that of its surrounding medium. Choice C is wrong because stomata tend to *open* in the presence of water. Choice D is wrong because chloroplast activity is irrelevant to the question.

165. Among the following, which statement(s) can be said to apply to the molecule depicted schematically below?

$$
\begin{array}{c}
\text{Br} \\
| \\
\text{H} - \text{C} - \text{CH}_3 \\
| \\
\text{CH}_2\text{Cl}
\end{array}
$$

    I. It rotates the plane of polarized light to the left.

    II. It exhibits chirality.

    III. It is optically active.

A. I only

B. I and II only

C. I and III only

D. II and III only

   D is correct. The molecule is made up of a carbon bonded to four different substituents. A carbon so situated constitutes a "chiral center" and the entire molecule itself is "chiral." A chiral molecule is optically active, which means that it rotates the plane of polarized light *either* to the right or left. However, one cannot ascertain the actual direction of rotation except by resorting to a polarimeter or by knowing *a priori* the direction in which the molecule's enantiomer ("mirror image molecule") rotates polarized light. That's why options II and III apply and option I does not.

166. Which statement below most accurately describes the characteristic features of striated muscle cells?

    A. Striated muscle cells are stimulated by the autonomic nervous system and contain few mitochondria.
    B. Striated muscle cells are mononucleate and arranged in syncytial bundles.
    C. Striated muscle cells have alternating A-bands and I-bands arranged in a transverse pattern.
    D. Striated muscle cells are similar to smooth muscle cells except they lack internal stores of calcium.

C is correct. After reviewing the musculoskeletal system, you'll know that striated muscle cells contain "thick filaments" that correspond to the sarcomere's A-band and "thin filaments" that correspond to its I-band.

The wrong answer choices: Choice A is wrong because striated muscle cells are not stimulated by the *autonomic* nervous system. They're stimulated by the *somatic* nervous system. Choices B and D are wrong because striated muscle cells are multinucleate and are structurally dissimilar to smooth muscle cells (although both smooth and striated muscle cells store calcium).

Passage IV (Questions 167-171)

167. Which of the following treatments would NOT effectively treat candidal infections?

    A. Administration of a drug that attacks the outer cell wall of the fungus
    B. Administration of a drug that interferes with fungal replication and transcription
    C. Exposure to a bacteriotoxic agent
    D. Exposure to oral fungistatic drugs

C is correct. The passage states that candidiasis is caused by a fungus, not a bacteria, so a bacteriotoxic agent would not effectively treat the condition.

The wrong answer choices: Choices A, B, and D all describe an *effective* treatment for candidal infection.

168. Attacking the gamete-producing stage of candida does NOT rid the body of candidal infection because:

A. the fungus does not reproduce by the formation of gametes.
B. the fungus can be killed only during periods of asexual reproduction via budding.
C. the fungus produces gametes that are insensitive to all known drugs.
D. the fungus most often exists in a form that reproduces asexually.

D is correct. This question requires that you read paragraph 2, which tells you that candida can divide asexually. Asexual reproduction involves *no* gametes. Therefore, one could *not* control the infection by attacking candida's gamete-producing stage.

The wrong answer choices: Choice A is wrong because paragraph 2 tells you that candida do produce gametes. Choices B and C should be eliminated because they represent false statements. The passage does not state that asexual reproduction is the only target of drugs, nor does it mention a drug-insensitive gamete.

169. 5-FC attacks the candida fungus by decreasing:

A. the availability of ATP.
B. the availability of DNA and RNA precursors.
C. the availability of necessary amino acids.
D. the availability of 5-FU.

B is correct. Paragraph 3 tells you that 5-FC leads to a decrease in thymidine formation. After reviewing molecular biology you'll know that thymidine is a precursor to *both* DNA and RNA.

The wrong answer choices: Choices A, C, and D are wrong. With reference to the effect of 5-FC, the passage does not mention ATP availability, amino acid availability, or 5-FU availability.

170. After absorption of 5-FC, which step must then occur for 5-FC to terminate DNA synthesis?

   A. One pyrimidine must be substituted for another pyrimidine.
   B. A purine must be converted into a pyrimidine.
   C. Uracil must be converted into thymidine.
   D. Thymidylate synthetase must be phosphorylated to be inactivated.

A is correct. Paragraph 4 provides the relevant text. It tells you that candida cells convert 5-FC to 5-FU. After reviewing cell biochemistry you'll know that both cytosine and uracil are pyrimidines.

The wrong answer choices: Choice B is incorrect because 5-FC is not a purine; it's a pyrimidine. Choice C should be eliminated because it distorts information in the passage. You're told that 5-FU *inhibits* production of thymidine. It doesn't *become* thymidine. Choice D should be eliminated too; with reference to thymidylate synthetase, phosphorylation and inactivation are not mentioned.

171. According to the passage, the yeast form of candida in the human body reproduces by retaining:

   A. the same number of chromosomes per nucleus, while randomly dividing the genome between two daughter cells.
   B. the same number of chromosomes per nucleus, without randomly dividing the genome between two daughter cells.
   C. half the number of chromosomes per nucleus, without randomly dividing the genome between two daughter cells.
   D. half the number of chromosomes per nucleus, while randomly dividing the genome between two daughter cells.

B is correct. The relevant text is in paragraph 2, which tells you that candida divide primarily by asexual budding. After reviewing cell division, you'll recall that mitosis gives rise to *non*random division of the genome.

The wrong answer choices: Choice A can be eliminated because asexual reproduction proceeds by mitosis. In the process of mitosis, genetic material is *not* divided randomly. Choice C is also incorrect. Mitosis does not involve a halving of genetic material. Choice D represents *both* inaccuracies set forth in choices A and C.

Passage V (Questions 172-178)

172. Which of the following ovarian cell organelles will show the greatest levels of activity during the secretion of estrogen?

    A. Lysosomes
    B. Golgi apparatus
    C. Centrioles
    D. Ribosomes

B is correct. The question is entirely unrelated to the passage. It requires that you remember that the Golgi apparatus *packages* steroids (and other substances) destined for secretion. In an actively secreting cell, the Golgi apparatus is busy.

The wrong answer choices: Choice A is incorrect because lysosomes contain and degrade "old and worn-out" cell structures. Choice C is wrong because centrioles are involved in reproduction (microtubules). Choice D can be eliminated because ribosomes are active in *protein* synthesis.

173. Which test groups showed the greatest levels of estrogen synthesis and secretion?

    I. Onset of menstruation
    II. Ovulation peak
    III. Pregnancy, 160 days
    IV. Pregnancy, term

    A. I and III only
    B. I and IV only
    C. II and III only
    D. III and IV only

D is correct. This question requires that you consider Table 1, keeping a particularly close watch over the relevant units. Look at the test groups labeled "pregnancy, 160 days" and "pregnancy, term." For these two groups, estrogen secretion is measured in mg. In all other test groups, estrogen level is measured in µg, a smaller unit. Once you're alerted to the units, you can see that the two named test groups do show the highest levels of estrogen synthesis and secretion. That's why options III and IV are correct.

174. From Table 1, which variable would prove to be the best marker for the term stage of normal pregnancy, as indicated by the Kober test?

   A. The oxidation of estradiol
   B. The presence of estriol
   C. The presence of 16∝-hydroxyestrone
   D. A positive Kober reaction

C is correct. The question calls for some common sense. Table 1 shows you that 16∝-hydroxyestrone appears only for the test group labeled "pregnancy, term." Hence, it would *tell you* that a patient is in the term stage of pregnancy. That's another way of saying 16∝-hydroxyestrone acts as an *indicator* for the term stage of pregnancy.

The wrong answer choices: Choice A should be eliminated. With reference to the term stage of pregnancy, the passage does not mention estradiol oxidation. Choice B is incorrect because estriol is present in *all* test groups. Choice D is also wrong. A positive Kober test indicates only that estrogen is present, and estrogen is present in *all* test groups.

175. Would estrogen levels in males increase at the onset of puberty?

   A. Yes, because the increased levels of testosterone in the pubertal male are partially converted to estrogens.
   B. Yes, because estrogen is the predominant male sex hormone produced by pubertal males.
   C. No, because estrogen hormones are not produced in human males.
   D. No, because estrogen concentration does not vary from pre-puberty to puberty in the male.

A is correct. Your review of the endocrine system will remind you that in males testosterone can be converted to estrogen.

The wrong answer choices: Choices B and C should be eliminated. Testosterone, not estrogen, is the main sex hormone produced by pubertal males, and choice C is false. Choice D makes a false statement because estrogen levels may vary from previous levels at the onset of male puberty.

176. In Table 1, which of the following pairs of subject groups showed the greatest difference in the ratio of estrone to 16-epiestriol levels?

    A. Pregnancy/160 days and post-menopause

    B. Pregnancy/term and pregnancy/160 days

    C. Post-menopause and pregnancy/160 days

    D. Onset of menstruation and post-menopause

B is correct. Only one of the choices sets forth a ratio of estrone to 16-epiestriol levels. That's because only one choice considers the test group "pregnancy, term"—the only stage of the cycle at which 16-epiestriol appears.

177. What change in the ratio of estrone to estradiol is expected to occur as women enter post-menopause, according to the passage?

    A. The ratio increases, because estradiol levels decrease relatively more than estrone levels decrease.

    B. The ratio increases, because estradiol levels decrease while estrone levels are unaffected.

    C. The ratio is unchanged, because both estrogen hormone levels decrease in the postmenopausal period.

    D. The ratio decreases, because estrone levels decrease more than estradiol levels.

A is correct. Table 1 provides the relevant information. For premenopausal women, the ratio of estrone to estradiol levels is approximately 2:1. For postmenopausal women, it's about 4:1.

178. Researchers further studied estrogen levels in subjects at the luteal minimum of estrogen secretion and at the 210th day of pregnancy. Which findings would NOT indicate a trend similar to that found during the original procedures?

A. The levels of estriol are greater than the levels of estradiol in both pregnant and luteal minimum groups.
B. The levels of estradiol are lower than those of estrone in the pregnant group.
C. The estrone levels are elevated in the pregnant group compared with the luteal minimum group.
D. The ratio of 16-epiestriol levels between the pregnant and luteal minimum groups is 1:2.

D is correct. According to Table 1, 16-epiestriol appears *only* at the term stage of pregnancy and not at anything called the "luteal minimum stage." The results listed in choice D would contradict the data in the table.

The wrong answer choices: Choices A, B, and C are wrong because each of the named findings is consistent with the data set forth in Table 1.

Passage VI (Questions 179-184)

179. When alkyl halides react with potassium hydroxide to yield alkene derivatives, the potassium hydroxide acts as:

   A. an acid.
   B. a base.
   C. a proton donor.
   D. a reductant.

B is correct. Once you review elimination reactions, you'll recall that an alkene may be formed from an alkyl halide in the presence of a strong base, like OH⁻. Consider, for example, ethylchloride:

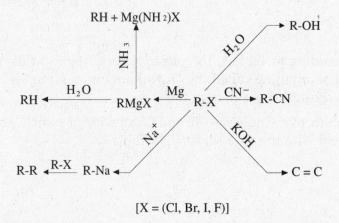

[X = (Cl, Br, I, F)]

The OH⁻ removes a proton from the first carbon, leaving it with a lone pair of electrons. This lone pair then moves between the two carbons, where it forms a double bond and simultaneously removes the chloride atom from the second carbon.

The wrong answer choices: Choices A and C should be eliminated because OH⁻ is not an acid and certainly cannot *donate* a proton. Choice D is wrong because the OH⁻ does not *reduce* the carbon.

180. If one were to substitute heavy water D_2O in the last steps of the Grignard reaction, the reaction would lead to the synthesis of:

A. R-R.
B. R-OD.
C. R-D.
D. R-H.

C is correct. After you study alkyl halides and their reactions, you'll know that alkyl halides can react with water (undergo hydrolysis) to yield a hydrocarbon and a metal hydroxide. Remember that "heavy water" is designated: D_2O.

So, $RX + D_2O \rightarrow RD + XOD$.

The wrong answer choices: Choice A should be eliminated since individual alkyl groups won't react with one another. Choice B is wrong because water's oxygen provides a *binding site* for the halide. The oxygen does not *replace* the halide or bond with the central carbon. You would also eliminate Choice D pretty quickly if you remembered that heavy water is D_2O and contains deuterium instead of hydrogen.

181. Alkyl halides are not usually prepared by direct halogenation of alkanes because:

A. alkanes are not very reactive compounds.
B. alkanes have low boiling points.
C. alkanes are desaturated by halogenation.
D. alkanes do not dissolve in polarized solutions.

A is correct. After you study the alkanes and their reactions, you'll know that alkanes are *not* terribly reactive. Direct halogenation of an alkane occurs only under special conditions of extremely high temperatures or in the presence of certain light wavelengths.

The wrong answer choices: Choice B makes a true statement, but it does not explain why direct halogenation is not generally used to prepare alkyl halides. Choice C is wrong because desaturation refers to the addition of multiple bonds. Alkanes don't have double bonds. Choice D makes a true statement, but, like Choice B, it fails to answer the question.

182. The synthesis of ethane from methyl bromide
     requires the addition of:

   A. Mg and H_2O.
   B. Mg and RCH_2Cl.
   C. Na^+ and RCH_2Cl.
   D. Na^+ and CH_3Br.

A is correct. The question requires that you refer to Figure 1. It shows that R-X becomes a Grignard reagent (RMgX) when Mg is added. When H_2O is added, the Grignard reagent is converted to an alkane.

The wrong answer choices: Choice B is wrong because a Grignard reagent does not react with an alkyl halide. Organometallic compounds like Grignard's reagent generally react with water, diatomic halogens, oxygen, or metal salts (MX) only. Figure 1 shows you that Choices C and D are wrong. Reaction of R-X with Na^+ and then with R-X produces an elongated alkane.

183. Alkyl halides are insoluble in water because:

   A. they are hydrophilic.
   B. they are ionic compounds.
   C. they are unable to form hydrogen bonds.
   D. they contain electron-withdrawing groups.

C is correct. This question is unrelated to the passage. It requires that you know something about hydrogen bonding, polarity, and their relationship to water solubility. Solubility in water *requires* polarity. If alkyl halides could form hydrogen bonds they would necessarily be polar and, hence, soluble in water.

The wrong answer choices: Choice A is wrong because hydrophilic *means* water-soluble. Choice B is wrong because alkyl halide bonds are generally covalent. Choice D is true, but it is irrelevant and does not answer the question.

184. Identification of alkyl halides is based on all of the following physical properties EXCEPT:

    A. boiling point.
    B. density.
    C. spectroscopy.
    D. mass.

D is correct. Compounds do not have inherent mass. Any given *sample* of a compound has a mass. But there is no such thing as a "compound's mass." (Compounds do, of course, have density and specific gravity, but that is not the same as mass.)

The wrong answer choices: Choices A and B are wrong because alkanes do have boiling points and densities. When you review alkane chemistry you'll know that, and such properties are useful in identifying alkanes. Choice C is wrong because a spectrum of IR absorptions positively identifies the presence of the "R-X stretch."

Passage VII (Questions 185-190)

185. Which of the following would NOT account for elevated levels of insulin in the blood?

    A. Ingesting a heavy meal
    B. Injecting insulin at bedtime
    C. Arising after an all-night fast
    D. Breaking a fast

C is correct. Paragraph 2 provides the relevant information. You're told that insulin is secreted into the blood stream in response to high glucose levels. After a fast, glucose levels would be *low*, not high.

The wrong answer choices: Choices A and D are wrong because ingesting a meal or *breaking* a fast would increase blood glucose. The increased glucose concentration would precipitate insulin secretion. Choice B is wrong because an insulin injection would naturally elevate insulin blood levels.

186. Which of the following individuals would have the highest levels of glucagon in the blood stream?

    A. A man running in the last third of a marathon
    B. A pregnant woman after eating breakfast
    C. A bedridden patient two hours after a meal
    D. A child after eating dessert

A is correct. The relevant text is in paragraph 2, which states that glucagon secretion follows from low blood glucose levels. Exercising would tend to reduce blood glucose levels and hence trigger secretion of glucagon.

The wrong answer choices: Choices B, C, and D are all wrong because they describe situations in which individuals have eaten, thus increasing blood glucose levels.

187. The administration of insulin in Experiment 2 is able to reverse hyperglycemia because:

    A. insulin inhibits glucose uptake by body cells.
    B. insulin enhances glucose uptake by body cells.
    C. glucagon production by the liver is inhibited by insulin.
    D. levels of intracellular glucose are reduced by insulin.

B is correct. Paragraph 2 tells you that insulin causes glucose to move from blood to cells. Insulin administration reverses hyperglyclemia because it removes glucose from the blood (and admits it to the cells).

The wrong answer choices: Choice A makes a false statement. The passage establishes that insulin *increases* uptake of glucose by body cells. Choice C also makes a false statement. Insulin reverses hyperglycemia by directly increasing cellular glucose uptake, not by inhibiting glucagon production. Choice D is wrong because insulin causes the body cells to experience *increased* glucose concentration.

188. Which of the following best supports the premise that insulin and glucagon are produced by two different types of pancreatic islet cells?

    A. Certain islet cells have secretory products similar to those secreted by nervous system cells.

    B. High blood glucose increases the activity of some islet cells while low blood glucose increases the activity of different islet cell types.

    C. Insulin and glucagon have opposing actions in the body.

    D. Insulin and glucagon are composed of different polypeptide chains.

B is correct. The passage tells you that *high* blood glucose concentration is associated with insulin secretion and *low* blood glucose concentration is associated with glucagon secretion. Once you realize that, the question itself, together with simple logic, tells you that the two hormones must arise from different cell types.

The wrong answer choices: Choice A is wild and irrelevant. Choices C and D make false statements. Neither provides evidence that insulin and glucagon arise from distinctly separate cell types.

189. Body cells can respond in vivo to exogenously administered insulin because insulin is a polypeptide that interacts with cells via:

    A. a bilayer membrane that allows simple inward diffusion of insulin.

    B. a bilayer membrane that allows endocytosis of insulin.

    C. cell receptors that are activated in close association with insulin.

    D. cell receptors that degrade insulin on contact.

C is correct. The question is unrelated to the passage. After reviewing cell membranes, you'll know that polypeptides cross cell membranes only with the participation of cell receptors.

The wrong answer choices: Choice A can be eliminated because insulin cannot cross the cell membrane by simple diffusion. Choice B also is wrong. Endocytosis is a process through which cells take in large molecules and particulate matter. Choice D also is incorrect: insulin would *never* affect cell function if it were systematically degraded upon contact with the cell membrane.

190. What happened to the blood glucose levels in the blood after insulin administration in Experiment 1?

    A. Glucose was moved primarily into the liver and not other body tissues.

    B. Glucose was moved primarily into the kidneys, as in diabetes insipidus.

    C. Glucose was moved into body cells because insulin prevented blood cell degradation of glucose.

    D. Glucose was moved into body cells because insulin increased the cells' uptake of glucose.

D is correct. Paragraph 2 tells you that insulin promotes cellular glucose uptake. It's that simple.

The wrong answer choices: Choices A and B are wrong because neither the liver nor the kidneys selectively takes in glucose, and the passage does not indicate that they do. Choice C is wrong because insulin does not affect blood cell degradation of glucose.

Questions 191 through 195 are NOT based on a descriptive passage

191. Bacteriophages are viruses that attack bacteria. They attach to the surface of a bacterium and inject their genetic material into the host. Bacteriophages differ from other organisms in that:

    A. they only contain RNA, which replicates inside a host cell.

    B. they have only RNA and must utilize a host cell's machinery to generate DNA.

    C. they lack the cellular metabolic machinery found in both eukaryotic and prokaryotic organisms.

    D. they possess bounding membranes and internal organelles including ribosomes and vacuoles.

C is correct. Your review of microbiology will remind you that viruses do *not* possess all of the cellular machinery that facilitates independent existence. Viruses rely on "host cells" to provide them with the apparatus necessary for reproduction.

The wrong answer choices: Choices A and B are wrong because bacteriophages proliferate by replicating within a host cell and their genetic material is DNA. Choice D should be eliminated because bacteriophages do not possess the named organelles.

192. Consider the reaction below.

$$CH_3CH_2CH_2OH \xrightarrow[CH_2Cl_2]{PCC} CH_3CH_2CHO$$

Which of the following observations about the infrared spectrum of the reaction mixture would indicate that the reaction shown above occurred?

A. The appearance of a C=O stretch and C–H stretch

B. The appearance of an aliphatic C–H stretch

C. The appearance of an O–H stretch

D. The disappearance of an N–H stretch

A is correct. The compound on the left is an alcohol and the compound on the right is an aldehyde. Once you review infrared and nuclear magnetic resonance spectroscopy, you'll know that *infrared* spectroscopy would reveal the *disappearance* of the –OH group and the *appearance* of the C=O and C–H groups.

The wrong answer choices: Choice B is wrong because neither the reactant nor the product represents an aliphatic compound. Choice C is wrong because the O–H stretch will *dis*appear. Choice D is wrong because nitrogen does not belong to either the product or reactant.

193. The process of respiration consists of both inspiration and expiration. Inspiration is:

A. a passive process due to negative pressure in the thoracic cavity.

B. a passive process due to positive pressure in the thoracic cavity.

C. an active process due to negative pressure in the thoracic cavity.

D. an active process due to positive pressure in the thoracic cavity.

C is correct. Once you review respiratory physiology, you'll remember that inspiration is active and that it follows from the negative pressure that's created when the diaphragm contracts.

194. Sickle cell anemia is a blood disorder due to a point mutation in a single gene. It is inherited as an autosomal recessive trait. A woman is heterozygous for the disorder, having one normal allele on the genome and one allele affected by the point mutation. She most likely has:

A. full-blown sickle cell anemia.
B. sickle cell trait, a carrier disease.
C. no signs or symptoms of the disease.
D. a predominance of sickle-shaped red blood cells.

B is correct. An individual with sickle cell *trait* (as opposed to full-blown sickle cell disease) has certain adverse symptoms associated with sickled blood cells, but she does not have fulminant sickle cell anemia.

The wrong answer choices: Choices A and D are wrong because the woman *carrying* sickle cell trait has one normal allele which tends to produce red blood cells of normal shape. Choice C is wrong because the woman carrying sickle cell trait has one allele that tends to produce sickle-shaped blood cells.

195. Which of the following is NOT a resonance structure of phenol?

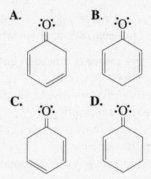

D is correct. When you review the chemistry of benzene, you'll know that benzene and its derivatives are "resonating" molecules. Benzene itself is a six-carbon ring with three double bonds dispersed about the ring. With reference to benzene, "resonance" refers to the dispersion of the double bonds. A simple *phenol* is benzene with an OH group attached to one of the ring carbons. The attachment of the OH group eliminates one of the ring's double bonds. The ring's two *remaining* double bonds continue to be dispersed throughout the ring. A drawing will correctly depict a phenol resonance structure only if it shows both bonds distributed about the ring with charge appropriately assigned. Choice D is correct because it shows only one double bond within the ring and thus *fails* to represent a phenol accurately.

Passage VIII (Questions 196-200)

196. High total serum cholesterol puts a patient at risk for myocardial infarction because it reflects:

   A. low blood content of high-density lipoproteins.
   B. low blood content of low-density lipoproteins.
   C. high blood content of high-density lipoproteins.
   D. high blood content of low-density lipoproteins.

D is correct. Paragraphs 3 and 6 contain the relevant information. Together they tell you that low-density lipoprotein, the particle most associated with heart attack, makes up 60 to 70 percent of serum cholesterol.

The wrong answer choices: Choices A and C are wrong because paragraph 4 tells you that high-density lipoproteins create no risk of myocardial infarction. Choice B is wrong because as stated in the passage, cholesterol is composed largely of LDL.

197. If an elderly woman with abnormally high levels of LDL has little coronary atherosclerosis, she most likely:

   A. has high levels of HDL, counteracting the effects of the LDL.
   B. follows a diet that is low in cholesterol-containing foods.
   C. has no atherosclerosis in arteries outside the heart.
   D. has failed to undergo a complete diagnostic screening for blood lipid status.

A is correct. The relevant information is in paragraph 4, in which you're told that a high *ratio* of LDL to HDL is associated with high risk of atherosclerosis.

The wrong answer choices: Choice B should be eliminated because it represents a false implication. A low-cholesterol diet would explain low levels of LDL. It would not explain the absence of atherosclerosis in the face of high LDL levels. Choices C and D should be eliminated because they represent unwarranted conclusions.

198. Coronary atherosclerosis constitutes a medical problem because it threatens to:

    A. render the heart less sensitive to stress.
    B. produce imbalance in the patient's blood lipid profile.
    C. compromise the heart muscle's oxygen supply.
    D. subject the patient to high blood pressure.

C is correct. In paragraph 1 you learn that coronary atherosclerosis involves an accumulation of plaques within the coronary arteries. In paragraph 2 you learn that the coronary arteries give the heart its blood supply. Since blood is the medium through which all tissues derive oxygen, any impairment of blood supply also compromises *oxygen* supply.

The wrong answer choices: Choices A and D should be eliminated because they distort information in the passage. In paragraph 1 you're told that high blood pressure and stress may increase the risk of heart attack. You're *not* told that atherosclerosis causes high blood pressure or stress. Choice B also distorts the passage's meaning. In paragraph 4 you learn that an unbalanced blood lipid profile might lead to atherosclerosis. You *don't* learn that atherosclerosis leads to the unbalanced profile.

199. Coronary atherosclerosis is virtually unknown among peoples living in nonindustrialized nations. This indicates that in comparison with industrialized populations these peoples probably have:

    A. a lower incidence of heart attack.
    B. a lower incidence of hypertension.
    C. higher levels of VLDL.
    D. higher levels of IDL.

A is correct. Paragraph 1 has the information you need. It tells you that coronary atherosclerosis is the leading cause of heart attack. Absence of atherosclerosis implies that fewer heart attacks will occur.

The wrong answer choices: Choice B should be eliminated because the passage makes no reference to the effect of atherosclerosis on blood pressure. Choices C and D should also be eliminated because the passage states that LDL and HDL affect the risk of atherosclerosis and heart attack. It makes no such statement about VLDL or IDL.

200. If coronary atherosclerosis produces myocardial infarction, what is the status of the affected heart muscle?

    A. High pH
    B. Low pH
    C. High O_2 concentration
    D. Low CO_2 concentration

B is correct. After reviewing the biochemistry associated with respiration and circulation, you'll know that low blood supply leads to increased metabolic waste formation. Metabolic waste (principally CO_2) in turn, produces acid (principally H_2CO_3). That, of course, *reduces* pH.

The wrong answer choices: Choice A is wrong because, as just explained, increased waste production *lowers* pH. Choices C and D are wrong because the decreased blood supply produced by atherosclerosis would impair *delivery* of oxygen and *removal* of carbon dioxide to and from the affected heart muscle.

Passage IX (Questions 201-207)

201. Based on the passage, one could estimate a dicarboxylic acid's K_1 value by determining:

    A. its concentration in a nonequilibrium mixture.
    B. its stability in anion form.
    C. its tendency to undergo decarboxylation.
    D. its crystallization structure.

B is correct. When you deal with chemical equilibria, you must remember: The more stable the products, the more likely it is that the reaction will proceed to completion. This means that K_1 is determined by the *relative stabilities* of a dicarboxylic acid's protonated and deprotonated forms.

The wrong answer choices: Choices A, C, and D are wrong because none of the named factors characterizes or influences equilibrium. Equilibrium is characterized by the *ratio of products to reactants*.

202. Glutaric acid is a dicarboxylic acid with the formula $HOOC(CH_2)_3COOH$. This acid is most likely to have a K_1 constant closest in value to which substance listed in the table?

   A. Fumaric acid
   B. Maleic acid
   C. Succinic acid
   D. Oxalic acid

C is correct. If you know that K_1 values decrease with increased number of double bonds, you'll realize that you should be looking for a compound whose structure is similar to that of glutaric acid. Among the choices, glutaric acid's molecular formula is most like that of succinic acid. (Glutaric acid has one more $[CH_2]$ group than does succinic acid.)

203. If equal concentrations of succinic acid, malonic acid, and maleic acid were heated in a weakly basic solution, which of the following products would be in the greatest concentration at equilibrium?

   A. $HOOCCH_2COO^-$
   B. $HOOC(CH_2)_2COO^-$
   C. $HOOCCH=CHCOOH$
   D. $HOOC–COOH$

C is correct. The question requires that you understand, to some degree, the meaning of K_1 and that you read the table provided in the passage. Among succinic, malonic, and maleic acids, maleic has the highest K_1. That means its *de*protonated form will predominate.

The wrong answer choices: Choices A and B are wrong because they represents the deprotonated form of succinic acid, and maleic which have a lower K_1 than does malonic acid. Choice D is wrong because they represent the protonated form of fumaric acid and oxalic acid, neither of which is present in solution.

204. Based on the information in the passage, it would be difficult to estimate K_1 for a molecule with the formula $HOOCCH_2NHCOOH$ because:

    A. its anion stability is not directly comparable to that of succinic acid.

    B. it cannot exist in the deprotonated form.

    C. it must form an insoluble compound.

    D. it represents an unstable compound.

A is correct. The anion of the indicated compound is not directly comparable to any structure listed on the table for the simple reason that *it contains an N-H group*.

205. In an aqueous mixture of maleic and fumaric acid, the equilibrium proportions can best be determined by which method?

    A. Radioactive tagging of the corresponding alkene

    B. Hydration of the anion solution

    C. Acidification of the solution

    D. Nuclear magnetic resonance spectroscopy of the equilibrium solution

D is correct. After you study NMR spectroscopy, you'll know that it is well suited to differentiate between *cis* and *trans* configurations.

The wrong answer choices: Answer choices A, B, and C are wrong for the simple reason that none of the named processes distinguishes between *cis* and *trans* configurations.

206. The value of K_1 of the dicarboxylic compound glutamic acid is substantially lower than the K_1 of glutaric acid because:

    A. glutamate is readily convertible into a non-polar zwitterion.

    B. glutamate's deprotonated form is less stable than the glutarate anion.

    C. glutamate is an amino acid.

    D. glutamic acid is a stronger acid than glutaric acid.

B is correct. From the passage you learn that lower K_1 value indicates a relatively lower tendency to deprotonate. After you study equilibria phenomena and acid-base organic chemistry, you'll know that the tendency to deprotonate, in turn, is a function of anion stability. Glutamic acid has a K_1 substantially lower than that of glutaric acid, which means that its anion is less stable than that of glutaric acid.

The wrong answer choices: Choices A, C, and D are all wrong because the phenomena to which they refer are irrelevant to the question.

207. One can most reasonably estimate the value of K_2 for acetic acid (CH_3COOH) to be:

    A. higher than K_1 for acetic acid.

    B. higher than K_2 for maleic acid.

    C. lower than K_2 for oxalic acid.

    D. less than zero.

C is correct. A reading of the passage teaches you that K_2 reflects a molecule's willingness to undergo double deprotonation. Thus, K_1 is larger than K_2. The more ionized an acid is, the larger the K_a value. pK_a is defined as the negative log of [H+] so pKa equals the negative log of K_a. As K_a gets larger pK_a gets smaller. That means that pK_1 is smaller than pK_2.

Passage X (Questions 208-215)

208. If a segment of the denatured viral DNA strand had a base sequence ATAA, what would have been the complementary RNA sequence?

   A. GTGG
   B. TATT
   C. UAUU
   D. TUTT

C is correct. The question has nothing to do with the passage. Your review of cell biochemistry will remind you of this: In the process of DNA-RNA transcription, a DNA adenine residue pairs with an RNA uracil residue. A DNA thymine residue pairs with an RNA adenine residue.

The wrong answer choices: Choices A, B, and D should be eliminated quickly because RNA never contains thymine. (It contains uracil instead.)

209. At the end of Experiment 3, how many off-spring reproduced through the formation of gametes?

   A. 0
   B. 2
   C. 4
   D. 12

A is correct. The descriptions of Experiments 2 and 3 provide the relevant information. You're told that reproduction occurred *asexually*. Asexual reproduction does not involve gametes.

The wrong answer choices: Choices B, C, and D are wrong because *none* of the organisms underwent any form of sexual reproduction.

210. Suppose the lower-density Light strand mutant in Figure 1 cannot undergo transcription. The most likely explanation is that it does not:

A. bind DNA.
B. bind RNA.
C. bind protein.
D. replicate.

B is correct. The description of Experiment 1 provides the necessary information. You're told that the lower-density Light strand is viral DNA. The process of transcription requires that an RNA molecule align itself with a molecule of DNA. The Light strand's failure to undergo transcription means that the DNA cannot bind to RNA.

The wrong answer choices: Choices A and C are wrong because transcription requires that DNA bind to *RNA*, not to DNA or to protein. Choice D is wrong because transcription does not require DNA replication.

211. All of the following are true with regard to bacteriophage SP8 EXCEPT:

A. it infects the *B. subtilis* bacterium
B. gram-staining its cell wall helps to permit its identification.
C. It contains viral DNA.
D. It possesses a tail structure.

B is correct. Paragraph 1 reminds you that a bacteriophage is a virus. Viruses do not have cell walls (bacteria do).

The wrong answer choices: Choices A, C, and D are not accurate statements regarding SP8. Paragraph 1 states that it infects *B. subtilis*, and that it contains viral DNA. A review of viruses will remind you that bacteriophages possess a tail structure which helps them to latch on to their host.

212. Which of the following findings best supports the conclusion that the viral DNA Heavy strand normally produces transcribed mRNA, whereas the viral DNA Light strand does not?

   A. Neither the Heavy strand nor the Light strand of viral DNA can excise point mutations.
   B. Neither the Heavy strand nor the Light strand of viral DNA hybridizes with labeled RNA.
   C. Only the viral DNA Light strand can direct protein synthesis.
   D. Only the mutated viral DNA Heavy strand produces phenotypic changes.

D is correct. The question has nothing to do with the passage. Transcription produces mRNA, which produces protein, and protein gives rise to phenotype (visible trait).

The wrong answer choices: Choices A and B should be eliminated because neither describes a *distinction* between the Light and Heavy viral DNA strands. Choice C is wrong because it would support the contrary conclusion: that viral DNA Light strand could produce transcribed mRNA.

213. How can one determine that mutations of the viral DNA Light strand do not affect phenotypic expression in the host?

   A. By locating the mutation on the host DNA
   B. By comparing Light strand mutants to Heavy strand mutants
   C. By comparing the mutant phenotype with the unmutated form
   D. By studying the production of RNA polymerase

C is correct. The question is unrelated to the passage. Instead, it requires simple common sense. In order to determine that mutation does or does not affect phenotype, one must simply *compare* the mutant and unmutated phenotype.

The wrong answer choices: Choice A is wrong because a mutation's location does not, of itself, indicate whether it will alter the host phenotype. Choice B is wrong because it describes the wrong comparison. The comparison should be between mutated and unmutated phenotypes. Choice D is wild and irrelevant.

214. By studying Figures 1 and 2, a scientist decided that the normal bacteriophage SP8 DNA consists of a double-stranded chromosome. For this conclusion to be true, which of the following assumptions must be correct?

   A. Hybridization of DNA with RNA involves the formation of covalent bonds.
   B. Radiolabeling affects the size of the RNA-DNA hybrid produced.
   C. Mutation does not lead to changes in DNA sequence.
   D. Denaturation breaks apart the double helix without hydrolyzing covalently attached base pairs.

D is correct. The question requires that you read Figure 1 strategically. The appearance of two peaks suggests the existence of two strands. That, in turn, indicates that the double-stranded chromosome separated without losing the covalently bonded base pairs on each strand.

The wrong answer choices: Choices A, B, and C are all wild and irrelevant.

215. For bacteriophage SP8, if the mutated Heavy strand codes for a protein that destroys DNA polymerases while the Light strand does not, then the mutant will:

   A. show increased production of DNA.
   B. show decreased evolutionary "fitness" compared with the Light strand mutant.
   C. show increased evolutionary "fitness" compared with the normal virus.
   D. show an increased tendency to undergo meiosis.

B is correct. The question is answerable without reference to the passage. It requires that you remember the meaning of evolutionary "fitness." If the Heavy strand mutant loses its DNA polymerase, *its ability to reproduce is impaired*, which means it's less "fit" than the Light strand mutant.

The wrong answer choices: Choices A and C are incorrect. The defective heavy strand would experience *decreased* production of DNA and, hence, show *decreased* evolutionary fitness. Choice D should be eliminated because it's wild and irrelevant.

Questions 216 through 219 are NOT based on a descriptive passage

216. Which of the following processes does NOT occur on the ribosomes during protein synthesis?

A. Translation of mRNA
B. Peptide bond formation
C. Attachment of tRNA anticodons to mRNA codons
D. Transcription of mRNA

C is correct. After you study cell biochemistry, you'll remember that protein synthesis begins when transfer RNA (tRNA) "anticodons" align themselves with the codons of messenger RNA (mRNA).

The wrong answer choices: Choices A, B, and D are wrong because each of the named processes *does* play a role in protein synthesis. During translation, a polypeptide is created from the mRNA template. Peptide bonds are the "glue" that holds a protein molecule together, and messenger RNA is created from a DNA template in transcription.

217. During embryonic gastrulation, invagination occurs as a result of which of the following processes?

A. Release of a hormone
B. Migration of cells
C. Reproduction of cells
D. Asymmetric division of cells

B is correct. After studying developmental biology, you'll know that in the process of gastrulation, cells *adjust their relative positions* to create three distinct germ layers (ectoderm, mesoderm, and endoderm).

The wrong answer choices: Choice A is wrong because hormones do not (as far as the MCAT is concerned) play any role in invaginating the blastula. Choices C and D are wrong because cell migration, not cell *reproduction*, is the event that characterizes gastrulation.

218. Surgically implanted pacemakers are frequently used in the treatment of heart disease. Which of the following normal heart structures carries out the same function as a pacemaker?

    A. The bundle of His
    B. The atrioventricular node
    C. The sinoatrial node
    D. The sinoventricular node

C is correct. Your review of mammalian physiology will tell you that the sinoatrial node generates the heartbeat and is thus known as the heart's natural "pacemaker."

The wrong answer choices: Choices A and B are wrong because each of the named structures fulfills functions other than pacemaking. The bundle of His conveys the heartbeat's electrical impulse outward along the walls of the ventricles. The atrioventricular node conducts the impulse from atria to ventricles. Choice D is wrong because there is no such thing as the sinoventricular node.

219. The hormone that most directly stimulates the formation of sperm in the testes is which of the following?

    A. Estrogen
    B. Testosterone
    C. Luteinizing hormone
    D. Follicle-stimulating hormone

B is correct. After reviewing the endocrine system you'll know that sperm production requires testosterone.

The wrong answer choices: Choice A is wrong because estrogen does not play a role in sperm production. Choices C and D can be eliminated because luteinizing hormone and follicle-stimulating hormone are only indirectly related to sperm production. The two substances *regulate* testosterone secretion.

PART FOUR

THE PRINCETON REVIEW
MCAT
DIAGNOSTIC TEST II

Verbal Reasoning II

Time: 85 Minutes
Questions 1–65

VERBAL REASONING

DIRECTIONS: There are nine passages in the Verbal Reasoning test. Each passage is followed by several questions. After reading a passage, select the one best answer to each question. If you are not certain of an answer, eliminate the alternatives that you know to be incorrect and then select an answer from the remaining alternatives. Indicate your selection by blackening the corresponding oval on your answer sheet.

Passage I (Questions 1–6)

The ubiquitous and vexing problem of solid waste disposal acquires special dimensions in the Caribbean territories of the United States. Because land surface area is severely
5 limited, and potable water at a premium, the usual complications of landfill abuse are magnified a thousand fold. Every piece of ground on such relatively small islands holds present and future potential for human habitation
10 and/or some other form of commercial development. Moreover, the economy of the region depends largely on its appeal as a vacation paradise: landfill stench and marine environmental destruction would pose a se-
15 rious threat to the tourist dollar.

Some analysts have proposed the construction of "destructive distillation" biomass treatment plants in the territory to turn garbage and sludge into methane gas, and to
20 provide electricity and desalinated water to the Water and Power Authority (W.A.P.A.) at rates lower than those the utility presently charges its customers. Such an approach integrates bottom-line pragmatism with
25 environmental strategy, a combination deemed essential by government and business representatives.

According to its proponents, the destructive distillation system involves shredding
30 of the bulk waste or biomass, separating out the iron content, drying the remains and distilling it to carbon char and methane gas.

Twenty percent of the methane product is diverted to fuel the system itself; the rest
35 would be used to generate electricity for consumers, and to power a desalinization plant. Because the distillation process entails no burning of waste, the biomass treatment plants will protect the ecosystem against the
40 unnecessary health hazards and adverse environmental effects normally associated with solid waste incineration.

Supporters of distillation technology believe it will contribute to environmental
45 preservation in ways beyond the primary applications. For example, carbon char leftover from distillation might be used to filter ecological poisons—leachate presently running from landfills into the sea—which are
50 toxic and fatal to the coral, and which, some environmentalists claim, have already destroyed most of the mahogany in Stalley Bay. These analysts propose that digging slurries against the sea wall and backfilling with car-
55 bon char will provide an activated charcoal system to filter, deodorize, and clarify the leachate that's running into the sea. Iron separated out in the distillation process might also prove a salable by-product.

60 The Department of Capital Improvements is currently considering a plan to build such model distillation plants on St. Thomas and St. Croix. Proponents estimate an 18-month construction period for both model plants,
65 which, through the hiring of local contractors and labor, and the local purchasing of

GO ON TO THE NEXT PAGE

materials, would generate some $24-million directly into the V.I. economy. Planners cal-culate that after completion the project will
70 provide 40 permanent jobs with congregate salaries of $1.3-million per island.

W.A.P.A. would derive an additional $2.2-million per island each year from the resale of electricity and potable water to its custom-
75 ers. Adding in an estimated $1-million annual miscellaneous operating expenses for each plant buttresses an already dramatic mon-etary argument in support of the project: approximately $4.5 million per island, or a
80 total $9-million in new revenues annually for the Territory's on-going economy.

Moreover, these two pilot plants could serve as models for stateside projects, and for export of the technology throughout the
85 Caribbean Basin. As the designated training center for the biomass destructive distilla-tion technology, the University of the Virgin Islands would offer a nine-week course—at $5-thousand per student—for all technicians
90 training to staff stateside and international installations, endowing the University with a long-term technological mission. Such a mission might prove vital to the University's long-term fiscal well-being, and serve to de-
95 crease its dependence on federal tax dollars.

Some policy-makers, however, remain cautious, concerned about taxpayer abuses that might occur by granting contracts pre-maturely. They cite an integrated solid waste
100 management evaluation, prepared three years ago by an independent consulting company, which determined that previous analyses had limited their scope to seasonal or extrapola-tive data. This independent evaluation
105 recommended that a new, comprehensive waste characterization study be undertaken, including real, year-round data to qualify and

quantify the kinds of waste going into the territorial dumps. Deliberaters insist that
110 only such a comprehensive analysis will pro-vide the information necessary to determine whether the distillation plant to the solid waste disposal will meet the needs of the islands.

1. Each of the following factors is explicitly cited in the passage to support the idea that destructive distillation combines pragma-tism with sound environmental strategy EXCEPT:

    A. The technology will provide electricity for the island at lower than prevailing rates.
    B. Extrapolative waste stream studies do not contraindicate the technology.
    C. Plant construction and maintenance will add millions of dollars to the local economy.
    D. It will provide a long-term teaching mis-sion to the local university.

2. According to the passage, which of the fol-lowing is most likely to be true about the solid waste disposal problem in the Carib-bean Basin?

    A. The Caribbean Islands do not face much of a solid waste crisis.
    B. Disposal problems in the Caribbean Ba-sin are much the same as they are elsewhere.
    C. A limited population and premium warm saltwater bays lessen the region's problem.
    D. Scarcities of land mass and drinking water magnify the problem.

GO ON TO THE NEXT PAGE

3. Which of the following statements, if true, would most WEAKEN the author's argument that the use of destruction distillation as described in the passage will contribute to environmental health in ways beyond the technology's primary applications?

A. Construction costs to tax-payers will overrun estimates by fifty percent.

B. The cost for exporting scrap iron will exceed the profit margin from its sale.

C. Because of the noise produced by the distillation process nearby hotels will be forced to relocate.

D. Mahogany in Stalley Bay will regenerate and surpass previous growth levels.

4. Suppose two major hurricanes causing severe, widespread damage to real estate and buildings, and eight minor hurricanes causing less but still significant damage, had struck the Virgin Islands during the last six years. This new information would most CHALLENGE the claim(s) that:

I. Technological success in the Virgin Islands could be exported to other nations in the Caribbean.

II. Approval of the proposal represents a wise long-term investment for the territories.

III. Plant construction will bring significant new revenues to the territory's economy.

A. II only
B. I and III only
C. II and III only
D. I , II, and III

5. According to the passage, proponents of the distillation technology claim that such a waste disposal system is environmentally superior to incineration in each of the following ways EXCEPT:

A. It will generate a byproduct to build a filtering system for landfill toxins.

B. It will qualify for increased federal subsidies under the Clean Air Clear Water Act.

C. It will serve as a new source for low-cost drinking water.

D. It produces significantly less environmental pollution than incineration.

6. Based on reading of the passage, officials who urge a more cautious approach because "previous analyses had limited their scope to seasonal or extrapolative data" are probably most concerned that:

A. year-round residents of the island might be distrustful of new methods of waste disposal.

B. registered voters might resent the job dislocations involved in altering the waste disposal system

C. the tourist industry might suffer because of travellers' fears that the system does not ensure adequate sanitary conditions year-round.

D. total annual waste flow might be better disposed of using a different system.

GO ON TO THE NEXT PAGE

Passage II (Question 7–13)

Federal law requires that states articulate guidelines for establishing the size of child support awards to be paid by a non-custodial parent to a custodial parent. The law
5 was enacted in response to a widespread perception that many states lacked meaningful criteria through which child support awards were to be established. In enacting the law, Congress has been generally concerned that
10 child support orders might be either inadequate or unjust. Congress has found that some awards are economically inadequate to facilitate adequate child rearing. Others reflect a pattern of inconsistency wherein two
15 noncustodial parents similarly situated might find themselves paying very different child support awards.

As to the matter of inadequacy, a recent study showed that the nation's noncustodial
20 parents would have paid more than $30 billion in a recent fiscal year if support awards took realistic account of the cost of child rearing. Census data, however, indicate that only $10.1 billion was due in that year and, more-
25 over, that only $7.1 billion was actually paid. The situation thus revealed an adequacy gap of $20 billion and a compliance gap of $3 billion. Without congressional action, the adequacy gap would likely increase. The
30 compliance gap is likely to increase regardless.

It is a matter of fundamental fairness that like parties should be treated alike, and as individuals, most state judges are fairly con-
35 sistent in the standards and criteria they apply in setting child support awards. Yet studies show that within a given state, judges do not necessarily exhibit similar patterns in setting their awards. The quality of life for a sepa-
40 rating couple and their children will depend on the judge who sets the support award rather than on preestablished criteria. It was found that in Colorado one parent might be required to make a support payment equal to
45 6 percent of income, while a similarly situated parent before another court might be required to pay a full third of income.

As the new federal law takes hold, states face a choice regarding the model on which they wish to base their criteria. The "flat
50 rate" model imposes on all paying parents a payment equal to a flat percentage of income, adjusted for the number of children at issue. Rates might be, for example, 8 percent for one child, 15 percent for two children, and 20
55 percent for three children. Under such a flat rate structure, all paying parent with one child would pay 8 percent of their income in support. The actual rates, of course, would depend on the states.

60 Conversely, the "income shares" model embodies the idea that each child should receive that percentage of total parental income as would have been received had the parents not separated. Each parent, in turn, is ex-
65 pected to contribute out of his or her income pro rata according to his or her contribution to total income. Suppose, for example, a separating couple has one child. Spouse A is the custodial spouse and has income of $20,000.
70 Spouse B has income of $60,000, which makes for a total parental income of $80,000. Twenty-five percent of the total derives from spouse A and 75 percent from spouse B. If the court determined that the child would
75 ordinarily enjoy the benefit of 20 percent of total income ($16,000), the parents would be required to provide that amount pro rata. Spouse A would be expected to contribute 25 percent ($4,000), and Spouse B would pay 75
80 percent ($12,000).

Flat rate and income shares awards reflect different values and thus lead to different awards. Where two children live with a payee spouse and the payee spouse has no income,
85 Wisconsin's flat rate approach, for example, would require monthly payments of $186 from a payor spouse whose monthly income is $600. In the same situation, the income shares approach would require a monthly
90 payment of $90. Because the approach to guidelines may differ from state to state, guidelines will not bring about parity in support orders across state lines.

GO ON TO THE NEXT PAGE

7. Given the ideas in the passage, which of the following statements accurately describes the quote "adequacy gap" and/or the "compliance gap?"

A. The compliance gap measures the court costs of child support proceedings unpaid by litigants and covered by state budgets.

B. The adequacy gap measures the court costs of child support proceedings unfunded by state budgets and covered by federal assistance.

C. The compliance gap measures the child support dollar amount awarded in courts and unpaid by parents.

D. The adequacy gap measures the child support dollar amount awarded in courts and unpaid by parents.

8. The author cites a specific study to support which of the following types?

   I. Judges do not always rely on the same criteria when setting child support awards even within the same state.

   II. Fairness dictates that noncustodial spouses in comparable circumstances should be treated alike.

   III. The quote "compliance gap" is likely to increase

A. I only
B. I and III only
C. II and III only
D. I, II, and III

9. Suppose Spouse A has custody of three children and a monthly of income of $6,000, while Spouse B has a monthly income of $2,000. A court has determined that the children would ordinarily enjoy benefit of 15% of total parental income. Which of the following statements would reflect appropriate child support payment alternatives as discussed in the passage?

A. Under the income shares model, a contribution of $300 monthly would be required, with Spouse B as the payee spouse.

B. Under the income shares model, a contribution of $300 monthly would be required, with Spouse A as the payee spouse.

C. Under the flat rate model, a contribution of $900 monthly would be required, with Spouse A as the payee spouse.

D. Under the flat rate model, a contribution of $900 monthly would be required, with Spouse B as the payee spouse.

10. The relationship between the flat rate model and the income shares model, as discussed in the passage, might best be analogized to which of the following?

A. Local telephone charges at a monthly flat rate or a rate based on amount of monthly usage

B. Long distance telephone rates based on a flat rate per minute or based on mileage between the call origination phone and the call destination phone

C. Monthly loan interest at a fixed rate or at a variable rate

D. An income tax system based on a single tax rate or on a graduated rate that escalates with income.

GO ON TO THE NEXT PAGE

11. Individuals opposed to leaving legislation regarding child support arrangements up to the individual states probably base their objections on their belief that:

    A. the federal government has an important and necessary role in protecting the welfare of children.

    B. divorced individuals often do not live in the same part of the country as do their former spouses.

    C. the federal government can best evaluate statistical variations in the cost of living index from state to state.

    D. the federal government has a constitutional obligation to ensure due process of law for all persons, including those involved in divorce proceedings.

12. A recent theory suggests that children of divorced spouses whose custodial parent received regular and sufficient child support payments will score higher on scales measuring self-esteem and self-confidence than those whose parents do not comply with court ordered support. Social workers who accept this theory would be LEAST likely to support which of the following?

    A. Support groups at the local level to help parents who do not meet child support obligations deal with their resulting psychological issues

    B. Support groups at the local level for custodial parents and their children who do not receive regular and sufficient child support

    C. Federal regulations making it more difficult for parents to avoid compliance with court ordered support judgments

    D. State laws requiring automatic deductions from payroll checks of parents convicted of failing to pay child support

13. In Self Reliance, Ralph Waldo Emerson wrote, "A foolish consistency is the hobgoblin of little minds." Given the ideas in the passage, Emerson would probably believe that:

    A. the goal of achieving consistency in child support awards through legislation is foolish.

    B. the process of achieving consistency through legislation should be left to people with little imagination.

    C. the goal of achieving consistency in child support awards through legislation is the obsession of vengeful litigants.

    D. the goal of consistency is not foolish in every circumstance.

GO ON TO THE NEXT PAGE

Passage III (Questions 14–19)

African art includes houses, masks, costumes, uniforms, and the decorations that adorn clothing. We cannot understand it without first abandoning some conventional
5 notions. African art goes beyond monuments and beyond that which one might observe in a museum.

The mbari house is filled with sculptures and probably represents a religious offering.
10 The construction of the house is conducted in ritualistic fashion, and, once built, the house and its sculptures are never maintained. They are permitted to deteriorate and to become once again a part of the ground
15 from which they came. Typically, a mbari house contains upwards of seventy sculptures. Usually the sculptures depict significant deities of the community. The front of a mbari house, for example, will usu-
20 ally feature the sculpted figure of the goddess of the Earth. The sculpture is a veritable complex showing not only the goddess herself, but also her children seated nearby. Her servants, too, are figured in poses that clearly
25 illustrate their function as her guards. Away from the front of the house other sculptures are usually found. These may assume a variety of forms. They may represent gods and they may depict human figures of myth or
30 history.

Close to the Ivory Coast, there lives a tribe called "Dan." The Dan are inveterate mask makers and have what amounts to a mask-making club that they call "poro." Masks
35 play a significant role in the operation of Dan society. Members of poro tend to hold functional political offices, and they generally regulate community affairs. They wear masks while executing their functions, and commu-
40 nity regard for the masks aids them in their work as does the anonymity that the mask provides. For example, the Dan have developed a mask that represents justice or judging, and the community judge, a mem-
45 ber of poro, wears the mask when performing his official function. Other functionaries

called on to perform unpopular tasks are similarly protected by anonymity when they wear the masks that represent their offices.

50 The Yoruba Gelade is another mask-making group. Gelade refers to a mysterious group of persons who devote themselves to the appeasement of gods whom they believe to be the sponsors of witchcraft. Gelade
55 masks are costumes and nothing more. They are worn by masqueraders who don them in connection with performances and cult activities. The masks themselves represent a diverse number of personages with whom
60 the Yoruba are familiar. Some masks represent merchants. Others represent motorists, hunters, physicians, and in general, the varied array of characters to whom the Yoruba are exposed. The Gelade give performances
65 in which they use the masks to partake of social commentary. In this respect, then, the masks constitute graphic art, and the performances constitute literature.

One should not try to understand African
70 art by resorting to the usual classifications and subdivisions. The classifications "fine art," "decorative art," and "craft" do not do it justice. The African culture differs from the European in that artwork is not separate
75 from utilitarian objects. The designation "African art" describes elaborately adorned eating utensils, simple furniture, clothing, usable pottery, and basketry. African art is thus an "art of life."

14. What is the main theme of the passage?

   A. African art serves as a barrier between the artist class and the community.
   B. African art is essentially inaccessible to students of Western art.
   C. African art participates in diverse functional ways in the community's daily life.
   D. Western art is divorced from the community's daily functioning.

GO ON TO THE NEXT PAGE

15. To emphasize the idea that African art is unlike Western art the author explicitly cites all of the following information EXCEPT:

    A. Structures housing African art are built according to ritual practices and laws.
    B. Once completed, African sculptures are allowed to crumble and rot.
    C. African sculptures often depict historical heroes.
    D. African art includes common objects of daily household use.

16. The word "literature" (line 68) most closely means:

    A. an unbound collected body of tribal writings.
    B. a catalogue of religious sculptures and myths.
    C. family stories passed down through generations of oral tradition.
    D. cultural narratives based on tribal values and beliefs.

17. Which of the following circumstances, if true, would most CHALLENGE the notion that the Dan poro masks serve to protect their wearers while executing official duties in the community?

    A. Members of the poro are selected through a democratic process rather than on the basis of clan affiliation.
    B. Community officers are chosen in tribal electoral campaigns instead of designated from within the poro.
    C. The poro's mask-making activities begin to consume twice the amount of time it had previously.
    D. The poro gradually evolves into a guild of craftspersons which instituted bylaws and secret oaths.

18. Based on the passage it is reasonable to conclude that the masks of the Dan tribe differ from those of the Yoruba Gelade in that a Dan mask:

    A. might accurately describe the role of the person who wears it.
    B. is rarely designed by the person who wears it.
    C. is designed to mollify the cult of magic practitioners.
    D. has a special relationship to social function.

19. If a member of the Yoruba community were kidnapped and transported to a Dan village, one might reasonably expect that in participating in the daily activities of the Dan:

    A. The Yoruban might confuse governance with ceremony.
    B. The Yoruban might confuse governance with utilitarianism.
    C. The Yoruban might confuse reality with the unconscious.
    D. The Yoruban might confuse reality with satire.

GO ON TO THE NEXT PAGE

Passage IV (Questions 20–29)

"Socialization" relates to the processes and dynamics by which children come to understand their position in relation to the positions of others. In the process of socialization, the
5 child learns to respect the rights and properties of others..[and] ideally, to recognize, gradually, the need to control impulses and appetites, to accept and fulfill responsibilities, and to conform behavior to the
10 circumstances that surround him at any given time. The six-month old infant taken by a parent to the theater does not think it inappropriate to cry loudly during the performance, but the six-year-old may will
15 restrain herself even if experiencing discomfort or discontent.

Classical sociologists view the socialization process as occurring in discrete stages. At one stage, it is said, the child learns that
20 she is not the center of all activity and ceases to be in demand from adults. Later she learns to cope with absences and separations. Still further on, she learns something about boundaries and territory—that all things do
25 not belong to her and that her wish is not always another's command. In time, she comes to appreciate that she is not the only person with unmet needs, and later still, develops a bona fide wish to help meet the
30 needs of others. At a yet later stage, the child learns to process complex information at higher levels of reasoning and abstraction.

Matthew Speier, among others perhaps, feels that socialization might be profitably
35 understood in different terms. Specifically, he suggests that the child's integration into her social environment requires, fundamentally, that she learn to interact. Speier believes that the achievement of any and all develop-
40 mental milestones identified by classic sociology (and psychology) reflects a more deeply lying development of interactional competence—the ability to conduct communication with the world outside the self. He
45 chose to study socialization in terms of the interactional process and the child's development of an ability to interact.

Speier wrote, "It is my firm belief that no investigation of acquisition processes can ef-
50 fectively get underway until the concrete features of interactional competencies are analyzed as topics in their own right." He thus sought to reduce human interaction to its essential components in order then to
55 study the child's development of interactional ability. In one of his papers, for example, Speier studied a seemingly simple interaction between an eight-year-old child and his playmate's mother. The child knocked at the
60 front door of the playmate's home. The mother answered and asked who was there. The child did not state his name but instead asked whether "your son" might come out to play. The mother, in turn, responded that the
65 playmate (her son) was not at home. The child said, "O.K.," and departed.

With reference to this episode Speier noted that the eight-year-old child had developed some interactional competencies but not oth-
70 ers, thus establishing that interactional competence involves the acquisition of discrete skills. The mother had asked the boy to identify himself, and the boy offered no direct response. Instead, he stated his request,
75 his own particular need of the moment, which was for his friend to come outside and join him. The child, Speier suggests, had his own purpose in mind and did not fully appreciate the need and propriety of interacting with
80 another in order to pursue it. On the one hand he understood the need to knock at the door and to say something of his own active purpose to the person who answered, but he did not process the interactive question from
85 that person as to his own identity.

Most impressively, however, the child had identified his playmate not by name, but as "your son." That means, first of all, that the child drew conclusions as to the identity of
90 his questioner: He concluded that she was his playmate's mother. Second, he related to this woman in referent terms—terms that would refer the interaction to her (the interactive other), not to himself or his playmate.
95 He did not speak of "Johnny," or "my friend," but of "your son."

GO ON TO THE NEXT PAGE

At the age of eight this child had learned to increase the efficacy of interaction by resorting to references with which the other party is familiar. He had in some primitive fashion coached himself to interact in a way that would be meaningful to the party with whom he sought to communicate. He recognized in some primitive way the need to express his need in terms of the interactive other's frame of reference . . . to speak her "language."

At the same time, however, he had not yet learned to appreciate the importance of responding to the purpose of the interactive other with his own interaction, by identifying himself in some objective way. Rather, when asked who he was, he disregarded the other's need, and simply stated his own purpose.

20. The central thesis of the passage is that:

A. interaction is only one of many competencies essential to the formation of a fully socialized human being.

B. diverse interactional abilities cause children of similar age to vary sharply in their development.

C. interactional development offers a sound model for the understanding of the socialization process.

D. the competence of intervention strategies by parents, counselors and teachers will improve significantly by understanding children's interactional disabilities.

21. Implicit in the statement that a child learns about boundaries and territories is the idea that these perceptions:

A. prepare children to cope in a society composed of a growing immigrant population.

B. enable children to deal with the sociopolitical fact of intermittent military confrontation with foreign nations.

C. permit children to explore and admire foreign cultures without losing their own identities.

D. teach children to function according to society's rules and regulations without feeling victimized or exploited.

22. The author probably compares the situations of a six-month old taken to the theater with that of a six-year-old in order to demonstrate that:

A. fully interactionalized adults must take responsibility for less socialized children.

B. children who are exposed to art and music will develop interactional competence at an earlier age than those without such experiences.

C. older children have greater appreciation for cultural interaction than do younger children.

D. an older child is likely to be more socialized than a younger child.

GO ON TO THE NEXT PAGE

23. The ideas discussed in this passage would be of most use to:

    A. parents of multi-sibling families wanting to promote more productive interactions among their children.
    B. professional sociologists expanding their understanding of socialization dynamics.
    C. primary school teachers designing foreign language programs for young children.
    D. pre-school teachers designing a reading curriculum for learning-disabled children.

24. Suppose by the age of six months a child has developed the ability to wave "bye-bye" to departing persons. Professor Speier would most likely view this development as:

    A. an achievement of a specific interactional skill.
    B. a reflex activity essentially peripheral to the process of socialization.
    C. a milestone in the child's information-processing abilities.
    D. an indication of the child's ability to cope with separations and absences.

25. Given the ideas in the passage, the phrases "a people person," "good telephone skills," and "ability to communicate" as seen in many help wanted ads, most probably refer to:

    A. individuals who manage others by communicating their own competence
    B. individuals who put the needs of others before their own.
    C. individuals who validate others' perspectives even as they assert their own.
    D. individuals who put their own needs before those of others.

26. Each of the following behaviors is specifically cited to explain Speier's concept of discrete interactional competencies EXCEPT:

    A. A six-year-old does not whine and carry on in the theater during a performance
    B. An eight-year-old does not fail to draw conclusions about an unseen questioner's identity
    C. An eight-year-old does not identify himself in response to a direct question
    D. An eight-year-old does not refer to his friend by the friend's own name

27. As used in the passage, the phrase "referent terms" means:

    A. expressions with which people of diverse backgrounds are likely to be familiar.
    B. words that enable a listener to relate a subject to himself.
    C. phrases that allow a speaker to describe diverse relationships in a single communication.
    D. sentences that do not employ proper names.

28. Suppose two brothers, ages six and seven, have occasionally been given ice cream popsicles by a friend's mother from a freezer in her garage. One day the brothers enter the garage uninvited and unseen, and take two popsicles. Given the ideas in the passage, this behavior would most likely represent:

    A. the brothers' belief that it was unnecessary to ask permission to enter the garage and take ice cream.
    B. the brothers' lack of recognition of the individual prerogatives and property of others.
    C. the brothers' feeling that they were treated like members of the family in their friend's home.
    D. a failure of the brothers' parents to teach them right from wrong.

GO ON TO THE NEXT PAGE

29. According to the information in the passage, which of the following statements best describes the essential difference between Speier's analysis of the socialization process and that of classical sociology?

   A. Classical sociology views the child fundamentally as a conformist adapting to social expectations.
   B. Classical sociology views society as a laboratory in which the child tests her reality perceptions.
   C. Speier considers the child as a potentially competent individual within a referent context.
   D. Speier identifies the child primarily as an actor in diverse social circumstances.

GO ON TO THE NEXT PAGE

Passage V (Questions 30–35)

Frequently we refer to the idea of "commitment" without appreciating its whole meaning or its vital significance to individuals and to the social structure as a whole.
5 What, we may then ask, is the true role of commitment in human life? Indeed, what is commitment? To think of commitment simply as one among many valuable character traits is probably not sufficiently judicious.
10 Rather, commitment likely represents...[the] fundamental underpinning of all valuable character traits. It is, one might contend, the "mother" of all valuable character traits: for in the absence of commitment human exist-
15 ence would represent no more than vegetative life.

The development of character fully depends on the skill of commitment. In order to gain identity—a true self—a person must
20 make choices day to day, month to month, and year to year. Many of these choices carry irreversible consequences...[and] so commit the individual to one or another unalterable course of action. The need to make such
25 choices may produce pleasure, or it may produce anguish...[but] such is the fabric of character...and so one's moral structure becomes the product of his or her decisions.

Therein does humanity differ from other
30 forms of life. The kernel becomes a corn plant simply on the basis of programmed genetic development: The plant makes no decisions, and except in the absence of water, nutrient soil and sunlight, does not hesitate to grow.
35 The puppy gives rise to the dog through aging and physical maturation, not, we should say, through will. Until our understanding of the psychology and selfhood of dolphins and whales is somewhat more advanced, we
40 are safe to say that only men and women attain their selfhood by virtue of decision making, and decision making imports commitment, ultimately, making us what we are: As Arnold Howe observes, commitment is
45 "the sine qua non of social life."

Commitment is not uniform in its manifestations, for it assumes a variety of forms. Most people probably think of commitment as devoting one's time and energy to a par-
50 ticular project or activity. Certainly we may agree that this concept represents one form of commitment. One may, for example, devote herself to a social cause, to the welfare of some other person or persons, to her own
55 professional endeavors, to a sport or perhaps to a hobby. Let us keep room in our minds, however, for another sort of commitment, that conceit which we may justly term the "societal commitment." Persons imbued with
60 the latter generally promote values of tolerance and pluralism. They reject violence as they persevere in the face of antagonism and adversity. Seralius, for example, continued to produce his essays despite imprisonment
65 and torture. Those with societal commitment seem to possess a genuine ability to feel for others. Often that ability is a product of the suffering they themselves have endured.

Another form of commitment is that which
70 we may call "interpersonal commitment." One makes this kind of commitment when one allows oneself to truly trust another person. Sometimes the trust will lead to intimacy and sometimes to betrayal. One can never
75 know in advance how another person might use or abuse one's trust. The only certainty is that having trusted another, one will not remain unchanged. Hence, trust constitutes taking an irreversible course of action, the
80 consequences of which are not known a priori. Interpersonal commitment differs from societal commitment in that the latter involves a quest for a better civilization, whereas the former entails the investment of one's self in
85 another.

Commitment is not only the basis of character, it is a prerequisite to art, literature, music, and even to technological and economic progress. No socially useful product
90 or advance is achieved without a commitment on some person's behalf. The writer chooses to write and thus foregoes other professional and personal pursuits. The scientific

GO ON TO THE NEXT PAGE

researcher, the entrepreneur, the statesman, 95 and the financier likewise make decisions to direct their inspiration to some particular pursuit, and those decisions ultimately create insight and innovation.

30. According to the passage, commitment is a quality that:

    A. means more to an individual than to a society.
    B. is the root of animal and vegetable life.
    C. is a substructure, not a trait.
    D. has no fundamental underpinnings.

31. The author states that interpersonal commitment is essentially different and distinct from societal commitment. Based on your reading of the passage, this statement probably derives from the author's belief that:

    A. societal commitment requires no investment of self.
    B. societal commitment requires no genuine concern for others.
    C. interpersonal commitment requires no genuine concern for others.
    D. interpersonal commitment requires one to put faith in another.

32. Based on your reading of the passage, which of the following phenomena, if true, would most WEAKEN the claim that only humans must make commitments in order to develop their characters?

    A. Documentation that the frontal lobes of some animals are more intricately convoluted than those of humans
    B. Evidence that animals experience lasting gratification and pain over the need to make choices
    C. Indications that all animals have certain inborn instincts
    D. Proof that dogs can reason abstractly

33. As used in the passage, the word "conceit" means:

    A. idea
    B. fantasy
    C. boastfulness
    D. surrender

34. It is often said that commitment requires persistence. Which of the following ideas from the passage to directly supports that assertion?

    A. All hobbies require skill that takes years to develop.
    B. People are required to make choices throughout life.
    C. Seralius continued to write even though he was tortured.
    D. There can be no commitment of time without commitment of energy.

GO ON TO THE NEXT PAGE

35. According to the passage, individuals such as Seralius dedicate themselves to the promotion of social harmony and universal humanism, and persevere in their commitment despite relentless scorn and harsh treatment from society. Which of the following individuals best embodies that kind of commitment?

   A. The Aztec emperor Montezuma, because even after his capture by the Spanish he continued to rule as chieftain, and was eventually stoned to death by his own people
   B. The first U.S. Treasury Secretary Alexander Hamilton, because after years of bitter civic strife on behalf of his party, he lost his life in a gun duel with a political rival
   C. American cleric Martin Luther King, because he gave his life to a hard and painful struggle for human rights in the face of political abuse and official penalties
   D. Nun and social worker Mother Teresa, because she persists in her campaign to dignify and humanize the life of the destitute in the midst of disease and deprivation

Passage VI (Questions 36-45)

Assigning the label of structuralist to the totality of literary criticism born of theoretical speculation usually reflects an uninformed perspective rather than a malicious one, al-
5 though even within this ignorant reductionism we find a useful presupposition:...that structuralism's crucial facets are common to and inherent in each of those theoretical literary strategies which rep-
10 resent a significant uprooting of the critical enterprise from its traditional homeground. Nevertheless, this precept does not usually motivate those literary commentators who tend to view theoretical strategies as mani-
15 festations of opposition to the established criteria of the New Criticism...which itself generally focuses on a humanistic consideration of human affairs through the lens of common values and shared ethical
20 assumptions..as expressed by a given artist's aesthetic and medium. Such opposition... seeks to undermine and subjugate literature by denying its ontological mission, and, under the theoretical academic guise of
25 interdisciplinary scholarship, by supplanting its uniquely interpretive text with a multitude of diverse, alien and/or tangential discourses: a usurpation, according to these commentators, which negates the existence
30 of a given work's discrete essence, devalues the critic's elucidative task, and ultimately defiles the artist's creative act.

Theoretical inclusiveness, however, is not a purpose wholly uncelebrated by the New
35 Criticism. Indeed, Wellek and Warren's classic critical overview, Theory of Literature, represents New Criticism as a sophisticated and multilateral..[application] of the critic's imaginative powers in the service of textual
40 exegesis. Their scholarly commitment to humanism stood as a bulwark against academic and epistemological usurpation by natural science, and against...[its] empirical method of inquiry;...New Critics honored aesthetic
45 sensibility and artistic expression as fundamental aspects of the human experience...necessary and sufficient in their

GO ON TO THE NEXT PAGE

own right, independent and distinct from other...projects of civilization's institutions.

50   When theoretical, "structuralist" critics apply social-scientific modes of reasoning to literature—say, concentrating on themes of class conflict in Steinbeck's Of Mice and Men, or deploying feminist ideology in a discus-
55   sion of women's plight throughout Shakespeare's dramatic opus—traditionalists feel the call anew to defend literature from intellectual violation by extra-literary preda-tors. (The phenomenon appears not unlike
60   the scientific establishment's insistence on the self-justifying necessity of pure science: as a rallying cry, "Science for the sake of Science!" bears essential symmetry to the mobilizing maxim, "Literature for its own sake!")

65   Interdisciplinary theoreticians, infiltrating literary study with the methods and objec-tives of the social sciences, abandon the concerns and interests of thematic aestheticism..[in favor] of a configurative
70   analysis focused not on the structures and processes integral to the work's operation, but rather on those external to it: not, that is, on the work's interior conditions of charac-terization, development, motive and
75   significance, but rather on the ambient cul-tural politics and socioeconomic factors which empower, inform and determine the act of signification. For traditionalists, this exterior theoretical approach amounts to intellectual
80   desertion and cultural betrayal, and raises the fundamentalist, anti-intellectual specter of literature's cremation.

     The "global", multifaceted "inclusivity" of interdisciplinary theory, then, seemingly
85   proposes an intensively bounded dominion, apportioning validity to virtually any dis-cursive or ideological critical advocacy, while excluding and consigning to the margins only those approaches committed to a humanis-
90   tic, universalist exploration of the artistic object itself! Such narrowly defined legiti-macy nicely conforms with the reactionary

apartheidism espoused and embraced by the fashionable tenets of identity politics, the doc-
95   trines and proponents of which are seen by traditionalists as the disinformation and dupes of a...resurgent, unscrupulous segregationalist agenda. In this perspective, identity apartheidism collaborates with reac-
100   tionary fundamentalism, instilling its disciples with an obsessive dependence on restriction and taboo, and exploiting their compulsively narcissistic rejection of holistic imagination.

105   Whereas the underlying objective of deconstruction implies the systematic repu-diation of literature's enterprise, reducing meaning and emotion to semiotics and me-chanics, traditionalists remain committed to
110   diversely interpretive excursions, providing they remain integral to—and not intrusive on—the literary work itself. Thus, a feminist scholar who discovers the painful horrors of women's oppression explicitly...[described]
115   in the shadow of artistically perfected and objectively glorified female images will be applauded by traditionalists for remaining faithful to the literary text, even as she or he delineates an oppressive element of intoxi-
120   cating poetic beauty, and of the critical canon so bedazzled by the latter as to be blinded to the former. In this way, through a critical act of faith, identity inclusion contributes to the reform of established analytical domains, and
125   in so doing, rehabilitates and transforms it-self as a vitally integrative element of the holistic imagination.

GO ON TO THE NEXT PAGE

36. The author's claim that "structuralist" criticism represents an attempt to "uproot the critical enterprise" rests on the New Critics' belief that:

    A. the complexities of theoretical disciplines should inform all literary commentary.
    B. theoretical foundations are totally useless to the task of literary criticism.
    C. the essential mission of literature unmasks disguises of similitude and dissimilitude.
    D. literary criticism should focus primarily on the literary work.

37. The author most likely believes that New Critics view their opponents as undermining and subjugating literature by:

    A. placing a fundamental emphasis on humanistic interpretation.
    B. substituting external texts as the basis for the critical endeavor.
    C. negating the usurpation of literature's unique discourse.
    D. rejecting interdisciplinary methodology as a basis for discourse.

38. According to the passage, the author believes that empirical reasoning represents:

    A. a diversion for traditionalist literary critics.
    B. a threat to "structuralist" critics.
    C. a rebuttal to feminist extrapolations of 18th century novels.
    D. a mode of analysis antithetical to traditional literary concerns.

39. Based on information in the passage, students who are drawn to a humanistic interpretive approach:

    A. ignore the metatextual domains of the literary universe.
    B. reject the traditionalist school of literary criticism.
    C. are excluded by the theoretical structuralists.
    D. are animated by the nihilistic exclusivity of ideological analysis.

40. Based on information in the passage, "inclusivity" as conceived by theoretical advocates conforms with:

    A. an identity politics unwittingly serving the forces of reactionary populism.
    B. an identity politics serving to liberate its disciples from restriction and taboo.
    C. a universalist humanism tending to embrace multicultural perspectives.
    D. a universalist humanism working to defuse reactionary apartheidism.

41. The author implies that the underlying objectives of deconstruction inevitably distort literary expression because they:

    A. can never effectively negate the humanistic principles of literary criticism.
    B. infer a semiotic relationship to the mechanics of novelistic form.
    C. impart meaning to a narrative's emotional content.
    D. reject inherent meaning and motive as appropriate subjects for critical consideration.

42. As used in the passage, the word "opus" (line 56) most nearly means:

    A. foul and sordid deeds
    B. sweet, pre-adolescent male characters
    C. operatic plays
    D. collected plays

GO ON TO THE NEXT PAGE

43. The author argues that structuralist analysis poses an anti-intellectual threat to literature's existence. Which of the following circumstances, if true, would most WEAKEN the argument?

   A. A multidisciplinary committee urges that the Literature faculty be dispersed among other Humanities and Social Science departments.

   B. An associate dean of Academic Affairs proposes that Literature course offerings be cut in half.

   C. A feminist critic of Chaucer's poetry offers his course through the Women's Studies department.

   D. A Freudian critic of James Joyce's novels offers her course through the Literature department.

44. The author's attitude to non-traditional criticism is best described as:

   A. reverent

   B. critical

   C. dispassionate

   D. exuberant

45. Suppose a course description in a college bulletin promises "an in-depth literary examination of the novels of William Faulkner and Mark Twain." Students later find that the course focuses nearly exclusively on themes of cultural injustice. Based on your reading of the passage, this new information would probably lead the author to:

   A. support a student who accused the professor of false advertising.

   B. organize a boycott of the course the following semester.

   C. publish an article defending the professor's academic freedom.

   D. oppose a dean who suggested moving the course to the Political History department.

GO ON TO THE NEXT PAGE

Passage VII (Questions 46–51)

According to newspaper accounts, certain activist participants in the recent community anti-violence summit appeared to indict the entire "Western Civilization" value system
5 as the prime reason behind "a scarcity of morality" among adolescents from economically deprived environments, and a major cause of the recent, insane escalation of deadly violence among the community's
10 youth. To lay the blame for such terror at the feet of "Western Civilization" values is not only inflammatory, it is also so poorly conceived and even irresponsible as properly to be called fatuous. Because it seems improb-
15 able that the summit participants quoted in the article are capable of hurling such ignorant slurs, the most likely explanation for the story is that the comments were quoted out of context.

20 But let us consider the larger theme: If there really exists such an ethical system as so-called " Western Civilization" values (as opposed to, say, human values), it must revolve around the concept of individual rights
25 exercised within a "team" context of family and community, and based on Biblical religious and/or ethical-humanist ideals. In such a system, self-worth and peer esteem derive from the setting of constructive goals, and
30 the application of creative, individual effort and "team play" cooperation towards their realization.

In this system of beliefs, self-improvement and community empowerment through
35 education and moral commitment are highly prized, and genuine compassionate concern for one's fellow being—particularly for the poor, the infirm, the defenseless and the bereft—is regarded as especially noble.
40 Recognition of individual dignity, regardless of a person's socioeconomic 'status', is given primary importance under this value system, and respect is earned and granted on the basis of character, conviction and courage,
45 and not because of twisted "macho" acts of reckless mayhem.

How can such "Western Civilization" values be viewed as somehow unnatural and inappropriate for, or alien to, the citizens of
50 our society and communities? That some folks of various and diverse cultural backgrounds might distort those values to the point of extreme greed, or apathy, or violence towards others, is not the fault of the
55 value system itself, but of those individuals' inadequate understanding of the ethical concepts involved.

Nonetheless, no one can argue that "Western Civilization"—a quasi-sociological
60 designation mangled beyond recognition by some rhetorician's delusions—any more than any other quasi-geocultural conglomeration, is always successful at fulfilling the ideals of their value system. (As the Book of Genesis relates,
65 for example, when paranoid jealousy and obsessive hate overwhelmed Joseph's brothers and drove them to cast him into a ditch and sell him in chains to slave traders, they were betraying—not affirming—Old Testament
70 values.) Still, people who sell illegal, addictive narcotics to children, adolescents, or pregnant and nursing women, or who illegally distribute, sell, and use handguns and semiautomatic weapons in the street, or who believe that vio-
75 lence and deadly force are appropriate responses to emotional quarrels, personal tiffs and differences of opinion, can no more be said to be representative of "Western Civilization" values than can those ancient nobles and mer-
80 cenaries who participated for profit in the inexcusable sale of their own neighboring tribesfolk as slaves be considered representative of their continental values, controversial as such a reflection might appear.

85 Similarly, and more important, those relatively few but fearsome young people who seem determined to destroy their own neighborhoods, and—in the process—their own lives, together with the lives of their neigh-
90 bors, or those older folks who foster and empower such deadly notions of self-aggrandizement and peer reputation, are no more representative of the economically deprived than is Jack the Ripper representative of West-
95 ern values.

GO ON TO THE NEXT PAGE

46. The author's main point about "Western Civilization values" is that:

    A. they are superior to the value systems of other cultural groups.
    B. they are entirely inappropriate as moral guidelines for other cultural groups.
    C. their imposition on economically deprived communities is responsible for maladaptive behaviors among some adolescents.
    D. they contain many elements accepted across many cultures.

47. The author contends that remarks of summit speakers who blamed "Western Civilization values" for antisocial behavior among today's youth:

    A. imply that Western Civilization values teach inequality and injustice.
    B. should have been censored.
    C. were probably imprecisely reported.
    D. have led to a general decline in moral civility.

48. With which of the following statements would the author most likely agree?

    A. "Western Civilization" is a term more useful to sociology than to everyday reality.
    B. "Western Civilization" is most useful as a rhetorical term.
    C. "Western Civilization" refers to a distinct geographical group.
    D. "Western Civilization" refers to a distinct cultural group.

49. The author suggests that the true reason(s) for antisocial behavior among some adolescents is/are:

    I. the principle that respect is earned on the basis of character
    II. the distortion of a humanistic value system
    III. the active corruption of youth by criminal elements
    A. I only
    B. II only
    C. II and III only
    D. I, II, and III

50. Among the following, the author most likely believes that much of the responsibility for urban social maladies is due to:

    A. Western Civilization values.
    B. Non-Western Civilization values.
    C. Ancient mercenaries of diverse backgrounds.
    D. People who sell guns on the streets.

51. The author argues that "Western Civilization values" are founded on true belief, personal bravery and moral action. Which of the following findings, if true, would most WEAKEN the author's contention?

    A. Many Americans believe that violence is the most appropriate way to resolve personal disputes.
    B. Many Americans learn moral commitment as a part of their religious training.
    C. Most Americans believe that bravery is the most important of all values.
    D. Most Americans believe that bravery, honesty, and commitment are the keys to a civilized society.

GO ON TO THE NEXT PAGE

Passage VIII (Questions 52–58)

Since the early days of the scientific study of computers, researchers have been fascinated by the subspecialty of artificial intelligence (AI). The notion that a non-or-
5 ganic information processor might independently accomplish certain tasks theretofore deemed unachievable without the direct involvement of a living human intelligence enthralled pioneers in the field. To date,
10 the kinds of tasks submitted to artificial intelligence have largely been limited to the understanding and/or translation of language, learning of game strategy, provision of professional counsel, defect analysis, and
15 robotics.

Rudimentary efforts to teach computers language translation relied solely on word equivalences programmed in the computer's dictionary and linked to automated syntax
20 substitution. With this approach, however, even in the case of linguistically related languages, such as French and Spanish, the sentences generated usually defied grammatical, syntactical, and logical sense.

25 In the area of game strategy, computers have realized considerably more success than in language translation. Chess, for example, has been extensively investigated as a channel for the exercise and expression of artificial
30 intelligence. Over the years, computerized tactical chess programs have evolved with such expertise and proficiency that the only human beings who can now prevail over them are among the international elite masters of
35 the game. Artificial intelligence has demonstrated similar capabilities in other systems of strategic learning and interaction as well.

In these rule-based searches, initial gross analysis is achieved by cueing the artificial
40 memory with a specific array of symptoms. Through a process of reductive elimination informed by operator responses to a rule-based question series, the computer generates a set of possible diagnoses consistent with
45 the encoded symptomatic profile and ranked according to programmed probability. This

kind of expert defect analysis, in which specific compartments of memory within an extensive body of knowledge are accessible
50 to the computer's search only on the basis of compliance with logical rules of inclusion and exclusion, today represents an area of significant accomplishment for artificial intelligence, and continues to generate a con-
55 siderable amount of enthusiastic research and development in a wide variety of fields.

A strategic approach to problem-solving is essential to the ability to provide professional caliber counsel. The ability to include
60 or exclude knowledge compartments from an ongoing processor search endows artificial intelligence with a trait something akin to human judgment and analytical discretion, and is achieved by organizing the
65 elements of expert knowledge within categorical frames. The particular elements comprising each framed category within a larger knowledge base bear some shared relation to a specific input event or data
70 constellation: i.e., they form an encapsulated informational object. (In a case of medical diagnosis, for example, a data constellation might consist of a non-productive hacking cough with spiking fever and systemic ener-
75 vation.) In this regard, frames are not unlike traditional databased tuples or file archives, with the essential difference, however, that framed memory accessibility derives from data linkage, itself regulated and encapsu-
80 lated according to procedural production syllogisms.

Linkage between and among frames proceeds in accordance with the restrictions of analytical logic: IF a particular data require-
85 ment is fulfilled, THEN a specified frame of memory is made accessible to the computer. (In the case of patient diagnosis, the presence of a non-productive cough with fever might open up certain frames of knowledge con-
90 taining pertinent and possible diagnoses for the computer's search, whereas a productive cough with fever would direct the computer to alternate memory compartments and other possible syndrome specifications.) The study
95 of coherent linkage of knowledge frames

GO ON TO THE NEXT PAGE →

through syllogistic requisites has led computer scientists to the invention of semantic or neural networks, programmatic learning systems patterned after a learning model
100 originally delineated for the human brain.

In neural networks, data constellations or elements are stored as nodes, integral knowledge objects interconnected by definitive informational relationships. Even more so-
105 phisticated applications can equip the computer with the ability to derive its own rules of linkage—and relative regulatory influence among contrasting and/or complimentary rules—in accordance with its
110 individual input experience base. (For instance, a node labelled "implement of silverware" might relate with identical probability to the particular elements "knife," "fork," and "spoon." However, the computer
115 might be programmed to learn that a greater probability should be linked to "fork" if the silverware object is pronged, or to "spoon" if it is curved.) Neural network learning programs are currently undergoing prolific
120 development in the areas of military technology, business cycle projection and fluctuation forecast, and microscopic recognition of medical pathology. This area of computer science represents one of the most promising hori-
125 zons on the frontier of technology's future.

52. According to the passage, the facet of artificial intelligence that particularly intrigued early computer scientists was the fact that:

   A. a mechanical apparatus could be taught to translate human languages.

   B. a computer could learn to accomplish thinking tasks completely independently of any live human being.

   C. a machine could perform tasks that required learning intelligence without the immediate operative participation of humans.

   D. a machine could teach human beings artificial modes of mental activity.

53. According to the passage, artificial intelligence programmers solved initial problems in language translation by:

   A. providing computers with independent memory of diverse systems of semiotic linguistic representation.

   B. liberating computers from confinement in semantic-free meaning.

   C. eliminating from translation programs languages with similar vocabulary and parallel syntax .

   D. teaching computers to recognize a word-based message independent of textual representation.

54. In relation to playing games, the author suggests that:

   A. computers will never be able to master the game of chess as well as humans.

   B. chess is the only game in which computers can effectively compete with humans.

   C. computer learning has been generally more effective in the area of game playing than language translation.

   D. computers usually prevail over human opponents in chess, except against internationally elite linguists.

55. According to the passage, computerized defect analysis functions differently from simple data retrieval in that:

   A. it incorporates a program of guidelines to selectively retrieve stored data.

   B. it excludes reductive elimination as a retrieval tool.

   C. it requires interactive inputs as retrieval prompts.

   D. there is no essential difference between the two processes.

GO ON TO THE NEXT PAGE

56. According to the passage, knowledge frames modulate memory accessibility by:

    A. compartmentalizing linkage instructions within larger informational contexts.
    B. restricting bounded knowledge packets to logically interconnected predictor inputs.
    C. limiting computer searches to encoded probability analysis.
    D. providing unencumbered scanning modes within relatively extensive bases of knowledge.

57. Discussing the relation of analytical logic to artificial intelligence, the author explains that:

    A. coherent linkage of knowledge frames occurs independently of IF/THEN propositions.
    B. syllogistic procedures define tuple-based information retrieval.
    C. syllogistic principles provide the basis for connecting integral knowledge objects.
    D. it is impossible to arrange tuples for medical diagnosis logically correlated objects.

58. According to the passage, which of the following statements regarding neural networks is accurate?

    A. Established informational relationships are generally inadequate to bridge nodal synapses.
    B. Established informational relationships are wholly unaffected by inputted information.
    C. For computers to construct neural links between information nodes human operators must provide programmed rules of relative probability.
    D. Through empirical learning methods computers can decide and apportion weighted linkage without preprogramming.

GO ON TO THE NEXT PAGE

Passage IX (Question 59–65)

Before the sun evolved into the Earth-sustaining and life-giving body that it is today, it underwent the same process of stellar formation by which other stars come into being.
5 Astronomers generally divide that formative process into three recognizable phases, distinguished from each other on the basis of the star's approximate diameter and other physical characteristics. Our sun presently
10 occupies the third, or "main sequence" phase, which will likely come to an end some five billion years from now, when, obliterating the inner planets, it will transform into a "red giant."

15 As a "G-dwarf" class star some 4.8 billion years old, the sun's current, main sequence diameter is roughly 700-thousand kilometers. In its first phase, the "protosun" measured some 150 million kilometers—equal to one
20 Astronomical Unit (AU)—in diameter. As an intermediate phase T-Tauri class star, the sun's diameter contracted to 28 hundred-thousand kilometers. An ongoing process of "dense hydrogen cloud collapse" powers this
25 transformative contraction of stars, producing, in the case of the sun, a main sequence G-dwarf star approximately one-eighth its original size.

Although astronomers previously believed
30 that protostellar hydrogen clouds obey a "power law" of molecular distribution—by which the vast majority of molecular material would coalesce around a hyperdense center— recent investigations have rather shown that
35 Gaussian (bell-shaped) rules prevail. Applying high-resolution astroradiometry in wavelengths of less than a millimeter, Ward-Thompson et al., concluded that the density at the center of protostellar hydrogen clouds is significantly
40 lower than previously estimated. One interesting sidelight to this discovery, detailed by Myhill and Boss, demonstrates that the absence of such a Gaussian distribution would make the creation of binary star systems—so-called
45 "double" stars—virtually impossible.

As recently as four years ago, astrophysicists believed that binary star systems represented an exceptional astrophysical phenomena. The recognition of Gaussian
50 distributions of hydrogen in the protostellar dense clouds, however, set the molecular stage for a universe where star pairs predominate over single suns. Given the requisite angular momentum and a gravita-
55 tional energy more than twice its thermal energy (below 10 Kelvin), Boss calculated that the cloud's gravitational collapse will result in a "fragmentation" of protostellar material, ultimately yielding two protostars bound to-
60 gether by mutual gravitational attraction—a protobinary system. Because such forces and energies are more the norm than otherwise in protostellar dense hydrogen cloud formations, double stars should far outnumber
65 singles.

Spectroscopic measurements of the periodic Doppler shift of all G-dwarf stars within 72 light-years from the Earth, in fact, validate those findings. Duquennoy and Mayor
70 determined that in a sample of 164 representative G-dwarfs in our galaxy, companion systems occurred at a frequency nearly twice that of lone stars. Spectroscopy also revealed that multiple stars—triples or quadruples—
75 appeared much less frequently than binaries, about one-seventh and one-thirtieth as often, respectively.

Investigators have proposed a two-stage collapse mechanism in the formation of com-
80 panion systems. Binary protostars separated by at least 10 AU in space contracted during the first step of collapse-fragmentation to produce a diameter of approximately 20 AU for each star of the pair. These stage-I paired
85 protostars then collapse a second time, a process during which a second fragmentation may occur, and a second companion system may emerge. The resulting distance between emergent stage-II protobinaries is
90 similar to that between the most proximate main sequence doubles.

Richard Muller et al., have suggested that even our sun represents one half of a binary

GO ON TO THE NEXT PAGE →

system with a separation distance so enor-
95 mous as to make the doubles essentially
invisible and unknown to each other. Such a
vast separation would mean that the sun and
its companion orbit each other once approximately every 30 million years. As the sun's
100 companion unleashes gravitational disturbances on every perihelion approach, comet
showers from the farthest ranges of the solar
system could tumble down to Earth, conceivably resulting in planetary extinctions every
105 30 million years, such as that which extermi-
nated the dinosaurs. Because no detectable
star lies close enough to the sun to enforce
gravitational orbit, however, most astrophysicists doubt the plausibility of Muller's
110 solar-pair hypothesis.

59. According to the passage, modern scientists
believe that star formation involves all of
the following EXCEPT:

A. processes that tend to form star pairs
more often than single stars.
B. separation of protostellar material to
yield protostars.
C. diminution in size facilitated by
Gaussian rules.
D. the aggregation of molecular matter
around a highly dense core.

60. According to the passage, the research of
Duquennoy and Mayor showed that:

A. Quadruples occur more often than
triples.
B. Triples occur less often than singles.
C. Singles occur more often than doubles.
D. Doubles occur less often than triples.

61. Compared to a star in the main sequence
phase, a T-Tauri star is, according to the
passage:

A. younger and larger.
B. younger and smaller.
C. older and larger.
D. older and smaller.

62. According to the passage, the "power law"
of molecular distribution is challenged by
the observation that:

A. our own sun is a G-dwarf class star.
B. some stars are formed as pairs.
C. protostars have centers of very high
density.
D. astroradiometry may be employed in
extremely small wavelengths.

63. According to the passage, it is considered
improbable that our own sun is part of a
star pair because:

A. the other star of the pair would have to
exist outside our own galaxy.
B. comet showers are known to occur with
a frequency greater than once every 30
million years.
C. the other star of the pair would cause
the extinction of most of Earth's animal
species.
D. investigations reveal no star sufficiently
close to the sun to exert significant gravitational force on it.

64. According to the passage, the termination
of the phase now occupied by our sun will
cause the planets to:

A. become red giants.
B. enter their main sequence phase.
C. shrink in diameter.
D. disappear.

65. The discovery that star formation is governed not by the "power law" but by Gaussian rules might best be analogized to the finding that:

   A. a given disease spreads not directly from one patient to another, but by an insect bite, which explains why a person could contract the disease without exposure to an afflicted patient.

   B. left-handedness corresponds not to longer life span, but to shorter life span, which explains the fact that left-handed persons tend to have a greater facility for artistic and verbal creativity.

   C. the first carts and wagons tended to break apart on encountering bumps, which led to the installation of springs and, later, of shock absorbers.

   D. certain isolated societies have no concept of property or ownership, which explains why such peoples never developed weapons of mass destruction.

STOP
IF YOU FINISH BEFORE TIME IS CALLED, YOU MAY CHECK YOUR WORK ON THIS TEST ONLY. DO NOT TURN TO ANY OTHER TEST IN THIS BOOK.

Physical Sciences II

Time: 100 Minutes
Questions 66-142

PHYSICAL SCIENCES

DIRECTIONS: Most questions in the Physical Sciences test are organized into groups, each preceded by a descriptive passage. After studying the passage, select the one best answer to each question in the group. Some questions are not based on a descriptive passage and are also independent of each other. You must also select the one best answer to these questions. If you are not certain of an answer, eliminate the alternatives that you know to be incorrect and then select an answer from the remaining alternatives. Indicate your selection by blackening the corresponding oval on your answer document. A periodic table is provided for your use. You may consult it whenever you wish.

PERIODIC TABLE OF THE ELEMENTS

1 H 1.0																	2 He 4.0
3 Li 6.9	4 Be 9.0											5 B 10.8	6 C 12	2 N 14.0	8 O 16	9 F 19.0	10 Ne 20.0
11 Na 22.0	12 Mg 24.3											13 Al 27.0	14 Si 28.1	15 P 31.0	16 S 32.1	17 Cl 35.5	18 Ar 39.0
19 K 39.1	20 Ca 40.1	21 Sc 45.0	22 Ti 47.9	23 V 50.9	24 Cr 52.0	25 Mn 54.9	26 Fe 55.8	27 Co 58.9	28 Ni 58.7	29 Cu 63.5	30 Zn 65.4	31 Ga 69.7	32 Ge 72.6	33 As 74.9	34 Se 79.0	35 Br 79.9	36 Kr 83.8
37 Rb 85.5	38 Sr 87.6	39 Y 88.9	40 Zr 91.2	41 Nb 92.9	42 Mo 95.9	43 Tc 97.0	44 Ru 101.0	45 Rh 102.9	46 Pd 106.4	47 Ag 107.9	48 Cd 112.4	49 In 114.8	50 Sn 118.7	51 Sb 121.8	52 Te 127.6	53 I 126.9	54 Xe 131.3
55 Cs 132.9	56 Ba 137.3	57 La 138.9	72 Hf 178.5	73 Ta 180.9	74 W 183.9	75 Re 186.2	76 Os 190.2	77 Ir 192.2	78 Pt 195.1	79 Au 197.0	80 Hg 200.6	81 Tl 204.4	82 Pb 207.2	83 Bi 209.0	84 Po 209.0	85 At 210.0	86 Rn 222.0
87 Fr 223.0	88 Ra 226.0	89 Ac 227.0															

58 Ce 140.1	59 Pr 140.9	60 Nd 144.2	61 Pm 145.0	62 Sm 150.4	63 Eu 152.0	64 Gd 157.3	65 Tb 158.9	66 Dy 162.5	67 Ho 164.9	68 Er 167.3	69 Tm 168.9	70 Yb 173.0	71 Lu 175.0
90 Th 232.0	91 Pa 231.0	92 U 238.0	93 Np 237.0	94 Pu 244.0	95 Am 243.0	96 Cm 247.0	97 Bk 247.0	98 Cf 251.0	99 Es 254.0	100 Fm 253.0	101 Md 256.0	102 No 253.0	103 Lr 257.0

GO ON TO THE NEXT PAGE

Passage I (Questions 66–72)

The rate at which a reaction takes place, the reaction rate, is a measure of the rate at which reactants disappear. For a first-order chemical reaction this rate varies according to the reaction rate law:

rate = k [A], where k is the rate constant for the reaction.

The rate of a reaction at any point in the progress of the reaction can be found experimentally by taking the ratio:

$$\frac{\text{change in molar concentration}}{\text{time}}$$

The rate constant, k *of reactant*, is constant for any given temperature, but increases with increasing temperature. For most reactions it very nearly doubles for every 10°C by which temperature is increased.

Reaction I was allowed to proceed under controlled conditions and the concentration of reactant A was measured at regular intervals until the reactants and products came to equilibrium.

$$A_{(aq)} \rightleftharpoons B_{(aq)} + C_{(aq)}$$

Reaction 1

The forward reaction is endothermic, with $\Delta H = 150$ kJ.

Figure 1 depicts change in the concentration of A as the reaction proceeded at 25°C and 1 atm pressure in a chamber containing 2 liters of solution.

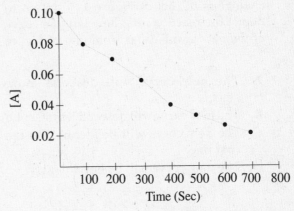

Figure 1

The process was later repeated in a chamber whose temperature was maintained at 60°C.

66. What is the approximate initial rate of the reaction 1 at 25°C?

   A. 1×10^{-4} M/sec
   B. 2×10^{-4} M/sec
   C. 1×10^{-2} M/sec
   D. 2×10^{-2} M/sec

67. According to figure 1, how many moles of A are present in the solution after 600 seconds have elapsed?

   A. 0.01 moles
   B. 0.03 moles
   C. 0.06 moles
   D. 0.09 moles

GO ON TO THE NEXT PAGE

68. If reaction 1 is run at 60°C and a graph analogous to that of Figure 1 is drawn to depict the reaction rate, how will the curve of the new graph differ from that of Figure 1?

   A. The new curve will descend more steeply.
   B. The new curve will descend less steeply.
   C. The new curve will be identical to the first line.
   D. The new curve will be horizontal.

69. How would increasing the temperature at which the reaction takes place affect the rates of the forward and reverse reactions and the eventual equilibrium?

   A. It would increase the rate of the forward reaction, decrease the rate of the reverse reaction, and shift the equilibrium towards the formation of products.
   B. It would decrease the rate of the forward reaction, increase the rate of the reverse reaction, and shift the equilibrium towards the formation of reactants.
   C. It would increase the rate of the forward reaction, increase the rate of the reverse reaction, and shift the equilibrium towards the formation of products.
   D. It would increase the rate of the forward reaction, increase the rate of the reverse reaction, and shift the equilibrium towards the formation of reactants.

70. As the forward reaction proceeds, the reaction rate:

   A. decreases.
   B. increases.
   C. remains constant.
   D. decreases, then increases.

71. If 2 moles each of B and C are formed in Reaction 1, the enthalpy change of the reaction is:

   A. 75 kJ.
   B. 150 kJ.
   C. 300 kJ.
   D. 600 kJ.

72. If the initial concentration of A is doubled, what will be the effect on the initial rate of reaction and the rate constant?

   A. The rate of reaction and the rate constant will double.
   B. The rate of reaction and the rate constant will not change.
   C. The rate of reaction will double and the rate constant will not change.
   D. The rate of reaction will not change and the rate constant will double.

Passage II (Questions 73–78)

The apparatus shown below was used by James Joule to demonstrate the equivalence of gravitational potential energy and thermal energy.

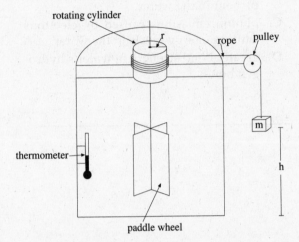

Water is contained in a thermally insulated container. The block, with mass m, is released. The descending block pulls the rope, which causes the cylinder to rotate, which, in turn, rotates the paddle wheel. The block's gravitational potential energy is dissipated in the friction between the paddles and the water. Acceleration due to gravity g is 9.8 m/s².

Joule found that the increase in temperature of the water caused by the rotating paddles was proportional to the potential energy of the block.

It was found that one calorie, the amount of heat needed to raise the temperature of one gram of water by 1°C, is equal to 4.19 J.

The following table gives the specific heats of various materials under standard conditions.

Material	Specific heat (cal/g°C)
Aluminum	0.22
Copper	0.09
Glass	0.20
Ice	0.50
Iron	0.11
Mercury	0.03
Water	1.00

Table 1

73. When 1 gram of each of the following materials is subjected to a given amount of heat, which will undergo the greatest temperature increase?

    A. Aluminum
    B. Copper
    C. Iron
    D. Mercury

74. Where m = the mass of the block, g = acceleration due to gravity, and r = radius of the rotating cylinder, which of the following expressions gives the magnitude of the torque exerted on the cylinder by the hanging block at the moment it begins to fall?

    A. 1/2 mgr
    B. mgr
    C. 1/2 $mghr$
    D. $mghr$

GO ON TO THE NEXT PAGE

75. Which of the following is true regarding the water in the insulated container?

    A. Fluid pressure is greater near the bottom of the container than near the top.
    B. Fluid pressure is greater near the top of the container than near the bottom.
    C. Fluid pressure is the same at all points within the container.
    D. Fluid pressure is zero at all points.

76. Using the apparatus shown in Figure 1, an investigator wishes to use a 1 kg mass to raise the temperature of 1 g of water by 1°C. From what height, approximately, must she drop the 1kg mass?

    A. 20 cm
    B. 40 cm
    C. 60 cm
    D. 80 cm

77. In an experiment, 500 cal are required to raise the temperature of a sample of glass by 10°C. How much heat would be required to raise, also by 10°C, the temperature of a sample of water with the same mass?

    A. 50 cal
    B. 100 cal
    C. 1000 cal
    D. 2500 cal

78. When the experiment described in the passage is complete, the initial gravitational potential energy of the hanging block has been converted to:

    A. increased kinetic energy of the water molecules.
    B. increased electrical energy of the ions present in the water.
    C. photon emissions caused by electrons shifting energy levels in the water.
    D. greater bond strength of water's hydrogen bonds.

GO ON TO THE NEXT PAGE

Passage III (Questions 79–84)

Human teeth are covered by a layer of enamel that serves to protect them. This enamel is composed of the mineral *hydroxyapatite*, whose empirical formula is $Ca_5(PO_4)_3OH(s)$.

When tooth decay occurs, hydroxyapatite is dissolved into the saliva as shown in the following reaction:

$$Ca_5(PO_4)_3OH(s) \longrightarrow 5\,Ca^{2+}(aq) + 3\,PO_4^{3-}(aq) + OH^-(aq)$$

Reaction 1

The forward reaction represents tooth decay. However, the reverse reaction normally occurs at a faster rate than does the forward reaction, and under normal conditions, teeth do not decay in saliva.

The consumption of food with a large sugar content promotes tooth decay because the digestion of sugar , which begins in the mouth, produces acid. Acid, in turn, affects the equilibrium of Reaction 1.

Fluoride is used to fight tooth decay because it can replace hydroxide in the enamel formation process to form a compound called fluorapatite, $Ca_5(PO_4)_3F(s)$, which undergoes this reaction:

$$Ca_5(PO_4)_3F(s) \Rightarrow 5\,Ca^{2+}(aq) + 3\,PO_4^{3-}(aq) + F^-(aq)$$

Reaction 2

The fluoride ions produced in Reaction 2 are much less likely to react in an acidic environment than are the hydroxide ions produced in reaction 1.

79. The process of tooth decay is most likely to occur in saliva maintained at which of the following pH values?

A. 6.0
B. 7.0
C. 8.0
D. 9.0

80. The oxidation state of calcium in the hydroxyapatite molecule is:

A. –1
B. 0
C. +1
D. +2

81. Fluorapatite is more resistant to tooth decay than is hydroxyapatite because the fluoride ion is:

A. a strong base that has little interaction with hydrogen ions in saliva.
B. a weak base that has little interaction with hydrogen ions in saliva.
C. a strong base that reacts with hydrogen ions in solution.
D. a weak base that reacts with hydrogen ions in solution.

GO ON TO THE NEXT PAGE

82. The presence of acid in saliva acts to promote tooth decay because acid in saliva will:

    A. increase the hydroxide concentration, shifting the equilibrium of Reaction 1 to the right.
    B. increase the hydroxide concentration, shifting the equilibrium of Reaction 1 to the left.
    C. decrease the hydroxide concentration, shifting the equilibrium of Reaction 1 to the right.
    D. decrease the hydroxide concentration, shifting the equilibrium of Reaction 1 to the left.

83. The pH of saliva is normally about 6.5. The normal pOH of saliva is:

    A. 6.0
    B. 6.5
    C. 7.0
    D. 7.5

84. Reaction 2 is examined under controlled conditions in order to examine how changes in various factors will affect its equilibrium. An increase in the pressure in the vessel in which the reaction occurs would be expected to:

    A. have no effect on the equilibrium.
    B. shift the equilibrium to the right.
    C. shift the equilibrium to the left.
    D. prevent the reaction from occurring.

Passage IV (Questions 85–91)

A researcher conducted several experiments designed to examine the principles of projectile motion.

Experiment 1

In eight trials, a projectile was launched from a level surface at an initial speed of 20 m/sec. With each trial, the angle of elevation was varied. Maximum height, horizontal distance, and flight time were recorded in Table 1.

Trial	Angle of elevation	Flight time (sec)	Height (m)	Distance (m)
1	10°	0.7	.05	14.0
2	20°	1.4	2.5	26.5
3	30°	2.0	5.0	35.0
4	40°	2.6	8.5	40.0
5	50°	3.1	12.0	39.5
6	60°	3.5	15.5	35.0
7	70°	3.8	18.0	26.0
8	80°	4.0	20.0	14.0

Table 1

Experiment 2

In five repeated trials, a projectile was launched horizontally—with 0° angle of elevation—from a platform raised 50 m above a level surface. With each trial, the projectile's initial speed was varied. Flight time and horizontal distance were recorded in Table 2.

GO ON TO THE NEXT PAGE

Trial	Speed (m/s)	Flight time (sec)	Distance (m)
1	10	3.2	32
2	20	3.2	64
3	30	3.2	96
4	40	3.2	128
5	50	3.2	160

Table 2

85. In the absence of air resistance, which of the following quantities remains constant throughout the flight of a projectile?

    I. Horizontal speed
    II. Vertical speed
    III. Acceleration

A. I only.
B. II only.
C. I and II only.
D. I and III only.

86. Which of the following conclusions is most justifiably drawn from the data gathered in Experiment 1?

A. Horizontal distance increases with increasing angle of elevation.
B. Horizontal distance decreases with increasing angle of elevation.
C. Flight time increases with increasing angle of elevation.
D. Flight time decreases with increasing angle of elevation.

87. If a ninth projectile had been launched in Experiment 1 and had traveled a horizontal distance of 31.0 m, its angle of elevation would most likely have been:

A. 25° or 65°.
B. 25° or 75°.
C. 35° or 65°.
D. 35° or 75°.

88. Which of the following expressions represents the horizontal speed of the projectile launched in Trial 3 of Experiment 1?

A. 20 m/s
B. 20 (cos 30°) m/s
C. 20 (sin 30°) m/s
D. 20 (tan 30°) m/s

89. As the angle of elevation is increased from 10° to 80° in Experiment 1, assuming air resistance to be negligible, the kinetic energy of the projectiles as they strike the ground:

A. increases.
B. decreases.
C. increases, then decreases.
D. remains the same.

90. A researcher examining the results of Experiment 2 could properly draw the conclusion that:

A. flight time is independent of horizontal speed.
B. flight time is independent of initial height.
C. horizontal distance is independent of initial height.
D. horizontal distance is independent of flight time.

GO ON TO THE NEXT PAGE

91. If Experiment 2 were performed a second time, with the initial height set at 25 m, what would be the expected flight time for the projectiles?

   A. 1.6 sec
   B. 2.3 sec
   C. 3.2 sec
   D. 5.1 sec

Questions 92 through 96 are **NOT** based on a descriptive passage.

92. A bucket with mass m is suspended from a rope that hangs straight downward. If g represents the acceleration due to gravity, and the rope pulls the bucket upward at a constant speed, what is the tension in the rope?

   A. $mg/2$
   B. mg
   C. $2mg$
   D. $4mg$

93. A chamber at constant temperature contains 10 moles of helium gas and 1 mole of neon gas. Which of the following is NOT true?

   A. The average speed of the helium atoms is greater than the average speed of the neon atoms.
   B. The partial pressure due to the helium atoms is greater than the partial pressure due to the neon atoms.
   C. The total mass of helium present in the chamber is greater than the total mass of neon present in the chamber.
   D. The average kinetic energy of the helium atoms is greater than the average kinetic energy of the neon atoms.

94. A 320 gram sample of sodium-25 decays through the emission of a beta particle, forming magnesium-25. If 40 g of sodium-25 remain after 3 minutes of decay, what is the half life of sodium-25?

   A. 1 min.
   B. 2 min.
   C. 3 min.
   D. 4 min.

95. A light ray first travels through water and then encounters a second medium. If the ray's angle of incidence is 30°, its angle of refraction will be:

   A. less than 30°.
   B. equal to 30°.
   C. greater than 30°.
   D. dependent on the refractive index of the second medium.

96. A student prepares a 1 molal aqueous solution of several salts. Among the following which solution will show the greatest boiling point elevation?

   A. NaCl
   B. $MgCl_2$
   C. $NaNO_3$
   D. $MgCO_3$

Passage V (Questions 97–102)

A student attempts to identify the metals involved in several oxidation-reduction reactions of the form:

$$Y^{2+}(aq) + Z(s) \rightarrow Y(s) + Z^{2+}(aq)$$

Reaction 1

The student examines three separate galvanic cells, all of which are designed as shown in Figure 1.

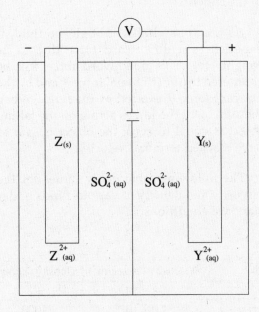

Half Reaction	$E°(V)$
$Ba^{2+}(aq) + 2\ e^- \rightarrow Ba(s)$	−2.9
$Mg^{2+}(aq) + 2\ e^- \rightarrow Mg(s)$	−2.4
$Be^{2+}(aq) + 2\ e^- \rightarrow Be(s)$	−1.9
$Mn^{2+}(aq) + 2\ e^- \rightarrow Mn(s)$	−1.2
$Zn^{2+}(aq) + 2\ e^- \rightarrow Zn(s)$	−0.8
$Cd^{2+}(aq) + 2\ e^- \rightarrow Cd(s)$	−0.4

Table 1

The student has been told that all half-reactions occurring in the cells are listed in Table 1.

Experiment 1

The voltmeter is connected to the electrodes of one cell and registers a potential difference of 0.5 V.

Experiment 2

The voltmeter is connected to the electrodes of a second cell and registers a potential difference of 0 V.

Experiment 3

The voltmeter is connected to the electrodes of a third cell and registers a potential difference of 1.6 V.

97. Regarding the reaction taking place in Experiment 1, which of the following statements must be true?

A. The free energy change is positive.
B. The free energy change is negative.
C. The free energy does not change.
D. The free energy change is equal to the voltage.

GO ON TO THE NEXT PAGE

98. If it is known that Z(s) for Experiment 1 is solid magnesium, the student should determine that the identity of Y(s) is:

A. barium.
B. beryllium.
C. zinc.
D. cadmium.

99. Which of the following could be the identities of $Y^{2+}(aq)$ and Z(s) in Experiment 2?

A. $Be^{2+}(aq)$ and Mn(s)
B. $Mg^{2+}(aq)$ and Ba(s)
C. $Cd^{2+}(aq)$ and Zn(s)
D. $Zn^{2+}(aq)$ and Be(s)

100. During the experiments, Reaction 1 proceeds in the forward direction. As Reaction 1 proceeds:

A. $Y^{2+}(aq)$ is oxidized and Z(s) is reduced.
B. $Y^{2+}(aq)$ is reduced and Z(s) is oxidized.
C. Y(s) is oxidized and $Z^{2+}(aq)$ is reduced.
D. Y(s) is reduced and $Z^{2+}(aq)$ is oxidized.

101. Among the species listed in Table 1, which is the strongest reducing agent?

A. $Cd^{2+}(aq)$
B. Cd(s)
C. $Ba^{2+}(aq)$
D. Ba(s)

102. The positive electrode in Figure 1 is the:

A. anode, where reduction takes place.
B. anode, where oxidation takes place.
C. cathode, where reduction takes place.
D. cathode, where oxidation takes place.

Passage VI (Questions 103–107)

When an object falls through a fluid, it experiences a frictional force tending to oppose its downward motion. This force's magnitude depends on the object's speed, size and shape, and the fluid's viscosity.

For a small sphere falling through a viscous fluid, the frictional force is given by the formula: $F_f = 6\rho grv$, where g is the viscosity of the fluid, r is the radius of the sphere, ρ is the density of the fluid, and v is the velocity of the sphere.

As the sphere falls through the fluid, it experiences a downward force due to its weight mg. This downward force will be countered by the frictional force F_f and by the buoyant force F_b exerted by the fluid. When the sum of all the forces acting on the falling object is equal to zero, the object is said to have reached terminal velocity.

The following table gives values for the viscosity and density of various fluids under standard conditions.

Fluid	Viscosity (N-sec/m²)	Density (kg/m³)
Air	1.8×10^{-5}	1.3
Water	1.0×10^{-3}	1000
Glycerine	8.3×10^{-1}	1260
Ethyl alchohol	1.2×10^{-3}	800

Table 1

103. For a small sphere falling through a fluid, which of the following equations describes the relationship between the magnitude of the forces as they act on the sphere at terminal velocity?

A. $F_f + F_b = mg$
B. $F_f + mg = F_b$
C. $F_b + mg = F_f$
D. $F_f = F_b = mg$

GO ON TO THE NEXT PAGE

104. For an object descending through fluid, which of the following graphs depicts the change in frictional force as speed varies?

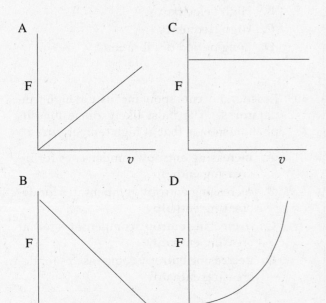

A

F

v

C

F

v

B

F

v

D

F

v

105. Two spherical drops with equal radii fall through the air. One is composed of glycerin and the other of ethyl alcohol. Which would be expected to reach the greater terminal velocity?

A. Ethyl alcohol, because it has the lower viscosity.
B. Ethyl alcohol, because it has the lower density.
C. Glycerine, because it has the higher viscosity.
D. Glycerine, because it has the higher density.

106. Which of the following will affect the buoyant force experienced by a solid object falling through a fluid?

A. The density of the object.
B. The density of the fluid.
C. The viscosity of the object.
D. The viscosity of the fluid.

107. Which statement must be true of an object sinking in a fluid?

A. The weight of the object is greater than the buoyant force.
B. The weight of the object is less than the buoyant force.
C. The frictional force is greater than the buoyant force.
D. The frictional force is less than the buoyant force.

GO ON TO THE NEXT PAGE

Passage VII (Questions 108–115)

Solar energy offers several advantages over the combustion of fossil fuels. Chief among these are the facts that its supply is virtually unlimited and that it need not produce hazardous waste products. One disadvantage of solar energy is the inconsistency of its availability. Figure 1 illustrates a device designed to store solar energy through the use of a reversible chemical process.

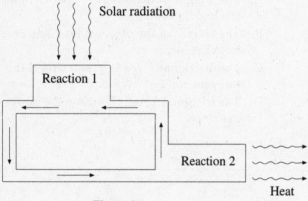

Figure 1

$$2 SO_3(g) \rightarrow 2 SO_2(g) + O_2(g) \quad \Delta H = 198 \text{ kJ}$$
Reaction 1

Reaction 1 is endothermic and occurs at high temperatures.

$$2 SO_2(g) + O_2(g) \rightarrow 2 SO_3(g) \quad \Delta H = -198 \text{ kJ}$$
Reaction 2

Reaction 2 is exothermic and occurs only in the presence of a catalyst.

The device is closed to the outside and gas is circulated around the system. Energy is stored in the endothermic process of Reaction 1 and can be later released by initiating the exothermic process of Reaction 2.

108. Solar radiation with which of the following properties will make the most energy available for storage by the device?

   A. Long wavelength.
   B. High velocity.
   C. High frequency.
   D. Long period of vibration.

109. Reaction 1 occurs spontaneously at high temperatures. The most likely cause for this phenomenon is that at high temperatures:

   A. increasing entropy compensates for increasing enthalpy.
   B. increasing entropy compensates for decreasing enthalpy.
   C. decreasing entropy compensates for increasing enthalpy.
   D. decreasing entropy compensates for decreasing enthalpy.

110. The heat of formation of $SO_3(g)$ is –396 kJ/mol. What is the heat of formation of $SO_2(g)$?

   A. –396 kJ/mol
   B. –297 kJ/mol
   C. –198 kJ/mol
   D. –495 kJ/mol

111. Which of the following best describes the energy conversion that takes place as solar radiation is taken into the device and converted?

   A. Kinetic to electrical to heat
   B. Kinetic to chemical to electrical
   C. Light to electrical to chemical
   D. Light to chemical to heat

GO ON TO THE NEXT PAGE

112. One of the advantages of the solar energy conversion device is that the energy can be stored indefinitely and released when desired. That is because:

   A. all of the reactants and products are in the gas phase.
   B. the endothermic reaction takes place only at high temperatures.
   C. the exothermic reaction takes place only in the presence of a catalyst.
   D. the exothermic reaction releases more energy than is stored by the endothermic reaction.

113. The formation of oxygen gas in Reaction 1 would be promoted by:

   A. increasing the pressure of the reaction chamber.
   B. decreasing the pressure of the reaction chamber.
   C. increasing the concentration of sulfur dioxide in the reaction chamber.
   D. decreasing the concentration of sulfur trioxide in the reaction chamber.

114. If one mole of oxygen gas is consumed by Reaction 2 over the course of 1 hour, what is the power of the conversion device?

   A. 3 W
   B. 22 W
   C. 55 W
   D. 330 W

115. Which of the following is NOT an advantage of the solar energy conversion device?

   A. Energy need not be used at the same time it is absorbed.
   B. The gases in the system are reused.
   C. Energy can be absorbed in the absence of solar radiation.
   D. Energy can be released in the absence of solar radiation.

Questions 116 through 120 are **NOT** based on a descriptive passage.

116. What is the ground state electron configuration of a neutral silicon atom?

   A. $1s^2\, 2s^2\, 2p^6\, 3s^2\, 3p^1$
   B. $1s^2\, 2s^2\, 2p^6\, 3s^2\, 3p^2$
   C. $1s^2\, 2s^2\, 2p^6\, 3s^2\, 3d^1$
   D. $1s^2\, 2s^2\, 2p^6\, 3s^2\, 3d^2$

117. An object is placed in front of a converging lens with a focal length f. At what distance from the lens must the object be placed in order to form a virtual, upright image twice the object's size?

   A. $\dfrac{f}{2}$

   B. f

   C. $\dfrac{3f}{2}$

   D. $2f$

118. Which of the following subatomic particles would experience the greatest force when exposed to an electric field?

   A. Alpha particle
   B. Beta particle
   C. Proton
   D. Neutron

119. The pH of an acidic solution is 3.5. Which of the following expresses the solution's hydrogen ion concentration?

   A. $10^{-3.5}$
   B. $10^{3.5}$
   C. $\log 3.5$
   D. $-\log 3.5$

GO ON TO THE NEXT PAGE

120. Which of the following best explains why sound travels faster through water than through air?

    A. Water is more dense than air.
    B. Water is less dense than air.
    C. Water is more resistant to compression than air.
    D. Water is less resistant to compression than air.

Passage VIII (Questions 121–126)

Between the top of the Earth's atmosphere and the surface of the Earth, there is a potential difference of approximately 400,000 V. This voltage gradient comes about because near the top of the atmosphere there exists a uniform layer of positively charged ions, whereas the earth's surface is negatively charged.

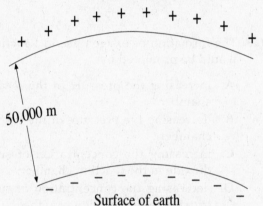

The degree of ionization of particles in the atmosphere is not constant. The number of ionized particles increases dramatically near the top of the atmosphere, which causes the electric field to grow stronger near the surface of the earth. Except near the top of the atmosphere, the electric field near the earth's surface is approximately 100 V/m. Human beings are not affected by this field because the human body is, for the most part, an equipotential surface. That is, all parts of the body are at the same voltage.

Although air is not normally thought to be a conductor, positive ions perpetually travel through the atmosphere to the surface of the Earth. At any given time, the total current reaching the Earth's surface is about 1800 A. Lightning strikes send negative charge to the earth and prevent it from becoming saturated with positive charge.

GO ON TO THE NEXT PAGE

121. What is the approximate resistance of the earth's atmosphere?

    A. 10 Ω

    B. 50 Ω

    C. 100 Ω

    D. 200 Ω

122. Which of the following statements best explains the increase in ionization near the top of the Earth's atmosphere?

    A. Ionization in the atmosphere is caused by radioactive decay at the Earth's surface.

    B. Ionization in the atmosphere is caused by collisions among air molecules.

    C. Ionization in the atmosphere is caused by solar radiation.

    D. Ionization in the atmosphere is greater over land masses than over large bodies of water.

123. The human body forms an equipotential surface and is unaffected by the atmospheric electric field because the human body is:

    A. a perfect insulator.

    B. a relatively good conductor.

    C. at a higher potential than its surroundings.

    D. at a lower potential than its surroundings.

124. Which picture best represents the direction of the electric field surrounding the Earth?

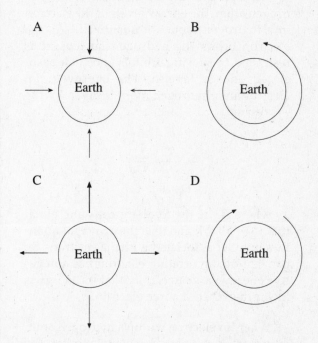

125. Where 1 MW is equal to 1 megawatt (1 million watts) what is the average power of the electrical system created by the Earth and its atmosphere?

    A. 20 MW

    B. 70 MW

    C. 200 MW

    D. 700 MW

126. How much work must be done to lift an object with a mass of 1 kg and a positive charge of 1C to a height of 5m above the Earth's surface?

    A. 50 J

    B. 550 J

    C. 1100 J

    D. 5500 J

GO ON TO THE NEXT PAGE

Passage IX (Questions 127–131)

According to the Bohr model of the hydrogen atom, the energy levels of the electron in a hydrogen atom are quantized. As the electron orbits the hydrogen nucleus, it is restricted to specific orbitals and their associated energy levels. The energy of an electron in a hydrogen atom is given by the expression:

$$E_n = {}^-R_H\left(\frac{1}{n^2}\right)$$

Equation 1

where R_H is the Rydberg constant, equal to 2.18×10^{-18} J, and n is the principal quantum number associated with the electron. By convention, an orbiting electron has a negative energy value to signify that its energy is lower than that of a free electron.

When an electron within a hydrogen atom moves from one energy level to another, the change in energy is given by the equation:

$$\Delta E = R_H\left(\frac{1}{n_i^2} - \frac{1}{n_f^2}\right)$$

Equation 2

where n_i and n_f are the initial and final quantum numbers. When the atom absorbs energy and the electron moves to a higher energy level, ΔE has a positive value. When the atom releases energy and the electron moves to a lower energy state, ΔE has a negative value and light energy is released.

An atom releases energy in the form of electromagnetic radiation whose frequency is given by the equation:

$$\Delta E = hf$$

where f is the frequency of the radiation and h is Planck's constant, equal to 6.63×10^{-34} J-sec.

Some of the electromagnetic radiation emitted by a hydrogen atom falls in the visible spectrum. Figure 1 shows a line emission spectrum for hydrogen.

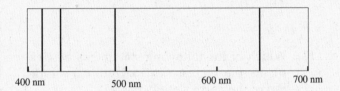

Figure 1

127. What is the energy of an electron occupying the third quantum level ($n = 3$) of a hydrogen atom?

A. -1.96×10^{-17} J
B. -2.42×10^{-19} J
C. -6.54×10^{-18} J
D. -7.27×10^{-19} J

128. Which of the lists below could represent the wavelengths of the electromagnetic radiation emitted by hydrogen atoms?

A. 410 nm, 434 nm, 486 nm, 580 nm.
B. 410 nm, 434 nm, 486 nm, 656 nm.
C. 410 nm, 486 nm, 580 nm, 656 nm.
D. 410 nm, 486 nm, 628 nm, 656 nm.

129. When an electron moves, within a hydrogen atom, from the third quantum level ($n = 3$) to the second quantum level ($n = 2$) which of the following is true?

A. ΔE will be positive and a photon will be emitted.
B. ΔE will be positive and a photon will be absorbed.
C. ΔE will be negative and a photon will be emitted.
D. ΔE will be negative and a photon will be absorbed.

GO ON TO THE NEXT PAGE

130. A photon of light will have the highest frequency if it is associated with which of the following wavelengths?

    A. 400 nm

    B. 500 nm

    C. 600 nm

    D. 700 nm

131. Increase in an electron's quantum number will produce:

    A. increased stability and increased energy.

    B. increased stability and decreased energy.

    C. decreased stability and decreased energy.

    D. decreased stability and increased energy.

GO ON TO THE NEXT PAGE

Passage X (Questions 132–137)

A mass undergoing undamped oscillation caused by a spring on a frictionless surface will obey the law of conservation of energy. An apparatus is set up as shown in Figure 1.

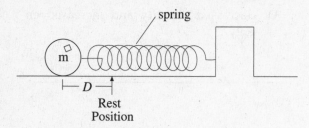

spring

Rest
Position

Figure 1

The oscillation of the mass is set in motion by displacing the mass an initial distance D from the rest position of the spring system as shown in Figure 1.

As oscillation proceeds the total energy of the mass and spring is unchanged. Its value depends on initial displacement, D—the distance between the spring's resting position and the point at which oscillation is begun. The energy of spring and mass undergoes conversion between kinetic energy and elastic potential energy.

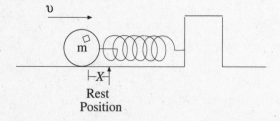

v

Rest
Position

Figure 2

The speed v of a mass m undergoing undamped oscillation can be found at any distance from rest X if the spring constant k and the initial displacement D are known.

$$v = \sqrt{\frac{k}{m}\left(D^2 - X^2\right)}$$

Equation 1

132. Which of the following graphs best relates total energy of the spring and mass system to the initial displacement from rest position?

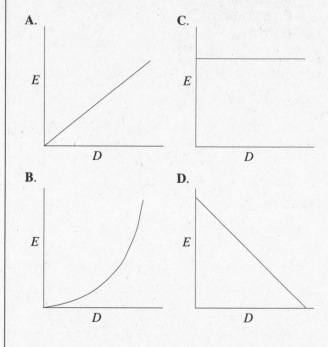

A.

C.

B.

D.

133. As the mass passes through the spring's resting position during the course of its oscillation:

A. kinetic and potential energies are at a minimum.

B. kinetic and potential energies are at a maximum.

C. kinetic energy is at a minimum and potential energy is at a maximum.

D. kinetic energy is at a maximum and potential energy is at a minimum.

GO ON TO THE NEXT PAGE

134. Which of the following changes to the system would produce the greatest increase in the block's speed at any given displacement from the resting position?

    A. Increase the mass of the block and the spring constant of the spring.
    B. Decrease the mass of the block and the spring constant of the spring.
    C. Increase the mass of the block and decrease the spring constant of the spring.
    D. Decrease the mass of the block and increase the spring constant of the spring.

135. As the block moves through the point shown in Figure 2, the magnitude of its acceleration:

    A. increases.
    B. decreases.
    C. remains unchanged with a positive value.
    D. is equal to zero.

136. Which expression gives the force required to hold the mass in equilibrium at a displacement D from the resting position before the start of oscillations?

    A. $\frac{1}{2}kD$
    B. kD
    C. $\frac{1}{2}kD^2$
    D. kD^2

137. In which of the following situations will the block's velocity have a magnitude of zero?

    A. $x > D$
    B. $x = D$
    C. $D > x > 0$
    D. $x = 0$

Questions 138 through 142 are **NOT** based on a descriptive passage.

138. Samples of which of the following molecules will exhibit the strongest intermolecular interactions?

    A. O_2
    B. N_2
    C. CO_2
    D. H_2O

139. Three cables are attached together as shown below.

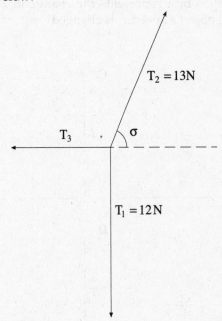

The cables are in equilibrium. If the tensions in the cables T_1 and T_2 are as shown in the diagram, and $\sin \sigma = \frac{12}{13}$, what is the magnitude of T_3 ?

    A. 1 N
    B. 5 N
    C. 15 N
    D. 25 N

GO ON TO THE NEXT PAGE

140. Barium fluoride is a slightly soluble salt with $K_{sp} = 1.7 \times 10^{-6}$. If the concentration of barium ions in a saturated aqueous solution is equal to $4.3 \times 10^{-3}\,M$, what is the concentration of fluoride ions in the solution?

    A. $4.0 \times 10^{-4}\,M$
    B. $2.0 \times 10^{-2}\,M$
    C. $4.0 \times 10^{-2}\,M$
    D. $2.0 \times 10^{-1}\,M$

141. An object of mass m is tied to a string of length r. The object is whirled around and maintained in a circular path by the tension T in the string. Which of the following graphs best represents the change in T as the object's speed, v, is changed?

A.
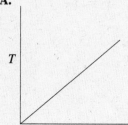

B.
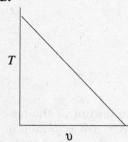

C.
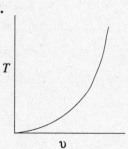

D.
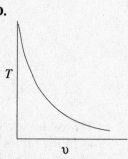

142. Which of the following units expresses power?

    A. $kg \bullet m^2/s^3$
    B. $kg \bullet m^2/s^2$
    C. J^2/sec
    D. J^2/sec^2

STOP

IF YOU FINISH BEFORE TIME IS CALLED, YOU MAY CHECK YOUR WORK ON THIS TEST ONLY.
DO NOT TURN TO ANY OTHER TEST IN THIS BOOK.

Writing Sample II

Time: 60 Minutes
2 Prompts, Separately Timed:
30 Minutes Each

WRITING SAMPLE

DIRECTIONS: This is a test of your writing skills. The test consists of two parts. You will have 30 minutes to complete each part.

Your responses to the Writing Sample prompts will be written on the following pages. Your response to Part 1 must be written only on the answer sheets marked "1," and your response to Part 2 must be written only on the answer sheets marked "2." You may work only on Part 1 during the first 30 minutes of the test and only on Part 2 during the second 30 minutes. If you finish writing on Part 1 before time is up, you may review your work on that part, but do not begin work on Part 2. If you finish writing on Part 2 before time is up, you may review your work only on that part of the test.

Use your time efficiently. Before you begin writing each of your responses, read the assignment carefully to understand exactly what you are being asked to do. You may use the space beneath each writing assignment to make notes in planning each response.

Because this is a test of your writing skills, your response to each part should be an essay of complete sentences and paragraphs, as well organized and clearly written as you can make it in the allotted time. *You may make corrections or additions neatly between the lines of your responses, but do not write in the margins of the answer booklet.*

There are four pages in your answer booklet to write your responses, two pages for each part of the test. You are not expected to use all of the pages, but to ensure that you have enough room for each essay, do not skip lines.

Essays that are illegible cannot be scored.

Part 1

Consider this statement:

The greatest and most lasting reward of education is the personal pleasure of understanding.

Write a unified essay in which you perform the following tasks. Explain what you think the above statement means. Describe a specific situation in which you think the greatest and most lasting reward of education might <u>not</u> be the pleasure of understanding. Discuss what you think determines whether or not the highest reward of education is the personal pleasure of understanding.

_____

_____

_____

_____

_____

_____

_____

_____

_____

_____

_____

_____

_____

_____

_____

_____

_____

_____

_____

_____

_____

STOP
IF YOU FINISH BEFORE TIME IS CALLED, YOU MAY CHECK YOUR WORK ON PART 1 ONLY.

Part 2

Consider this statement:

Concern for the possibility of failure interferes with success.

Write a unified essay in which you perform the following tasks. Explain what you think the above statement means. Describe a specific situation in which you think concern over failure does not interfere with success. Discuss what you think determines whether or not worrying about failure interferes with success.

_____

_____

_____

_____

_____

_____

_____

_____

_____

_____

_____

_____

_____

_____

_____

_____

_____

_____

_____

_____

_____

_____

_____

_____

_____

_____

_____

_____

_____

_____

_____

_____

_____

_____

_____

_____

_____

_____

_____

_____

_____

_____

STOP
IF YOU FINISH BEFORE TIME IS CALLED, YOU MAY CHECK YOUR WORK ON PART 2 ONLY.

Biological Sciences II

Time: 100 Minutes
Questions 143-219

BIOLOGICAL SCIENCES

DIRECTIONS: Most questions in the Biological Sciences test are organized into groups, each preceded by a descriptive passage. After studying the passage, select the one best answer to each question in the group. Some questions are not based on a descriptive passage and are also independent of each other. You must also select the one best answer to these questions. If you are not certain of an answer, eliminate the alternatives that you know to be incorrect and then select an answer from the remaining alternatives. Indicate your selection by blackening the corresponding oval on your answer document. A periodic table is provided for your use. You may consult it whenever you wish.

PERIODIC TABLE OF THE ELEMENTS

1 H 1.0																	2 He 4.0
3 Li 6.9	4 Be 9.0											5 B 10.8	6 C 12	2 N 14.0	8 O 16	9 F 19.0	10 Ne 20.0
11 Na 22.0	12 Mg 24.3											13 Al 27.0	14 Si 28.1	15 P 31.0	16 S 32.1	17 Cl 35.5	18 Ar 39.0
19 K 39.1	20 Ca 40.1	21 Sc 45.0	22 Ti 47.9	23 V 50.9	24 Cr 52.0	25 Mn 54.9	26 Fe 55.8	27 Co 58.9	28 Ni 58.7	29 Cu 63.5	30 Zn 65.4	31 Ga 69.7	32 Ge 72.6	33 As 74.9	34 Se 79.0	35 Br 79.9	36 Kr 83.8
37 Rb 85.5	38 Sr 87.6	39 Y 88.9	40 Zr 91.2	41 Nb 92.9	42 Mo 95.9	43 Tc 97.0	44 Ru 101.0	45 Rh 102.9	46 Pd 106.4	47 Ag 107.9	48 Cd 112.4	49 In 114.8	50 Sn 118.7	51 Sb 121.8	52 Te 127.6	53 I 126.9	54 Xe 131.3
55 Cs 132.9	56 Ba 137.3	57 La 138.9	72 Hf 178.5	73 Ta 180.9	74 W 183.9	75 Re 186.2	76 Os 190.2	77 Ir 192.2	78 Pt 195.1	79 Au 197.0	80 Hg 200.6	81 Tl 204.4	82 Pb 207.2	83 Bi 209.0	84 Po 209.0	85 At 210.0	86 Rn 222.0
87 Fr 223.0	88 Ra 226.0	89 Ac 227.0															

58 Ce 140.1	59 Pr 140.9	60 Nd 144.2	61 Pm 145.0	62 Sm 150.4	63 Eu 152.0	64 Gd 157.3	65 Tb 158.9	66 Dy 162.5	67 Ho 164.9	68 Er 167.3	69 Tm 168.9	70 Yb 173.0	71 Lu 175.0
90 Th 232.0	91 Pa 231.0	92 U 238.0	93 Np 237.0	94 Pu 244.0	95 Am 243.0	96 Cm 247.0	97 Bk 247.0	98 Cf 251.0	99 Es 254.0	100 Fm 253.0	101 Md 256.0	102 No 253.0	103 Lr 257.0

GO ON TO THE NEXT PAGE

Passage I (Questions 143–148)

Cholesterol is a steroid widely found in animal tissues. It is a major component of human gallstones and egg yolks. Cholesterol is an important intermediate in the biosynthesis of steroid hormones such as testosterone and estradiol. It has received much popular attention because of its association with atherosclerosis or "hardening of the arteries."

Cholesterol

143. How many functional groups does the cholesterol molecule feature?

    A. 1

    B. 2

    C. 3

    D. 4

144. What is the product of the reaction shown below?

145. When cholesterol reacts with CH_3COOH it forms:

    A. a carboxylic acid and water.

    B. a carboxylic acid and an alcohol.

    C. an ester and water.

    D. an ester and an alcohol.

146. A student believes that cholesterol will readily undergo electrophilic substitution when reacted with Bromine (Br_2). Is the belief reasonable?

    A. Yes, because cholesterol is a conjugated diene.

    B. Yes, because cholesterol undergoes a hydrogenation reaction.

    C. No, because cholesterol is not aromatic.

    D. No, because electrophilic substitution requires catalysis.

GO ON TO THE NEXT PAGE

147. Which of the following is the most likely product when cholesterol undergoes ozonolysis?

C₈H₁₇
CH₃
CH₃
HO
+ O₃ →(Zn, H₃O⁺)

A.

CH₃ C₈H₁₇
CH₃
O   O

B.

CH₃ C₈H₁₇
CH₃
HO   O   O

C.

CH₃ C₈H₁₇
CH₃
HO   O

D.

CH₃ C₈H₁₇
CH₃
O

148. Suppose an investigator attempts to produce 5-cholestene-3-one from cholesterol. Which of the following infrared spectroscopic findings would inform the investigator that the reaction has occurred?

HO
Cholesterol

Jones' reagent →

O
5-Cholestene-3-one

A. The disappearance of OH absorption from the reactant.

B. The disappearance of the carbonyl group in the product

C. The disappearance of a double bond from the reactant

D. The disappearance of a methyl group from the reactant

Passage II (Questions 149–156)

The stomach is composed of circular and longitudinal layers of smooth muscle. Like all tubular structures it has an internal space termed the *lumen*. Its glands, composed of secretory cells, contribute to gastric juices in the lumen. Parietal cells produce hydrochloric acid, which gives the gastric juices an approximate pH of 1.0. Parietal cells also secrete intrinsic factor, which is necessary to vitamin B12 absorption. Chief cells produce pepsinogen, and mucous cells contribute soluble and insoluble forms of mucus. The mucus serves to lubricate the stomach, to protect its internal walls from mechanical injury, and to shield its mucosal lining from digestion by acid and enzyme activity. Endocrine cells called G cells secrete the hormone gastrin, which stimulates acid secretion. A model of acid secretion by the parietal cells of the stomach is presented in Figure 1.

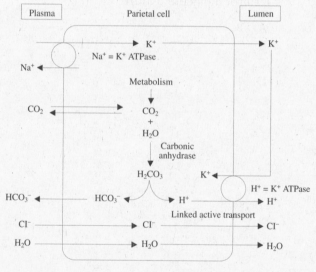

Figure 1

An H^+, K^+, ATPase located on the luminal surface of the parietal cells facilitates secretion of H^+ ions into the lumen against their concentration gradient, with Cl^- ions actively secreted in conjunction with them. For every H^+ ion secreted into the lumen, one HCO_3^- ion is secreted into the plasma.

Acetylcholine, gastrin, and histamine stimulate gastric acid secretion. These substances have a synergistic effect. Parasympathetic stimulation promotes gastric motility and gastric acid secretion. These effects are inhibited by several factors, including low pH within the gastric juice and low levels of the hormone secretin, (which normally *increases* pepsin secretion).

149. All of the following statements regarding pepsinongen are true EXCEPT that:

A. it is an inactive zymogen.
B. gastric acid facilitates conversion of pepsinogen to the active enzyme pepsin.
C. it is secreted by gastric chief cells.
D. it initiates the digestion of lipids.

150. Sympathetic stimulation of the gastrointestinal tract probably:

A. stimulates gastric acid secretion.
B. inhibits gastric acid secretion.
C. acts synergistically with parasympathetic stimulation.
D. produces peristalsis of the smooth muscle.

151. According to Figure 1, which ion shows lower concentration in gastric secretions than in plasma?

A. Potassium
B. Chloride
C. Hydrogen
D. Sodium

152. Hydrogen and chloride ions in the stomach draw water into the lumen so that gastric secretions are isotonic to plasma. This form of transport is most appropriately termed:

A. active transport.
B. passive transport.
C. osmosis.
D. facilitated transport.

153. Which among the following do NOT serve an exocrine function?

A. Parietal cells.
B. Chief cells.
C. G cells.
D. Mucous cells.

154. Studying the gastric activities of a volunteer, a group of researchers monitor the stomach's venous blood and report a transitory period during which it is highly basic. With which of the following is the period of basicity most likely associated?

A. Active acid secretion
B. Reduced gastrin secretion
C. Active secretin secretion
D. Reduced pepsinogen secretion

GO ON TO THE NEXT PAGE

155. Carbonic acid that is secreted into the plasma is formed from:

    A. carbon dioxide and hydrogen ion with facilitation by carbonic anhydrase.
    B. carbon dioxide and hydrogen ion with facilitation by ATPase.
    C. carbon dioxide and water with facilitation by carbonic anhydrase.
    D. carbon dioxide and water with facilitation by ATPase.

156. Which of the following pharmacological agents would most likely stimulate gastric motility?

    A. An agent that mimics the action of secretin
    B. An agent that acts as a terminal parasympathetic transmitter
    C. An agent that blocks parasympathetic transmission
    D. An agent that acts as a sympathetic transmitter.

Passage III (Questions 157–162)

A primary amine, RNH_2, adds to an aldehyde or ketone to yield a substituted imine, a molecule that contains a carbon-nitrogen double bond. The reaction constitutes nucleophilic addition involving the elimination of water and the formation of a new double bond between carbon and a nucleophile. The formation of a substituted imine occurs in two steps:

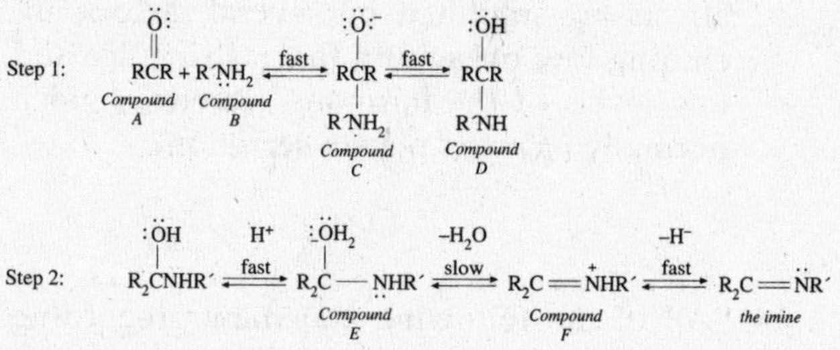

Figure 1

157. Which step(s) is (are) acid-catalyzed?

    A. Step 1
    B. Step 2
    C. Steps 1 and 2
    D. Neither step 1 nor step 2

158. Which of the following compounds undergoes nucleophilic attack?

    A. Compound A
    B. Compound B
    C. Compound C
    D. Compound D

GO ON TO THE NEXT PAGE

159. In step 2, the first intermediate is protonated to produce the carbanolamine, Compound E, in order to:

    A. decrease the pH of the solution.
    B. allow compound E to yield a neutral amino product.
    C. provide the intermediate with a better leaving group.
    D. initiate the nucleophilic addition reaction.

160. Among the following, step 2 of the reaction most resembles:

    A. a substitution reaction.
    B. a bimolecular elimination reaction.
    C. a unimolecular elimination reaction.
    D. a homogeneous catalysis.

161. With reference to the reaction described in the passage, what will likely occur if the reaction solution is highly acidic?

    A. The nucleophile will not attack the initial carbonyl compound.
    B. The solution will have a high pH.
    C. The intermediate will not be protonated.
    D. The amine nucleophile will be completely protonated.

162. The addition of an amine to an aldehyde or ketone is pH dependent. According to the graph below, what pH is most favorable to reaction rate?

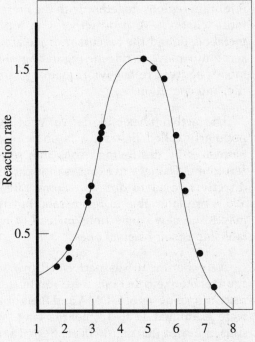

Dependence on pH of the rate of reaction

    A. 0.5
    B. 1.5
    C. 2.0
    D. 4.5

GO ON TO THE NEXT PAGE

Passage IV (Questions 163–169)

Neurons within the brain stem synthesize and release serotonin to serotonergic cells throughout areas of the central nervous system. Targets of the neurotransmitter include the nearby amygdala, hypothalamus, and midbrain regions, together with the more remote cortex. A product of tryptophan metabolism and the precursor of melatonin, serotonin plays a role in regulating sleep, mood, aggressive behavior, memory, appetite, and cognition.

The methamphetamine derivative MDMA, popularly called Ecstasy, acts on serotonin pathways by destroying axons that release serotonin. Damage to axons is thought to be directly related to dosage. Some affected axons are later able to regenerate, but they may forge new connections instead of reestablishing their original ones.

An experiment was performed in which squirrel monkeys and rats were administered recreational doses of MDMA and their brains were examined 12 to 18 months later. Results indicated that regrowth of affected axons reinstated previous synaptic connections in rats. In squirrel monkeys, however, reconnections presented a pattern that differed from that shown by the rats. The extent of axonal restoration in the monkeys also differed, depending on the connecting target. Results from the study are presented in Table 1.

Table 1: Axonal restoration 12-18 months after MDMA administration

Serotonergic target	Rat	Squirrel monkey
amygdala	++	+++
hypothalamus	++	+++
cortex	++	+

Key:

Axonal regrowth from brain stem to brain targets

+   less than number of original connections

++   equal to number of original connections

+++   surpasses number of original connections

163. Serotonin is derived from:

   A. an amino acid.

   B. an enzyme.

   C. another neurotransmitter.

   D. a hormone.

164. Among the following, which graph best describes the degree of axonal degeneration as a function of MDMA dose?

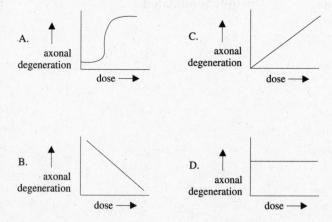

GO ON TO THE NEXT PAGE

165. If MDMA is found to produce insomnia, the reason might be that:

    A. it inhibits serotonin synthesis in brain stem neurons.

    B. it destroys serotonin-containing axons in the brain stem.

    C. it competes for serotonin binding sites on serotonergic neurons.

    D. it causes degeneration of cell bodies of serotonin-producing neurons.

166. The most likely explanation for the differences between axonal regeneration in rats and squirrels monkeys as shown in Table 1 is that:

    A. excessive axonal repair to the amygdala and hypothalamus inhibits reconnection to the cortex

    B. dendrites of neurons in the cortex can compensate for axonal deficiencies.

    C. longer axonal projections regenerate more easily than do shorter ones.

    D. shorter axonal projections regenerate more easily than do longer ones.

167. A drug that prevented the re-uptake of serotonin would most likely:

    A. produce an action potential in the presynaptic neuron by binding to receptors on the axonal membrane.

    B. reduce the intensity of an action potential in the postsynaptic neuron.

    C. prevent the postsynaptic neuron from undergoing frequent action potentials.

    D. increase the amount of stimulation received by dendrites of the postsynaptic neuron.

168. The most likely explanation for the differences in axonal regeneration of various brain stem neurons in squirrel monkeys as shown in Table 1 is that:

    A. excessive axonal repair to the amygdala and hypothalamus inhibits reconnection to the cortex.

    B. dendrites of neurons in the cortex can compensate for axonal deficiencies in brain stem neurons.

    C. longer axonal projections in brain stem neurons can regenerate more easily than shorter ones.

    D. shorter axonal projections in brain stem neurons can regenerate more easily than longer ones.

169. All of the following statements correctly describe events associated with synaptic transmission of a nerve impulse EXCEPT:

    A. Mitochondria supply the ATP needed for synthesis of neurotransmitter.

    B. Neurotransmitters are released into the synaptic cleft in direct response to an action potential.

    C. Calcium is actively sequestered in direct response to an action potential.

    D. Neurotransmitters bind to receptors on the postsynaptic membrane and cause a change in permeability of the membrane.

GO ON TO THE NEXT PAGE

Questions 170 through 175 are **NOT** based on a descriptive passage.

170. The graph below depicts the changes in sodium and potassium conductance that take place during an action potential in a giant squid axon.

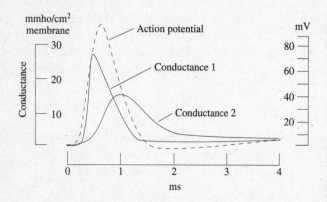

Conductance 2 depicts the movement of:

    A. sodium ions.
    B. chloride ions.
    C. potassium ions.
    D. magnesium ions.

171. Within the cell, protein turnover reflects a balance between the rates of protein synthesis and degradation. For a given protein the rate of synthesis is regulated by which of the following factors?

    A. The amount of DNA available for transcription
    B. The amount of RNA available for translation
    C. The number of ribosomes available for protein synthesis
    D. The number of tRNA molecules available for transport of amino acids

172. Which of the following pathways of cellular respiration occurs in the cytosol?

    A. The Krebs cycle
    B. Oxidative phosphorylation
    C. Glycolysis
    D. Electron transport chain

173. The orientation of substituent groups on a cyclohexane ring may be axial or equatorial. For halogen substituents which orientation is favored?

    A. Equatorial because of reduced steric hindrance.
    B. Axial because of reduced steric hindrance.
    C. Axial because the bonds have more mobility.
    D. Equatorial because it displays more staggered than eclipsed conformation.

174. The likelihood of a given allele's sudden predominance within a small isolated population independent of adaptive advantage is best attributed to:

    A. the Hardy-Weinberg law.
    B. genetic drift.
    C. adaptive radiation.
    D. survival of the fittest.

175. Alcohols show characteristic absorptions in the ^1H NMR spectrum. If 1-propanol is subjected to ^1H NMR the protons on the oxygen-bearing carbon will be split into a:

    A. singlet
    B. doublet
    C. triplet
    D. quadruplet

GO ON TO THE NEXT PAGE

Passage V (Questions 176–180)

Isopropanol is a colorless liquid with an odor characteristic of alcohols. It melts at –89.5°C and boils at 82.5°C. The compound is soluble in water, ethanol, and ether. It is often used as a disinfectant and as a skin-cooling agent, "rubbing alcohol." Many alcohols are made commercially by the hydration of alkenes. Isopropanol is prepared by reacting propylene ($CH_3CH=CH_2$) with a strong acid such as sulfuric acid, followed by treatment with water.

The initial steps are shown below:

$$CH_3- CH=CH_2 + H^+ + HSO_4^- \longrightarrow \text{Intermediate}$$

The reaction of the intermediate with water then yields isopropanol.

$$\text{Intermediate} + H_2O \longrightarrow CH_3 - \overset{\displaystyle OH}{\underset{\displaystyle H}{C}} - CH_3 + H_2SO_4$$

176. In the preparation of isopropanol what is the role of sulfuric acid?

A. It acts as a catalyst.
B. It increases the pH of the solution.
C. It ionizes the alkene.
D. It causes a reduction of the alkene.

177. How many chiral centers are featured within the isopropanol molecule?

A. 0
B. 1
C. 2
D. 3

178. What property of isopropanol makes it most useful as a rubbing alcohol?

A. It forms hydrogen bonds.
B. It is weakly acidic.
C. It is relatively volatile.
D. It acts as a proton donor.

179. Between isopropanol or 1-butanol, which compound likely has the higher boiling point?

A. 1-butanol because it has the higher molecular weight
B. 1-butanol because it is a straight chain alcohol
C. Isopropanol because its density is higher than that of 1-butanol
D. Isopropanol because its carbon chain branches

180. All of the following are isomers of isobutanol EXCEPT:

A. $(CH_3)_3COH$
B. $CH_3CH_2COC_3$
C. $CH_3CH_2CH_2CH_2OH$
D. $CH_3CH_2OCH_2CH_3$

GO ON TO THE NEXT PAGE ⟩

Passage VI (Questions 181–187)

Drug therapy ideally establishes therapeutic yet nontoxic levels of drug in target tissues. Factors determining drug levels in the body include the mechanisms of and extent to which a drug is absorbed from the site of administration, distributed into interstitial and intracellular fluids, and metabolized prior to its excretion from the body (Figure 1).

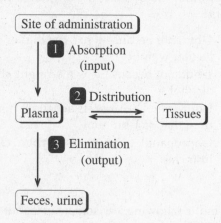

Figure 1

Enteral drug administration is achieved via the oral, sublingual, and rectal routes. Of the three, the oral route is most common, but creates the most complicated pathway to target tissues.

A drug given by mouth must first dissolve in the gastrointestinal fluid and then cross the epithelial cells of the intestinal mucosa, where most absorption takes place. Drug absorption from the duodenal mucosa is by diffusion or active transport. A schematic representation of drug transport mechanisms across an epithelial cell membrane of the gastrointestinal mucosa is depicted in Figure 2.

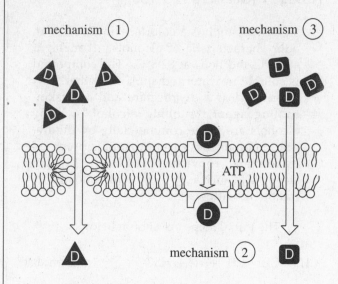

Figure 2

Sublingual administration permits a drug to enter the systemic circulation directly by diffusion into the capillary network under the tongue. The drug bypasses the liver and thus avoids inactivation by hepatic metabolic activity. With rectal administration, one-half of the rectal region bypasses the hepatic portal circulation, minimizing the biotransformation of drugs that are metabolized by the liver. Sublingual and rectal routes of drug administration also prevent destruction of a drug by intestinal enzymes or by gastric pH.

Parenteral administration of drugs, by intravenous, intramuscular, and subcutaneous routes, allow for greater control of dosage delivered to target tissues. Candidates for parenteral routes are drugs that are poorly absorbed from or unstable in the gastrointestinal tract, or those that require a rapid onset of action, such as epinephrine given during anaphylaxis (a severe and life-threatening form of allergic reaction). Patients who are unconscious also require parenteral drug administration.

GO ON TO THE NEXT PAGE

181. Excessive peristalsis and rapid emptying of the small intestine will most likely have which of the following effects on the absorption of a drug taken orally?

   A. Increase the absorption of the drug, because it would accelerate transport from the stomach to the intestines.
   B. Increase the absorption of the drug, because the drug could then bypass low pH and enzymatic environments of the stomach and the intestines.
   C. Decrease the absorption of the drug, because it would prolong gastric emptying into the duodenum.
   D. Decrease the absorption of the drug, because it would accelerate transport through the gastrointestinal tract.

182. The drug insulin is unstable in the gastrointestinal tract. As a result it is administered parenterally. The effect of insulin on target tissues is to:

   A. decrease blood glucose levels.
   B. increase blood glucose levels.
   C. mobilize release of glycogen from storage.
   D. initiate synthesis of glucose by gluconeogenesis.

183. Of the mechanisms depicted in Figure 2, which mechanism would most likely demonstrate saturation kinetics similar to that of an enzyme-catalyzed reaction?

   A. Mechanism 1
   B. Mechanism 2
   C. Mechanism 3
   D. Mechanisms 2 and 3

184. With reference to Figure 2, mechanism 3 differs from Mechanism 2 in that:

   A. Mechanism 3 requires hydrolysis of ATP.
   B. Mechanism 3 involves a carrier molecule.
   C. Mechanism 3 involves movement from a region of higher concentration to one of lower concentration.
   D. Mechanism 3 shows a high structural specificity.

185. A decision to administer nitroglycerine sublingually would be most justified by a finding that nitroglycerine is:

   A. not metabolized by the liver and is excreted in the urine unchanged.
   B. highly susceptible to inactivation by hepatic enzymes.
   C. well tolerated by the stomach and is relatively immune to degradation by acid.
   D. susceptible to rapid absorption from intestinal mucosa.

186. Which of the following sites offers the greatest area of absorption due to its comparatively large surface area?

   A. the esophagus, because of its length.
   B. the stomach, because of its gastric mucosa.
   C. the small intestine, because of its microvilli.
   D. the large intestine, because of its large circumference.

GO ON TO THE NEXT PAGE

187. A student assumes that a highly hydrophilic drug will be poorly absorbed across the cell membrane. Is the assumption well founded?

 A. Yes; a highly hydrophilic drug will be unable to cross hydrophobic portions of the lipid bilayer.

 B. Yes; a highly hydrophilic drug will be repelled by the hydrophilic heads of the lipid bilayer.

 C. No; a highly hydrophilic drug can readily cross both the hydrophilic and the hydrophobic portions of the lipid bilayer.

 D. No; the hydrophilic character of a drug has no bearing on its ability to cross the lipid bilayer.

Passage VII (Questions 188–194):

The intoxication that follows ingestion of wine, beer, and "hard liquor" is due to cerebral effects of ethyl alcohol, a small, neutral water soluble molecule with the structure shown in Figure 1.

$$H_3C—CH_2—OH$$

Ethyl alcohol is rapidly absorbed from the stomach. Blood levels reach a peak at approximately 40 minutes after ingestion and absorption is complete after about 1 hour.

Ingested alcohol reaches the tissues via the blood. Distribution about the body is proportional to water content in the various tissues. In the alveolar blood vessels small amounts pass into the lung according to an equilibrium between alveolar air and alveolar blood. The concentration of alcohol in expired air (Figure 1) closely parallels concentration in the blood. Alcohol is also excreted in the urine to some degree, but urine concentrations do not correspond well to blood concentrations at the time a urine specimen is collected.

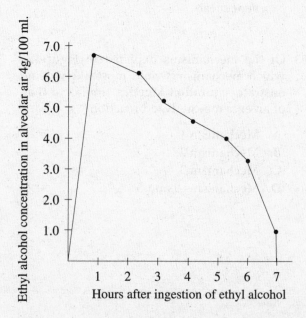

Figure 1

GO ON TO THE NEXT PAGE

The primary site of alcohol metabolism is the liver, where conversion to acetaldehyde is mediated by the enzyme alcohol dehydrogenase. Aldehyde dehydrogenase within the liver and other tissues then catalyzes the oxidation of acetaldehyde to acetyl co-A which enters the Krebs acid cycle for ultimate oxidation to water and carbon dioxide.

$$\underset{\text{ethyl alcohol}}{H_3C-CH_2-OH} \xrightarrow{\text{alcohol dehydrogenase}} \underset{\text{acetaldehyde}}{H_3C-C=O} \xrightarrow{\text{aldehyde dehydrogenase}} \text{acetyl}-CoA$$

The conversion of alcohol to acetaldehyde represents the rate limiting step and is very much slower than the subsequent conversion of acetaldehyde to acetyl co-A. When blood levels of alcohol reach approximately 0.1%, the acetaldehyde dehydrogenase system is saturated and the rate at which alcohol is converted to acetaldehyde reaches a maximum.

188. Among the following properties, a sample of ethyl alcohol is most likely to demonstrate:

- **A.** relatively low solubility in polar solvents due to small molecular size.
- **B.** relatively high solubility in polar solvents due to hydrogen bonding.
- **C.** relatively high boiling points due to weak van der Waals forces.
- **D.** relatively low boiling points due to strong van der Waals forces.

189. Excessive ethyl alcohol intake is often associated with poor nutrition and vitamin deficiency. Among the following proposed explanations for the association, which is LEAST likely to be accurate?

- **A.** Ethyl alcohol does not generate metabolic fuel for body cells.
- **B.** Persons who ingest high quantities of ethyl alcohol derive their calories from alcohol and do not experience hunger for other foods.
- **C.** Chronic alcohol ingestion interferes with conversion of ingested vitamins to their active forms.
- **D.** Prolonged excessive alcohol intake is associated with psychological and social dysfunction that causes the individual to fail in caring for himself.

190. Among the following, which would most dramatically reduce the rate at which the body eliminates ingested ethyl alcohol?

- **A.** Decreased respiratory rate
- **B.** Increased ingestion of water
- **C.** Moderate inhibition of *aldehyde* dehydrogenase
- **D.** Moderate inhibition of *alcohol* dehydrogenase

GO ON TO THE NEXT PAGE

191. An investigator studies the oxidative metabolism of ethyl alcohol in an experimental animal. He artificially increases the liver concentration of alcohol dehydrogenase to the point that the oxidation of acetaldehyhde to acetyl co-A becomes the rate limiting step. If the liver concentration of alcohol dehydrogenase is then increased further, which of the following graphs will most likely depict the relationship between alcohol dehydrogenase concentration and the rate of alcohol elimination?

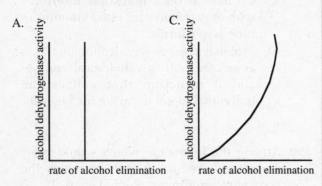

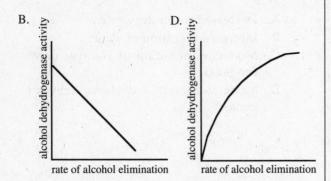

192. If ethyl alcohol and acetaldehyde are compared in terms of molecular weight, boiling point, acidity, and polarity, which of the following will LEAST likely be observed?

   A. The molecular weight of ethyl alcohol is higher than that of acetaldehyde.

   B. The boiling point of acetaldehyde is higher than that of ethyl alcohol.

   C. Ethyl alcohol is more acidic than acetaldehyde.

   D. The acetaldehyde molecule shows greater polarity than does the ethyl alcohol molecule.

193. In an effort to enforce laws relating to blood alcohol concentrations and motor vehicle operation, a state wishes to devise a procedure that will provide for relatively simple, immediate and, above all, *accurate* estimations of blood alcohol content. Scientist 1 advocates a "dipstick" test that measures urine alcohol concentration. Scientist 2 advocates a machine that measures the alcohol concentration of expired air. From which scientist should the state take advice?

   A. Scientist 1, because the dipstick is simpler than a mechanism designed to measure alcohol concentration in the blood.

   B. Scientist 1, because urinary alcohol concentrations will likely provide the more accurate data regarding blood alcohol concentration.

   C. Scientist 2, because an individual breathes continuously but does not produce urine continuously

   D. Scientist 2, because blood alcohol concentrations will likely provide the more accurate data regarding blood alcohol concentration.

194. Among the following, the highest point on the curve shown in Figure 1 most nearly represents:

   A. peak levels of blood alcohol.

   B. peak respiratory clearance of alcohol.

   C. complete absorption of ingested alcohol.

   D. the equilibrium between alcohol concentrations in alveolar blood and the lung.

GO ON TO THE NEXT PAGE

Passage VIII (Questions 195–199)

Catalases are a group of functionally and structurally similar iron-containing enzymes especially prominent in erythrocytes and in the lysosomes and peroxisomes of the liver. They constitute one of a number of groups of enzymes that catalyze the decomposition of hydrogen peroxide to water and oxygen:

$$2H_2O_2 \longrightarrow 2H_2O + O_2$$

Hydrogen peroxide arises from photorespiration and degradation of cellular waste products. It is highly toxic to cells, producing free radicals which attack nucleic acids and proteins. Catalase is important to cell survival due to its rapid elimination of hydrogen peroxide. The turnover rate of catalase is high; a single catalase molecule reacts with up to five million substrate molecules per minute.

Experiment

In a first trial, hydrogen peroxide was titrated with potassium permanganate in the absence of catalase. In a second trial, hydrogen peroxide and potassium permanganate were once again mixed in a reaction vessel and catalase was added. The following observations were made.

Trial 1

Finding 1. 28 milliliters of potassium permanganate were required to titrate 5 milliliters of 0.005 M hydrogen peroxide to water.

Trial 2

Finding 2. Three minutes after the addition of catalase, the amount of potassium permanganate required for titration was one-third of the amount required in the absence of catalase.

Finding 3. Data obtained for the first fifteen minutes following addition of catalase indicated a nearly constant rate of hydrogen peroxide decomposition, evidenced by a decline in amount of permanganate required for titration.

195. The substrate in the experiment is:

A. catalase.
B. potassium permanganate.
C. hydrogen peroxide.
D. water.

196. The primary function of lysosomes is to:

A. sequester degradative enzymes from the cytoplasm.
B. store water and other materials.
C. digest worn cells and organelles.
D. modify secretory enzymes before they are sent from the cell.

197. With reference to the experiment, which of the following did NOT occur during the three-minute period following the introduction of catalase?

A. The substrate bound to the enzyme.
B. A substrate-enzyme complex was formed.
C. The reaction proceeded.
D. New enzyme was synthesized.

198. Reduction of temperature would have which of the following affects on the second trial?

A. It would impair catalase activity.
B. It would enhance catalase activity.
C. It would prevent regeneration of the catalase at the conclusion of the reaction
D. It would convert the catalase to an inorganic catalyst.

GO ON TO THE NEXT PAGE

199. Extreme high temperature would have which of the following effects on the second trial?

   A. It would increase the required potassium permanganate to approximately 18 milliliters.
   B. It would increase the required potassium permanganate to approximately 28 milliliters.
   C. It would maintain the required potassium permanganate at approximately 9 milliliters.
   D. It would reduce the required potassium permanganate to approximately 1 milliliter.

Questions 200 through 204 are **NOT** based on a descriptive passage.

200. Which of the following is NOT true of erythrocytes?

   A. They contain the protein hemoglobin, which transports oxygen to the tissues.
   B. They are a constituent of whole blood but not of plasma.
   C. They contain no nuclei but contain cellular organelles.
   D. They form a part of the immune system, providing cellular immunity.

201. The amino acids serine, threonine, and tyrosine frequently undergo phosphorylation of a free OH group on their side chains. Phosphorylation of the OH group serves to regulate the activity of the protein, causing activation or inactivation depending on the protein. Phosphorylation involves formation of a(n):

   A. covalent bond, with accompanying hydrolysis of ATP.
   B. hydrogen bond, without accompanying hydrolysis of ATP.
   C. ionic bond, without accompanying hydrolysis of ATP.
   D. noncovalent bond, with accompanying hydrolysis of ATP.

GO ON TO THE NEXT PAGE

202. Muscle contraction requires all of the following EXCEPT for:

    A. release of calcium from the sarcoplasmic reticulum.
    B. hydrolysis of ATP.
    C. depolarization produced by stimulus from a motor neuron.
    D. binding of tropomyosin to actin.

203. Which of the following represents an effect of antidiuretic hormone (ADH) on the renal nephron?

    A. It increases water loss by reducing the permeability of the collecting tubule to water.
    B. It reduces water loss by increasing the permeability of the collecting tubule to water.
    C. It reduces water loss by increasing the permeability of the loop of Henle to water.
    D. It increases water loss by reducing the permeability of the loop of Henle to water.

204. When methane is burned to form carbon dioxide and water, its hydrogen atoms:

    A. acquire negative charge.
    B. lose negative charge.
    C. acquire positive charge.
    D. lose positive charge.

GO ON TO THE NEXT PAGE

Passage IX (Questions 205–209):

Physical Properties of Anasthetics

	Flammable and Explosive	Concentrations for Surgical Anesthesia		Ostwald Solubility Coefficients		
		Inhaled Concentration (Vol%)	Blood Level (mg/100ml)	Blood / Air	Brain / Blood	Oil (Fat) / Blood
Ether	Yes	5–10	130–150	12–15	1.1	5.4
Halothane	No	1–3	5–25	2.3	2.6	97
Cyclopropane	Yes	10–25	10–20	0.42	1.3	26.7
Nitrous oxide	No	80–85	30–50	0.47	1.1	3

Table 1

Anesthetics act principally at the medulla within the brain. In addition to anesthesia itself, most but not all anesthetics produce muscular relaxation and depressed respiratory rate. Muscular relaxation is desirable for surgery but depressed respiration is not.

Maximum anesthetic affect corresponds positively with partial pressure of the anesthetic agent within the brain. Anesthesia and maximum partial pressure are achieved by the intake of an inspired mixture of anesthetic and oxygen through a process schematically represented in Figure 1.

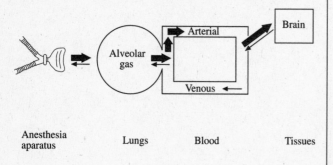

Anesthesia aparatus Lungs Blood Tissues

Figure 1

Principal factors that affect the rate at which the brain achieves a given partial pressure of anesthetic gas are (1) concentration within the inspired mixture, (2) alveolar concentration, (3) uptake by blood from the alveoli, and (4) uptake by brain tissue from the blood. The brain achieves maximum concentration when there is equilibrium of movement from alveoli to blood, and from blood to brain. Between alveoli and blood, the equilibrium corresponds closely (but not exactly) to the "knee" in Figure 2. High blood/air Ostwald solubility coefficient increases the time required to reach the "knee."

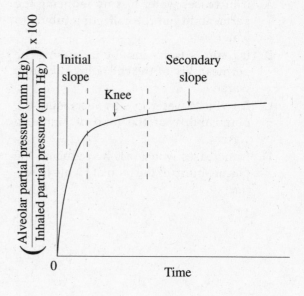

Figure 2

GO ON TO THE NEXT PAGE

Diethyl ether and halothane have the chemical structures shown in Figure 3.

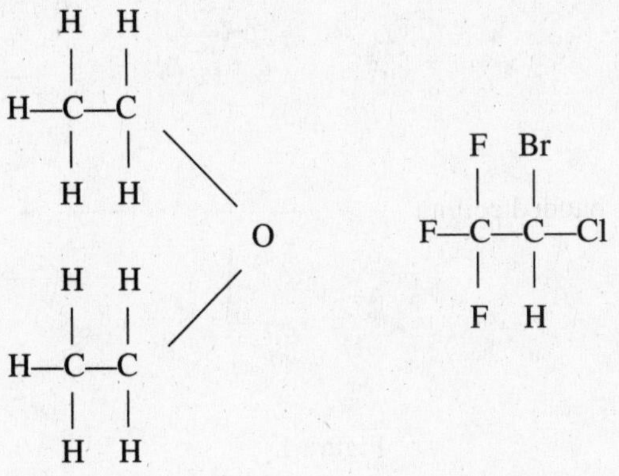

diethyl ether   halothane

Figure 3

205. Some investigators have theorized that water soluble molecules tend not to be effective anesthetics. Regarding the diethyl ether molecule (shown in Figure 3), which of the following facts is LEAST consistent with such a theory?

A. The molecule is composed solely of carbon, oxygen, and hydrogen.
B. All of the molecule's carbon atoms are saturated.
C. The bond angle formed where two carbon atoms are joined by a central oxygen atom generates a dipole moment of approximately 1.18 debye.
D. The molecule is achiral.

206. If figure 1 were drawn to represent a point in time corresponding to the knee in Figure 2, movement of gas between alveoli and blood would be shown to be:

A. absent.
B. in the direction of alveoli to blood only.
C. in the direction of blood to alveoli only.
D. roughly equal in both directions.

207. Which of the following phrases most accurately describes the halothane molecule?

A. Branched phenyl derivative
B. Unsaturated alkyl derivative
C. Halogenated alkene
D. Substituted hydrocarbon

208. Among the following, equilibrium concentrations between alveoli and blood are achieved LEAST quickly with:

A. ether
B. halothane.
C. cyclopropane.
D. nitrous oxide.

209. Which of the following measures will tend to increase the equilibrium concentration of anesthetic within the brain?

I. Increasing the anesthetic's solubility within the brain
II. Increasing the concentration of anesthetic within the inspired mixture
III. Increasing respiratory rate

A. I only
B. II only
C. I and II only
D. I, II, and III

GO ON TO THE NEXT PAGE

Passage X (Questions 210–214)

Spiral cleavage is a feature of most developing molluscs, all annelids, turbellarian flatworms, and nemertean worms. Unlike radial cleavage, in which cell division is in parallel or perpendicular orientation to the animal-vegetal axis of the egg, spiral cleavage involves cell division at oblique angles, so that daughter cells form a spiral. Viewed from the animal pole of the embryo, the upper ends of the mitotic spindle alternate from a clockwise orientation to a counterclockwise one. Cytoplasmic factors in the oocyte determine the orientation of the cleavage plane to the left or to the right.

In snails, shell coiling is either right-handed or left-handed, with each orientation developing as a mirror image of the other (Figure 1). The rotation of coiling is consistent for all members of a species. However, mutations produce individuals that display an orientation opposite to that which is normal for their species. The reverse orientation in mutants originates at the second cell division of cleavage, when the mitotic spindle shows abnormal positioning.

Researchers have identified a single pair of genes that control the direction of snail shell coiling. By mating rare left-handed coil mutants of the snail *Limnaca peregra* with wild-type snails, they determined that the right-handed allele (D) was dominant to the left-handed allele (d). It is the genotype of the mother, however, and not of the developing offspring, that determines the direction of cleavage in the offspring.

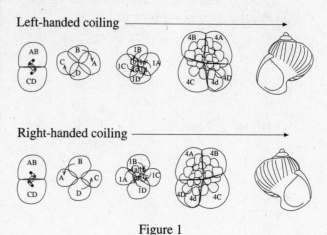

Left-handed coiling

Right-handed coiling

Figure 1

210. Which of the following does NOT occur at the same time that the mitotic spindle assembles in the dividing cell?

   A. Chromosomes condense and become visible when viewed with a microscope.
   B. The nuclear membrane begins to disintegrate.
   C. Chromosomes line up along the cell's equator.
   D. Centrioles divide and each one moves to an opposite pole of the cell.

211. The mating shown below would create offspring that exhibit which of the following shell coiling patterns?

DD (male) x dd (female) ⟶ Dd (offspring)

   A. All right-coiling
   B. All left-coiling
   C. 50% right-coiling and 50% left-coiling
   D. Cannot be determined from the information provided

GO ON TO THE NEXT PAGE

212. In mammals, oogenesis involves:

    A. two divisions that ultimately produce one haploid ovum.

    B. two divisions that ultimately produce four haploid ova.

    C. one division that ultimately produces one haploid ovum.

    D. one division that ultimately produces two haploid ova.

213. When scientists injected a low-molecular-weight yellow dye into a single cell of a 16-cell mollusc embryo, they discovered that the dye was confined to that cell and its progeny. When they injected the dye into a single cell of a 32-cell embryo, they located the dye in that cell as well as in adjacent cells. Based on these findings, it is most reasonable to conclude that communication between cells of a developing mollusc embryo develops at the:

    A. zygote stage.

    B. neurula stage.

    C. gastrula stage.

    D. blastula stage.

214. Members of the same species:

    A. have identical genotypes.

    B. have identical phenotypes.

    C. are unable to breed with one another to produce viable offspring.

    D. are unable to produce fertile offspring with members of another species.

Questions 215 through 219 are **NOT** based on a descriptive passage.

215. A man whose mother is a carrier for color-blindness and whose father was color-blind has a male child with a normal female. What are the chances that the male child will be color-blind?

    A. 0%

    B. 25%

    C. 50%

    D. 100%

216. A virus that employs reverse transcriptase to carry out its infective cycle within a host cell has as its nucleic acid core:

    A. RNA.

    B. DNA.

    C. Either RNA or DNA.

    D. Neither RNA nor DNA.

217. Which of the following represents the addition of H_2SO_4 to propylene (C_3H_6) according to Markovnikov's rule?

A.

$$CH_3-\underset{\underset{H}{|}}{\overset{\overset{OSO_3}{|}}{C}}-CH_3$$

B.

$$CH_3-\underset{\underset{H}{|}}{\overset{\overset{H}{|}}{C}}-CH_3$$

C.

$$CH_3-\underset{\underset{H}{|}}{\overset{\overset{H}{|}}{C}}-CH_2OSO_3H$$

D.

$$CH_3-\underset{\underset{H}{|}}{\overset{\overset{OSO_3H}{|}}{C}}-CH_3$$

GO ON TO THE NEXT PAGE →

218. The increased stability that characterizes a resonance structure is due to:

   A. conformational isomerization.
   B. ortho and meta isomerization
   C. electron delocalization.
   D. increased van der Waals attraction.

219. If a sample of a chiral substance fails to rotate the plane of polarized light, the sample most likely contains:

   A. equal amounts of two optical isomers.
   B. unequal amounts of two optical isomers.
   C. equal amounts of two structural isomers.
   D. unequal amounts of two structural isomers.

STOP
IF YOU FINISH BEFORE TIME IS CALLED, YOU MAY CHECK YOUR WORK ON THIS TEST ONLY. DO NOT TURN TO ANY OTHER TEST IN THIS BOOK.

MCAT
DIAGNOSTIC TEST II
ANSWERS AND EXPLANATIONS

DIAGNOSTIC TEST II ANSWERS

Section 1 Verbal Reasoning		Section 2 Physical Sciences		Section 3 Biological Sciences	
1. B	34. C	66. B	105. D	143. B	182. A
2. D	35. C	67. C	106. B	144. C	183. B
3. B	36. D	68. A	107. A	145. C	184. C
4. A	37. B	69. C	108. C	146. C	185. B
5. B	38. D	70. A	109. A	147. B	186. C
6. D	39. C	71. C	110. B	148. A	187. A
7. C	40. A	72. C	111. D	149. D	188. B
8. A	41. D	73. D	112. C	150. B	189. A
9. B	42. D	74. B	113. B	151. D	190. D
10. D	43. C	75. A	114. C	152. C	191. A
11. B	44. B	76. B	115. C	153. C	192. B
12. A	45. A	77. D	116. B	154. A	193. D
13. D	46. D	78. A	117. A	155. C	194. A
14. C	47. C	79. A	118. A	156. B	195. C
15. C	48. B	80. D	119. A	157. B	196. C
16. D	49. C	81. B	120. C	158. A	197. D
17. B	50. D	82. C	121. D	159. C	198. A
18. A	51. A	83. D	122. C	160. C	199. B
19. D	52. C	84. A	123. B	161. D	200. D
20. C	53. D	85. D	124. A	162. D	201. A
21. D	54. C	86. C	125. D	163. A	202. D
22. C	55. A	87. A	126. B	164. C	203. B
23. B	56. B	88. B	127. B	165. B	204. B
24. A	57. C	89. D	128. B	166. B	205. C
25. C	58. D	90. A	129. C	167. D	206. D
26. A	59. D	91. B	130. A	168. D	207. D
27. B	60. B	92. B	131. D	169. C	208. A
28. A	61. A	93. D	132. B	170. C	209. C
29. D	62. B	94. A	133. D	171. B	210. C
30. C	63. D	95. D	134. D	172. C	211. B
31. D	64. D	96. B	135. B	173. A	212. A
32. B	65. A	97. B	136. B	174. B	213. D
33. A		98. B	137. B	175. C	214. D
		99. A	138. D	176. A	215. A
		100. B	139. B	177. A	216. A
		101. D	140. B	178. C	217. D
		102. C	141. C	179. B	218. C
		103. A	142. A	180. B	219. A
		104. A		181. D	

VERBAL REASONING EXPLANATIONS II

Passage I (Questions 1–6)

1. Each of the following factors is explicitly cited in the passage to support the idea that destructive distillation combines pragmatism with sound environmental strategy EXCEPT:

    A. The technology will provide electricity for the island at lower than prevailing rates.
    B. Extrapolative waste stream studies do not contraindicate the technology.
    C. Plant construction and maintenance will add millions of dollars to the local economy.
    D. It will provide a long-term teaching mission to the local university.

B is correct. Paragraphs 2, 5, 6, and 7 contain text rephrased in choices A, C, and D, respectively. Choice B is tempting because the final paragraph mentions the likelihood that current extrapolative waste flow studies are insufficient to support the proposal. So, while they might not contraindicate the technology, neither do they particularly represent pragmatism united with environmentalism.

2. According to the passage, which of the following is most likely to be true about the solid waste disposal problem in the Caribbean Basin?

    A. The Caribbean Islands do not face much of a solid waste crisis.
    B. Disposal problems in the Caribbean Basin are much the same as they are elsewhere.
    C. A limited population and premium warm saltwater bays lessen the region's problem.
    D. Scarcities of land mass and drinking water magnify the problem.

D is correct. The justification for this choice appears unambiguously in the second sentence.

The wrong answer choices: Choice A inverts the meaning of the first sentence (disposal problems are "ubiquitous"). Choice B also inverts meaning in that sentence (the problem "acquires special dimensions") in the Islands. Choice C seeks to tempt the reader with an assertion that makes superficial sense, but is false, and unsupported by the passage.

3. Which of the following statements, if true, would most WEAKEN the author's argument that the use of destruction distillation as described in the passage will contribute to environmental health in ways beyond the technology's primary applications?

A. Construction costs to tax-payers will over-run estimates by fifty percent.

B. The cost for exporting scrap iron will exceed the profit margin from its sale.

C. Because of the noise produced by the distillation process nearby hotels will be forced to relocate.

D. Mahogany in Stalley Bay will regenerate and surpass previous growth levels.

B is correct. The final sentence of paragraph 4 refers to the possible resale of scrap iron by-product. But if market conditions made such an industry unprofitable, the Islands would be left with unsightly and burdensome accumulations of scrap metal.

The wrong answer choices: Choices A, C, and D are appealing; each makes a kind of superficial sense. Sentence 1 of the final paragraph does refer to a concern about "taxpayer abuses"; but this question speaks of "environmental" health, not economic soundness. Therefore, choice A is incorrect. The passage nowhere mentions noise levels produced by the technology, so choice C is unsupported. Choice D suggests a development that would strengthen, not WEAKEN the author's argument about the environment.

4. Suppose two major hurricanes causing severe, widespread damage to real estate and buildings, and eight minor hurricanes causing less but still significant damage, had struck the Virgin Islands during the last six years. This new information would most CHALLENGE the claim(s) that:

   I. Technological success in the Virgin Islands could be exported to other nations in the Caribbean.
   II. Approval of the proposal represents a wise long-term investment for the territories.
   III. Plant construction will bring significant new revenues to the territory's economy.

   A. II only
   B. I and III only
   C. II and III only
   D. I , II, and III

A is correct. Think logically. If the Islands are geographically vulnerable to hurricanes, as the question says, then the wisdom of making a large infrastructure investment as discussed in the passage seems questionable. The export of technology to other Caribbean islands would not necessarily be affected by the Virgin Islands' storm experience (especially if the technology were a "success"), even though one might be tempted to make the connection. Hurricanes would only increase the amount of revenues from plant construction since a destructive storm would require rebuilding and the inflow of new funding. Therefore, only statement II applies.

5. According to the passage, proponents of the distillation technology claim that such a waste disposal system is environmentally superior to incineration in each of the following ways EXCEPT:

   A. It will generate a byproduct to build a filtering system for landfill toxins.
   B. It will qualify for increased federal subsidies under the Clean Air Clear Water Act.
   C. It will serve as a new source for low-cost drinking water.
   D. It produces significantly less environmental pollution than incineration.

B is correct. The assertion in choice A rephrases text from paragraph 4, sentence 2. Choice C rewords meaning from the first sentence of paragraph 2. And choice D is represented in paragraph 3, sentence 3.

6. Based on your reading of the passage, officials who urge a more cautious approach because "previous analyses had limited their scope to seasonal or extrapolative data" are probably most concerned that:

   A. year-round residents of the island might be distrustful of new methods of waste disposal.
   B. registered voters might resent the job dislocations involved in altering the waste disposal system
   C. the tourist industry might suffer because of travellers' fears that the system does not ensure adequate sanitary conditions year-round.
   D. total annual waste flow might be better disposed of using a different system.

D is correct. The relevant text is found in sentences 3 and 4 of the final paragraph, which states that independent evaluators had advised a year-round study "to qualify and quantify the kinds of waste going into the territorial dumps" and determine if the technology discussed in the passage is "adequate" to the territory's needs.

The wrong answer choices: None of the other choices is anywhere supported in the passage, although each of them might tempt you with a kind of superficial sense. Furthermore, choice C distorts the reference to "year-round" concerns mentioned above.

Passage II (Questions 7–13)

7. Given the ideas in the passage, which of the following statements accurately describes the quote "adequacy gap" and/or the "compliance gap?"

   A. The compliance gap measures the court costs of child support proceedings unpaid by litigants and covered by state budgets.
   B. The adequacy gap measures the court costs of child support proceedings unfunded by state budgets and covered by federal assistance.
   C. The compliance gap measures the child support dollar amount awarded in courts and unpaid by parents.
   D. The adequacy gap measures the child support dollar amount awarded in courts and unpaid by parents.

C is correct. The question requires that you infer from your reading the meaning of the two phrases. "Adequacy gap" seems to refer to the difference between the "realistic...cost of child rearing" (paragraph 1, sentence 1) and the amounts awarded. The "compliance gap" can only mean the difference between the amounts awarded and the amounts actually paid.

The wrong answer choices: Choices A and B seek to mislead you with information which, true or false, is not directly relevant to the passage. Choice D confuses the two concepts.

8. The author cites a specific study to support which of the following types?

   I.   Judges do not always rely on the same criteria when setting child support awards even within the same state.
   II. Fairness dictates that noncustodial spouses in comparable circumstances should be treated alike.
   III. The quote "compliance gap" is likely to increase

   A. I only
   B. I and III only
   C. II and III only
   D. I, II, and III

A is correct. Sentence 3 of paragraph 3 presents the meaning of statement I in different words and refers to studies in support of the claim. The author asserts statement II in sentence 1 of that same paragraph as a given ethical precept and does not support it by citing a study. Similarly, the author's forecast about the science gap (paragraph 2, last sentence) is not buttressed by statistical analysis.

9. Suppose Spouse A has custody of three children and a monthly of income of $6,000, while Spouse B has a monthly income of $2,000. A court has determined that the children would ordinarily enjoy benefit of 15 percent of total parental income. Which of the following statements would reflect appropriate child support payment alternatives as discussed in the passage?

   A. Under the income shares model, a contribution of $300 monthly would be required, with Spouse B as the payee spouse.
   B. Under the income shares model, a contribution of $300 monthly would be required, with Spouse A as the payee spouse.
   C. Under the flat rate model, a contribution of $900 monthly would be required, with Spouse A as the payee spouse.
   D. Under the flat rate model, a contribution of $900 monthly would be required, with Spouse B as the payee spouse.

B is correct. Even though Spouse A has a larger income the income shares model requires that each parent contribute a percentage of the total amount by which the child would benefit if his parents had not divorced (paragraph 5, sentence 1). In the situation given, the total income for both parents was $8,000 per month of which Spouse B earned 25%. Since the court decreed a 15% benefit rate in child support, the total benefit rate would be 15% of $8,000 or $1,200 per month. Twenty-five percent of that, or $300 per month, would be Spouse B's obligation as payor to the custodial spouse and payee Spouse A.

The wrong answer choices: Choice A inverts the payee-payor relationship which is described in sentence 2 of the final paragraph. The guideline cited in the passage for a flat rate model (paragraph 4) would entitle a custodial spouse with 3 children to receive 20% of the paying parent's income. In the case at question, 20% of the noncustodial parent's monthly income would be $400, not $90 (choice C). Choice D is wrong because, in addition to mangling the flat rate contribution for support of 3 children, it inverts the payee-payor relationship.

10. The relationship between the flat rate model and the income shares model, as discussed in the passage, might best be analogized to which of the following?

   A. Local telephone charges at a monthly flat rate or a rate based on amount of monthly usage
   B. Long distance telephone rates based on a flat rate per minute or based on mileage between the call origination phone and the call destination phone
   C. Monthly loan interest at a fixed rate or at a variable rate
   D. An income tax system based on a single tax rate or on a graduated rate that escalates with income.

D is correct. The essential difference between the flat rate and income shares models is that the latter is calculated based on relative incomes. An analogous relationship exists between a flat rate tax system and a graduated system where rate increases with income.

The wrong answer choices: Choice A presents a relationship which might be analogous if the income shares models based support contributions on the amount of time each parent spent with the children. Choice B might be analogous if the income shares model were based on the amount of time each parent had to travel to visit with the children. Choice C might be analogous if the income shares model based support obligations on a number of economic factors including the inflation rate, the unemployment rate, and, most important, the Federal Reserve's prime rate.

11. Individuals opposed to leaving legislation regarding child support arrangements up to the individual states probably base their objections on their belief that:

A. the federal government has an important and necessary role in protecting the welfare of children.

B. divorced individuals often do not live in the same part of the country as do their former spouses.

C. the federal government can best evaluate statistical variations in the cost of living index from state to state.

D. the federal government has a constitutional obligation to ensure due process of law for all persons, including those involved in divorce proceedings.

B is correct. The final sentence of the passage mentions the author's concern that approaches which vary from state to state "will not bring about parity."

The wrong answer choices: All other choices make assertions because they not only sound logical but are probably true. They mislead you in that none is directly responsive to the question or specifically relevant to issues discussed in the passage. (Although choice A has general support in paragraph 1, sentences 2 and 3, it is not so specifically supported in the passage as is choice B.)

12. A recent theory suggests that children of divorced spouses whose custodial parent received regular and sufficient child support payments will score higher on scales measuring self-esteem and self-confidence than those whose parents do not comply with court ordered support. Social workers who accept this theory would be LEAST likely to support which of the following?

A. Support groups at the local level to help parents who do not meet child support obligations deal with their resulting psychological issues

B. Support groups at the local level for custodial parents and their children who do not receive regular and sufficient child support

C. Federal regulations making it more difficult for parents to avoid compliance with court ordered support judgments

D. State laws requiring automatic deductions from payroll checks of parents convicted of failing to pay child support

A is correct. Given the sense of the question, social workers would less likely be concerned about the psychological needs of payment avoiders than about those who do not receive adequate support (choice B).

The wrong answer choices: Choices C and D both present propositions designed to improve child support compliance and social workers would be likely to support them.

13. In Self Reliance, Ralph Waldo Emerson wrote, "A foolish consistency is the hobgoblin of little minds." Given the ideas in the passage, Emerson would probably believe that:

   A. the goal of achieving consistency in child support awards through legislation is foolish.
   B. the process of achieving consistency through legislation should be left to people with little imagination.
   C. the goal of achieving consistency in child support awards through legislation is the obsession of vengeful litigants.
   D. the goal of consistency is not foolish in every circumstance.

D is correct. This question is tangential to the passage in the sense that it can answered apart from the text. The question quotes Emerson as having written that "a foolish consistency is the hobgoblin of little minds," implying that consistencies which are not foolish do not necessarily warrant that characterization.

The wrong answer choices: We cannot know what Emerson might think in relation to the other choices, and certainly there is nothing in the passage to assist us in making that determination.

Passage III (Questions 14–19)

14. What is the main theme of the passage?

   A. African art serves as a barrier between the artist class and the community.
   B. African art is essentially inaccessible to students of Western art.
   C. African art participates in diverse functional ways in the community's daily life.
   D. Western art is divorced from the community's daily functioning.

C is correct. Sentence 3 of paragraph 3 states that Dan masks play "a significant role" in daily community life.

The wrong answer choices: The final two sentences of the passage emphasize the importance of African art in daily life. Both of those references also rule out choice A, which inverts the relationship of artists with their communities. Choice B might tempt those who believe that differences between distinct cultures are unbridgeable, but the author would likely not have bothered to write the essay at all if choice B were his central idea. Although choice D offers an idea that some might infer from the author's words (paragraph 1, sentence 3; and paragraph 5, sentence 1), it represents an absolute statement not directly related to the passage's central theme.

15. To emphasize the idea that African art is un-like Western art the author explicitly cites all of the following information EXCEPT:

    A. Structures housing African art are built according to ritual practices and laws.
    B. Once completed, African sculptures are allowed to crumble and rot.
    C. African sculptures often depict historical heroes.
    D. African art includes common objects of daily household use.

C is correct. In both African and western art, heroes are often the subject, so this fact does not emphasize the difference between the two. Western museums are built according to architectural plans, not religious rituals. Western cultures usually do everything they can to preserve ancient sculptures, not let them crumble through natural deterioration. And, despite the popularity of Peter Max sunglasses and Swatch watches, most Western art is valued for its truth and its beauty, not because it is useful in daily life.

16. The word "literature" (line 71) most closely means:

    A. an unbound collected body of tribal writings.
    B. a catalogue of religious sculptures and myths.
    C. family stories passed down through generations of oral tradition.
    D. cultural narratives based on tribal values and beliefs.

D is correct. We are told that "performances constitute literature." Combining that information with your own insight into the word, you should arrive at choice D. You might also select D by eliminating the other choices.

The wrong answer choices: The passage clearly states (paragraph 4, final sentence) that the Gelade "performance constitutes literature." That observation rules out both choices A and B, which refer to written work, not performances. Although it is possible that some Gelade performances draw, in part, on family stories and oral traditions, the author notes that social commentary is the masker's primary focus (paragraph 4, sentence 8). Narratives relevant to the Yoruba culture, observing foibles and failings of various familiar characters (paragraph 4, sentence 7) who fail—or surpass—in one way or another the community's shared values and beliefs, seem closer to what the author had in mind by social commentary.

17. Which of the following circumstances, if true, would most CHALLENGE the notion that the Dan poro masks serve to protect their wearers while executing official duties in the community?

   A. Members of the poro are selected through a democratic process rather than on the basis of clan affiliation.
   B. Community officers are chosen in tribal electoral campaigns instead of designated from within the poro.
   C. The poro's mask-making activities begin to consume twice the amount of time it had previously.
   D. The poro gradually evolves into a guild of craftspersons which instituted bylaws and secret oaths.

B is correct. According to the passage, the masks hide the identities of Dan officials from the community, protecting those who must perform unpopular duties from the revenge of those adversely affected.

The wrong answer choices: Public electoral campaigns to choose officials would obviously prevent Dan officials from maintaining their anonymity. But a democratic election to the poro, as offered in choice A, would not necessarily identify specific officials publicly. The passage does not indicate that the identities of the maskmaking poro are unknown to the community, only that of a specific member performing a specific duty. Options C and D are not directly relevant to the question of Dan anonymity as discussed in the passage.

18. Based on the passage it is reasonable to conclude that the masks of the Dan tribe differ from those of the Yoruba Gelade in that a Dan mask:

A. might accurately describe the role of the person who wears it.

B. is rarely designed by the person who wears it.

C. is designed to mollify the cult of magic practitioners.

D. has a special relationship to social function.

A is correct. The author describes the Dan and Yoruba masks in paragraphs 3 and 4. Among the Dan, a judge wears a judge's mask. Among the Yoruba, masks are used as performance costumes. In the Dan community the mask represents the actual role of the person wearing it. In the Yoruba community, the role represented buy the mask is make-believe.

The wrong answer choices: Choice B distorts the information (paragraph 3) about the poro mask-making activities and their relationship to the person who might wear a particular mask. Choice C inverts the author's meaning. Sentence 2 of paragraph 4 states that the Yoruba Gelade, not the Dan poro, use masks to appease the forces of sorcery. Choice D also distorts information regarding the function of masks in each culture. As has been explained, although the function of the mask differs according to the culture, in both cultures—not just the Dan—the masks serve "a special function."

19. If a member of the Yoruba community were kidnapped and transported to a Dan village, one might reasonably expect that in participating in the daily activities of the Dan:

A. The Yoruban might confuse governance with ceremony.

B. The Yoruban might confuse governance with utilitarianism.

C. The Yoruban might confuse reality with the unconscious.

D. The Yoruban might confuse reality with satire.

D is correct. As discussed above, a member of the Yoruba would be accustomed to seeing masks used to offer social commentary, including, it may be assumed, satirical comment. In the Dan village, masks are used in actual, not make-believe proceedings.

The wrong answer choices: Choice A confuses the largely ceremonial use of art described in paragraph 2, with the theatrical use of masks among the Yoruba. A Yoruban witnessing an act of Dan governance might mistake the proceedings for social commentary, but probably not for ceremony. Choice B distorts the reference in the final paragraph to utilitarianism, which is a characteristic of African art common to each of the communities described by the author. Choice C confuses the purpose of Gelade theater with that of western theater.

Passage IV (Questions 20–29)

20. The central thesis of the passage is that:

    A. interaction is only one of many competencies essential to the formation of a fully socialized human being.
    B. diverse interactional abilities cause children of similar age to vary sharply in their development.
    C. interactional development offers a sound model for the understanding of the socialization process.
    D. the competence of intervention strategies by parents, counselors and teachers will improve significantly by understanding children's interactional disabilities.

C is correct. The question requires that you understand the author's central purpose and distinguish it from ancillary points. The passage points out, primarily, that socialization might be viewed in terms of interaction.

The wrong answer choices: Choice A is wrong because it represents a view that the author never expresses. Choices B and D are tempting because they sound sensible and "nice." Unfortunately, they have nothing whatsoever to do with the passage.

21. Implicit in the statement that a child learns about boundaries and territories is the idea that these perceptions:

    A. prepare children to cope in a society composed of a growing immigrant population.
    B. enable children to deal with the sociopolitical fact of intermittent military confrontation with foreign nations.
    C. permit children to explore and admire foreign cultures without losing their own identities.
    D. teach children to function according to society's rules and regulations without feeling victimized or exploited.

D is correct. Paragraph 2 explains that learning about "boundaries and territory" refers not to frontiers between different countries or cultures, but to the rights and prerogatives of different people. Some things belong to the child, and some belong to others. Certain behaviors and desires are appropriate, and likely to be met without difficulty, while others might cross parental limits.

The wrong answer choices: Choices A, B, and C all distort the author's sense of boundaries and territory.

22. The author probably compares the situations of a six-month old taken to the theater with that of a six-year-old in order to demonstrate that:

   A. fully interactionalized adults must take responsibility for less socialized children.
   B. children who are exposed to art and music will develop interactional competence at an earlier age than those without such experiences.
   C. older children have greater appreciation for cultural interaction than do younger children.
   D. an older child is likely to be more socialized than a younger child.

D is correct. In paragraph 1, the author makes a general point: "In the process of socialization, the child learns to respect the rights and property of others." The very next sentence tells you what socialization is. The socialized child is able to "conform behavior to the circumstances that surround him or her at any given time." In order to answer this question, you must see that the illustration involving the theater supports the point that an older child is better able than a younger child to "conform behavior to the circumstances." In other words, the author intends to demonstrate that an older child is better socialized than a younger child.

The wrong answer choices: Choice A is wrong because it is irrelevant to the main thrust of the paragraph and the passage. Choices B and C are also wrong because they bear no connection to the author's points.

23. The ideas discussed in this passage would be of most use to:

    A. parents of multi-sibling families wanting to promote more productive interactions among their children.

    B. professional sociologists expanding their understanding of socialization dynamics.

    C. primary school teachers designing foreign language programs for young children.

    D. pre-school teachers designing a reading curriculum for learning-disabled children.

B is correct. The passage offers a new approach to the understanding of socialization. Figure out that a sociologist might use the information to gain a better understanding of socialization.

The wrong answer choices: Choices A and C are wrong because they incorporate the author's words but distort his meaning. The author refers to language, interactions, and parents, but never makes points relevant to the matters described in choices A and C. Choice D is wrong because it (1) distorts the author's reference to an eight-year-old learning to speak another person's "language" (paragraph 7, sentence 3) and (2) is far removed from the author's discussions.

24. Suppose by the age of six months a child has developed the ability to wave "bye-bye" to departing persons. Professor Speier would most likely view this development as:

    A. an achievement of a specific interactional skill.

    B. a reflex activity essentially peripheral to the process of socialization.

    C. a milestone in the child's information-processing abilities.

    D. an indication of the child's ability to cope with separations and absences.

A is correct. Speier's main point is this: Socialization is a process in which children develop their ability to interact. Choice A makes a similar statement. Choice B is contrary to the passage's central purpose and Speier's view points. Choice C sounds sensible, but it is unrelated to the points made in the passage. Choice D borrows the words "separation" and "absence" from paragraph 2, but thoroughly distorts the author's meaning. The author noted only that the ability to accept temporary absence and separation marked developmental progress. There is nothing in the passage to suggest that a child's ability to wave good-bye has bearing on her ability to accept separation or absence.

25. Given the ideas in the passage, the phrases "a people person," "good telephone skills," and "ability to communicate" as seen in many help wanted ads, most probably refer to

    A. individuals who manage others by communicating their own competence
    B. individuals who put the needs of others before their own.
    C. individuals who validate others' perspectives even as they assert their own.
    D. individuals who put their own needs before those of others.

C is correct. The passage describes discrete skills of interaction, including both the skill of responding to the needs and concerns of other people (paragraph 4, sentence 4), as well as the skill of communicating to others one's own needs (paragraph 4, sentence 3). The ideas in the passage indicate that such interactional skills form the basis of good communication abilities.

The wrong answer choices: Individuals who communicate their own competence (choice A) do not necessarily take the needs of others into account, and their communication skills lack that ability to empathize. Those who always put the needs of others before their own (choice B) would probably not be very effective communicators. An individual who always puts his or her own needs before those of others, could hardly be called "a people person."

26. Each of the following behaviors is specifically cited to explain Speier's concept of discrete interactional competencies EXCEPT:

    A. A six-year-old does not whine and carry on in the theater during a performance
    B. An eight-year-old does not fail to draw conclusions about an unseen questioner's identity
    C. An eight-year-old does not identify himself in response to a direct question
    D. An eight-year-old does not refer to his friend by the friend's own name

A is correct. Although the restraint shown by a six-year old who behaves herself well in a theater is offered in paragraph as an example of socialization, it is not cited later in the passage where the author discusses Speier's "discrete interactional skills."

The wrong answer choices: The eight-year-old who concluded he was talking to his friend's mother, as mirrored in choice B, showed a certain level of interactional skill (paragraph 6, sentence 2). The boy's failure to identify himself in response to the mother's question (choice C) demonstrated a lack of interactional skill (paragraph 5, sentence 4), but the author uses that failure to help explain Speier's concept (paragraph 7, sentence 4). Choice D reflects the author's explanation of Speier's concept of referent terms (paragraph 6).

27. As used in the passage, the phrase "referent terms" means:

   A. expressions with which people of diverse backgrounds are likely to be familiar.
   B. words that enable a listener to relate a subject to himself.
   C. phrases that allow a speaker to describe diverse relationships in a single communication.
   D. sentences that do not employ proper names.

B is correct. In the last paragraph, the author implicitly explains the meaning of referent terms. You are told that the phrase "your son" was a referent term because it allowed the mother to refer the child's statement to herself. A referent term is one that allows a listener to relate a subject to himself.

The wrong answer choices: Choice D distorts the importance of the child's failure to use his friend's proper name in responding to the friend's mother (paragraph 6). Choices A and C are wild and irrelevant.

28. Suppose two brothers, ages six and seven, have occasionally been given ice cream popsicles by a friend's mother from a freezer in her garage. One day the brothers enter the garage uninvited and unseen, and take two popsicles. Given the ideas in the passage, this behavior would most likely represent:

   A. the brothers' belief that it was unnecessary to ask permission to enter the garage and take ice cream.
   B. the brothers' lack of recognition of the individual prerogatives and property of others.
   C. the brothers' feeling that they were treated like members of the family in their friend's home.
   D. a failure of the brothers' parents to teach them right from wrong.

A is correct. The question presents a situation in which two young boys have not, in Speier's terms, learned certain interactional skills: specifically, the necessity to take into account another person's needs and concerns. Because it did not occur to the boys that their friend's mother might wish to keep the popsicles in her freezer for an occasion of her own choosing, they did not believe it was necessary to interact with her before taking the ice cream for themselves.

The wrong answer choices: The statement presented in choice B is more in keeping with a traditional analysis of socialization than with the interactional model. Choice C also suggests that the boys had a mistaken notion about boundaries and territory, and choice D reflects a still more advanced level of traditional socialization.

29. According to the information in the passage, which of the following statements best describes the essential difference between Speier's analysis of the socialization process and that of classical sociology?

    A. Classical sociology views the child fundamentally as a conformist adapting to social expectations.
    B. Classical sociology views society as a laboratory in which the child tests her reality perceptions.
    C. Speier considers the child as a potentially competent individual within a referent context.
    D. Speier identifies the child primarily as an actor in diverse social circumstances.

D is correct. This is a difficult question because all of the choices seem sensible. After all, Speier would probably agree that the interactional child will learn the skill of respecting certain social norms (choice A) and will sharpen interactional skills through a gradual process of reality testing (choice B). And Speier would be unlikely to dispute the idea offered in choice C. But keeping in mind his concept of interacting, his view of the child as an actor in diverse social circumstances seems the best choice here.

Passage V (Questions 30–35)

30. According to the passage, commitment is a quality that:

    A. means more to an individual than to a society.
    B. is the root of animal and vegetable life.
    C. is a substructure, not a trait.
    D. has no fundamental underpinnings.

C is correct. In paragraph 1 the author states, basically, that commitment is not "just another" trait. Rather, it is a "fundamental underpinning" from which all traits arise. Choice C represents, more or less, the same statement. "Substructure" is intended to mean the same thing as "fundamental underpinning."

The wrong answer choices: Choice A is wrong because the passage indicates that commitment is valuable to both the individual and the society. Choice B is wrong because the author distinguishes between animal and vegetable life, noting that vegetable life is incapable of commitment. Choice D takes the author's words and distorts their meaning. According to the passage, commitment is a "fundamental underpinning." The passage does not say that commitment lacks underpinnings.

31. The author states that interpersonal commitment is essentially different and distinct from societal commitment. Based on your reading of the passage, this statement probably derives from the author's belief that:

    A. societal commitment requires no investment of self.
    B. societal commitment requires no genuine concern for others.
    C. interpersonal commitment requires no genuine concern for others.
    D. interpersonal commitment requires one to put faith in another.

D is correct. Paragraph 4 presents the relevant text. The author distinguishes interpersonal commitment from societal commitment, noting that one involves devotion to the society and that another involves trust or "investment" in another. Choice D represents, more or less, the same statement.

The wrong answer choices: Choice C distorts the meaning of the author's words. Nowhere does the passage indicate that interpersonal commitment does not require genuine concern for others. Choices B and A are absolutes not supported by the passage.

32. Based on your reading of the passage, which of the following phenomena, if true, would most WEAKEN the claim that only humans must make commitments in order to develop their characters?

    A. Documentation that the frontal lobes of some animals are more intricately convoluted than those of humans
    B. Evidence that animals experience lasting gratification and pain over the need to make choices
    C. Indications that all animals have certain inborn instincts
    D. Proof that dogs can reason abstractly

B is correct. In paragraph 2, the author associates the importance of commitment with the fact that it may "produce pleasure as it may produce anguish." He says that such pleasure and anguish are the "fabric of character." If it turns out that dolphins also experience pain and pleasure over the need to make decisions, then it would begin to appear that commitment plays an important role in their development too. It would WEAKEN the author's claim that commitment is important only to human development.

The wrong answer choices: Choice A is very tempting because frontal lobe complexity may well be related to human decision-making capabilities. But the passage does not discuss that idea. Choice C is essentially irrelevant to the question. The ability to reason abstractly is associated with the higher functions of the cerebral cortex, and so a dog who had that ability might also challenge the author's claim that commitment is uniquely human issue. Yet nothing in the passage connects abstract reasoning with commitment, and choice D is incorrect.

33. As used in the passage, the word "conceit" means:

    A. idea
    B. fantasy
    C. boastfulness
    D. surrender

A is correct. The word appears in paragraph 4, sentence 5, in the context of a discussion of the idea of societal commitment. There is nothing fantastic (choice B) or boastful (choice C) about the author's discussion, and unless you confuse the word "concede" with "conceit" you will not have chosen D.

34. It is often said that commitment requires persistence. Which of the following ideas from the passage to directly supports that assertion?

    A. All hobbies require skill that takes years to develop.

    B. People are required to make choices throughout life.

    C. Seralius continued to write even though he was tortured.

    D. There can be no commitment of time without commitment of energy.

C is correct. If you realize that "persistence" means, more or less, "perseverance," you will turn your attention to paragraph 3. The author discusses the importance of perseverance to social commitment and for illustration describes Seralius.

The wrong answer choices: Choices A and D distort the author's meaning. In paragraph 3 the author refers briefly to hobbies, but he never makes a statement that resembles choice A. Also in paragraph 3, the author refers to "time and energy." But he never states that a commitment of one requires a commitment of the other (even though we might think it does). Choice B accurately reflects the author's view, but it is wholly unresponsive to the question.

35. According to the passage, individuals such as Seralius dedicate themselves to the promotion of social harmony and universal humanism, and persevere in their commitment despite relentless scorn and harsh treatment from society. Which of the following individuals best embodies that kind of commitment?

A. The Aztec emperor Montezuma, because even after his capture by the Spanish he continued to rule as chieftain, and was eventually stoned to death by his own people

B. The first U.S. Treasury Secretary Alexander Hamilton, because after years of bitter civic strife on behalf of his party, he lost his life in a gun duel with a political rival

C. American cleric Martin Luther King, because he gave his life to a hard and painful struggle for human rights in the face of political abuse and official penalties

D. Nun and social worker Mother Teresa, because she persists in her campaign to dignify and humanize the life of the destitute in the midst of disease and deprivation

C is correct. No doubt the lives of each of the individuals cited in the choices represent genuine societal commitments, but the question asks which one best embodies committed determination in the face of social rejection and political adversity. As described in choice C (and as is generally known), Dr. King answers that description.

The wrong answer choices: Few would question the depth or vitality of Mother Theresa's societal commitment (choice D), but it is also true that she is much admired and beloved by most of the world. She probably does not face social ridicule and political danger on a daily basis. Alexander Hamilton (choice B) did give his life for what he probably felt was service to his country, but a duel to defeat a political rival is not the same as promoting "values of tolerance and pluralism." Montezuma (choice A) perhaps attempted to maintain his commitment to his people under difficult conditions, but his enemies restored him to his throne, even though his position depended on his subservience. And some have criticized Montezuma for surrendering to the invaders from Europe. Perhaps he did attempt to promote understanding and harmony between the Spaniard conquistadors and his own people, but not enough recorded fact is known about Montezuma's motives to draw that conclusion. Martin Luther King (choice C), on the other hand, is famous for his life-long struggle, against great odds and at great personal cost, to bring about a society based on racial equality and social harmony.

Passage VI (Questions 36–45)

36. The author's claim that "structuralist" criticism represents an attempt to "uproot the critical enterprise" rests on the New Critics' belief that:

   A. the complexities of theoretical disciplines should inform all literary commentary.
   B. theoretical foundations are totally useless to the task of literary criticism.
   C. the essential mission of literature unmasks disguises of similitude and dissimilitude.
   D. literary criticism should focus primarily on the literary work.

D is correct. By paraphrase it accurately describes the New Critics' beliefs, as discussed throughout the passage. Choice A inverts the statement in the passage about the New Critics' appreciation of theoretical approaches. Choice B is an absolute, unsupported by the passage, and choice C distorts the information in the passage.

37. The author most likely believes that New Critics view their opponents as undermining and subjugating literature by:

   A. placing a fundamental emphasis on humanistic interpretation.
   B. substituting external texts as the basis for the critical endeavor.
   C. negating the usurpation of literature's unique discourse.
   D. rejecting interdisciplinary methodology as a basis for discourse.

B is correct. In the first paragraph the author states that the structuralists subvert "the New Criticism's interpretive text with a multitude of diverse and often tangential discourses," which is paraphrased in choice B as "emphasizing the importance of factors external to literary works and neglecting the literary work itself."

The wrong answer choices: Choice A inverts the passage's assertions regarding humanistic interpretation. Choice C distorts the concept of usurpation as described in the passage. Choice D reverses the passage's observations about the opponents of New Criticism and their use—not rejection—of interdisciplinary methodology.

38. According to the passage, the author believes that empirical reasoning represents:

   A. a diversion for traditionalist literary critics.
   B. a threat to "structuralist" critics.
   C. a rebuttal to feminist extrapolations of 18th century novels.
   D. a mode of analysis antithetical to traditional literary concerns.

D is correct. It takes statements from the passage and rewords them.

The wrong answer choices: Choice A inverts the author's assertion to the effect that traditionalists feel the need "to defend" their discipline against systems of empirical inquiry. Choice B substitutes "structuralists" for "traditionalists." Choice C distorts the passage's reference to a feminist approach to Shakespeare.

39. Given the information in the passage, students who are drawn to a humanistic interpretive approach:

   A. ignore the metatextual domains of the literary universe.
   B. reject the traditionalist school of literary criticism.
   C. are excluded by the theoretical structuralists.
   D. are animated by the nihilistic exclusivity of ideological analysis.

C is correct. The relevant information is found in paragraph 7. According to the author, the humanistic interpretive approach is consigned "to the margins." They are, in other words, excluded by theoretical and ideological analysts.

The wrong answer choices: Choice A represents an absolute that is not supported in the passage. Choice B distorts the passage's discussion of the relationship between "the traditionalist school" and humanistic interpretation. Choice D is wrong because students interested in the humanistic approach would hardly be animated by ideologues who exclude them.

40. Given the information in the passage, "inclusivity" as conceived by theoretical advocates conforms with:

    A. an identity politics unwittingly serving the forces of reactionary populism.
    B. an identity politics serving to liberate its disciples from restriction and taboo.
    C. a universalist humanism tending to embrace multicultural perspectives.
    D. a universalist humanism working to defuse reactionary apartheidism.

A is correct. It rewords information set forth in paragraph 5 where the author writes that such "inclusivity" "nicely conforms with the reactionary apartheidism espoused and embraced by the fashionable tenets of identity politics."

The wrong answer choices: Choice B reverses the role that identity politics play vis-a-vis restriction and taboo. Choice C inverts information set forth in the passage. The passage states that humanism is consigned to the margins by theoretical inclusivity. Choice D also distorts the author's meaning. The passage indicates that identity politics, not universalist humanism, collaborates with apartheidism.

41. The author implies that the underlying objectives of deconstruction inevitably distort literary expression because they:

    A. can never effectively negate the humanistic principles of literary criticism.
    B. infer a semiotic relationship to the mechanics of novelistic form.
    C. impart meaning to a narrative's emotional content.
    D. reject inherent meaning and motive as appropriate subjects for critical consideration.

D is correct. It accurately paraphrases the information found in lines 125-129 of the passage. Choice A is an absolute. Choice B distorts the passage's reference to "semiotics." Choice C inverts the author's statements relating deconstruction and emotional content, and stands in virtual opposition to choice D.

42. As used in the passage, the word "opus" (line 55) most nearly means:

   A. foul and sordid deeds
   B. sweet, pre-adolescent male characters
   C. operatic plays
   D. collected plays

D is correct. As the author speaks of Shakespeare's "opus" in the passage, she is referring to the entire body of his work, not to a single great play. None of the other choices approximates the meaning of the word.

43. The author argues that structuralist analysis poses an anti-intellectual threat to literature's existence. Which of the following circumstances, if true, would most WEAKEN the argument?

   A. A multidisciplinary committee urges that the Literature faculty be dispersed among other Humanities and Social Science departments.
   B. An associate dean of Academic Affairs proposes that Literature course offerings be cut in half.
   C. A feminist critic of Chaucer's poetry offers his course through the Women's Studies department.
   D. A Freudian critic of James Joyce's novels offers her course through the Literature department.

C is correct. The author's basic argument with the "structuralists" is that they take ideas from other disciplines and use literature to teach those belief systems.

The wrong answer choices: The author would view someone who wants to teach Freudian psychology as a course in the literature department (choice D) as a person willing to substitute psychology for literature. That substitution would confirm, not weaken, the author's argument. On the other hand, a person who believes that Chaucer can be used as a vehicle to teach feminist ideas, and who offers such a course in the Women's Studies department, would not be pretending to teach Chaucer, only feminism, and so would not threaten literature's own identity. Choices A and B would strengthen the author's argument that literature's being is under attack.

44. The author's attitude to non-traditional criticism is best described as:

A. reverent
B. critical
C. dispassionate
D. exuberant

B is correct. Throughout the passage the author indicates that the various structuralist ie, non-traditional) approaches to literary criticism fail in various respects to provide a useful framework for analyzing literature. This generally negative tone makes choices A and D incorrect. Answer choice C is contrary to the author's rather passionate critique of the non-traditional approaches. The author probably would not write such an essay if he or she were truly dispassionate or unconcerned with the topic?

45. Suppose a course description in a college bulletin promises "an in-depth literary examination of the novels of William Faulkner and
Mark Twain." Students later find that the
course focuses nearly exclusively on themes of
cultural injustice. Based on your reading of
the passage, this new information would probably lead the author to:

A. support a student who accused the professor of false advertising.
B. organize a boycott of the course the following semester.
C. publish an article defending the professor's
academic freedom.
D. oppose a dean who suggested moving the
course to the Political History department.

A is correct. A professor who ignored the richly varied themes of Faulkner and Twain to concentrate exclusively on questions of cultural injustice would not be teaching literature, in the view of the passage author. Thus, he might well support a student who accused such a professor of falsely describing the course in the catalogue.

The wrong answer choices: Although nothing in the passage indicates that the author would deny academic freedom to such a professor, it is unlikely, given the ideas in the passage, that he would go out of his way to defend that professor (choice C). The author would probably applaud, not oppose, a dean who felt that such a course belonged more appropriately to a Political History curriculum (choice D). The author would most likely believe that the boycott described in choice B would violate the principles of academic freedom.

Passage VII (Questions 46-51)

46. The author's main point about "Western Civilization values" is that:

   A. they are superior to the value systems of other cultural groups.
   B. they are entirely inappropriate as moral guidelines for other cultural groups.
   C. their imposition on economically deprived communities is responsible for maladaptive behaviors among some adolescents.
   D. they contain many elements accepted across many cultures.

D is correct. Paragraphs 2 and 3 provide information supporting this choice.

The wrong answer choices: Nothing in the passage is said about the relative superiority (choice A) of one system of cultural values vis-a-vis another. The rhetorical question which opens paragraph 4 rules out choice B which reverses the author's true opinion. Some readers may find an oblique reference to choice C in the passage's opening sentence, but the very next sentence—and the rest of the text— makes clear that the view it expresses does not coincide with the author's.

47. Based on the passage, the author contends that remarks of summit speakers who blamed "Western Civilization values" for antisocial behavior among today's youth:

   A. imply that Western Civilization values teach inequality and injustice.
   B. should have been censored.
   C. were probably imprecisely reported.
   D. have led to a general decline in moral civility.

C is correct. Choice C is directly supported in sentence 3 of paragraph 1.

The wrong answer choices: Choice A distorts the reported comments' reference to the problems of immorality and violence among some economically deprived youth (paragraph 1, sentence 1). The author certainly expresses her disapproval in sentence 2 of that same paragraph but nowhere calls for censorship. Her disapproval may imply that she feels a decline in civility due to the reported rhetoric, but she does not say so directly. For that reason, choice C is the better choice.

48. With which of the following statements would the author most likely agree?

    A. "Western Civilization" is a term more useful to sociology than to everyday reality.
    B. "Western Civilization" is most useful as a rhetorical term.
    C. "Western Civilization" refers to a distinct geographical group.
    D. "Western Civilization" refers to a distinct cultural group.

B is correct. The opening sentence of paragraph 5 makes B the best answer to this question, and rules out choices C and D which inverts the author's meaning. Choice A distorts the reference to "quasi-sociological" in an attempt to mislead you.

49. The author suggests that the true reason(s) for antisocial behavior among some adolescents is/are:

    I. the principle that respect is earned on the basis of character
    II. the distortion of a humanistic value system
    III. the active corruption of youth by criminal elements

    A. I only
    B. II only
    C. II and III only
    D. I, II, and III

C is correct. Paragraph three of the text mentions the relationship between character and respect (statement I), but nowhere is that relationship linked to antisocial behavior. To do so would be to completely invert the author's idea. Paragraphs 4 and 5 support statements II and III, respectively. Thus, only statements II and III are connected by the author to antisocial behavior.

50. Among the following, the author most likely believes that much of the responsibility for urban social maladies is due to:

   A. Western Civilization values.
   B. Non-Western Civilization values.
   C. Ancient mercenaries of diverse backgrounds.
   D. People who sell guns on the streets.

D is correct. Sentence 3, paragraph 5, makes this choice the best of the choices offered.

The wrong answer choices: Choice A asserts the exact opposite of the author's main thesis. Choice B is essentially irrelevant to the passage and constitutes a distortion of the author's themes. Although some readers may feel there is a case to be made for the aptness of choice C, it is not supported by the text.

51. The author argues that "Western Civilization values" are founded on true belief, personal bravery and moral action. Which of the following findings, if true, would most WEAKEN the author's contention?

   A. Many Americans believe that violence is the most appropriate way to resolve personal disputes.
   B. Many Americans learn moral commitment as a part of their religious training.
   C. Most Americans believe that bravery is the most important of all values.
   D. Most Americans believe that bravery, honesty, and commitment are the keys to a civilized society.

A is correct. This question is tangential to the passage. It requires only that the reader understand the question stem and then apply her own logic to it. Choices A and B do not relate directly to the author's arguments as given in the question. Choice D would probably strengthen, not weaken, those arguments.

Passage VIII (Questions 52–58)

52. According to the passage, the facet of artificial intelligence that particularly intrigued early computer scientists was the fact that:

   A. a mechanical apparatus could be taught to translate human languages.
   B. a computer could learn to accomplish thinking tasks completely independently of any live human being.
   C. a machine could perform tasks that required learning intelligence without the immediate operative participation of humans.
   D. a machine could teach human beings artificial modes of mental activity.

C is correct. The passage discusses machines performing tasks without the direct participation of human beings, as set forth in choice C. Choice A distorts the text's reference to computerized language translation. Choice B offers an absolute that is not contained in the passage, and choice D inverts the teaching relationship between humans and computers.

53. According to the passage, artificial intelligence programmers solved initial problems in language translation by:

   A. providing computers with independent memory of diverse systems of semiotic linguistic representation.
   B. liberating computers from confinement in semantic-free meaning.
   C. eliminating from translation programs languages with similar vocabulary and parallel syntax .
   D. teaching computers to recognize a word-based message independent of textual representation.

D is correct. It rephrases the author's statement, made in the second paragraph: "Rudimentary efforts to teach computers language translation relied solely on word equivalences programmed in the computer's dictionary and linked to automated syntax substitution."

The wrong answer choices: Choice A inverts the author's meaning. The passage clearly indicates that semiotic memory of independent vocabularies proved insufficient to the translation task. Choice B reverses the passage's description of disrupted translation: words, not meaning, limited computer effectiveness. Choice D distorts the reference to languages with similar structures.

54. In relation to playing games, the author suggests that:

    A. computers will never be able to master the game of chess as well as humans.

    B. chess is the only game in which computers can effectively compete with humans.

    C. computer learning has been generally more effective in the area of game playing than language translation.

    D. computers usually prevail over human opponents in chess, except against internationally elite linguists.

C is correct. It reflects a statement made in the third paragraph: " In the area of game strategy, computers have realized considerably more success than in language translation."

The wrong answer choices: Choices A and B are both absolutes, and choice B inverts the text's reference to other game strategies. Choice D subtly distorts the statement regrading the elite international chess masters, in that the passage makes no reference to the frequency with which computers defeat chess champions. Choice D implies that computers do not "usually" defeat those experts.

55. According to the passage, computerized defect analysis functions differently from simple data retrieval in that:

    A. it incorporates a program of guidelines to selectively retrieve stored data.

    B. it excludes reductive elimination as a retrieval tool.

    C. it requires interactive inputs as retrieval prompts.

    D. there is no essential difference between the two processes.

A is correct. It reflects a statement made in paragraph 4, where the author reports that defect identification "includes a set of rules as well, which serve to direct the computer's search according to interactive inputs."

The wrong answer choices: Choice B inverts the author's meaning. The passage explicitly describes reductive elimination as a tool in the service of defect analysis. Choice C distorts the author's text, which nowhere implies that interactive prompts are uncharacteristic of simple data retrieval as well. Choice D contradicts the passage.

56. According to the passage, knowledge frames modulate memory accessibility by:

    A. compartmentalizing linkage instructions within larger informational contexts.

    B. restricting bounded knowledge packets to logically interconnected predictor inputs.

    C. limiting computer searches to encoded probability analysis.

    D. providing unencumbered scanning modes within relatively extensive bases of knowledge.

B is correct. The phrase "logically interconnected predictor inputs" paraphrases the text. Choices A and C present confused versions of the author's statements. Choice D inverts the text's description of retrieval accessibility within an extensive knowledge memory.

57. Discussing the relation of analytical logic to artificial intelligence, the author explains that:

    A. coherent linkage of knowledge frames occurs independently of IF/THEN propositions.

    B. syllogistic procedures define tuple-based information retrieval.

    C. syllogistic principles provide the basis for connecting integral knowledge objects.

    D. it is impossible to arrange tuples for medical diagnosis logically correlated objects.

C is correct. It paraphrases information set forth in paragraph 6, where the author discusses the relevance of the IF/THEN process and states that: "The study of coherent linkage of knowledge frames through syllogistic requisites has led computer scientists to the invention of . . ."

The wrong answer choices: Choice A reverses the relationship between coherent linkage and IF/THEN statements. Choice B distorts the reference to database retrieval. Choice D reverses the textual information.

58. According to the passage, which of the following statements regarding neural networks is accurate?

  A. Established informational relationships are generally inadequate to bridge nodal synapses.
  B. Established informational relationships are wholly unaffected by inputted information.
  C. For computers to construct neural links between information nodes human operators must provide programmed rules of relative probability.
  D. Through empirical learning methods computers can decide and apportion weighted linkage without preprogramming.

D is correct. The passage refers to a "computer with the ability to derive its own rules of linkage," and the capacity to determine "relative regulatory influence among contrasting and/or complementary rules." Choice D expresses that idea. Choice A, B, and C make statements opposite to those made by the author.

Passage IX (Questions 59–65)

59. According to the passage, modern scientists believe that star formation involves all of the following EXCEPT:

  A. processes that tend to form star pairs more often than single stars.
  B. separation of protostellar material to yield protostars.
  C. diminution in size facilitated by Gaussian rules.
  D. the aggregation of molecular matter around a highly dense core.

D is correct. The answer is found in sentence 1 of paragraph 3, where the author states the exact opposite of choice D: the "highly dense core" was part of previous theories. Paragraph 4, sentence 2 contains information supporting the accuracy of choice A. Choice B is upheld in paragraph 4, sentence 3. Paragraph 4, sentences 2 and 3 confirm the truth of choice C.

60. According to the passage, the research of Duquennoy and Mayor showed that:

    A. Quadruples occur more often than triples.
    B. Triples occur less often than singles.
    C. Singles occur more often than doubles.
    D. Doubles occur less often than triples.

B is correct. The fifth paragraph describes data of Duquennoy and Mayor showing that singles occur about half as often as doubles (eliminating choice C), triples occur about one-seventh as often as doubles (eliminating choice D and supporting choice B), and quadruples occur about one-thirtieth as often as doubles (eliminating choice A).

61. Compared to a star in the main sequence phase, a T-Tauri star is, according to the passage:

    A. younger and larger.
    B. younger and smaller.
    C. older and larger.
    D. older and smaller.

A is correct. Sentence 2, paragraph 1 identifies our sun as a main sequence star, and Sentence 3, paragraph 2 states that it contracted from its previous size as a T-Tauri star. Therefore, in its present main sequence phase it is older and smaller than its T-Tauri ancestor. That means that the T-Tauri star is younger and larger than a main sequence star.

62. According to the passage, the "power law" of molecular distribution is challenged by the observation that:

    A. our own sun is a G-dwarf class star.
    B. some stars are formed as pairs.
    C. protostars have centers of very high density.
    D. astroradiometry may be employed in extremely small wavelengths.

B is correct. The final sentence of paragraph 4 points out that the Gaussian distribution of protostellar molecular material—which directly challenges the "power law" in question—is a necessary condition for the creation of paired stars. The existence star pairs, then, confirms the Gaussian distribution, which in turn negates the "power law." The final sentence of paragraph 1 refers to "dense hydrogen cloud collapse" having formed our sun as a G-class star.

The wrong answer choices: If one confused "dense hydrogen cloud collapse with the "power law" theory of a hyperdense cloud center, he might choose A. Choice C inverts the sense of sentence 3 in paragraph 4. Protostars are produced by "fragmentation," and are held together by gravity. The following sentence says protostellar clouds—not protostars—are "dense . . . formations." Choice D attempts distorts the importance of small wavelength astroradiometry as discussed in the passage (paragraph 3, sentence 3). While that technology led Ward-Thompson's team to discard the "power law" hypothesis, it was the findings of the experiment—not the mechanism of its technology (small waves)—which permitted them to do that.

63. According to the passage, it is considered improbable that our own sun is part of a star pair because:

   A. the other star of the pair would have to exist outside our own galaxy.
   B. comet showers are known to occur with a frequency greater than once every 30 million years.
   C. the other star of the pair would cause the extinction of most of Earth's animal species.
   D. investigations reveal no star sufficiently close to the sun to exert significant gravitational force on it.

D is correct. It paraphrases the final sentence of the last paragraph.

The wrong answer choices: Choice A distorts the information regarding the enormous distance between our sun and its hypothetical pair (final paragraph, sentence 1). Choice B refers out of context to the period of 30 million years. The author does not associate that period with the frequency of comet showers. A star pair might cause comet showers similar to those which are theorized to have caused the dinosaur extinction (final paragraph, sentence 4), but the passage nowhere indicates that serial extinctions of that kind would be an inevitable consequence of intermittent comet showers caused by a sun twin.

64. According to the passage, the termination of the phase now occupied by our sun will cause the planets to:

   A. become red giants.
   B. enter their main sequence phase.
   C. shrink in diameter.
   D. disappear.

D is correct. The information is set forth explicitly in the final sentence of paragraph 1.

The wrong answer choices: Choice A inverts the reference to red giant stars. Planets will not become red giants, but when the sun becomes one, it will obliterate the planets. Choice B distorts the reference to a main sequence phase. Stars, like our sun, enter main sequence phases; planets do not (paragraph 1, sentence 3). Choice C distorts the information regarding contraction in a star's formation. In fact, the author does not tell us whether a G-dwarf star, like our sun, will shrink or expand as it becomes a red giant. Since we are told that it will obliterate the planets at that stage, the passage implies the latter.

65. The discovery that star formation is governed not by the "power law" but by Gaussian rules might best be analogized to the finding that:

   A. a given disease spreads not directly from one patient to another, but by an insect bite, which explains why a person could contract the disease without exposure to an afflicted patient.

   B. left-handedness corresponds not to longer life span, but to shorter life span, which explains the fact that left-handed persons tend to have a greater facility for artistic and verbal creativity.

   C. the first carts and wagons tended to break apart on encountering bumps, which led to the installation of springs and, later, of shock absorbers.

   D. certain isolated societies have no concept of property or ownership, which explains why such peoples never developed weapons of mass destruction.

A is correct. The passage indicates that measuring molecular densities in protostellar clouds by using astroradiometry (paragraph 3, sentence 3) revealed a physical fact previously "invisible" to researchers: that densities at the center of hydrogen clouds were considerably lower than had been estimated. That which had been invisible became visible. Choice A describes a discovery of similar significance. Before its discovery, the insect bite was an invisible force affecting the spread of epidemic disease.

The wrong answer choices: Choice C is not so good as choice A because, the bumps were not invisible. Choices B and D are—by and large—babble.

PHYSICAL SCIENCES EXPLANATIONS II

Passage I (Questions 66–72)

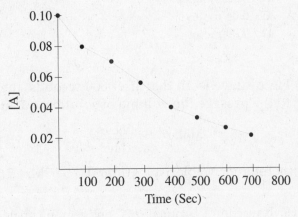

Figure 1

66. What is the approximate initial rate of reaction/1 at 25⁰C?

    A. 1×10^{-4} M/sec
    B. 2×10^{-4} M/sec
    C. 1×10^{-2} M/sec
    D. 2×10^{-2} M/sec

B is correct. The passage's first sentence tells you that reaction rate is a measure of the rate at which reactant(s) disappear. *Initial* reaction rate refers to the rate at the beginning of the reaction. Figure 2 depicts reactant concentration as a function of time. Ascertain initial reaction rate by examining the left most portion of Figure 2. Between 0 and 100 seconds, the concentration of substance A falls in near-linear fashion from 0.10 M to 0.08 M.

$$\text{Rate} = \frac{\text{change in concentration}}{\text{time}} = \frac{0.02\text{M}}{100 \text{ sec}} = 2 \times 10^{-4} \text{M/sec}$$

67. According to Figure 1, how many moles of A are present in the solution after 600 seconds have elapsed?

    A. 0.01 moles
    B. 0.03 moles
    C. 0.06 moles
    D. 0.09 moles

C is correct. From Figure 2 we learn that after 600 seconds the concentration of A is 0.03 M. According to the passage the volume of solution is 2 liters.

$$\text{Molarity} = \frac{\text{moles}}{\text{liter}}$$

Number of moles, therefore, = (molarity) × (liters) = $0.03M \times 2\ell = 0.06$ mol

68. If reaction 1 is run at 60°C and a graph analogous to that of Figure 1 is drawn to depict the reaction rate, how will the curve of the new graph differ from that of Figure 1?

    A. The new curve will descend more steeply.
    B. The new curve will descend less steeply.
    C. The new curve will be identical to the first line.
    D. The new curve will be horizontal.

A is correct. Higher temperature increases reaction rate. That means the concentration of reactants decreases more swiftly. For any given time period (depicted on the X axis), the concentration of reactants (depicted on the Y axis) will experience a greater fall. The curve's slope steepens.

69. How would increasing the temperature at which the reaction takes place affect the rates of the forward and reverse reactions and the eventual equilibrium?

A. It would increase the rate of the forward reaction, decrease the rate of the reverse reaction, and shift the equilibrium towards the formation of products.

B. It would decrease the rate of the forward reaction, increase the rate of the reverse reaction, and shift the equilibrium towards the formation of reactants.

C. It would increase the rate of the forward reaction, increase the rate of the reverse reaction, and shift the equilibrium towards the formation of products.

D. It would increase the rate of the forward reaction, increase the rate of the reverse reaction, and shift the equilibrium towards the formation of reactants.

C is correct. For this reaction, enthalpy change, ΔH, is positive and the reaction therefore, is endothermic; it absorbs heat from the surroundings. You might think of heat as belonging to the left side of the equation: $\text{Heat} + A \rightleftharpoons B + C$.

Adding heat to the reaction system drives the equilibrium to the right and increases equilibrium concentrations of the products. Increased temperature also increases the rate constant for both the forward reaction *and* the reverse reaction which causes reaction rate to increase as well.

70. As the forward reaction proceeds, the reaction rate:

A. decreases.
B. increases.
C. remains constant.
D. decreases, then increases.

A is correct. Examine Figure 2. The slope represents the reaction rate, and it decreases over time. As reactants are depleted the rate of reaction decreases.

71. If 2 moles each of B and C are formed in Reaction 1, the enthalpy change of the reaction is:

    A. 75 kJ.
    B. 150 kJ.
    C. 300 kJ.
    D. 600 kJ.

C is correct. Treat enthalpy change stoichiometrically as you would any of the products or reactants. Since $\Delta H = 150$ kJ when the reaction yields 1 mole of B and 1 mole of C, it is twice that number when the reaction yields 2 moles of B and 2 moles of C.

$$2 \times 150 \text{ kJ} = 300 \text{ kJ}$$

72. If the initial concentration of A is doubled, what will be the effect on the initial rate of reaction and the rate constant?

    A. The rate of reaction and the rate constant will double.
    B. The rate of reaction and the rate constant will not change.
    C. The rate of reaction will double and the rate constant will not change.
    D. The rate of reaction will not change and the rate constant will double.

C is correct. The rate constant does not change with concentration of the reactant, (although it does change with temperature). As you learn at the beginning of the passage (and from your own review of chemical kinetics) rate = k [A], which means that rate is directly proportional to the concentration of reactant(s). If the initial concentration of substance A is doubled, then the initial reaction rate is doubled as well.

Passage II (Questions 73–78)

73. When 1 gram of each of the following materials is subjected to a given amount of heat, which will undergo the greatest temperature increase?

   A. Aluminum
   B. Copper
   C. Iron
   D. Mercury

D is correct. Specific heat is proportional to the ratio $\dfrac{\text{heat absorbed}}{\text{temperature increase}}$. The greater that ratio, the smaller will be the temperature increase for any given amount of heat absorbed. The smaller the ratio, the greater will be the increase in temperature for any given amount of heat absorbed. The correct answer, therefore, is that which reflects the smallest ratio—the lowest specific heat. Table 1 shows that among the four listed elements, mercury has the lowest specific heat (0.03cal/g°C).

74. Where m = the mass of the block, g = acceleration due to gravity, and r = radius of the rotating cylinder, which of the following expressions gives the magnitude of the torque exerted on the cylinder by the hanging block at the moment it begins to fall?

   A. $1/2\,mgr$
   B. mgr
   C. $1/2\,mghr$
   D. $mghr$

B is correct. For a body in rotatory motion, torque refers to the quantity: (force) × (lever arm). Force imposed on (and by) the falling block is equal to (block's mass) × (acceleration due to gravity). For a rotating cylindrical body, lever arm is equal to the radius of the cylinder (r). In this instance, therefore, torque exerted on the cylinder = $(m)(g)(r)$.

75. Which of the following is true regarding the water in the insulated container?

    A. Fluid pressure is greater near the bottom of the container than near the top.

    B. Fluid pressure is greater near the top of the container than near the bottom.

    C. Fluid pressure is the same at all points within the container.

    D. Fluid pressure is zero at all points.

A is correct. Fluid pressure is given by the expression $P = \rho g h$, where h is the *depth below* the surface of the fluid above the point being discussed. Therefore, fluid pressure increases with increasing depth.

The wrong answer choices: If you were tempted to choose C you may have been thinking of the fact that *at any depth* within a closed container of fluid, fluid pressure is the same at all points. That is, at a depth of 2 feet into a closed container of fluid, fluid pressure is equal at all points. This is true even if the container is irregularly shaped. However, at different depths, fluid pressure differs.

76. Using the apparatus shown in Figure 1, an investigator wishes to use a 1 kg mass to raise the temperature of 1 g of water by 1°C. From what height, approximately, must she drop the 1 kg mass?

    A. 20 cm

    B. 40 cm

    C. 60 cm

    D. 80 cm

B is correct. The passage tells you that 1 cal raises the temperature of 1 g of water by 1°C. The block must therefore be raised to such a height as will provide it a gravitational potential energy of 1 cal which, you are told, is equal to 4.19 J. Therefore, (h) must be such that the product (m)(g)(h) = 4.19 J. The question becomes an algebraic problem: Since m = 1 kg and g = 9.8 m/s^2, 4.19 J = (1 kg) (9.8 m/s^2) (h); h = 0.42 m ≈ 40 cm

77. In an experiment, 500 cal are required to raise the temperature of a sample of glass by 10°C. How much heat would be required to raise, also by 10°C, the temperature of a sample of water with the same mass?

   A. 50 cal
   B. 100 cal
   C. 1000 cal
   D. 2500 cal

D is correct. Table 1 shows you that the specific heat of water (1.0) is five times that of glass (0.2). For any two samples of glass and water *of equivalent mass*, the quantity of heat required to raise the water's temperature by a given amount is equal to five times that which is required to raise the glass's temperature by the same amount. (5)(500 cal) = 2500 cal.

78. When the experiment described in the passage is complete, the initial gravitational potential energy of the hanging block has been converted to:

   A. increased kinetic energy of the water molecules.
   B. increased electrical energy of the ions present in the water.
   C. photon emissions caused by electrons shifting energy levels in the water.
   D. greater bond strength of water's hydrogen bonds.

A is correct. Temperature is a function of kinetic energy. The increase in water temperature reflects an increase in the kinetic energy of water molecules.

The wrong answer choices: Choices B and C are wrong because the energy released by friction takes the form not of electrical energy or photon emission, but of heat. Choice D is wrong. The addition of heat to the water does not increase hydrogen bond strength.

Passage III (Questions 79–84)

79. The process of tooth decay is most likely to occur in saliva maintained at which of the following pH values?

    A. 6.0
    B. 7.0
    C. 8.0
    D. 9.0

A is correct. The passage tells you that acid promotes tooth decay. That means, simply, that the lower the pH, the greater the decay.

The wrong answer choices: Choices B–D reflect higher pH values than does choice A. Moreover Choice B reflects a neutral saliva, and choices C and D reflect basic saliva.

80. The oxidation state of calcium in the hydroxyapatite molecule is:

    A. –1
    B. 0
    C. +1
    D. +2

D is correct. The oxidation states of all atoms within a neutral molecule must sum to zero. You should know that the oxidation state of PO_4 is (-3) and that of OH is (-1).

$(5) \times$ [(Oxidation state of Ca)] $+ 3(-3) + 1(-1) = 0$ Oxidation state of Ca $= +2$. You would also have arrived at this answer by knowing that calcium has two valence electrons that it tends to lose in chemical bonding or by looking at Reaction I.

81. Fluorapatite is more resistant to tooth decay than is hydroxyapatite because the fluoride ion is:

   A. a strong base that has little interaction with hydrogen ions in saliva.
   B. a weak base that has little interaction with hydrogen ions in saliva.
   C. a strong base that reacts with hydrogen ions in solution.
   D. a weak base that reacts with hydrogen ions in solution.

B is correct. For any aqueous solution, K_w (hydrogen ion concentration × hydroxide ion concentration) is always equal to 1×10^{-14} m/L. That value is called water's ion product. When protons are added to an aqueous solution reducing pH, some react with OH^- ions (hydroxide ions) in order to maintain water's ion product. Reaction 1 produces OH^- ions on the right side. For a solution in which reaction 1 occurs, therefore, the *removal* of OH^- ions by protons drives the reaction equilibrium to the right—promoting tooth decay. Reaction 2 generates not OH^- ions but F^- instead. HF is a strong acid which is highly ionized in aqueous solution. F^- its conjugate base tends *not* to react with protons; it is a *weak base*. When protons are added to a solution in which reaction 2 occurs, they react not with F^- ions but with free OH^- ions (or hydronium ions) within the solution (again, in order to maintain water's ion product). *That*, however, does *not* drive the equilibrium of Reaction 2 to the right.

82. The presence of acid in saliva acts to promote tooth decay because acid in saliva will:

   A. increase the hydroxide concentration, shifting the equilibrium of Reaction 1 to the right.
   B. increase the hydroxide concentration, shifting the equilibrium of Reaction 1 to the left.
   C. decrease the hydroxide concentration, shifting the equilibrium of Reaction 1 to the right.
   D. decrease the hydroxide concentration, shifting the equilibrium of Reaction 1 to the left.

C is correct. As explained in connection with question 81, the addition of protons to a solution in which reaction 1 occurs tends to reduce the concentration of hydroxide ions and thus drive reaction 1's equilibrium to the right.

83. The pH of saliva is normally about 6.5. The normal pOH of saliva is:

    A. 6.0
    B. 6.5
    C. 7.0
    D. 7.5

D is correct. As noted in connection with question 16, for any aqueous solution, K_w (hydrogen ion concentration × hydroxide ion concentration) is always equal to 1 x 10^{-14} m/L. That value is called water's ion product. Since pH represents the (-) log $[H^+]$ and pOH = (-) log $[OH^-]$, pH + pOH = 14; 6.5 + pOH = 14; pOH = 7.5

84. Reaction 2 is examined under controlled conditions in order to examine how changes in various factors will affect its equilibrium. An increase in the pressure in the vessel in which the reaction occurs would be expected to:

    A. have no effect on the equilibrium.
    B. shift the equilibrium to the right.
    C. shift the equilibrium to the left.
    D. prevent the reaction from occurring.

A is correct. Ambient pressure affects only those reactions involving gases. For reaction 2, all reactants and products are in aqueous solution. Surrounding pressure is insignificant to equilibrium.

Passage IV (Questions 85–91)

Trial	Angle of elevation	Flight time (sec)	Height (m)	Distance (m)
1	10°	0.7	.05	14.0
2	20°	1.4	2.5	26.5
3	30°	2.0	5.0	35.0
4	40°	2.6	8.5	40.0
5	50°	3.1	12.0	39.5
6	60°	3.5	15.5	35.0
7	70°	3.8	18.0	26.0
8	80°	4.0	20.0	14.0

Table 1

Trial	Speed (m/s)	Flight time (sec)	Distance (m)
1	10	3.2	32
2	20	3.2	64
3	30	3.2	96
4	40	3.2	128
5	50	3.2	160

Table 2

85. In the absence of air resistance, which of the following quantities remains constant throughout the flight of a projectile?

   I. Horizontal speed
  II. Vertical speed
 III. Acceleration

  A. I only.
  B. II only.
  C. I and II only.
  D. I and III only.

D is correct. Option I applies because a projectile experiences no horizontal force—none to the right, and none to the left—its horizontal speed is constant throughout flight. Option II does not apply because a projectile experiences a downward vertical acceleration due to gravity. Its vertical speed therefore changes during flight. It slows during ascent and speeds up during descent. Option III applies, because the acceleration due to gravity is an unchanging 9.8 m/s^2 throughout flight.

86. Which of the following conclusions is most justifiably drawn from the data gathered in Experiment 1?

  A. Horizontal distance increases with increasing angle of elevation.
  B. Horizontal distance decreases with increasing angle of elevation.
  C. Flight time increases with increasing angle of elevation.
  D. Flight time decreases with increasing angle of elevation.

C is correct. In experiment 1, angle of elevation differs for each trial. Table 1 shows that as angle of elevation increases, flight time increases as well.

The wrong answer choices: Choices A and B are wrong because, as Table 1 reveals, horizontal distance first increases as angle of elevation increases from 10° to 40°, then *decreases* as angle of elevation further increases from 50° to 80°. Choice D is wrong because it directly contradicts data set forth in Table 1.

87. If a ninth projectile had been launched in Experiment 1 and had traveled a horizontal distance of 31.0 m, its angle of elevation would most likely have been:

    A. 25° or 65°.
    B. 25° or 75°.
    C. 35° or 65°.
    D. 35° or 75°.

A is correct. As noted for question 86, horizontal distance first increases as angle of elevation increases from 10° to 40°, then *decreases* as angle of elevation further increases from 50° to 80°. With respect to Table 1, interpolation reveals that a horizontal distance of 35.0 m corresponds to two angles of elevation: (1) approximately 25°, and (2) approximately 65°.

88. Which of the following expressions represents the horizontal speed of the projectile launched in Trial 3 of Experiment 1?

    A. 20 m/s
    B. 20 (cos 30°) m/s
    C. 20 (sin 30°) m/s
    D. 20 (tan 30°) m/s

B is correct. Table 1 shows that the projectile is launched with a speed of 20 m/s at an angle of 30°. The projectile's velocity vector may be resolved into horizontal and vertical components, with the *horizontal* component representing horizontal speed. Through vector analysis you ascertain the horizontal speed.

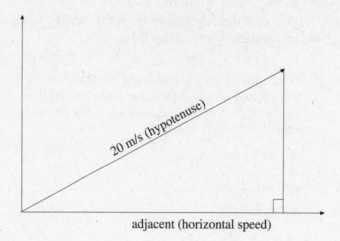

adjacent (horizontal speed)

$$\text{Cos } 30° = \frac{\text{horizontal speed}}{20 \text{ m/s}} \; ; \qquad\qquad \text{horizontal speed} = 20 \text{ (cos } 30°\text{) m/s.}$$

The wrong answer choices: Choice A is wrong because it represents the total speed which is greater than the horizontal speed. Choice C, too, is incorrect. It describes vertical speed. Choice D represents a nonsensical answer which could only be selected by guess.

89. As the angle of elevation is increased from 10° to 80° in Experiment 1, assuming air resistance to be negligible, the kinetic energy of the projectiles as they strike the ground:

   A. increases.
   B. decreases.
   C. increases, then decreases.
   D. remains the same.

D is correct. At the start of each flight in experiment 1, the projectile has kinetic energy equal to $\frac{1}{2}mv^2$ with v equal in each case to 20 m/s. During the ascending portion of each flight, the vertical velocity decreases, ultimately to zero, and the vertical contribution to the projectile's total kinetic energy is converted entirely to gravitational potential energy, reflected in the projectile's maximum height. The horizontal contribution remains unchanged since horizontal speed is constant. During *de*scent, gravitational potential energy is converted, once again, to a downward contribution toward total kinetic energy while the horizontal contribution continues unchanged. The final total kinetic energy with which the projectile lands is equal to that with which it started.

90. A researcher examining the results of Experiment 2 could properly draw the conclusion that:

   A. flight time is independent of horizontal speed.
   B. flight time is independent of initial height.
   C. horizontal distance is independent of initial height.
   D. horizontal distance is independent of flight time.

A is correct. Table 2 shows that variation in horizontal speed has no effect on flight time which remains, for each trial, 3.2 sec. Flight time is therefore independent of horizontal speed.

The wrong answer choices: Choice B is wrong because initial height is unchanged from one trial to the next. One cannot logically conclude that flight time is dependent or independent of initial height. Choice C is wrong for the same reason. The experiment involves no variation of initial height and allows for no conclusion regarding the dependence or independence of horizontal distance on initial height. Choice D is wrong because flight time is constant throughout the experiment. The experiment offers no data as to the dependence or independence of horizontal distance on flight time. (It does, however, show that *flight time* is independent of *horizontal distance*.)

91. If Experiment 2 were performed a second time, with the initial height set at 25 m, what would be the expected flight time for the projectiles?

   A. 1.6 sec
   B. 2.3 sec
   C. 3.2 sec
   D. 5.1 sec

B is correct. For any body in uniform accelerated motion, the relationships among distance, velocity, acceleration, and time are set forth in the equation: $x = v_o t + a t^2$ where x = distance, v_o = initial velocity, t = time, and a = acceleration. $x = v_o t + g t^2$; $(25 \text{ m}) = 0 + 1/2 (9.8 \text{ m/s}^2)(t^2)$; $t^2 = 5 \text{ sec}^2$; $t = 2.3 \text{ sec}$; $t = \sqrt{\dfrac{2x}{g}}$ for freefalling objects.

Questions 92 through 96 are NOT based on a descriptive passage.

92. A bucket with mass m is suspended from a rope that hangs straight downward. If g represents the acceleration due to gravity, and the rope pulls the bucket upward at a constant speed, what is the tension in the rope?

   A. $mg/2$
   B. mg
   C. $2mg$
   D. $4mg$

B is correct. If the bucket moves at constant speed it experiences no acceleration. The sum of all forces acting on it is zero. The downward force of its weight must be equal to the upward force exerted by the rope. Weight = mg and the tension in the rope, therefore, equals mg as well.

93. A chamber at constant temperature contains 10 moles of helium gas and 1 mole of neon gas. Which of the following is NOT true?

   A. The average speed of the helium atoms is greater than the average speed of the neon atoms.
   B. The partial pressure due to the helium atoms is greater than the partial pressure due to the neon atoms.
   C. The total mass of helium present in the chamber is greater than the total mass of neon present in the chamber.
   D. The average kinetic energy of the helium atoms is greater than the average kinetic energy of the neon atoms.

D is correct. You are searching for a false statement. For any gas, average kinetic energy is proportional to temperature. Choice D, therefore, represents a false statement.

The wrong answer choices: Choice A is wrong because it represents a true statement. Since the two gases have equal kinetic energy, and kinetic energy = $\frac{1}{2}mv^2$, the gas molecules of lesser mass must have greater velocity. Choice B, too, represents a true statement. The partial pressure of any gas, g, within a mixture of gases is equal to the fraction:

$$\frac{\text{\# moles of gas } g \text{ present in mixture}}{\text{total number of moles of all gases present in mixture}}$$

In this sample, the number of helium atoms is greater than the number of neon atoms, and helium's partial pressure is therefore greater than neon's. Choice C is wrong because it too makes a true statement:

$$(10 \text{ moles } H_2) \times (4 \text{ g/mole}) = 40 \text{ g; } (1 \text{ mole Ne}) \times (20 \text{ g/mole}) = 20 \text{ g.}$$

94. A 320 gram sample of sodium-25 decays through the emission of a beta particle, forming magnesium-25. If 40 g of sodium-25 remain after 3 minutes of decay, what is the half life of sodium-25?

A. 1 min.
B. 2 min.
C. 3 min.
D. 4 min.

A is correct. 40 g represents $\frac{1}{8}$ of 320 g. You must (1) determine how many half-lives are consumed when a sample of radioactive material decays so that only $\frac{1}{8}$ of the original sample remains, and (2) divide 3 minutes by the result. After 1 half life, $\frac{1}{2}$ of the original sample remains. After 2 half-lives $\frac{1}{4}$ of the original sample remains. After 3 half-lives $\frac{1}{8}$ of the original sample remains. You know, therefore, that 3 minutes represents 3 half-lives. One half life is equal to 3 minutes ÷ 3 = 1 minute.

95. A light ray first travels through water and then encounters a second medium. If the ray's angle of incidence is 30^0, its angle of refraction will be:

   A. less than 30^0.
   B. equal to 30^0.
   C. greater than 30^0.
   D. dependent on the refractive index of the second medium.

D is correct. When light moves from one medium to the next the refraction it undergoes depends on the refractive indices of the two media. Specifically,

$$\frac{\text{sine of angle of incidence}}{\text{sine of angle of refraction}} = \frac{\text{refractive index for medium 2}}{\text{refrective index for medium 1}}$$

   In this instance, if the refractive index of the second medium is greater than the refractive index for water, the angle of refraction will be less than 30^0. If the refractive index of the second medium is smaller than the refractive index for water, the angle of refraction will be greater than 30^0. If the refractive index of the second medium is equal to the refractive index for water, the angle of refraction will be 30^0.

96. A student prepares a 1 molal aqueous solution of several salts. Among the following which solution will show the greatest boiling point elevation?

   A. NaCl
   B. $MgCl_2$
   C. $NaNO_3$
   D. $MgCO_3$

B is correct. The degree of boiling point elevation (or freezing point depression) produced by any solute is proportional to the number of ions (or particles) into which its molecule dissociates when dissolved. On dissociation, the $MgCl_2$ molecule generates three separate ions: one Mg^+ ion and 2 Cl^- ions. All other listed salts generate two ions only.

Passage V (Questions 97–102)

97. Regarding the reaction taking place in Experiment 1, which of the following statements must be true?

   A. The free energy change is positive.
   B. The free energy change is negative.
   C. The free energy does not change.
   D. The free energy change is equal to the voltage.

B is correct. The voltmeter registers a voltage for the reaction which means that the reaction proceeds spontaneously; electrons are exchanged between the two compartments in the cell via the wire. For any spontaneous reaction, the free energy change, ΔG, is negative.

The wrong answer choices: Choice A is wrong because a positive free energy change would indicate a non-spontaneous reaction which would mean, in turn, that the voltmeter would fail to register a voltage. Choice C is wrong because, as explained, positive voltage indicates negative free energy. Choice D, too, is wrong. Voltage and free energy change are related by the equation: $\Delta G = -nFx$ where x is the cell potential or voltage.

98. If it is known that Z(*s*) for Experiment 1 is solid magnesium, the student should determine that the identity of Y(*s*) is:

    A. barium.
    B. beryllium.
    C. zinc.
    D. cadmium.

B is correct. For the reaction in experiment 1, voltage is 0.5 V. For the oxidation of magnesium, voltage = 2.4 V, as shown in table 1.

Recall that $E_{reaction} = E_{ox} + E_{red}$; 0.5 V = 2.4 V + E_{red}; E_{red} = –1.9 V. Examining Table 1 once again, you find that reduction potential of –1.9 V corresponds to the reduction of Be^{2+} to form Be^0.

99. Which of the following could be the identities of $Y^{2+}(aq)$ and Z(*s*) in Experiment 2?

    A. $Be^{2+}(aq)$ and Mn(*s*)
    B. $Mg^{2+}(aq)$ and Ba(*s*)
    C. $Cd^{2+}(aq)$ and Zn(*s*)
    D. $Zn^{2+}(aq)$ and Be(*s*)

A is correct. In Experiment 2 the reaction generates zero voltage, which means the reaction is non-spontaneous. The reaction potential for this cell must therefore be less than zero. Examining Table 1, together with the answer choices you learn that:

(Choice A:) $Be^{2+} + Mn^0 \rightarrow Be^0 + Mn^{2+}$ E = –0.7 V

(Choice B:) $Mg^{2+} + Ba^0 \rightarrow Mg^0 + Ba^{2+}$ E = +0.5 V

(Choice C:) $Cd^{2+} + Zn^0 \rightarrow Cd^0 + Zn^{2+}$ E = +0.4 V

(Choice D:) $Zn^{2+} + Be^0 \rightarrow Zn^0 + Be^{2+}$ E = +1.1 V

Among those listed in the choices, only the reaction involving beryllium and manganese show a reaction potential less than zero.

100. During the experiments, Reaction 1 proceeds in the forward direction. As Reaction 1 proceeds:

    A. $Y^{2+}(aq)$ is oxidized and $Z(s)$ is reduced.
    B. $Y^{2+}(aq)$ is reduced and $Z(s)$ is oxidized.
    C. $Y(s)$ is oxidized and $Z^{2+}(aq)$ is reduced.
    D. $Y(s)$ is reduced and $Z^{2+}(aq)$ is oxidized.

B is correct. Recall the mnemonic "LEO says GER." The **L**oss of **E**lectrons denotes **O**xidation and the **G**ain of **E**lectrons denotes **R**eduction.

Y^{2+} gains electrons to become Y^0; Y^{2+} is reduced.

Z^0 loses electrons to become Z^{2+}; Z^0 is oxidized.

101. Among the species listed in Table 1, which is the strongest reducing agent?

    A. $Cd^{2+}(aq)$
    B. $Cd(s)$
    C. $Ba^{2+}(aq)$
    D. $Ba(s)$

D is correct. A reducing agent is itself oxidized and an oxidizing agent is, itself, reduced. The strongest reducing agent is that which most readily undergoes oxidation. Ba^{2+} and Cd^{2+} are positively charged and are not likely to undergo further oxidation; they will not "want" to lose additional electrons. The answer, therefore, is neutral Ba or neutral Cd.

For the two half reactions involving Ba and Cd, ascertain the oxidation of the *reverse* half reaction by taking the reduction potential and changing its sign (negative to positive, or positive to negative).

$Ba^0 \rightarrow Ba^{2+} + 2e^-$ $E = +2.9$ V

$Cd^0 \rightarrow Cd^{2+} + 2e^-$ $E = +0.4$ V

Barium shows a greater oxidation potential than does cadmium.

102. The positive electrode in Figure 1 is the:

    A. anode, where reduction takes place.
    B. anode, where oxidation takes place.
    C. cathode, where reduction takes place.
    D. cathode, where oxidation takes place.

C is correct. In a galvanic cell, the positive electrode is the cathode.

Recall the mnenomic AN OX and RED CAT:

OXidation occurs at the ANode.

REDuction occurs at the CAThode.

Passage VI (Questions 103–107)

103. For a small sphere falling through a fluid, which of the following equations describes the relationship between the magnitude of the forces as they act on the sphere at terminal velocity?

    A. $F_f + F_b = mg$
    B. $F_f + mg = F_b$
    C. $F_b + mg = F_f$
    D. $F_f = F_b = mg$

A is correct. The object experiences upward forces of (1) friction, and (2) buoyancy. It experiences a downward force equal to its own weight which, for any object, is equal to (mass) × (acceleration due to gravity) = mg. At terminal velocity, the sum of the upward and downward forces equals zero. The magnitude of the upward forces $F_f + F_b$ must equal the magnitude of the downward force mg: $F_f + F_b = mg$

104. For an object descending through fluid, which of the following graphs depicts the change in frictional force as speed varies?

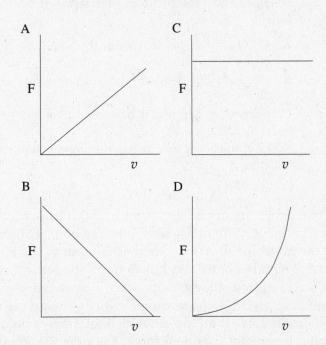

A is correct. From the passage you learn that F_f = 6pgrv, which means that frictional force is directly proportional to speed (just as it is directly proportional to radius and fluid viscosity). When two factors bear a proportional relationship a graph comparing one to the other yields a *straight line that slopes upward*.

105. Two spherical drops with equal radii fall through the air. One is composed of glycerin and the other of ethyl alcohol. Which would be expected to reach the greater terminal velocity?

   A. Ethyl alcohol, because it has the lower viscosity.
   B. Ethyl alcohol, because it has the lower density.
   C. Glycerine, because it has the higher viscosity.
   D. Glycerine, because it has the higher density.

D is correct. The two drops are of equal volume and fall through the same medium. Table 1 shows that glycerine is more dense than ethyl alcohol. This means that the mass and weight of the glycerine drop are greater than that of the ethyl alcohol drop. Because the drops are of equal volume and fall through the same medium, they experience identical forces of buoyancy. (Buoyancy = F_b = (density of the displaced fluid)(volume of fluid displaced)(g). At terminal velocity the glycerine drop must experience greater *frictional* force than the ethyl alcohol drop in order that its greater weight be compensated by greater frictional force. Examine the equation set forth in the passage. Frictional force is proportional to velocity, radius and viscosity (of the air). For these two equal-sized drops falling through the same medium, viscosity (of the air) and radius are equal. Differences in frictional force are attributable only to differences in velocity. Since, at terminal velocity, the frictional force for glycerine must exceed the frictional force for ethyl alcohol, the terminal velocity of the glycerine must exceed that of the ethyl alcohol.

The wrong answer choices: Choices A and C are wrong because in the equation set forth in the passage, viscosity refers to the viscosity of the medium through which the spheres travel, not to the viscosity of the spheres themselves. Choice B is wrong because lesser density will make not for a greater terminal velocity but for a lesser one.

106. Which of the following will affect the buoyant force experienced by a solid object falling through a fluid?

A. The density of the object.
B. The density of the fluid.
C. The viscosity of the object.
D. The viscosity of the fluid.

B is correct.. The buoyant force exerted on an object is given by the equation: $F_b =$ (density of the displaced fluid)(volume of fluid displaced)(g)

Among the listed factors, only density of the fluid affects buoyant force.

107. Which statement must be true of an object sinking in a fluid?

A. The weight of the object is greater than the buoyant force.
B. The weight of the object is less than the buoyant force.
C. The frictional force is greater than the buoyant force.
D. The frictional force is less than the buoyant force.

A is correct. An object will sink only if its weight exceeds the buoyant force it experiences. When weight and buoyant force are equal the object floats within the fluid. (It is stationary, therefore, and experiences no upward force of friction).

The wrong answer choices: Choice B is wrong; if the object's weight is less than buoyant force, the object rises within the fluid. Choices C and D are wrong because the relationships they describe have no bearing on the matter of sinking.

Passage VII (Questions 108–115)

108. Solar radiation with which of the following properties will make the most energy available for storage by the device?

    A. Long wavelength.
    B. High velocity.
    C. High frequency.
    D. Long period of vibration.

C is correct. For electromagnetic radiation, higher frequency is associated with greater energy.

The wrong answer choices: Choice B is wrong because in a given medium the speed of light is constant. In a vacuum it is 3.0×10^8 m/s. Choice A refers to long wavelength which, in turn, denotes low frequency, since (wavelength) × (frequency) = speed. The phrase "long period of vibration" indicates a cycle of relatively long endurance. That too denotes long wavelength and low frequency.

109. Reaction 1 occurs spontaneously at high temperatures. The most likely cause for this phenomenon is that at high temperatures:

    A. increasing entropy compensates for increasing enthalpy.
    B. increasing entropy compensates for decreasing enthalpy.
    C. decreasing entropy compensates for increasing enthalpy.
    D. decreasing entropy compensates for decreasing enthalpy.

A is correct. If a reaction is endothermic, its system absorbs heat from the surroundings, and the enthalpy of the reaction (ΔH) is positive. Positive enthalpy is disfavored, however, and an endothermic reaction will only proceed spontaneously if its entropy is sufficiently positive to generate, overall, a negative free energy. In reaction 1, the number of moles of products exceeds the number of moles of reactants which, in this case, indicates that entropy increases. The reaction is spontaneous because increased entropy compensates for increased enthalpy and generates, overall, negative free energy.

110. The heat of formation of $SO_3(g)$ is -396 kJ/mol. What is the heat of formation of $SO_2(g)$?

    A. -396 kJ/mol
    B. -297 kJ/mol
    C. -198 kJ/mol
    D. -495 kJ/mol

    B is correct. You may work the problem by reference to reaction 1 or reaction 2. Recall that the heat of formation of an element in its standard state is zero. Selecting reaction 1, remember that

$$H_{f\,reaction} = H_{f\,products} - H_{f\,reactants;}$$
$$198 \text{ kJ} = (2 \text{ mol})(H) - (2 \text{ mol})(-396 \text{ kJ/mol})$$
$$H = -297 \text{ kJ/mol}$$

111. Which of the following best describes the energy conversion that takes place as solar radiation is taken into the device and converted?

    A. Kinetic to electrical to heat
    B. Kinetic to chemical to electrical
    C. Light to electrical to chemical
    D. Light to chemical to heat

    D is correct. The energy emanating from the sun takes the form of electromagnetic radiation, and, more specifically, light. At the conclusion of reaction 1 the energy is housed within chemical bonds. At the conclusion of reaction 2 the energy is released as heat.

112. One of the advantages of the solar energy conversion device is that the energy can be stored indefinitely and be released when desired. That is because:

   A. all of the reactants and products are in the gas phase.
   B. the endothermic reaction takes place only at high temperatures.
   C. the exothermic reaction takes place only in the presence of a catalyst.
   D. the exothermic reaction releases more energy than is stored by the endothermic reaction.

C is correct. Reaction 2 requires a catalyst. Until the catalyst is supplied, energy remains housed within the chemical bonds resulting from reaction 1. When the catalyst is introduced, reaction 2 occurs and the energy is released as heat.

The wrong answer choices: Choices A and B make true statements but do not answer the question. The gas phase and high temperature do not explain how the device stores energy until its release is sought. Choice D makes a false statement. The exothermic reaction can release no more energy than is absorbed during the endothermic reaction; *recall that energy is conserved*.

113. The formation of oxygen gas in Reaction 1 would be promoted by:

    A. increasing the pressure of the reaction chamber.

    B. decreasing the pressure of the reaction chamber.

    C. increasing the concentration of sulfur dioxide in the reaction chamber.

    D. decreasing the concentration of sulfur trioxide in the reaction chamber.

B is correct. The left side of reaction 1 shows 2 moles of gas and the right side shows 3. Pressure on the right is therefore greater than pressure on the left. In a limited sense, pressure is a "product" of the reaction. Applying LeChatelier's principle, you know that the removal of any product drives a reaction to the right. Alternatively you may think of pressure as a "stress." Alleviation of the stress allows the reaction to move more readily in the direction that regenerates the stress. Since reduction of pressure drives the reaction forward, and oxygen is generated in the forward reaction, reducing pressure promotes the formation of oxygen.

The wrong answer choices: Choice A is wrong because increased pressure would drive the reaction to the left and reduce oxygen formation. Choice C is wrong as well. Sulfur dioxide appears on the right side of the reaction. Increasing its concentration will drive the reaction to the left and, once again, reduce oxygen formation. Choice D is wrong for analogous reasons. Sulfur trioxide is a reactant. Reducing the concentration of a reactant tends to drive a reaction to the left. That would mean, yet again, reducing the formation of oxygen.

114. If one mole of oxygen gas is consumed by Reaction 2 over the course of 1 hour, what is the power of the conversion device?

    A. 3 W
    B. 22 W
    C. 55 W
    D. 330 W

C is correct. For every mole of oxygen gas consumed, 198 kJ of energy are released. Power is measured in watts (W); 1 watt = 1 joule/second. Simple algebra reveals that:

$$\frac{198000 \text{ J}}{1 \text{hr}} \times \frac{1 \text{hr}}{3600 \text{ sec}} = 55 \text{ J/sec} = 55 \text{ W}.$$

115. Which of the following is NOT an advantage of the solar energy conversion device?

    A. Energy need not be used at the same time it is absorbed.
    B. The gases in the system are reused.
    C. Energy can be absorbed in the absence of solar radiation.
    D. Energy can be released in the absence of solar radiation.

C is correct. It makes a false statement. The passage notes that solar energy itself has, as a disadvantage, the fact that it is not consistently available. The device described in the passage is designed to harness solar radiation when it *is* available, and *store* it so that energy is usable on demand. Although the device effectively stores solar energy it *absorbs* it only when it is available. Like so many other useful and productive entities it must "make hay while the sun shines."

The wrong answer choices: Choices A, B, and D do represent the device's advantageous features.

Questions 116–120 are NOT based on a descriptive passage

116. What is the ground state electron configuration of a neutral silicon atom?

    A. $1s^2\ 2s^2\ 2p^6\ 3s^2\ 3p^1$
    B. $1s^2\ 2s^2\ 2p^6\ 3s^2\ 3p^2$
    C. $1s^2\ 2s^2\ 2p^6\ 3s^2\ 3d^1$
    D. $1s^2\ 2s^2\ 2p^6\ 3s^2\ 3d^2$

B is correct. Silicon has atomic number 14, which means that a neutral silicon atom has 14 protons in its nucleus with 14 electrons surrounding them. The total number of electrons represented in the configuration must be equal to 14. Knowing the order in which electron subshells are filled allows you to construct the ground state electron configuration shown in choice B. *The wrong answer choices*: Choices A and C show only 13 electrons each:

$2 + 2 + 6 + 2 + 1 = 13$. Choice D shows 14 electrons, but places the outer two in the 3d subshell, which is incorrect. They belong to the 3p subshell as shown in choice B.

117. An object is placed in front of a converging lens with a focal length f. At what distance from the lens must the object be placed in order to form a virtual, upright image twice the object's size?

    A. $\dfrac{f}{2}$
    B. f
    C. $\dfrac{3f}{2}$
    D. $2f$

A is correct. Apply the lens equation, remembering that (1) the image is virtual and the image distance is therefore negative, (2) the image is twice the size of the object so the image distance must be twice the object distance (3) for a converging lens, focal length is positive.

$$\frac{1}{f} = \frac{1}{ob} + \frac{1}{im} \ ; \ \frac{1}{f} = \frac{1}{x} - \frac{1}{2x} \ ; \ x = \frac{f}{2}$$

Alternatively, notice that for a converging lens to create a virtual image, the object must be placed inside the focal length. Only choice A conforms to this rule.

118. Which of the following subatomic particles would experience the greatest force when exposed to an electric field?

    A. Alpha particle
    B. Beta particle
    C. Proton
    D. Neutron

A is correct. A particle exposed to an electric field experiences a force proportional to the magnitude of its own charge. Recall the charge associated with each of the listed particles: Alpha : +2, Beta: –1, Proton : +1, Neutron: 0. The charge magnitude on the alpha particle is 2 and is greater than that on any of the other listed particles.

119. The pH of an acidic solution is 3.5. Which of the following expresses the solution's hydrogen ion concentration?

    A. $10^{-3.5}$
    B. $10^{3.5}$
    C. $\log 3.5$
    D. $-\log 3.5$

A is correct. pH represents (-) log [H⁺]. If for some solution hydrogen ion concentration is 10^{-5}, pH = 5. If for some other solution hydrogen ion concentration is 10^{-3}, pH = 3. If pH is 3.5, the hydrogen ion concentration is $10^{-3.5}$

120. Which of the following best explains why sound travels faster through water than through air?

    A. Water is more dense than air.
    B. Water is less dense than air.
    C. Water is more resistant to compression than air.
    D. Water is less resistant to compression than air.

C is correct. The speed of sound through any medium is a function of (1) the medium's density, and (2) the degree to which the medium resists compression. Speed decreases with increased density and increases with increased resistance to compression. Water is more dense than air, which tends to reduce the speed with which it conducts sound. However, water's resistance to compression is far greater than air's. That difference more than overcomes the difference in density. The net result is that sound travels more quickly through water than through air because of the greater resistance to compression.

Passage VIII (Questions 121–126)

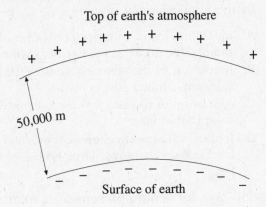

Figure 1

121. What is the approximate resistance of the earth's atmosphere?

A. 10 Ω
B. 50 Ω
C. 100 Ω
D. 200 Ω

D is correct. Your review of physics will remind you that Ohm's law provides a relationship among resistance, voltage, and current. Resistance = Voltage ÷ Current;

$$R = \frac{V}{I} = \frac{400000V}{1800A} = 200 \ \Omega.$$

122. Which of the following statements best explains the increase in ionization near the top of the Earth's atmosphere?

    A. Ionization in the atmosphere is caused by radioactive decay at the Earth's surface.

    B. Ionization in the atmosphere is caused by collisions among air molecules.

    C. Ionization in the atmosphere is caused by solar radiation.

    D. Ionization in the atmosphere is greater over land masses than over large bodies of water.

C is correct. The question calls for "common sense." If solar radiation produces the ionization then it follows that the concentration of positive ions will be at that position within the earth's atmosphere closest to the source—the top.

The wrong answer choices: Choice A is wrong. If ionization were caused by radioactive decay on the earth's surface, the highest concentration of positive ions would be *on* the surface of the earth. Choice B is wrong as well. If ionization were caused by collisions among air molecules, it would be greatest where the air is most dense—at the bottom of the atmosphere. The matter to which choice D alludes is entirely irrelevant.

123. The human body forms an equipotential surface and is unaffected by the atmospheric electric field because the human body is:

    A. a perfect insulator.

    B. a relatively good conductor.

    C. at a higher potential than its surroundings.

    D. at a lower potential than its surroundings.

B is correct. Recall that a good conductor carries the same electrical potential at all points. If the potential should be modified at one point, electrons will move toward or away from the modified area so that the potential alteration is "dispersed" evenly throughout the conductor .

124. Which picture best represents the direction of the electric field surrounding the Earth?

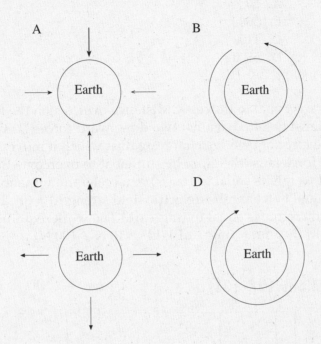

A is correct. By convention, an electric field is said to point from the area of positive charge to the area of negative charge, as shown in choice A.

125. Where 1 MW is equal to 1 megawatt (1 million watts) what is the average power of the electrical system created by the Earth and its atmosphere?

A. 20 MW
B. 70 MW
C. 200 MW
D. 700 MW

D is correct. Review physics and recall that power is a measure of work per time. It is measured in watts and in electrical contexts it may be ascertained according to the formula $P = IV = (1800 \text{ A}) \times (400{,}000 \text{ V}) = 720{,}000{,}000 \text{ W} \approx 700 \text{ MW}$

126. How much work must be done to lift an object with a mass of 1 kg and a positive charge of 1C to a height of 5m above the Earth's surface?

    A. 50 J

    B. 550 J

    C. 1100 J

    D. 5500 J

B is correct. Work is equal to (force) × (distance over which the force acts). In this instance the mass must be lifted against two downward forces (1) the force of its own weight, and (2) The force of positive charge against which it moves within the electric field. The upward force must therefore be sufficient to overcome the sum of those forces. The force of weight is equal to (mass) × (acceleration due to gravity) = mg. The electrical force is equal to (charge) × (electric field strength) = qE. The sum of the downward forces, therefore is equal to (mg + qE) The work required to lift the object is equal to (mg + qE) (height) = (mg + qE) (h) = (10 N + 100 N) × (5 m) = 550 joules.

Passage IX (Questions 127–131)

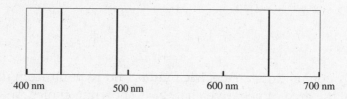

Figure 1

127. What is the energy of an electron occupying the third quantum level ($n = 3$) of a hydrogen atom?

    A. -1.96×10^{-17} J

    B. -2.42×10^{-19} J

    C. -6.54×10^{-18} J

    D. -7.27×10^{-19} J

B is correct.

Apply the equation set forth in the passage:

$$E_n = {}^-R_H \left(\frac{1}{n^2} \right) = {}^-(2.18 \times 10^{-18} \text{ J}) \times \left(\frac{1}{3^2} \right) = {}^-(2.18 \times 10^{-18} \text{ J}) \times \frac{1}{9} = {}^-2.42 \times 10^{-19}$$

Having recognized that the relevant calculation was 2.18×10^{-18} J $\times \frac{1}{9}$ you might have (1) divided the Rydberg constant by 10 to arrive at 2.18×10^{-19}, and (2) then looked among the answer choices for a slightly larger value.

128. Which of the lists below could represent the wavelengths of the electromagnetic radiation emitted by hydrogen atoms?

    A. 410 nm, 434 nm, 486 nm, 580 nm.
    B. 410 nm, 434 nm, 486 nm, 656 nm.
    C. 410 nm, 486 nm, 580 nm, 656 nm.
    D. 410 nm, 486 nm, 628 nm, 656 nm.

B is correct. The emitted wavelengths correspond to the energy levels that the electron is "permitted" to occupy and they correspond, also, to the emission spectrum shown in Figure 1. Figure 1 shows three bands between 400 nm and 500 nm and one band between 600 nm and 700 nm. Among the choices, only choice B satisfies that condition. The values 410 nm, 434 nm, 486 nm fall between 400 nm and 500 nm. The value 656 nm falls between 600 and 700 nm.

The wrong answer choices: Choice A is incorrect because it presents a value that falls between 500 nm and 600 nm. Moreover, it fails to present a value between 600 nm and 700 nm. Choices C and D are erroneous for analogous reasons.

129. When an electron moves, within a hydrogen atom, from the third quantum level($n = 3$) to the second quantum level ($n = 2$) which of the following is true?

    A. ΔE will be positive and a photon will be emitted.
    B. ΔE will be positive and a photon will be absorbed.
    C. ΔE will be negative and a photon will be emitted.
    D. ΔE will be negative and a photon will be absorbed.

C is correct. From the passage and your own review of inorganic chemistry you learn that an electron falling from a higher energy state to a lower energy state emits energy; ΔE is negative. You know also that the released energy may take the form of light. It is implausible that a photon should be *absorbed* when energy is released. A photon might, however, be emitted.

130. A photon of light will have the highest frequency if it is associated with which of the following wavelengths?

    A. 400 nm
    B. 500 nm
    C. 600 nm
    D. 700 nm

A is correct. Recall that the speed of electromagnetic radiation in any medium is constant, and in a vacuum is equal to 3.0×10^8 m/s. For an electromagnetic wave (and for any wave), (frequency) × (wavelength) = (speed). For electromagnetic radiation, $c = \lambda f$. When speed is constant, therefore, frequency and wavelength are inversely proportional. The larger the wavelength the lower the frequency. The smaller the wavelength the higher the frequency. The correct answer is that which describes the smallest wavelength.

131. Increase in an electron's quantum number will produce:

    A. increased stability and increased energy.
    B. increased stability and decreased energy.
    C. decreased stability and decreased energy.
    D. decreased stability and increased energy.

D is correct. Higher quantum number means higher energy state. Recall from your review of thermodynamics and subatomic chemistry, that lower energy is associated with greater stability (and that higher entropy is also associated with greater stability). Higher energy is associated with lesser stability (and lower entropy is associated with lesser stability).

Passage X (Questions 132–137)

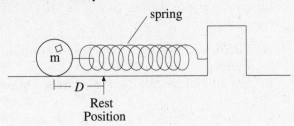

Figure 1

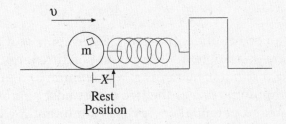

Figure 2

132. Which of the following graphs best relates total energy of the spring and mass system to the initial displacement from rest position?

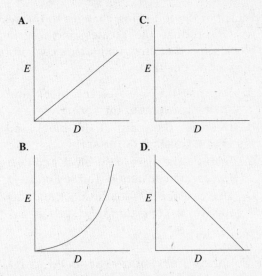

B is correct. The oscillation constitutes simple harmonic motion. The initial potential energy of a system in simple harmonic motion is equal to $E = \frac{1}{2}kx^2$. The initial potential energy is converted to kinetic energy, to potential energy, to kinetic energy, etc. The equation just presented shows that its value is directly proportional to the square of displacement. Recall that if one plots on the "y" axis a value that is directly proportional to the square of the value plotted on the "x" axis, he obtains a characteristic "exponential curve" as shown in choice B.

The wrong answer choices: Choice A depicts a graph wherein "x" and "y" values are directly proportional. Choice C depicts a graph wherein y does not vary with x, and choice D depicts a graph in which x and y values are inversely proportional.

133. As the mass passes through the spring's resting position during the course of its oscillation:

    A. kinetic and potential energies are at a minimum.

    B. kinetic and potential energies are at a maximum.

    C. kinetic energy is at a minimum and potential energy is at a maximum.

    D. kinetic energy is at a maximum and potential energy is at a minimum.

D is correct. When an object undergoes simple harmonic motion, it converts kinetic energy to potential energy and potential energy to kinetic energy. In the case of a pendulum, for example, potential energy is at a maximum and kinetic energy at a minimum when the pendulum reaches the two uppermost points in its arc. Kinetic energy is at a maximum and potential energy is at a minimum when it reaches the bottom-most, resting position of its arc. For the mass and spring apparatus described in this passage, potential energy is at a maximum and kinetic energy at a minimum when the spring reaches maximum expansion and compression. Potential energy is at a minimum and kinetic energy at a maximum as the mass traverses the spring's resting position.

134. Which of the following changes to the system would produce the greatest increase in the block's speed at any given displacement from the resting position?

    A. Increase the mass of the block and the spring constant of the spring.

    B. Decrease the mass of the block and the spring constant of the spring.

    C. Increase the mass of the block and decrease the spring constant of the spring.

    D. Decrease the mass of the block and increase the spring constant of the spring.

D is correct. Examine Equation 1 and note that speed, v, is directly proportional to the square root of k and inversely proportional to the square root of m. To increase the square root of any variable, the variable itself must be increased. To increase the value of a fraction the numerator must be increased and/or the denominator decreased. Choice D indicates that the numerator is increased *and* the denominator decreased.

The wrong answer choices: Choices A refers to increased denominator and numerator. Choice B refers to decreased denominator and numerator. Choice C refers to increased denominator and decreased numerator which surely would decrease the block's velocity.

135. As the block moves through the point shown
in Figure 2, the magnitude of its acceleration:

    A. increases.

    B. decreases.

    C. remains unchanged with a positive value.

    D. is equal to zero.

B is correct. Don't confuse velocity with acceleration. Acceleration follows from force. When the spring is fully compressed or fully expanded, it is "set" to deliver maximum force. As it then moves the block toward the resting position the acceleration *declines* although velocity increases until, *at* the resting position, acceleration is zero and velocity reaches its maximum. As the block then moves past the center, toward either compression or extension, the spring subjects it to a negative acceleration ("deceleration"). The negative acceleration increases as the spring undergoes increased compression or expansion. Velocity decreases until negative acceleration reaches a maximum and velocity is zero.

The wrong answer choices: Choice A refers to an increase and would be correct if the question concerned not acceleration, but velocity. Choice C refers to constancy and would be correct if the question concerned total energy of the system. Choice D refers to zero, and would be correct if the question concerned (1) acceleration at the resting position, or (2) velocity at the terminal positions.

136. Which expression gives the force required to
hold the mass in equilibrium at a displacement D from the resting position before the
start of oscillations?

    A. $\dfrac{1}{2}kD$

    B. kD

    C. $\dfrac{1}{2}kD^2$

    D. kD^2

B is correct. Recall your review of simple harmonic motion and know that the force required to maintain a spring is equal to (spring constant) × (displacement) = $F = kD$. The answer therefore is, simply, kD .

137. In which of the following situations will the block's velocity have a magnitude of zero?

    A. $x > D$
    B. $x = D$
    C. $D > x > 0$
    D. $x = 0$

B is correct. As explained for question 135, the block's speed is zero at points of maximum compression and expansion (just as a pendulum's speed is zero at the two high points in its arc). Since D represents the initial/maximum displacement, velocity has a magnitude of zero when $x = D$.

Questions 138–142 are NOT based on a descriptive passage

138. Samples of which of the following molecules will exhibit the strongest intermolecular interactions?

    A. O_2
    B. N_2
    C. CO_2
    D. H_2O

D is correct. Water exhibits hydrogen bonding, which makes its intermolecular attractions stronger than those of the other three molecules listed. As a consequence, water is the only one of the four that is liquid at room temperature.

139. Three cables are attached together as shown below.

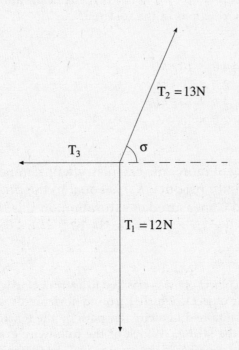

The cables are in equilibrium. If the tensions in the cables T_1 and T_2 are as shown in the diagram, and $\sin \sigma = \dfrac{12}{13}$, what is the magnitue of T_3 ?

A. 1 N
B. 5 N
C. 15 N
D. 25 N

B is correct. The 13N T_2 vector is resolved into a vertical component with magnitude of 12N and a horizontal component wth magnitude of 5N. Note that cables T_3 and T_1 are horizontal and vertical respectively. Since the system is in equilibrium, the vertical vector T_1 must have and does have a magnitude exactly equal to 12N so that it compensates for the vertical *component* of T_2. The horizontal vector T_3 must have a magnitude of 5N so that it compensates for the horizontal component of T_2.

140. Barium fluoride is a slightly soluble salt with $K_{sp} = 1.7 \times 10^{-6}$. If the concentration of barium ions in a saturated aqueous solution is equal to $4.3 \times 10^{-3}\ M$, what is the concentration of fluoride ions in the solution?

A. $4.0 \times 10^{-4}\ M$
B. $2.0 \times 10^{-2}\ M$
C. $4.0 \times 10^{-2}\ M$
D. $2.0 \times 10^{-1}\ M$

B is correct. Your review of inorganic chemistry will remind you that for any soluble salt $A_b C_d$ the solubility product, K_{sp} is equal to the product $[A]^b \times [C]^d$ with the concentrations of A and C measured at saturation. In this instance, the solubility product $= Ksp = [Ba^{2+}]^1 [F^-]^2 = 1.7 \times 10^{-6} = (4.3 \times 10^{-3})(x^2)$; $4.0 \times 10^{-4} = x^2$; $x = 2.0 \times 10^{-2}$

141. An object of mass m is tied to a string of length r. The object is whirled around horizontally and maintained in a circular path by the tension T in the string. Which of the following graphs best represents the change in T as the object's speed, v, is changed?

A.

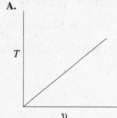

B.

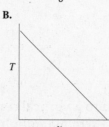

C.

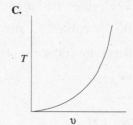

D.

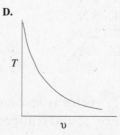

C is correct. The tension in the string exerts a centripetal force on the mass. Your review of physics will reveal that centrifugal force $= \dfrac{(\text{mass})(\text{velocity}^2)}{\text{radius}} = F_c = \dfrac{mv^2}{r}$. Examine the equation, and recognize that centripetal force is proportional to the square of velocity. Once again when a value plotted on the "y" axis is proportional to the square of a value plotted on the "x" axis a characteristic "exponential curve" results, as shown in choice C.

The wrong answer choices: Choice A shows a relationship of direct proportionality and choice B and D show relationships of inverse proportionality.

142. Which of the following units expresses power?

    A. $kg \bullet m^2/s^3$

    B. $kg \bullet m^2/s^2$

    C. J^2/sec

    D. J^2/sec^2

A is correct. Power is a function of work per time. It is normally expressed in the unit watt, where 1 watt = 1 joule/sec. Work, in turn, represents (force) × (the distance through which force acts). It is normally expressed in the unit joule, where 1 joule = 1 Newton • meter. Force, in turn, represents (mass) × (acceleration) and is normally expressed in the unit newton, where 1 newton = 1 $kg \bullet m/sec^2$ Making use of the most basic of units, we can express work as $(kg \bullet m/sec^2)$ (m) = $kg \bullet m^2/sec^2$. In order to express power, we must divide that unit by time to get:

$$\frac{kg \bullet m^2}{sec^2} \times \frac{1}{sec} = \frac{kg \bullet m^2}{sec^3} = kg \bullet m^2/sec^3$$

7

WRITING SAMPLE EXPLANATIONS II

The following essays were written according to The Princeton Review's MCAT Essay Formula. As described in Part I, they are designed to make a "good impression" on a reader who will spend approximately *ninety seconds* evaluating them. Notice that each essay:

- performs, in appropriate order, all three "tasks" described in the MCAT instructions,

- provides frequent paragraphing,

- uses formal language, and

- cites a quotation from some famed authority.

WRITING SAMPLE EXAMPLE #1

THE GREATEST AND MOST LASTING REWARD OF EDUCATION IS THE PERSONAL PLEASURE OF UNDERSTANDING.

Essay:

The statement indicates that education brings about "rewards," and, by suggesting that personal comprehension is the "greatest and most lasting" reward, implies a hierarchy of benefits that may be derived from education. By extension, the statement suggests that pragmatic yet ephemeral rewards of education are not as relevant as the ethereal yet psychologically gratifying gifts that learning bestows. (The statement likewise seems a refutation of the common assertion that "ignorance is bliss.")

If the advantages of education, when examined through the lens of personal pleasure, outweigh any immediate accolades that education might bring, then we may say that the veracity of this statement has been confirmed. For, if we are to subscribe to the view expressed in the above sentence, it is not simply the increase of comprehension skills which provide the more lasting rewards of education, but a corresponding rise in the pleasure that we derive from our newfound knowledge.

In order specifically to describe a situation in which the statement does not apply, one need only to recognize that the terms "reward" and "personal pleasure" are inherently ambiguous and subjective. The statement hinges on these two terms, and its applicability depends on the meanings attached to them.

As used in the statement, "reward" could be interpreted in various ways. While some individuals might consider financial or social advancement a pertinent "reward," others may seek education to quench the flames of doubt. Thus, the statement does not take into account the highly ambiguous nature of such a term, and is not clear in assigning a value judgment such as "greater" to the word "reward."

The term "personal pleasure" also harbors ambiguity. If it means "happiness," then there are a great many situations in which the statement does not apply. For instance, education may bring with it a greater awareness of the complexities of life, and may end up burdening a learned human being with an ennui which is not present in the less educated. This point is supported by the existential angst often found in the works of some of the great Continental philosophers of the twentieth century, many of whom became disillusioned when "education" failed to provide answers to the metaphysical questions that plagued them.

The preponderance of highly educated individuals with serious psychological and sociological maladjustments suggests that, at times, "understanding" does not necessarily lead to personal pleasure. The determining factor of an increase in such pleasure would be the healthy assimilation of the understanding gained from education, and its application to the personal lives of the educated.

Hence the pertinence of the statement depends in large measure on the meaning attached to its language. If the terms "reward" and "pleasure" refer to the utilitarian growth education can foster, then perhaps the statement represents a meaningful comment. If, however, "reward" and "personal pleasure" refer to emotional fulfillment, then the statement is not a useful insight.

WRITING SAMPLE EXAMPLE #2
CONCERN FOR THE POSSIBILITY OF FAILURE INTERFERES WITH SUCCESS.
Essay:

The above statement suggests that success is dependent on a cognitive state that can be routed by opposing thoughts. (The statement seems implicitly to oppose the statement by Truman Capote that "Failure is the condiment that gives success its flavor.") This statement is thus contrary to the popular notion that success often results from a fear of failure, by suggesting that this concern somehow impedes our achievements. In order specifically to describe a situation in which the statement does not apply, one need only observe the ambiguous nature of the words "concern," "failure," and "success." The meaning of this statement hinges on the interpretation of these words, and an evaluation of this statement should begin with an examination of their denotations. As used in this statement, "concern" is subject to interpretation. "Concern" might range from simple uneasiness, which may aid in motivating someone to prepare for a successful venture, to full-blown anxiety, which of course would greatly interfere with both the apprehension and enjoyment of success. Since the connotations of a term such as "concern" vary greatly, the persuasiveness of the statement is severely hampered.

Furthermore, the definitions of the words "success" and "failure" are open to numerous pragmatic interpretations. Supposed success may turn to failure, not due to the psychological state of one individual but rather due to a simple twist of fate. In many fields of human endeavor, success is influenced by the vicissitudes of causality as much as, if not more than, the concern for failure on the part of the human participant. For instance, concern for the possibility of failure has no effect of your potential to win the lottery. Likewise, the reason people play the lottery is not from concern of failure, but the desire to win.

The definitions of "success" and "failure" are further obscured by situations in which apparent failure turns into success, and vice versa. For instance, the success that Iraqi troops had during the invasion of Kuwait quickly transformed into abject failure during the Gulf War. The fleeting nature of achievement on any level makes generalized statements such as this one highly suspect.

The statement also excludes the possibility that a concern for failure may motivate an individual to prepare in such a way that success is more easily attainable. The concern for the possibility of failure caused the US-backed forces in the Gulf War to arguably overprepare, and helped bring about the most lopsided victory in the history of modern warfare. If concern for failure leads to a fruitful groundwork for success, then the stated proposition is refuted.

Thus, the pertinence of the statement depends in large part on the connotations of the language used. Because every event can be judged as either a success or a failure based on one's definitions of the given terms, and because multiple factors contribute to any end result, defining one of those conditions, in the above case, "concern," as the determining influence is unfeasible. If, however, "success" and "failure" are accepted on a purely subjective level, and "concern" is defined as excessive anxiety, then the statement furnishes an exceedingly useful insight.

BIOLOGICAL SCIENCES EXPLANATIONS II

Cholesterol

143. How many functional groups does the cholesterol molecule feature?

A. 1
B. 2
C. 3
D. 4

B is correct. Functional groups are those atoms or groups of atoms that tend most to serve as a chemical molecule's reactive sites. The cholesterol molecule features two functional groups: (1) the hydroxyl (OH) group and (2) carbon-carbon, double bond group.

144. What is the product of the reaction shown below?

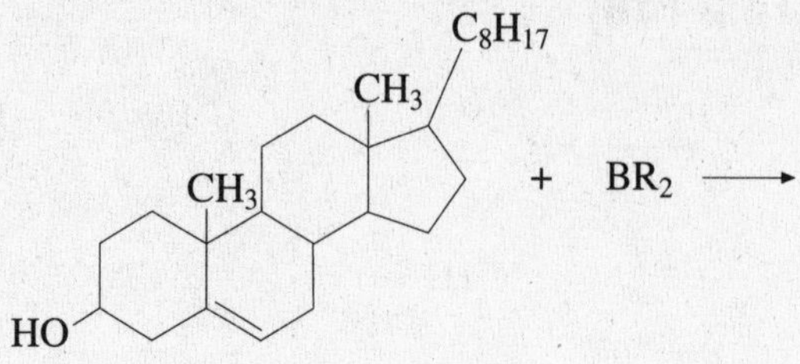

A.

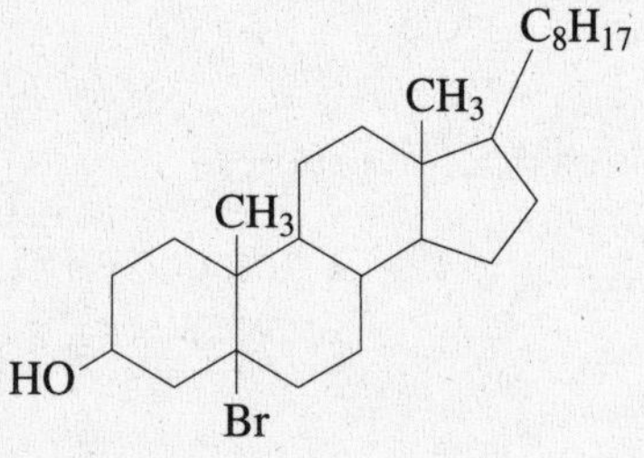

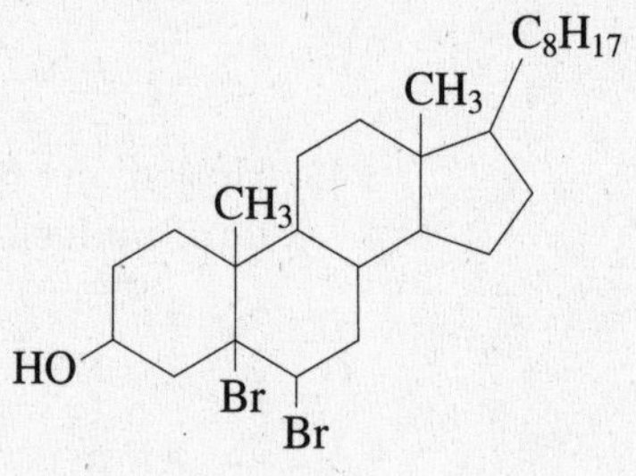

B.

C.

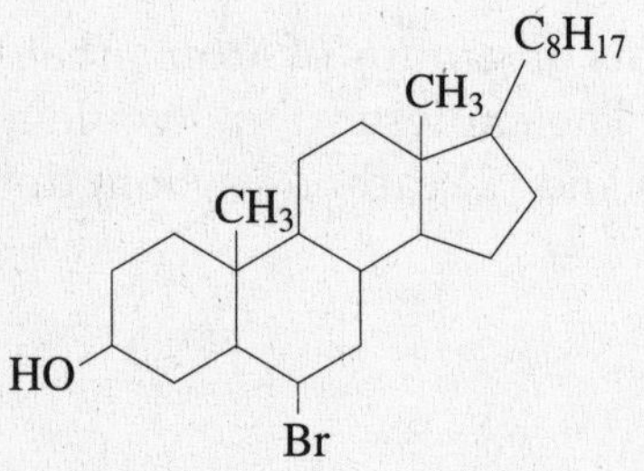

D.

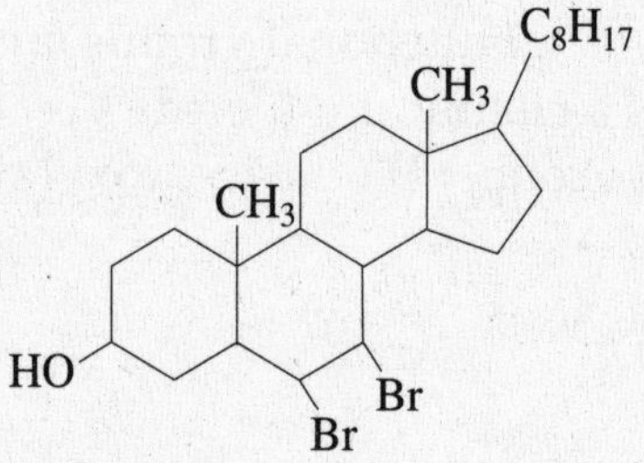

C is correct. Halogen molecules undergo electrophilic addition reactions with alkenes. In this case, the bromine molecule adds to the carbon-carbon double bond. As Br_2 approaches the double bond, the Br-Br bond is polarized and ultimately breaks.

The wrong answer choices: Choice A is wrong because it shows not two but one bromine atom bonded to the alkene. Choice B is wrong because bromine adds to the double bond, not to the hydroxyl group. Choice D is wrong as well. It shows the bromine atoms incorrectly positioned; they should be positioned on either side of the preexisting double bond.

145. When cholesterol reacts with CH_3COOH it forms:

    A. a carboxylic acid and water.
    B. a carboxylic acid and an alcohol.
    C. an ester and water.
    D. an ester and an alcohol.

C is correct. An ester (RCOOR) is a carboxylic acid derivative. It may be synthesized from a carboxylic acid and an alcohol. Cholesterol *is* an alcohol. (It is also a steroid.) When it reacts with a carboxylic acid it forms an ester and water, as shown in this illustration:

146. A student believes that cholesterol will readily undergo electrophilic substitution when reacted with Bromine (Br_2). Is the belief reasonable?

    A. Yes, because cholesterol is a conjugated diene.
    B. Yes, because cholesterol undergoes a hydrogenation reaction.
    C. No, because cholesterol is not aromatic.
    D. No, because electrophilic substitution requires catalysis.

C is correct. Only aromatic compounds—benzene and its derivatives—undergo electrophilic substitution. Cholesterol undergoes electrophilic *addition*.

The wrong answer choices: Choice A is wrong. A conjugated diene features single and double bonds in alternating series. Cholesterol does not. Choice B is incorrect because hydrogenation denotes the addition of hydrogen gas to an alkene. Choice D is wrong because it makes a false statement. Electrophilic substitution requires no catalyst.

147. Which of the following is the most likely product when cholesterol undergoes ozonolysis?

A.

B.

C.

D.

B is correct. Ozonolysis represents the cleavage of a molecule by ozone. When ozone is added to a carbon-carbon double bond in the pictured reaction, two carbonyl entities result, as shown in B.

148. Suppose an investigator attempts to produce 5-cholestene-3-one from cholesterol. Which of the following infrared spectroscopic findings would inform the investigator that the reaction has occurred?

Cholesterol → (Jones' reagent) → 5-Cholestene-3-one

A. The disappearance of OH absorption from the reactant.

B. The disappearance of the carbonyl group in the product

C. The disappearance of a double bond from the reactant

D. The disappearance of a methyl group from the reactant

A is correct. Infrared spectroscopy identifies a molecule's functional groups. Examine the illustration that depicts the reaction. The reactant features a hydroxyl group. The product shows a carbonyl group but no OH group. The investigator will know the reaction has occurred if IR spectroscopy shows the disappearance of an OH group.

The wrong answer choices: Choice B refers to the disappearance of a carbonyl group in the product. Since both product features a carbonyl group, such a finding is incorrect. Choice C refers to the disappearance of a carbonyl group from the reactant. Again, both reactant and product feature carbonyl groups; the carbonyl group does not disappear. Choice D refers to disappearance of the methyl group in the reactant, an event that does not arise with this reaction.

Passage II (Questions 149-156)

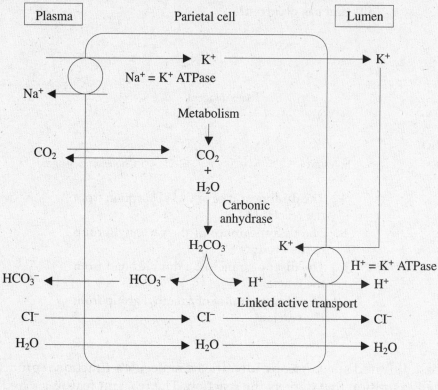

Figure 1

149. All of the following statements regarding pepsinogen are true EXCEPT that:

   A. it is an inactive zymogen.
   B. gastric acid facilitates conversion of pepsinogen to the active enzyme pepsin.
   C. it is secreted by gastric chief cells.
   D. it initiates the digestion of lipids.

D is correct. An acid environment transforms the enzyme precursor pepsinogen to the active enzyme pepsin. Pepsin cleaves the peptide bonds, that link the amino acid constituents of a protein. Pepsin therefore initiates the digestion not of lipid but of protein.

The wrong answer choices: A makes a true statement. Pepsinogen is an inactive zymogen; it is an enzyme precursor which requires some further modification, or environmental stimulus to facilitate its activity. Choice B also makes a true statement. The zymogen pepsinogen is rendered active by the stomach's acid environment. Choice C makes an accurate statement as well; pepsinogen is secreted by gastric chief cells.

150. Sympathetic stimulation of the gastrointestinal tract probably:

    A. stimulates gastric acid secretion.
    B. inhibits gastric acid secretion.
    C. acts synergistically with parasympathetic stimulation.
    D. produces peristalsis of the smooth muscle.

B is correct. Parasympathetic and sympathetic nervous systems tend to act antagonistically. The passage states that parasympathetic stimulation promotes gastrointestinal motility and increases gastric secretion. Sympathetic stimulation, therefore, would likely reduce gastrointestinal motility and gastric secretion.

The wrong answer choices: Choice A is wrong because it is opposite to the probable truth. Choice C is wrong because it implies that sympathetic and parasympathetic effects tend to augment each other. They don't. Choice D is incorrect because peristalsis is a localized phenomenon triggered by distension of the GI tract; it is not triggered by central nervous system stimuli.

151. According to Figure 1, which ion shows lower concentration in gastric secretions than in plasma?

    A. Potassium
    B. Chloride
    C. Hydrogen
    D. Sodium

D is correct. Figure 1 shows that potassium, hydrogen, and chloride are secreted from the luminal face of the parietal cell into the lumen of the stomach. The diagram also makes clear that the cell secretes none of these ions into the plasma. The concentration of all three ions must therefore be higher in the stomach than in the plasma. Sodium, on the other hand, is not secreted into the stomach but into the plasma by action of an ATPase (as shown at the upper left aspect of diagram). Sodium concentration, therefore, is lower in gastric secretions than in the plasma.

152. Hydrogen and chloride ions in the stomach draw water into the lumen so that gastric secretions are isotonic to plasma. This form of transport is most appropriately termed:

    A. active transport.
    B. passive transport.
    C. osmosis.
    D. facilitated transport.

C is correct. Osmosis denotes the passive movement of water along its concentration gradient in response to osmotically active ions.

The wrong answer choices: Choice A refers to active transport, which involves energy dependent movement of an electrolyte against its concentration or electrical gradient. Choice B refers to passive transport and refers to the movement of ions (not fluid) in accordance with their concentration or electrical gradient. Choice D refers to facilitated transport, a process in which lipid insoluble matter crosses a lipid membrane by combining with a lipid soluble "carrier molecule." Like osmosis and passive transport it is an energy <u>in</u>dependent phenomenon.

153. Which among the following do NOT serve an exocrine function?

    A. Parietal cells.
    B. Chief cells.
    C. G cells.
    D. Mucous cells.

C is correct. According to the passage, parietal cells (which secrete acid and intrinsic factor), chief cells (which secrete pepsinogen) and mucus cells (which secrete mucus)—all release their products into the lumen of the stomach, which is an external space. The passage also states that G cells are endocrine cells which secrete the hormone gastrin. The function served by G cells, therefore, is <u>endo</u>crine, not <u>exo</u>crine.

154. Studying the gastric activities of a volunteer, a group of researchers monitor the stomach's venous blood and report a transitory period during which it is highly basic. With which of the following is the period of basicity most likely associated?

A. Active acid secretion
B. Reduced gastrin secretion
C. Active secretin secretion
D. Reduced pepsinogen secretion

A is correct. Both the passage text and Figure 1 indicate that for every hydrogen ion secreted into the stomach's lumen, one HCO_3^- ion moves into the plasma. A high concentration of HCO_3^- in the blood produces an alkaline pH (above 7.0). A high HCO_3^- concentration in the gastric venous blood likely follows recent gastric acid secretion, since each release of H^+ into the lumen engenders a concomitant release of HCO_3^- to the plasma. *The wrong answer choices*: Choices B and D are wrong because secretion of gastric acid accompanies secretion of pepsinogen. Choice C is wrong because the passage states that secretin inhibits gastric secretions.

155. Carbonic acid that is secreted into the plasma is formed from:

A. carbon dioxide and hydrogen ion with facilitation by carbonic anhydrase.
B. carbon dioxide and hydrogen ion with facilitation by ATPase.
C. carbon dioxide and water with facilitation by carbonic anhydrase.
D. carbon dioxide and water with facilitation by ATPase.

C is correct. Your review of biology should remind you that carbonic acid is produced by reaction of carbon dioxide and water, with carbonic anhydrase as enzyme. Moreover, the diagram demonstrates that CO_2 and H_2O combine to produce H_2CO_3 with facilitation by carbonic anhydrase.

The wrong answer choices: Choice A is wrong. Hydrogen is not a substrate in the formation of carbonic acid. Choices B and D are wrong because, among other reasons, ATPases do catalyze only those reactions in which ATP is formed.

156. Which of the following pharmacological agents would most likely stimulate gastric motility?

- **A.** An agent that mimics the action of secretin
- **B.** An agent that acts as a terminal parasympathetic transmitter
- **C.** An agent that blocks parasympathetic transmission
- **D.** An agent that acts as a sympathetic transmitter.

B is correct. Acetylcholine is the neurotransmitter that mediates parasympathetic transmission at the neuromuscular junction. If an agent mimics acetylcholine it will likely "fool" the gastric muscle into contracting.

The wrong answer choices: Choice A is wrong because secretin is not a neurotransmitter but a hormone whose effects do not include the stimulation of gastric motility. Choice C is wrong because parasympathetic stimulation *promotes* gastric motility. Choice D is wrong as well. Sympathetic stimulation would likely oppose the effects of parasympathetic stimulation and therefore inhibit gastric motility.

Passage III (Questions 157–162)

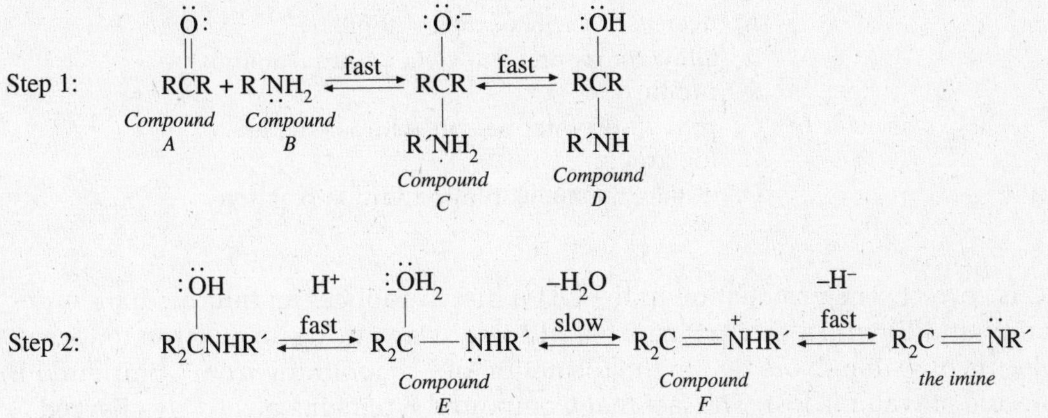

Step 1:

$$\underset{\substack{Compound \\ A}}{RCR} + \underset{\substack{Compound \\ B}}{R'NH_2} \overset{fast}{\underset{}{\rightleftarrows}} \underset{\substack{Compound \\ C}}{\overset{:\ddot{O}:^-}{\underset{R'NH_2}{|}}{RCR}} \overset{fast}{\underset{}{\rightleftarrows}} \underset{\substack{Compound \\ D}}{\overset{:\ddot{O}H}{\underset{R'NH}{|}}{RCR}}$$

Step 2:

$$\underset{}{\overset{:\ddot{O}H}{\underset{R_2CNHR'}{|}}} \overset{H^+}{\underset{fast}{\rightleftarrows}} \underset{\substack{Compound \\ E}}{\overset{:\ddot{O}H_2}{\underset{R_2C — \ddot{N}HR'}{|}}} \overset{-H_2O}{\underset{slow}{\rightleftarrows}} \underset{\substack{Compound \\ F}}{R_2C = \overset{+}{N}HR'} \overset{-H^-}{\underset{fast}{\rightleftarrows}} \underset{\substack{the\ imine}}{R_2C = \ddot{N}R'}$$

Figure 1

157. Which step(s) is (are) acid-catalyzed?

    A. Step 1

    B. Step 2

    C. Steps 1 and 2

    D. Neither step 1 nor step 2

B is correct. In step 2, a hydroxyl group is protonated to produce the OH_2 moiety shown in the intermediate "compound E." Moreover, the H^+ depicted over the arrow indicates catalysis by acid.

158. Which of the following compounds undergoes nucleophilic attack?

    A. Compound A

    B. Compound B

    C. Compound C

    D. Compound D

A is correct. In nucleophilic attack, a nucleophile ("lover of positive charge") donates an electron pair to an electrophile ("lover of negative charge"). At step 1, "Compound B," the nucleophilic amine ($R'NH_2$), attacks the electrophilic carbonyl of the ketone to eliminate the double bond and produce the intermediate "Compound C."

The wrong answer choices: Choices A, C, and D are wrong because in this reaction, none of the compounds to which they refer gives up electrons.

159. In step 2, the first intermediate is protonated to produce the carbanolamine, Compound E, in order to:

- **A.** decrease the pH of the solution.
- **B.** allow compound E to yield a neutral amino product.
- **C.** provide the intermediate with a better leaving group.
- **D.** initiate the nucleophilic addition reaction.

C is correct. The protonation of the OH moiety produces an intermediate (Compound E) with a group that is readily lost by acquiring an electron to form a molecule of water. (Note that in the formation of Compound F from Compound E, a molecule of water is lost. The fact that Compound F remains positively charged indicates that an electron has been taken from Compound E.) The protonated OH moiety is thus termed a "good leaving group." (The phrase is also used, commonly, to describe the halide atom in a halogenated alkane that undergoes nucleophilic substitution.)

The wrong answer choices: Choice A is wrong because the protonation that produces Compound E is unrelated to increase or decrease in pH. Choice B is incorrect because Compound E generates compound F, which is not neutral but *charged*. Choice D is incorrect because the nucleophilic attack occurs not at step 2 but at step 1.

160. Among the following, step 2 of the reaction most resembles:

- **A.** a substitution reaction.
- **B.** a bimolecular elimination reaction.
- **C.** a unimolecular elimination reaction.
- **D.** a homogeneous catalysis.

C is correct. As described in the passage and depicted in the illustration, the reaction involves the *elimination* of water from a ketone or aldehyde and the addition of a primary amine.

The wrong answer choices: Choice A is wrong because the reaction involves addition and elimination, but no true substitution. Choice B is wrong because bimolecular elimination (E_2) is favored for primary molecules. Choice D is wrong because catalytic hydrogenation involves the addition of hydrogen to an alkene.

161. With reference to the reaction described in the passage, what will likely occur if the reaction solution is highly acidic?

   A. The nucleophile will not attack the initial carbonyl compound.
   B. The solution will have a high pH.
   C. The intermediate will not be protonated.
   D. The amine nucleophile will be completely protonated.

D is correct. If pH is very low, the amine nucleophile is fully protonated.

$$R\ddot{N}H_2 + H^+ \longrightarrow R\acute{N}H_3^+$$

The reaction system is depleted of nucleophile (the amine) and the initial nucleophilic reaction does not occur.

The wrong answer choices: Choice A is wrong because, as noted, under highly acidic conditions the amine is fully protonated; there *is* no nucleophile. Choice B is wrong because high pH is contrary to the condition of high acidity. Choice C is wrong as well. Protonation of the nucleophile has no effect on the electrophile or its concentration.

162. The addition of an amine to an aldehyde or ketone is pH dependent. According to the graph below, what pH is most favorable to reaction rate?

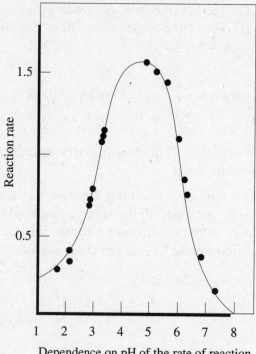

Dependence on pH of the rate of reaction

A. 0.5
B. 1.5
C. 2.0
D. 4.5

D is correct. The question requires a simple reading of the graph which shows that reaction rate is greatest when pH is 4.5

Passage IV (Questions 163–170)

Table 1: Axonal restoration 12-18 months
after MDMA administration

Serotonergic target	Rat	Squirrel monkey
amygdala	++	+++
hypothalamus	++	+++
cortex	++	+

Key:

Axonal regrowth from brain stem to brain targets

+   less than number of original connections

++   equal to number of original connections

+++   surpasses number of original connections

163. Serotonin is derived from:

    A. an amino acid.

    B. an enzyme.

    C. another neurotransmitter.

    D. a hormone.

A is correct. The third sentence of the first paragraph states that serotonin is a product of tryptophan metabolism. Review biochemistry, and recall that tryptophan is an essential amino acid.

164. Among the following, which graph best describes the degree of axonal degeneration as a function of MDMA dose?

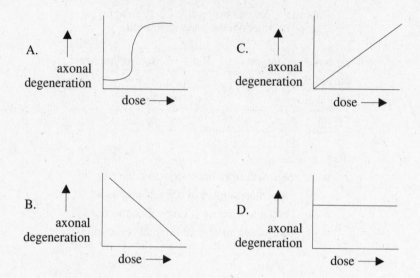

C is correct. The passage states that in all probability damage to serotonin-producing axons is most likely related to dosage. The graph depicted in choice C shows a linear relationship between dose of the drug and damage to axons. As dose increases, so does the damage.

The wrong answer choices: Choice A depicts a relationship in which dose produces increased damage at relatively higher doses, but produces little damage at relatively lower doses. Choice B depicts dose and damage as inversely proportional. Choice D indicates that dose has *no* affect on axonal health.

165. If MDMA is found to produce insomnia, the reason might be that:

A. it inhibits serotonin synthesis in brain stem neurons.

B. it destroys serotonin-containing axons in the brain stem.

C. it competes for serotonin binding sites on serotonergic neurons.

D. it causes degeneration of cell bodies of serotonin-producing neurons.

B is correct. If, as here, you must speculate, have your speculation conform to information supplied in the passage. The passage indicates that MDMA destroys axons that release serotonin. If an axon releases serotonin it must first contain serotonin.

The wrong answer choices: Choices A, C, and D are not inherently wrong, but they find no justification in the passage.

166. The most likely explanation for the differences between axonal regeneration in rats and squirrels monkeys as shown in Table 1 is that:

A. excessive axonal repair to the amygdala and hypothalamus inhibits reconnection to the cortex

B. dendrites of neurons in the cortex can compensate for axonal deficiencies.

C. longer axonal projections regenerate more easily than do shorter ones.

D. shorter axonal projections regenerate more easily than do longer ones.

B is correct. The passage states that MDMA "acts on serotonin pathways by destroying *axons* that release serotonin." Among the four statements only B refers to a compensation for deficient axons and calm, simple reasoning indicates that it must be correct.

167. A drug that prevented the re-uptake of serotonin would most likely:

A. produce an action potential in the presynaptic neuron by binding to receptors on the axonal membrane.

B. reduce the intensity of an action potential in the postsynaptic neuron.

C. prevent the postsynaptic neuron from undergoing frequent action potentials.

D. increase the amount of stimulation received by dendrites of the postsynaptic neuron.

D is correct. A drug that prevents the re-uptake of serotonin from the synaptic cleft would cause serotonin to remain there, prolonging the amount of stimulation received at the postsynaptic dendrites.

The wrong answer choices: Choice A is wrong because a nerve impulse travels in one direction only, from dendrite to axon within a neuron, and from axon to dendrite from one neuron to the next. Choice B is wrong because an action potential is an "all-or-none" phenomenon. When a stimulus reaches threshold, a neuron undergoes a full action potential whose intensity does not change as the action potential travels down the neuron. Choice C is wrong too. It describes an effect opposite to that which should be expected.

168. The most likely explanation for the differences in axonal regeneration of various brain stem neurons in squirrel monkeys as shown in Table 1 is that:

A. excessive axonal repair to the amygdala and hypothalamus inhibits reconnection to the cortex.

B. dendrites of neurons in the cortex can compensate for axonal deficiencies in brain stem neurons.

C. longer axonal projections in brain stem neurons can regenerate more easily than shorter ones.

D. shorter axonal projections in brain stem neurons can regenerate more easily than longer ones.

D is correct. The passage states that, relative to the brain stem neurons, the amygdala, hypothalamus, and midbrain regions are "nearby" while the cortex is more "remote." Table 1 shows that reconnection of brain stem neurons to the nearer amygdala and hypothalamus are made, but reconnections to the distant cortex are not. A plausible hypothesis is that reconnections to nearby targets are made more readily than those to distant targets. The connections are made by axonal regrowth, therefore shorter axons are more likely to recover than longer ones.

The wrong answer choices: Choices A and B are wrong because they are not supported by any information provided in the passage or by any experimental data. Choice C states that which is opposite to a logical interpretation of the passage and the data.

169. All of the following statements correctly describe events associated with synaptic transmission of a nerve impulse EXCEPT:

  A. Mitochondria supply the ATP needed for synthesis of neurotransmitter.
  B. Neurotransmitters are released into the synaptic cleft in direct response to an action potential.
  C. Calcium is actively sequestered in direct response to an action potential.
  D. Neurotransmitters bind to receptors on the postsynaptic membrane and cause a change in permeability of the membrane.

C is correct. When an action potential reaches the terminal end of an axon, it causes not sequestration but *release* of calcium from storage. The influx of calcium into the terminal end of the axon causes synaptic vesicles there to fuse with the axonal membrane. The vesicles exocytose (engulf) neurotransmitter and take it into the synaptic cleft. The neurotransmitter then diffuses across the cleft, binds to receptors on the postsynaptic dendrites, and causes a change in permeability to one or more ions.

Questions 170–175 are NOT based on a descriptive passage

170. The graph below depicts the changes in sodium and potassium conductance that take place during an action potential in a giant squid axon.

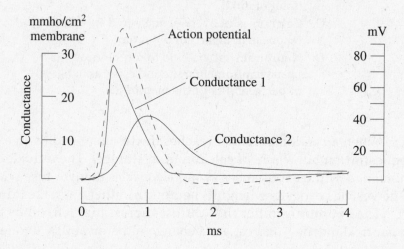

Conductance 2 depicts the movement of:

A. sodium ions.
B. chloride ions.
C. potassium ions.
D. magnesium ions.

C is correct. During the initial phase of an action potential, sodium channels open and sodium ion moves rapidly into the neuron down its concentration gradient. During the next phase of conductance, sodium channels close and potassium channels open. Potassium leaves the cell down *its* concentration gradient, helping to remove positive charge from the neuron.

171. Within the cell, protein turnover reflects a balance between the rates of protein synthesis and degradation. For a given protein the rate of synthesis is regulated by which of the following factors?

    A. The amount of DNA available for transcription
    B. The amount of RNA available for translation
    C. The number of ribosomes available for protein synthesis
    D. The number of tRNA molecules available for transport of amino acids

B is correct. Regulation of protein synthesis lies at the level of mRNA molecules. The number of copies of mRNA that are transcribed from a single DNA template (choice A) govern cellular production of a given protein.

172. Which of the following pathways of cellular respiration occurs in the cytosol?

    A. The Krebs cycle
    B. Oxidative phosphorylation
    C. Glycolysis
    D. Electron transport chain

C is correct. Review biochemistry and recall that glycolysis is the anaerobic phase of cellular respiration and it takes place in the cytosol. (Indeed, it is conducted by anaerobic organisms that lack mitochondria.) Its substrate is glucose and its end product is pyruvic acid which, under aerobic conditions generates acetyl co-A. The Krebs cycle acts on Cetyl–CoA.

The wrong answer choices: Choices A, B, and D refer to aerobic processes that occur within the mitochondrion.

173. The orientation of substituent groups on a cyclohexane ring may be axial or equatorial. For halogen substituents which orientation is favored?

A. Equatorial because of reduced steric hindrance.

B. Axial because of reduced steric hindrance.

C. Axial because the bonds have more mobility.

D. Equatorial because it displays more staggered than eclipsed conformation.

A is correct. Review organic chemistry and recall that in unsubstituted cyclohexane, some hydrogen atoms occupy equatorial positions and others occupy axial positions. An equatorially positioned substituent lies along the ring's equator. When two molecules differ only in axial or equatorial orientation of substituents, they are "conformational isomers." An axially positioned substituent lies along the axis perpendicular to the ring's plane. If a hydrogen atom is substituted by a larger atom it might theoretically occupy axial or equatorial positions. However, for all atoms other than hydrogen, the equatorial position produces lesser steric hindrance. The substituent has "more room" in the equatorial position.

The wrong answer choices: Choice B is wrong because axial and equatorial conformations may undergo interconversion or "ring flip." Choice C is incorrect because each orientation can convert itself to the other. Choice D is wrong because staggered and eclipsed conformation are unrelated to the stability of conformational isomers.

174. The likelihood of a given allele's sudden predominance within a small isolated population independent of adaptive advantage is best attributed to:

    A. the Hardy-Weinberg Law.
    B. genetic drift.
    C. adaptive radiation.
    D. survival of the fittest.

B is correct. Genetic drift occurs in small, isolated populations. It refers to the statistical possibility that deleterious alleles might nonetheless predominate. The limited gene pool associated with small populations contributes to random "genetic accidents of misfortune," and to the predominance of disadvantageous alleles.

The wrong answer choices: Choice A is incorrect because the Hardy-Weinberg Law applies to very large populations and predicts stability of the gene pool. Choice C refers to the likelihood that a given species may "radiate" to produce new ones as competing organisms "force" themselves to find environments and niches that reduce competition. Choice D mentions a time-weary phrase that is, in fact, contrary to the phenomenon described in the question.

175. Alcohols show characteristic absorptions in the ^1H NMR spectrum. If 1-propanol is subjected to ^1H NMR the protons on the oxygen-bearing carbon will be split into a:

    A. singlet
    B. doublet
    C. triplet
    D. quadruplet

C is correct. Review NMR spectroscopy and recognize that the signal attributable to the two protons associated with the molecule's 2 CH_2O moieties is split into a triplet by coupling with the neighboring CH_2 protons.

Passage V (Questions 176–180)

$$\text{Intermediate} + \text{H}_2\text{O} \longrightarrow \underset{\underset{\displaystyle H}{|}}{\overset{\overset{\displaystyle OH}{|}}{\text{CH}_3 - \text{C} - \text{CH}_3}} + \text{H}_2\text{SO}_4$$

176. In the preparation of isopropanol what is the role of sulfuric acid?

    A. It acts as a catalyst.
    B. It increases the pH of the solution.
    C. It ionizes the alkene.
    D. It causes a reduction of the alkene.

A is correct. Examine the two steps as set forth in the passage and note that sulfuric acid is present at the beginning of the first (in dissociated form, as H^+ and HSO4^-) and at the end of the reaction as well. That a substance should be necessary to a reaction and regenerated at its conclusion is strong evidence that it serves as a catalyst.

The wrong answer choices: Choice B is wrong because sulfuric acid is a strong acid and <u>de</u>creases ambient pH. Choices C and D are wrong because there is no basis to conclude that sulfuric acid ionizes or reduces the alkene.

177. How many chiral centers are featured within the isopropanol molecule?

    A. 0
    B. 1
    C. 2
    D. 3

A is correct. A chiral center is a carbon atom bonded to four substituents, none of which is identical to any other. The isopropanol molecule features three carbons. The central carbon is bound to two CH_3 moieties and cannot be chiral. The other two carbons are those of the CH_3 moieties themselves, and each, quite obviously is bound to 3 hydrogen atoms. None of the carbon atoms can "boast" four dissimilar substituents.

178. What property of isopropanol makes it most useful as a rubbing alcohol?

    A. It forms hydrogen bonds.
    B. It is weakly acidic.
    C. It is relatively volatile.
    D. It acts as a proton donor.

C is correct. "Rubbing alcohol" is designed to cool the skin. A volatile liquid—one that tends rapidly to vaporize—will cool the skin by drawing heat away from it as it moves from the liquid to the gaseous phase.

The wrong answer choices: Choices A, B, and D all represent isopropanol's properties, but they do not explain the cooling of skin.

179. Between isopropanol or 1-butanol, which compound likely has the higher boiling point?

    A. 1-butanol because it has the higher molecular weight
    B. 1-butanol because it is a straight chain alcohol
    C. Isopropanol because its density is higher than that of 1-butanol
    D. Isopropanol because its carbon chain branches

B is correct. Review organic chemistry and recognize that because 1-butanol is a straight chain alcohol its molecules experience increased van der Waals attractions.

The wrong answer choices: Choice A is true but B is a better answer. Choice C, too, makes a false statement. The density of isopropanol is not higher than that of 1-butanol. Choice D is wrong because branching tends to *reduce* boiling point.

180. All of the following are isomers of isobutanol EXCEPT:

    A. $(CH_3)_3COH$ **C.** $CH_3CH_2CH_2CH_2OH$

    B. $CH_3CH_2COCH_3$ **D.** $CH_3CH_2OCH_2CH_3$

B is correct. The term "isomer" refers to two compounds whose molecular formulas are identical but differ in the arrangement of their composite atoms. The isobutanol molecule is composed of 4 carbon atoms, 1 oxygen atom, and 10 hydrogen atoms. Examine the 4 molecules shown in the answer choices. Note that all have 4 carbon atoms, all have 1 oxygen atom, and all *except B* have 10 hydrogen atoms. The molecule shown in choice B has only 8 hydrogen atoms.

Passage VI (Questions 181–187)

181. Excessive peristalsis and rapid emptying of the small intestine will most likely have which of the following effects on the absorption of a drug taken orally?

    A. Increase the absorption of the drug, because it would accelerate transport from the stomach to the intestines.
    B. Increase the absorption of the drug, because the drug could then bypass low pH and enzymatic environments of the stomach and the intestines.
    C. Decrease the absorption of the drug, because it would prolong gastric emptying into the duodenum.
    D. Decrease the absorption of the drug, because it would accelerate transport through the gastrointestinal tract.

D is correct. A drug (or any other substance) will be absorbed by the duodenum only if it is exposed to the duodenal mucosal surface for an adequate period of time. If the small intestine (and hence the duodenum) moves very rapidly it reduces the time during which drug molecules are exposed to the duodenal mucosa. For that reason it decreases absorption.

The wrong answer choices: Choices A, B, and C refer to the stomach which, in relation to this question, is not involved in the excessive peristalsis or rapid emptying.

182. The drug insulin is unstable in the gastrointestinal tract. As a result it is administered parenterally. The effect of insulin on target tissues is to:

    A. decrease blood glucose levels.
    B. increase blood glucose levels.
    C. mobilize release of glycogen from storage.
    D. initiate synthesis of glucose by gluconeogenesis.

A is correct. Insulin is a hormone produced and released by the pancreas and, more particularly, by the islets of Langerhans. Release is stimulated by high levels of blood glucose. At most (but not all) body cells, insulin opens the "gates" that admit glucose and so, promotes uptake of glucose by body cells and concomitantly reduces glucose concentration in the blood.

The wrong answer choices: Choice B, C, and D are wrong but would be correct if the question referred not to insulin but to glucagon. Glucagon, also produced and released by the pancreas, tends to raise blood sugar as needed by promoting its synthesis, mobilization, and release from the liver.

183. Of the mechanisms depicted in Figure 2, which mechanism would most likely demonstrate saturation kinetics similar to that of an enzyme-catalyzed reaction?

    A. Mechanism 1
    B. Mechanism 2
    C. Mechanism 3
    D. Mechanisms 2 and 3

B is correct. Mechanism 2 depicts a drug that undergoes carrier-mediated transport. The drug can be transported only as fast as carrier molecules can serve it. When drug concentration exceeds carrier molecule availability, transport across the membrane must await the availability of newly freed carrier molecules. This form of saturation is analogous to that observed with enzyme-dependent reactions. When the number of substrate molecules exceeds the number of available enzyme molecules, the enzyme is said to be saturated, and the substrate must "await" the availability of enzyme. Under such conditions the addition of substrate will not increase the rate of reaction.

184. With reference to Figure 2, mechanism 3 differs from mechanism 2 in that:

    A. Mechanism 3 requires hydrolysis of ATP.
    B. Mechanism 3 involves a carrier molecule.
    C. Mechanism 3 involves movement from a region of higher concentration to one of lower concentration.
    D. Mechanism 3 shows a high structural specificity.

C is correct. Mechanism 2 depicts passive diffusion of a lipid-soluble drug through the lipid membrane. Passive diffusion always involves movement from a region of higher concentration to a region of lower concentration. For that reason, it requires no energy.

The wrong answer choices: Choices A, B, and D apply to mechanism 2 which, as noted on the figure, is ATP-dependent. ATP dependence denotes the need for energy and the transport shown as mechanism 2 is thus termed "active." The involvement of a carrier molecule gives rise to the name "carrier mediated active transport."

185. A decision to administer nitroglycerine sublingually would be most justified by a finding that nitroglycerine is:

A. not metabolized by the liver and is excreted in the urine unchanged.
B. highly susceptible to inactivation by hepatic enzymes.
C. well tolerated by the stomach and is relatively immune to degradation by acid.
D. susceptible to rapid absorption from intestinal mucosa.

B is correct. The passage states that sublingual drug administration facilitates bypass of the liver and its metabolic action. Therefore, it is particularly appropriate to drugs whose activity is jeopardized by hepatic activity. When administered sublingually, a drug is absorbed by capillaries apposing the sublingual area and so is not presented to the liver with any immediacy. (Such drugs do ultimately reach the liver because all blood "sooner or later" finds its way to the liver via the hepatic artery.)

The wrong answer choices: Choice A is wrong for the same reason that B is right. A drug that is not endangered by hepatic metabolism does not suggest the need for sublingual administration. Choice C is wrong because the finding to which it refers would militate in favor of the oral route. Choice D, too, is incorrect. Rapid absorption from intestinal mucosa would argue for administration via the oral or rectal routes.

186. Which of the following sites offers the greatest area of absorption due to its comparatively large surface area?

A. the esophagus, because of its length.
B. the stomach, because of its gastric mucosa.
C. the small intestine, because of its microvilli.
D. the large intestine, because of its large circumference.

C is correct. The small intestine is the primary site of absorption due to its high surface area. Its inner (luminal) surface is studded with projections called "microvilli." By monumental proportions, these increase absorptive surface area, making the small intestine for more suitable to absorption than any other portion of the gastrointestinal tract.

187. A student assumes that a highly hydrophilic drug will be poorly absorbed across the cell membrane. Is the assumption well founded?

   A. Yes; a highly hydrophilic drug will be unable to cross both the hydrophilic and hydrophobic portions of the lipid bilayer.
   B. Yes; a highly hydrophilic drug will be repelled by the hydrophilic heads of the lipid bilayer.
   C. No; a highly hydrophilic drug can readily cross both the hydrophilic and the hydrophobic portions of the lipid bilayer.
   D. No; the hydrophilic character of a drug has no bearing on its ability to cross the lipid bilayer.

A is correct. The cell membrane is composed of a lipid bilayer. Each lipid molecule of the bilayer contains a hydrophilic portion directed outward toward the extracellular or intracellular spaces, and a hydrophobic portion that is directed inward toward the center of the lipid bilayer. The biological adage "like dissolves like" applies. Hydrophobic molecules are generally lipid soluble, and hydrophilic molecules generally are not. This question, however, asks that you account for the amphoteric nature of some lipid molecules. A *highly* hydrophilic molecule would be largely unable to traverse the lipid portion of the cell membrane.

Passage VII (Questions 188-194):

188. Among the following properties, a sample of ethyl alcohol is most likely to demonstrate:

   A. relatively low solubility in polar solvents due to small molecular size.
   B. relatively high solubility in polar solvents due to hydrogen bonding.
   C. relatively high boiling points due to weak van der Waals forces.
   D. relatively low boiling points due to strong van der Waals forces.

B is correct. In its first sentence, the passage states that ethyl alcohol is a water-soluble molecule. Since water is itself a polar molecule the passage directly implies that ethyl alcohol has relatively *high* solubility in polar solvents. Choice B refers to high solubility in polar solvents due to hydrogen bonding. Hydrogen bonding does increase solubility in polar solvents (like water) and alcohol exhibits hydrogen bonding between hydroxyl groups.

The wrong answer choices: Choice A contravenes the passage by referring to *low* solubility in polar solvents. Choice C is wrong because weak van der Waals forces promote *low* boiling points. Choice D is incorrect because strong van der Waals forces tend to *raise* boiling points.

189. Excessive ethyl alcohol intake is often associated with poor nutrition and vitamin deficiency. Among the following proposed explanations for the association, which is LEAST likely to be accurate?

A. Ethyl alcohol does not generate metabolic fuel for body cells.

B. Persons who ingest high quantities of ethyl alcohol derive their calories from alcohol and do not experience hunger for other foods.

C. Chronic alcohol ingestion interferes with conversion of ingested vitamins to their active forms.

D. Prolonged excessive alcohol intake is associated with psychological and social dysfunction that causes the individual to fail in caring for himself.

A is correct. In its third paragraph the passage states that alcohol metabolism produces acetyl co-A, which enters the Krebs cycle and is oxidized to generate carbon dioxide and water. Alcohol does, therefore, constitute a metabolic fuel. Choice A represents a false statement. It cannot explain the association between alcohol intake and poor nutrition. It is, therefore, correct.

The wrong answer choice: Neither choices B, C, or D is inconsistent with information in the passage. Each *could*, conceivably, explain the connection between poor nutrition and the ingestion of alcohol.

190. Among the following, which would most dramatically reduce the rate at which the body eliminates ingested ethyl alcohol?

A. Decreased respiratory rate
B. Increased ingestion of water
C. Moderate inhibition of *aldehyde* dehydrogenase
D. Moderate inhibition of *alcohol* dehydrogenase

D is correct. In its third paragraph the passage describes the oxidative metabolism of ethyl alcohol. The *rate limiting step* is the conversion of ethyl alcohol to acetaldehyde, which is catalyzed by alcohol dehydrogenase. A moderate reduction in that enzyme's activity will significantly affect the rate of alcohol elimination.

The wrong answer choices: Choice A is incorrect because respiratory elimination of alcohol is relatively slight; "small amounts" pass from the alveolar vessels to the lungs. Reduced respiratory rate would produce far less a reduction in alcohol elimination than would inhibition of alcohol metabolism in the liver. Choice B is incorrect because increased ingestion of water would, if anything, *speed* the elimination of alcohol by increasing overall urinary excretion. Choice C is wrong for the same reason that choice D is right. In the metabolism of alcohol, oxidation of acetaldehyde is *not* the rate limiting step. A moderate reduction in the relevant enzyme—aldehyde dehydrogenase—would not affect the rate of elimination.

191. An investigator studies the oxidative metabolism of ethyl alcohol in an experimental animal. He artificially increases the liver concentration of alcohol dehydrogenase to the point that the oxidation of acetaldehyhde to acetyl co-A becomes the rate limiting step. If the liver concentration of alcohol dehydrogenase is then increased further, which of the following graphs will most likely depict the relationship between alcohol dehydrogenase concentration and the rate of alcohol elimination?

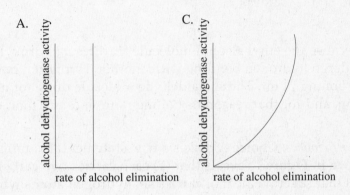

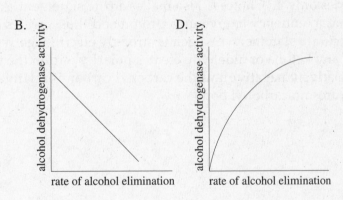

A is correct. Paragraphs 3 and 4 provide the relevant information. Oxidative metabolism of ethyl alcohol involves two steps: (1) The formation of acetaldehyde and (2) the formation of acetyl co-A. Normally the first step is slower than the second and is, therefore, the rate determining step. *But,* if the first step is made faster than the second, the second will become rate determiner. Further increase in the rate of the first step will have no affect on overall reaction rate.

The wrong answer choices: Choices B, C, and D all show a change in reaction rate with change in alcohol dehydrogenase activity. All are inconsistent, therefore, with the fact that alcohol dehydrogenase no longer catalyzes the rate determining step.

192. If ethyl alcohol and acetaldehyde are compared in terms of molecular weight, boiling point, acidity, and polarity, which of the following will LEAST likely be observed?

A. The molecular weight of ethyl alcohol is higher than that of acetaldehyde.

B. The boiling point of acetaldehyde is higher than that of ethyl alcohol.

C. Ethyl alcohol is more acidic than acetaldehyde.

D. The acetaldehyde molecule shows greater polarity than does the ethyl alcohol molecule.

B is correct. Because the ethyl alcohol molecule features a hydroxyl group one molecule will undergo hydrogen bonding with another. Hydrogen bonding, in turn, tends to increase boiling point. The acetaldehyde molecule does not undergo hydrogen bonding, and for that reason its boiling point is *lower* than that of ethyl alcohol.

The wrong answer choices: Choice A makes a true statement. Examination of the two molecules as shown in Figure 1 reveals that (1) each carries two carbon atoms and an oxygen atom, but that (2) ethyl alcohol carries six hydrogen atoms whereas acetaldehyde carries only 4. Choice C also makes a true statement. An alcohol's hydroxyl group has a tendency to give up a proton and thus creates acidity. Choice D also reflects an accurate statement. Oxygen is strongly electronegative and the carbonyl bond of any ketone or aldehyde creates polarity within the molecule; the oxygen atom is relatively negative and the carbonyl carbon is relatively positive. Ethyl alcohol features no carbonyl bond.

193. In an effort to enforce laws relating to blood alcohol concentrations and motor vehicle operation, a state wishes to devise a procedure that will provide for relatively simple, immediate and, above all, *accurate* estimations of blood alcohol content. Scientist 1 advocates a "dipstick" test that measures urine alcohol concentration. Scientist 2 advocates a machine that measures the alcohol concentration of expired air. From which scientist should the state take advice?

   A. Scientist 1, because the dipstick is simpler than a mechanism designed to measure alcohol concentration in the blood.

   B. Scientist 1, because urinary alcohol concentrations will likely provide the more accurate data regarding blood alcohol concentration.

   C. Scientist 2, because an individual breathes continuously but does not produce urine continuously

   D. Scientist 2, because blood alcohol concentrations will likely provide the more accurate data regarding blood alcohol concentration.

D is correct. The answer lies in the passage's second paragraph where you learn that "The concentration of alcohol in expired air closely parallels concentration in the blood," and that "...urine concentrations do not correspond well to blood concentrations at the time a urine specimen is collected."

The wrong answer choices: Choice A is inappropriate because the mere simplicity of a dipstick does not address the state's goal of achieving accurate estimations of blood alcohol concentration. Choice B is incorrect because it makes a false statement. Blood alcohol concentration is better reflected by the alcohol concentration of expired air than by that of urine. Choice C is incorrect as well. It is true that one does not continuously expel urine, but that statement does not relate to the state's goal of accuracy. Regardless of the frequency with which a patient urinates, urine alcohol concentration at the time a sample is collected does not correspond to the alcohol concentration of blood.

194. Among the following, the highest point on the curve shown in Figure 1 most nearly represents:

    A. peak levels of blood alcohol.
    B. peak respiratory clearance of alcohol.
    C. complete absorption of ingested alcohol.
    D. the equilibrium between alcohol concentrations in alveolar blood and the lung.

A is correct. Figure 1 relates to information provided in the passage's second paragraph where you learn that the oxygen concentration of expired air closely parallels that of the blood. Proper reading of the graph reveals that the highest point of its curve directly represents the oxygen content of expired air and *indirectly* represents the oxygen content of blood.

The wrong answer choices: Choices B, C, and D will tempt you if you have (1) not identified and carefully read the relevant section of the passage or (2) assumed, somehow, that the answer must be complicated rather than simple. The second paragraph does make references to respiratory elimination of alcohol, absorption of alcohol, and an "equilibrium." None of these answer choices, however, offers a correct response to the question.

Passage VIII (Questions 195–199)

195. The substrate in the experiment is:

    A. catalase.
    B. potassium permanganate.
    C. hydrogen peroxide.
    D. water.

C is correct. Catalase is an enzyme that acts on hydrogen peroxide, reducing it to water and oxygen. In an enzymatic reaction the substrate is that on which the enzyme acts.

The wrong answer choices: Choice A is clearly wrong; catalase is an enzyme. Choice B is wrong as well. Potassium permanganate serves in the titration but is not the substrate. Choice D refers to water, a product.

196. The primary function of lysosomes is to:

    A. sequester degradative enzymes from the cytoplasm.

    B. store water and other materials.

    C. digest worn cells and organelles.

    D. modify secretory enzymes before they are sent from the cell.

C is correct. Lysosomes digest worn cells and organelles, using degradative enzymes contained within their membranes.

The wrong answer choices: Choice A speaks to sequestration. Lysosomes do sequester enzymes, but that is not their principal function. Choice B refers to the storage of water, a function served by vacuoles. Choice D describes not lysosomes, but the Golgi apparatus.

197. With reference to the experiment, which of the following did NOT occur during the three-minute period following the introduction of catalase?

    A. The substrate bound to the enzyme.

    B. A substrate-enzyme complex was formed.

    C. The reaction proceeded.

    D. New enzyme was synthesized.

D is correct. Finding 2 indicates that much hydrogen peroxide disappeared from the reaction vessel *without* participation of potassium permanganate. The increased disappearance was attributable to the presence of catalase, and represents an enzyme catalyzed reaction. An enzyme molecule is characteristically regenerated at the conclusion of the reaction it catalyzes only to "reenlist in the service" and catalyze its reaction over and over again. Nothing in the experimental procedure or findings indicates that *new* enzyme was synthesized.

The wrong answer choices: The events described in choices A and B are characteristic of catalysis. Choice C, of course, makes a true statement since it is clear that the catalyzed decomposition of hydrogen peroxide did occur.

198. Reduction of temperature would have which of the following affects on the second trial?

    A. It would impair catalase activity.
    B. It would enhance catalase activity.
    C. It would prevent regeneration of the catalase at the conclusion of the reaction
    D. It would convert the catalase to an inorganic catalyst.

A is correct. Enzyme activity normally increases with increased temperature and decreases with decreased temperature.

The wrong answer choices: Choice B is contravenes scientific observation. Choice C is wrong because it is inherent in the nature of a catalyst however impaired its activity that is regenerated at the conclusion of catalysis. Option D is implausible. There is no basis on which to suppose that reducing the temperature of a protein will convert its chemical structure.

199. Extreme high temperature would have which of the following effects on the second trial?

    A. It would increase the required potassium permanganate to approximately 18 milliliters.
    B. It would increase the required potassium permanganate to approximately 28 milliliters.
    C. It would maintain the required potassium permanganate at approximately 9 milliliters.
    D. It would reduce the required potassium permanganate to approximately 1 milliliter.

B is correct. Although enzyme activity normally increases with increasing temperature, *extreme* high temperature denatures the enzyme and renders it inactive. Twenty-eight milliliters of potassium permanganate were required to titrate the hydrogen peroxide in the absence of enzyme (finding 1). With catalase rendered inactive by extreme high temperature, the reaction vessel would be functionally devoid of enzyme. As in the first trial, 28 milliliters of potassium permanganate solution would be required to titrate the hydrogen peroxide.

Questions 200–204 are NOT based on a descriptive passage

200. Which of the following is NOT true of erythrocytes?

   A. They contain the protein hemoglobin, which transports oxygen to the tissues.
   B. They are a constituent of whole blood but not of plasma.
   C. They contain no nuclei but contain cellular organelles.
   D. They form a part of the immune system, providing cellular immunity.

D is correct. Red blood cells or erythrocytes do not participate in immune function. (White blood cells do.)

The wrong answer choices: Choice A is wrong because erythrocytes bind oxygen at the lungs and release it to metabolizing tissues. The oxygen molecules bind to the iron-containing protein hemoglobin, located in within the erythrocytes. Choice B is wrong as well. Plasma represents blood without its cells. Erythrocytes are not, therefore, found in plasma. Choice C characterizes erythrocytes. They do feature organelles, but they do *not* contain nuclei; at maturity they are "anucleated."

201. The amino acids serine, threonine, and tyrosine frequently undergo phosphorylation of a free OH group on their side chains. Phosphorylation of the OH group serves to regulate the activity of the protein, causing activation or inactivation depending on the protein. Phosphorylation involves formation of a(n):

   A. covalent bond, with accompanying hydrolysis of ATP.
   B. hydrogen bond, without accompanying hydrolysis of ATP.
   C. ionic bond, without accompanying hydrolysis of ATP.
   D. noncovalent bond, with accompanying hydrolysis of ATP.

A is correct. Review biochemistry and recall that the phosphate bonds to oxygen by means of covalency. Energy needed to form the covalent bond is supplied by ATP.

202. Muscle contraction requires all of the following EXCEPT for:

    A. release of calcium from the sarcoplasmic
    reticulum.
    B. hydrolysis of ATP.
    C. depolarization produced by stimulus from
    a motor neuron.
    D. binding of tropomyosin to actin.

D is correct. Your review of muscle physiology will remind you that contraction
requires the binding of myosin to actin. Tropomyosin is first displaced from myosin
binding sites on actin so that myosin and actin may bind. When the muscle cell is
depolarized calcium ions are released from the sarcoplasmic reticulum. Calcium ions
bind to sites on troponin, causing a conformational change that moves tropomyosin
away from myosin binding sites on actin. ATP is required to disengage myosin from
actin and to sequester calcium in the sarcoplasmic reticulum.

203. Which of the following represents an effect of
antidiuretic hormone (ADH) on the renal nephron?

    A. It increases water loss by reducing the per-
    meability of the collecting tubule to water.
    B. It reduces water loss by increasing the per-
    meability of the collecting tubule to water.
    C. It reduces water loss by increasing the per-
    meability of the loop of Henle to water.
    D. It increases water loss by reducing the per-
    meability of the loop of Henle to water.

B is correct. ADH renders increased water permeability at the collecting tubule.
Because the fluid within the tubule is more concentrated than the interstitial fluid,
increased permeability causes water to move by osmosis from interstitium to tubule.
This in turn creates a relatively more voluminous and dilute urine.

The wrong answer choices: Choice A is opposite to fact. Choices C and D speak to
effects at the loop of Henle. ADH does not operate at that site.

204. When methane is burned to form carbon dioxide and water, its hydrogen atoms:

- **A.** acquire negative charge.
- **B.** lose negative charge.
- **C.** acquire positive charge.
- **D.** lose positive charge.

B is correct. With reference to the combustion of methane CH_4 it is commonly said that "methane is oxidized" and "oxygen is reduced."

$$CH_4 + 2O_2 \longrightarrow CO_2 + 2H_2O$$

It is difficult on any superficial examination to see how the methane has "lost" electrons in the usual sense of that word, since it does not even appear on the right side of the reaction. It is also difficult to see how oxygen has "gained" electrons since every oxygen atom on right and left sides of the equation has eight electrons "to its name." The truth is that methane's carbon atom "loses electrons" in that it is first bound to 4 hydrogen atoms and then to two oxygen atoms. The two oxygen atoms exert a greater pull on carbon's valence electrons than do the four hydrogen atoms. In that sense, the carbon "loses electrons." Similarly methane's 4 hydrogen atoms are first bound to a carbon atom and then to two oxygen atoms (2 hydrogen atoms per oxygen atom). Oxygen exerts a stronger pull on hydrogen's valence electrons than does carbon. In that sense, hydrogen "loses electrons."

Reciprocally, the oxygen atoms on the left side of the reaction are bound to one another. On the right side of the reaction they are bound to carbon and to hydrogen. They exert a greater pull on hydrogen and carbon's valence electrons than they do on the valence electrons of each other. In that sense the oxygen atoms "gain electrons."

You might, of course, apply the mnemonic "LEO says GER." Loss of electrons characterizes oxidation. Gain of electrons characterizes reduction. *You would do well, however, to understand* the "loss" and "gain" to which the mnemonic refers. Loss of electrons refers to greater separation between negative charge and nucleus. Gain of electrons refers to lesser separation between negative charge and nucleus.

Passage IX (Questions 205-209):

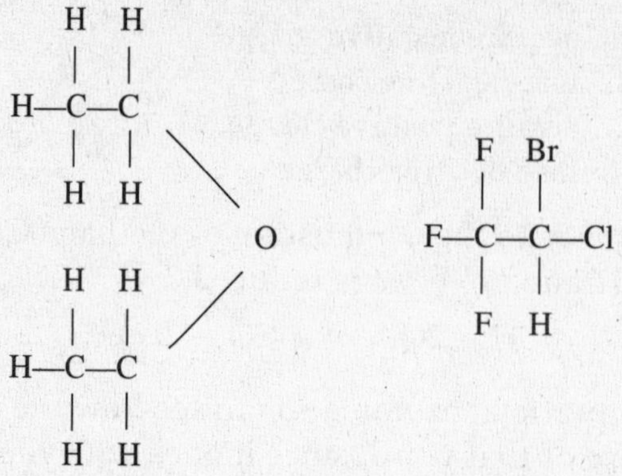

diethyl ether   halothane

Figure 3

205. Some investigators have theorized that water soluble molecules tend not to be effective anesthetics. Regarding the diethyl ether molecule (shown in Figure 3), which of the following facts is LEAST consistent with such a theory?

A. The molecule is composed solely of carbon, oxygen, and hydrogen.

B. All of the molecule's carbon atoms are saturated.

C. The bond angle formed where two carbon atoms are joined by a central oxygen atom generates a dipole moment of approximately 1.18 debye.

D. The molecule is achiral.

C is correct. Diethyl ether *is* an effective anesthetic. If it is water soluble the theory is cast in doubt. Look for some feature of the molecule that suggests water solubility. Water solubility tends strongly to correspond with polarity. The fact that the molecule is polar tends to make it water soluble. That, in turn, tends to contravene the theory that water solubility correlates negatively with anesthetic activity.

The wrong answer choices: Choices A, B, and D reflect true statements about the diethyl ether molecule, but none bears on its water solubility.

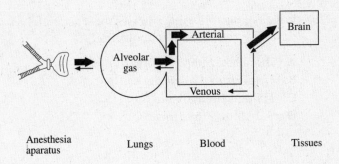

Anesthesia aparatus   Lungs   Blood   Tissues

Figure 1

206. If Figure 1 were drawn to represent a point in time corresponding to the knee in Figure 2, movement of gas between alveoli and blood would be shown to be:

A. absent.
B. in the direction of alveoli to blood only.
C. in the direction of blood to alveoli only.
D. roughly equal in both directions.

D is correct. At its third paragraph the passage indicates that the "knee" in Figure 2 corresponds roughly to equilibrium of movement between alveoli and blood, meaning that gas flows between alveoli and blood at equal rates. If Figure 2 were redrawn so that it corresponded to the knee, it would show that movement in one direction is equal to movement in the other.

The wrong answer choices : Choice A is wrong because it refers to the *absence* of movement. The "knee" in Figure 2 represents an equilibrium at which there is no *net* movement. Gas moves between blood and brain in both directions, but does so at equal rates. Choices B and C are clearly wrong, therefore, because they refer to movement in one direction only.

207. Which of the following phrases most accurately
describes the halothane molecule?

    A. Branched phenyl derivative
    B. Unsaturated alkyl derivative
    C. Halogenated alkene
    D. Substituted hydrocarbon

D is correct. The halothane (fluothane) molecule shows two singly bonded carbon atoms, each of which is bonded to the other and to three other atoms. The carbon atoms, therefore, are saturated. The halogen atoms, chlorine, bromine, and fluorine represent substituents; they "substitute" for hydrogen. You may conceive of the molecule as ethane, a hydrocarbon, in which all but one hydrogen atom has been replaced with a halogen atom.

ethane

The wrong answer choices: Choice A is wrong because halothane does not show the six membered ring characteristic of a phenyl moiety. Choice B describes an <u>un</u>saturated molecule. All carbons in the halothane molecule are saturated. Choice C refers to a halogenated alk<u>ene</u>, which denotes the presence of doubly bonded, unsaturated carbon atoms. (The halothane molecule is an unsaturated alk<u>ane</u>.)

208. Among the following, equilibrium concentrations between alveoli and blood are achieved
LEAST quickly with:

    A. ether.
    B. halothane.
    C. cyclopropane.
    D. nitrous oxide.

A is correct. In its third paragraph the passage states that (1) equilibrium between alveoli and air corresponds to the "knee" in Figure 2, and (2) that a high blood/air Ostwald solubility coefficient increases the time required to reach the knee. Table 1 shows that ether's blood/air solubility coefficient of 12-15 is higher than that for any other agent listed among the choices.

209. Which of the following measures will tend to increase the equilibrium concentration of anesthetic within the brain?

    I. Increasing the anesthetic's solubility within the brain

    II. Increasing the concentration of anesthetic within the inspired mixture

    III. Increasing respiratory rate

    A. I only
    B. II only
    C. I and II only
    D. I, II, and III

C is correct. Distinguish between (1) the *speed* at which a system attains equilibrium, and (2) the *concentrations* that prevail when it does. You might conceive of the system thus:

$$\text{tank} \rightleftharpoons \text{lung} \rightleftharpoons \text{blood} \rightleftharpoons \text{brain}$$

Apply LeChatelier's principle. Note that increased uptake on the right will drive this equilibrium *to* the right as will increased concentration on the left. Numbers I and II therefore reflect correct statements.

The wrong answer choices: Choice A omits number I and choice B omits number II. Choice D is wrong because it includes number III. Increasing the respiratory rate might increase the *speed* at which anesthetic is moved from tank to brain but it does not alter equilibrium *concentrations*. You might loosely analogize respiratory rate to a catalyst in the equilibrium:

$$A \xrightleftharpoons{\text{catalyst}} B$$

The catalyst increases the speed at which equilibrium is achieved but does not alter equilibrium concentrations.

Passage X (Questions 210–214)

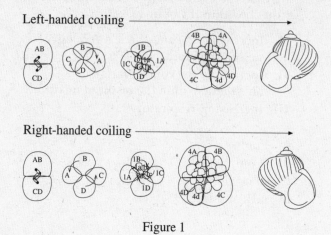

Left-handed coiling

Right-handed coiling

Figure 1

210. Which of the following does NOT occur at the same time that the mitotic spindle assembles in the dividing cell?

A. Chromosomes condense and become visible when viewed with a microscope.
B. The nuclear membrane begins to disintegrate.
C. Chromosomes line up along the cell's equator.
D. Centrioles divide and each one moves to an opposite pole of the cell.

C is correct. Review the stages of mitosis and recall that the spindle apparatus begins to appear and the chromosomes begin to align themselves along its fibers late in early metaphase.

The wrong answer choices: Choices A, B, and D describe events that occur during prophase. In prophase centrioles move to opposite sides of the cell, microtubules assemble to form the spindle apparatus, and the nuclear membrane begins to degenerate.

211. The mating shown below would create off-spring that exhibit which of the following shell coiling patterns?

DD (male) × dd (female) ⟶ Dd (offspring)

- **A.** All right-coiling
- **B.** All left-coiling
- **C.** 50% right-coiling and 50% left-coiling
- **D.** Cannot be determined from the information provided

B is correct. Although D (right-coiling) is the dominant allele, the passage states that direction of coiling in the offspring is governed not by the genotype of the offspring itself, but by that of its mother. In this case, the offspring's mother has a genotype that codes for left-handed coiling (dd). That is what the offspring will exhibit.

212. In mammals, oogenesis involves:

- **A.** two divisions that ultimately produce one haploid ovum.
- **B.** two divisions that ultimately produce four haploid ova.
- **C.** one division that ultimately produces one haploid ovum.
- **D.** one division that ultimately produces two haploid ova.

A is correct. Oogenesis is the meiotic process that produces the haploid female gamete, the ovum. Theoretically the first and second meiotic divisions should yield four haploid progeny. In mammalian oogenesis, however, the overwhelming mass of cytoplasm belonging to the progenitor cell is delivered to only one of its four progeny. The remaining three are dwarfed by comparison. They are termed "polar bodies" and degenerate. (In mammalian spermatogenesis, a single diploid progenitor does produce four haploid spermatozoa.)

213. When scientists injected a low-molecular-weight yellow dye into a single cell of a 16-cell mollusc embryo, they discovered that the dye was confined to that cell and its progeny. When they injected the dye into a single cell of a 32-cell embryo, they located the dye in that cell as well as in adjacent cells. Based on these findings, it is most reasonable to conclude that communication between cells of a developing mollusc embryo develops at the:

    A. zygote stage.
    B. neurula stage.
    C. gastrula stage.
    D. blastula stage.

D is correct. The blastula is a fluid-filled ball of cells that arises during cleavage. Choice A can be ruled out because the zygote is a single cell. Choices B and C can be ruled out because these constitute later developmental stages that involve many more cells than the 32-cell embryo examined in the experiment.

214. Members of the same species:

    A. have identical genotypes.
    B. have identical phenotypes.
    C. are unable to breed with one another to produce viable offspring.
    D. are unable to produce fertile offspring with members of another species.

D is correct. By definition two individuals belong to the same species if they can produce fertile offspring. And, if two individuals belong to different species they cannot produce fertile offspring. (Note that the dogma just described allows for breeding between individuals of two different species. The horse and the donkey, for example, belong to different species but might mate to produce a mule. The mule, however, is sterile.)

Questions 215–219 are NOT based on a descriptive passage.

215. A man whose mother is a carrier for color-blindness and whose father was color-blind has a male child with a normal female. What are the chances that the male child will be color-blind?

    A. 0%
    B. 25%
    C. 50%
    D. 100%

A is correct. Color blindness is a sex-linked (or "X linked") trait. It is carried on the X chromosome only. Since a father delivers only a Y chromosome to a male child, he cannot pass the gene for colorblindness to a male, even if he himself carries it. Put more broadly, an X-linked trait cannot pass from a male to a male. In this case, the father himself has a 50% chance of carrying the color-blind gene; from his own mother he might have received the mutant or normal gene. But, even if he did receive the mutant gene he cannot pass it to a male (although he can pass it to a female.)

216. A virus that employs reverse transcriptase to carry out its infective cycle within a host cell has as its nucleic acid core:

    A. RNA.
    B. DNA.
    C. Either RNA or DNA.
    D. Neither RNA nor DNA.

A is correct. Reverse transcriptase is an enzyme capable of producing DNA from an RNA template. Therefore, the virus in question contains RNA as its nucleic core.

The wrong answer choices: Choices B, C, and D are wrong because they refer to virons that contain DNA. Viruses that have DNA as their nucleic acid have no call for reverse transcriptase.

217. Which of the following represents the addition of H_2SO_4 to propylene (C_3H_6) according to Markovnikov's rule?

A.
$$CH_3 - \overset{\overset{\displaystyle OSO_3}{|}}{\underset{\underset{\displaystyle H}{|}}{C}} - CH_3$$

B.
$$CH_3 - \overset{\overset{\displaystyle H}{|}}{\underset{\underset{\displaystyle H}{|}}{C}} - CH_3$$

C.
$$CH_3 - \overset{\overset{\displaystyle H}{|}}{\underset{\underset{\displaystyle H}{|}}{C}} - CH_2OSO_3H$$

D.
$$CH_3 - \overset{\overset{\displaystyle OSO_3H}{|}}{\underset{\underset{\displaystyle H}{|}}{C}} - CH_3$$

D is correct. Propylene is an alkene

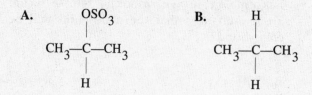

propylene

Markovnikov's rule provides: In the ionic addition of an acid to the carbon-carbon double bond of an alkene, the hydrogen of the acid preferentially attaches itself to the carbon atom that already holds the greater number of hydrogens. Carbon 2, the doubly bonded carbon on the "left" carries 1 hydrogen atom, and carbon 3, adjacent to it carries 2. The hydrogen therefore will bond preferentially to carbon 3 (and the deprotonated anion OSO_3H will bond to carbon 2) to yield the product shown in choice D.

218. The increased stability that characterizes a resonance structure is due to:

- **A.** conformational isomerization.
- **B.** ortho and meta isomerization
- **C.** electron delocalization.
- **D.** increased van der Waals attraction.

C is correct. Some molecules and moieties are so structured as to allow for movement of electrons within the molecule. The molecule may be conceived as interconverting rapidly between two conformations, each differing from the other in terms of electron localization. The classic example is benzene, whose three double bonds are "spread out" among the six bonding positions, so that each position has a measure of double bond character. The SO_2 moiety furnishes another example, as shown below.

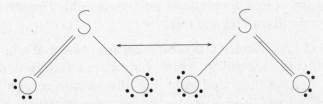

The carboxylate ion furnishes yet another example and is responsible for (1) the extraordinary stability of the ion and, concomitantly, (2) the pronounced acidity of carboxylic acids. In all events, you should associate the word "resonance" with the phrase "delocalization of charge."

The wrong answer choices: Choices A, B, and D refer to matters unrelated to resonance.

219. If a sample of a chiral substance fails to rotate the plane of polarized light, the sample most likely contains:

    A. equal amounts of two optical isomers.
    B. unequal amounts of two optical isomers.
    C. equal amounts of two structural isomers.
    D. unequal amounts of two structural isomers.

A is correct. A chiral molecule has one or more chiral centers. Such a molecule rotates the plane of polarized light to the right or left and has a mirror-image isomer that rotates it in the opposite direction. Each such isomer is "optically active," and the pair are termed "optical isomers." If each isomer is mixed with the other in equal quantity, the first's tendency to rotate the plane of polarized light in one direction fully opposes the second's te1.dency to rotate it in the other. Such a mixture is termed "racemic," and does not rotate the plane of polarized light. The sample to which the question refers is, evidently, a racemic mixture.

The wrong answer choices: Choice B is wrong because unequal amounts of optical isomers do not constitute a racemic mixture. A mixture so composed *will* be optically active, rotating the plane of polarized light in a direction corresponding to the isomer that predominates. Choices C and D are wrong because structural isomers have no bearing on the matter of optical activity.

ABOUT THE AUTHOR

THEODORE SILVER

Theodore Silver holds a medical degree from the Yale University School of Medicine, a bachelor's degree from Yale University and, in addition, a law degree from the University of Connecticut.

Dr. Silver has been intensely involved in the field of education, testing, and test preparation since 1976 and has written several books and computer tutorials pertaining to those fields. He became affiliated with The Princeton Review in 1988 and is chief author and architect of The Princeton Review MCAT preparatory course.

Dr. Silver is Associate Professor of Law at Touro College Jacob D. Fuchsberg Law Center where he teaches the law of medical practice and malpractice, contracts, and federal income taxation.

THE PRINCETON REVIEW WORLDWIDE

Each year, thousands of students from countries throughout the world prepare for the TOEFL and for U.S. college and graduate school admissions exams. Whether you plan to prepare for your exams in your home country or the United States, The Princeton Review is committed to your success.

INTERNATIONAL LOCATIONS

If you are using our books outside of the United States and have questions or comments, or want to know if our courses are being offered in your area, be sure to contact the Princeton Review office nearest you:

◆ HONG KONG	852-517-3016
◆ JAPAN (Tokyo)	8133-463-1343
◆ KOREA (Seoul)	822-508-0081
◆ MEXICO CITY	525-564-9468
◆ MONTREAL	514-499-0870
◆ PAKISTAN (Lahore)	92-42-571-2315
◆ SAUDI ARABIA	413-584-6849 (a U.S. based number)
◆ SPAIN (Madrid)	341-323-4212
◆ TAIWAN (Taipei)	886-27511293

U.S. STUDY ABROAD

Review USA offers international students many advantages and opportunities. In addition to helping you gain acceptance to the U.S. college or university of your choice, *Review USA* will help you acquire the knowledge and orientation you need to succeed once you get there.

Review USA is unique. It includes supplements to your test-preparation courses and a special series of *AmeriCulture* workshops to prepare you for the academic rigors and student life in the United States. Our workshops are designed to familiarize you with the different U.S. expressions, real-life vocabulary, and cultural challenges you will encounter as a study-abroad student. While studying with us, you'll make new friends and have the opportunity to personally visit college and university campuses to determine which school is right for you.

Whether you are planning to take the TOEFL, SAT, GRE, GMAT, LSAT, MCAT, or USMLE exam, The Princeton Review's test preparation courses, expert instructors, and dedicated International Student Advisors can help you achieve your goals.

For additional information about *Review USA*, admissions requirements, class schedules, F-1 visas, I-20 documentation, and course locations, write to:

The Princeton Review • Review USA
2315 Broadway, New York NY 10024
Fax: 212/874-0775

NOTES

NOTES

NOTES

NOTES

NOTES

NOTES